The American Collection

Selected Works from the Norton Museum of Art Collection

Edited and with an introduction by Christina Orr-Cahall

This publication was made possible by a grant from The Henry Luce Foundation. Additional support has been provided by The Ralph H. and Elizabeth C. Norton Philanthropic Trust and Sotheby's.

Norton Museum of Art • West Palm Beach, Florida

1451 S. Olive Avenue, West Palm Beach, Florida 33401

Library of Congress Catalogue Number: 95-71259
ISBN: 0-943411-29-7

Typeset in Florida, United States of America.
Printed and bound in Japan by Toppan Printing Co.

Table of Contents

Preface

In 1941 when the Norton Gallery of Art, now known as the Norton Museum of Art, was founded, the study of American art history was still in relative infancy. Although American collectors believed in American art, the world of art history primarily directed its research to European works, leaving the documentation and publication of American art to only a handful of visionary art historians. Although the study of American artworks has burgeoned over the last twenty-five years, this publication is the first to study the holdings of the Norton Museum, considered to be among the finer American museums. Although the addition is a belated one, the product will serve both the general museum visitor and the scholar in appreciating our holdings and their relationship to American art.

Beyond the publication itself, one of the most exciting aspects of this book has been the collaborative nature of its creation. The Norton Museum wished to foster the study of American art history in the South not only by documenting our own collections but also by nurturing research by young, Southern scholars. With the good countenance of The Henry Luce Foundation the museum worked with the Art History Graduate School of Emory University in Atlanta, Georgia, to research and write this publication. Dr. Dorinda Evans provided the academic leadership on behalf of the University, while five students, who were completing their graduate degrees in American art history, authored the entries. They are acknowledged by their initials at the end of each entry. The students were also paid for their work in an effort to assist with the costs of graduate school. For the students the project was, by and large, their first professional publication experience.

It is our hope that this publication will encourage the reader to learn more about the Norton's permanent collection and to visit the institution. Alternatively, for those who are familiar with the works but would like the substantive research information on the artists and on their specific works in our holdings, it is our hope that this book will also provide. Following our museum's original mission statement, "to educate and to enlighten" our public, this publication serves to bring our collections to all.

Acknowledgments

This publication has been a pleasure to create because of the many outstanding professionals who have helped to bring the project to fruition. It is important to acknowledge The Henry Luce Foundation, which from our first day of discussion has helped to encourage and frame the project while providing very substantial funds for its development and publication. In particular, I would like to thank Dr. Ellen Holtzman of The Henry Luce Foundation for her efforts and support.

Additional project funds were provided by the Ralph H. and Elizabeth C. Norton Philanthropic

Trust and by Sotheby's, which is to be commended for its dedication to providing funds for the support of museum publications and the documentation of permanent collections. Both David Ober and Katherine Ross of Sotheby's are to be thanked for their efforts on behalf of the project.

Emory University and, especially, the Art History Graduate School and Dr. Dorinda Evans, the eminent scholar of American art, were innovators in accepting our invitation to have five of their graduate students in American art history research and write the catalogue entries. The museum's goal in undertaking this cooperative project was to help support the study of art history in the South as well as to provide students with experience in publishing their work and with funds to assist them through graduate school. The students to be credited with fine work include Anne M. Bolin, Catherine M. Chastain, Lacey Taylor Jordan, and Diana McClintock who worked under the guidance of Dr. Evans and the direct supervision of their colleague, Jacqueline Francis, who also researched and wrote entries for the publication.

The editor for the project, Christine Droll, is also to be commended for her diligent work and her willingness to edit five writers. She has brought the publication to the point of reading as a unified text. The selection of the works to be included in the catalogue were made by the Norton staff, David Setford, senior curator and Olga Viso, assistant curator (now at the Hirshhorn Museum) with the students' perspective considered as well. Norton assistant curator Lisa Hurley undertook the task of coordinating and advising the writers and editor on behalf of our institution, a job which demanded considerable perseverance. All three curators served as readers in order to ensure a fully understandable text. It was my privilege to serve as senior editor for the project, and I greatly enjoyed the opportunity to work with graduate student research and writing once again. The calibre of work they produced is impressive, and the professional insights they gained in doing the project will serve them well in their future work.

Support staff are crucial to any publication, and I would like to acknowledge Pam Parry, the museum's registrar who with her assistant, Nancy Barrow, painstakingly confirmed details of each work, such as measurements, signature, and the like. Ms. Parry also supervised the photographing of the works which was expertly undertaken by Lucian Capehart. Kyle Zimmer, our director of public affairs, including publications, was responsible for selecting Molly Murphy, Red Letter Design Group, as the book's graphic designer. In addition, he skillfully interviewed and negotiated with printers, ultimately accepting Toppan Printing Co. Ms. Murphy did an outstanding job in interpreting the sense of the institution and the collection in the book's graphic presentation, and Toppan has again printed to the highest attainable calibre.

On behalf of all those who will benefit from this book, I would like to thank you all for your generosity and hard work on this project.

Christina Orr-Cahall
Museum Director

Introduction

A collector's understanding that possession of a work of art is fleeting—that his role is to serve as temporary custodian is the impetus behind most great museum collections. The Norton Museum of Art had such collectors as founders, Ralph Norton and his wife Elizabeth Calhoun Norton.

This publication presents for the first time a thoroughly researched documentation of sixty-five important works in the Norton Museum collection of American painting and sculpture. Selected as representative of the museum's holdings in American art, the works not only give a sense of the quality and range of the collection, but also provide a quick overview of the history of American art. Particular attention was given to the role of a work in its creator's oeuvre, as well as to the specific attributes of the work itself and to the artist's biography.

In 1941 when the Norton Gallery of Art (now known as the Norton Museum of Art) opened its doors to the public, southern Florida was still emerging from the Depression. Palm Beach County, which comprises more than 2,000 square miles, had 53,000 residents. The sophistication of the island of Palm Beach was in stark contrast to the agricultural communities of orange groves and to the bungalows of northern retirees. But Ralph Norton had a vision for Florida, and he understood that its growth would be phenomenal as travel became easier and leisure time more available. Above all, he believed that everyone needed the benefits of an art museum.

In 1935 Ralph Norton had moved to West Palm Beach, Florida, as a semi-retired businessman from Chicago. He was the son of

Oliver Norton, one of the first entrepreneurs to produce tin cans and whose company, Norton Brothers, eventually merged into the American Can Company. After graduation from the University of Chicago, Ralph Norton began his business career as a tool-and-machine designer at Acme Steel Goods Company. Through his exceptional business acumen, he eventually became the company's president and chairman of its board.

The tradition of the Norton family was one of philanthropy. In the cultural arena, family members were supporters of the Art Institute of Chicago, the Chicago Symphony, and Chautauqua, a movement and center that in its original mission supported the spread of culture to under served communities in the United States. The concept behind the original Chautauqua movement may have, in part, inspired the Nortons to make their generous contribution to the outpost of Florida.

The original Norton Gallery building was commissioned by Ralph Norton to be constructed on land that he acquired and donated to the City of West Palm Beach as a park. Norton selected Marion Sims Wyeth of the distinguished firm of Wyeth, King & Johnson as the architect for the museum building. Having graduated from Princeton University and having studied at the Ecole des Beaux Arts in Paris, Wyeth worked with the firms of Bertram Goodhue and Carrere & Hastings. He originally established his firm in New York City, but soon opened an office in Palm Beach which became the center for his work. Wyeth and Norton decided to ask Paul Manship, the renowned American sculpture, to create two bronzes for the front niches of the museum. Upon Manship's recommendation, they selected a large Diana and Actaeon pair of plaster casts that were then on display in "Gardens on Parade" at the 1939 World's Fair in New York. (Norton may also have been familiar with the monumental version of the pair at Brookgreen Gardens in South Carolina.) In addition, Norton commissioned three-bas reliefs in Alabama limestone representing "Inspiration," "Imagination," and "Interpretation" for the principal façade of the building. In 1995 the museum began its first major expansion of the building, selecting Chad Floyd, a principal in the firm of Centerbrook Architects of Essex, Connecticut, as its architect. The principal façade of the original Wyeth building, as well as the general integrity of the galleries—building footprint, room proportions, and the cypress-lined theater—will remain. The expansion of the museum will allow more of the permanent collection to be on view at any given time.

Ralph Norton's knowledge of museums was a sophisticated one. He had served as a trustee of the Art Institute of Chicago and thus fully understood the goals and the needs of an art museum. He was a close friend of Daniel Catton Rich, the legendary director of the Art Institute and one of the greatest of connoisseurs and art historians. Whether the Art Institute bemoaned the loss of the potential Norton gift to a new institution in Florida is not known, but to this day by our trust documents, the director of the Art Institute of Chicago serves on the R. H. Norton Trust acquisition committee for our museum, indicating generous initial and continued support for this institution.

As with most collectors, the Nortons' tastes matured as they travelled, talked with dealers, met artists, and visited the great museums of the world. Their initial collecting interests in the 1930s were aimed at decorating their new, large Chicago home, yet they resisted any temptation to acquire the merely fashionable or to embrace *retardataire*, safe tastes. Norton turned his attention to Chicago watercolorists whose work he could see firsthand in various galleries around town. Indeed, the Chicago Watercolor School is seen from today's perspective as having its own integrity as a regionalist school. As Norton became more certain of his eye, he began to collect American artists of greater reputation, often travelling to New York to select pieces for his collection. It quickly became known that Norton would not accept "any old work," simply based upon an artist's accomplishments, but that he demanded the highest quality works and would prefer not to have an artist represented at all than to have him represented by a mediocre piece. Ultimately, the Nortons turned their attention to European art, with Elizabeth Norton arguing for the acquisition of Impressionist works. Ralph Norton's taste tended consistently toward tougher, more questioning works, whether American or European. After Elizabeth's death in 1947, Ralph Norton subsequently married Ann Weaver, a sculptor and teacher at the museum's art school. It is generally thought that she influenced her husband to collect sculpture, which is well represented in the American and European collections by major works. Norton died in 1953, whereupon he gifted the balance of his collection to the museum, having donated 150 works at its opening in 1941. In addition, the R. H. Norton Fund, an endowment established for the purchase of works of art, has allowed the museum to more fully develop its American collection.

Although the history of the Norton and its collections is, to a major degree, the history of the Norton family, the institution has benefitted from the philanthropy of many other collectors of American art over the last half century. Included in this publication are important works by artists as diverse as Thomas Moran, Winslow Homer, Arthur Dove, Sam Francis, and Viola Frey, indicating hearty support for the development of the Norton's American collection from many generous donors in the community. Indeed, as this publication reached completion, a noteworthy collection—including major works by Frank Stella, Beverly Pepper, and Hans Hofmann to name but a handful of artists represented—was generously donated to the museum by Melvin and Barbara Nessel, substantially benefitting our holdings dating from the past three decades.

The strength of the Norton Museum collection is not in numbers but in quality. Norton's goal, when he had emerged as an informed, sophisticated collector, was to acquire the finest work by an artist. He particularly sought out those works which represented turning points or touchstones in an artist's career. As example, Georgia O'Keeffe's *Ranchos Church No. 1*, 1929, is her earliest painting of the adobe church at Ranchos de Taos that she made on her first visit to New Mexico. George Bellows' great painting, *Winter Afternoon*, 1929, is one of the earliest of the artist's snow scenes that Bellows considered vital to his work. He once remarked, "There has been none of my favorite snow. I must always (sic) paint the snow at least twice a year." Between the founding of the museum and his death in 1953, Norton systematically worked with the institution's director, Robert Hunter, to refine his collection, selecting only the finest works to remain as his legacy. This emphasis on quality in the collection has remained the guiding vision of the museum.

The development of the American collection has been carried out through the commitment of several fine directors and curators. Noteworthy among them are three directors: Edmund Robert Hunter (1943–1949 and 1962–1974), Willis Woods (1949–1952 and 1953–1962) and Richard Madigan (1974–1989). Trained at the Courtauld Institute in London, itself a password in the museum world, under esteemed mentors Kenneth Clark, Robert Fry, Herbert Read, and Anthony Blunt, Robert Hunter directed the Norton for a total of 18 years, taking time out to serve as director of the High Museum of Art in Atlanta. Hunter's own family, his grandfather on his maternal side, Sir Edmund Walker, had been the principal force behind the founding of the National Gallery of Canada (Ottawa), the Art Gallery of Toronto, and the Royal Ontario Museum. Unable to find museum work in Canada's tight economy, Hunter had moved to Chicago where Daniel Catton Rich personally introduced him to Ralph Norton and suggested that Norton consider him for the directorship of the new museum. Although there are many instances of the professionalism and connoisseurship which Hunter brought to the Norton, his vision can be clearly seen in his acquisition of Jackson Pollock's *Night Mist*, 1944, which he purchased in 1961, having saved three years of acquisition funds to do so. *Night Mist*, a transitional painting for Pollock, is still painted with a brush, but the paint itself is squeezed directly from the tube onto the canvas. Although seemingly abstract, it retains representational elements with vestiges of predatory birds and skeletal bones throughout.

Willis Franklin Woods, who had studied the history of art at Brown University, American University, and the University of Oregon, was lured to the Norton from an assistant directorship at the Corcoran Gallery in Washington, D.C., which has one of the most noted collections of American art and which has always been renowned for its scholarship in the field. Woods, in collaboration with Norton, purchased such important works as Winslow Homer's *Log Jam*, the previously mentioned O'Keeffe's *Ranchos Church*, and John Marin's robust painting, *Looking Up Fifth Avenue from 30th Street*. Richard Madigan, who had also been assistant director at the Corcoran Gallery, was recruited to the Norton from the founding directorship of the Brooklyn Children's Museum. Madigan characterized his directorship as "taking an activist sort of public or civic posture to bring about greater use of the museum." In addition, Madigan began to introduce contemporary art into the American collection, adding such admired works as Duane Hanson's *Young Worker*, an early polyester resin and fiberglass piece from 1975 and Claes Oldenburg's *Soft Screw*, while commissioning avant-garde installation/performance works by artists like Colette and Rockne Krebs.

Bruce Weber served as the museum's senior curator from 1981 to 1989, acquiring some exceptional works for the American collection and providing excellent scholarship in several special exhibitions of American art which garnered national attention. Weber's particular areas of interest were watercolors and silverpoint drawings. Robert Blum's delightful watercolor, *Figure of a Man in Middle Eastern Costume Leaning Against a Wall*, is an example of his skillful collecting. Since 1990 David Setford has served as the museum's senior curator, bringing to the position another European viewpoint of American art. Working together, our goal for the American collection has been to expand the contemporary holdings, to broaden the representation of works by minority artists, to strengthen the collection from the period 1949–1975, to acquire works by artists notably missing from the collection, and to broaden the range of works by acquiring examples of important regional artists, particularly Californians, whose importance to American art history has only recently been considered. There has also been a concerted effort to increase the quality and number of gifts to the collection, as witnessed by the recent Nessel gift of more than 80 works.

As the Norton Museum moves into the next century, the challenge of developing the American collection will pleasantly remain. New directors and curators will bring their specific vision, and generous collectors will choose to share their best works as gifts to the public. Generations of school children will reminisce about their first encounters with art at the Norton Museum, as they do today about the Norton past. The continuum will persist with this publication as a pausing point, a moment for assessment and for sharing, a time to praise the past, and a time to seek new horizons.

The American Collection

Selected Works

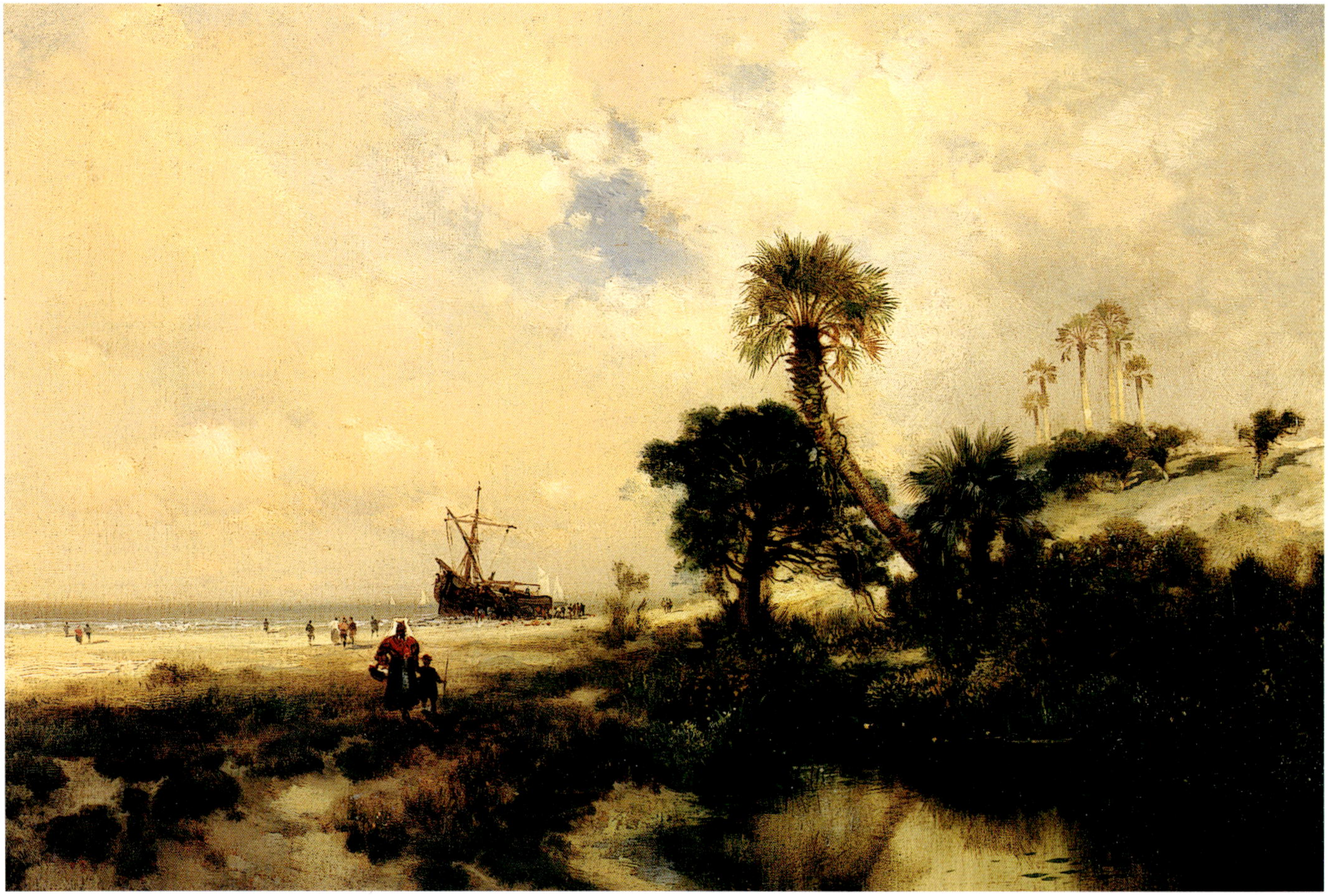

Florida Scene, ca. 1878
Oil on canvas
10 1/2 x 15 1/2 in.
Gift of Mr. Will Richeson, Jr.

Thomas Moran

1837–1926

Best known today, as in his lifetime, for his sublime paintings of the American West, Thomas Moran actually had a prolific and diverse career as an oil painter, watercolorist, illustrator and printmaker. Among the last of the nineteenth century's artist-explorers, Moran travelled extensively during his seventy-year career, capturing the essence of a wide array of landscapes.

Born in Bolton, England, Moran came to America with his family in 1844, settling in Philadelphia. At age sixteen, he began a three-year apprenticeship with a local wood-engraving firm, obtaining valuable experience for his later work as an illustrator and printmaker.

With the encouragement of his older brother Edward, a successful marine painter, Moran began painting in oils in 1855 and, the following year, began exhibiting landscapes at the Academy of Fine Arts in New York City. Essentially self-taught, Moran received some informal instruction from James Hamilton during this period. A well-established Philadelphia painter who specialized in marine subjects, Hamilton shared with Moran his appreciation of Joseph M.W. Turner's dramatic use of color and atmospheric effects, both of which Moran later incorporated into his own landscapes.

Although the French Barbizon style of landscape painting was then coming into vogue with many American painters and collectors, Moran generally painted in a style more closely allied with the Hudson River School. Like Frederic Edwin Church, whom he greatly admired, Moran sought uncultivated and unfamiliar landscapes as his subjects. After making detailed sketches and watercolors on location, Moran would return to his studio to create highly finished oil paintings which were true to nature in their particulars, but more artistic than literal in their composition.

Particularly in the 1870s, but continuing throughout his career, Moran maintained financial security through the sale of illustrations to popular magazines whose readers were eager for more knowledge of the American frontier. *Scribner's Monthly*, for example, financed several of Moran's sketching trips, including his 1871 participation in the government's Yellowstone expedition and his 1877 trip to Florida's Fort George Island. The publication of hundreds of Moran's sketches, by Scribner's and others, helped to establish him as a leading American landscape artist, a reputation which was firmly secured with his first monumental canvas, *The Grand Canyon of the Yellowstone.* Purchased by Congress for the then remarkable sum of $10,000, this panorama became the first American landscape painting to be acquired by the United States government.[1]

The enthusiastic patronage of publishers, the federal government and railroad companies who hired Moran to promote the West as a desirable destination, enabled Moran to travel widely for the rest of his career. He also painted scenery in Europe, Mexico, and other parts of the United States. Toward the end of his career, however, Moran focused once again on the American West and became increasingly vocal in his advocation of American scenery as the proper subject for American artists.

Lauded in the press in his final years as the "Dean of American Painters," Moran's reputation diminished rapidly after his death and was only revived with that of the Hudson River School. Today, Moran is appreciated for his superb draftsmanship and often daring use of color, and he is recognized as the artist who, more than any other, made the western frontier familiar and alluring to the rest of America.

Florida Scene, ca. 1878
Oil on canvas
10 1/2 x 15 1/2 in.
(no inscription)
Gift of Mr. Will Richeson, Jr. 79.43

Florida Scene represents an intriguing departure from Moran's more familiar style and subject matter. His 1877 trip to Florida was sponsored by *Scribner's Monthly* which had been running a series of articles on the post-Civil War South since 1873. Featuring the current social and political condition of the former Confederate States, each article included steel engravings of Southern scenery and society. Thus, Moran's assignment was to visit Fort George, one of the Sea Islands near the mouth of the St. John's River in Florida, and prepare illustrations for an upcoming article.[2] Upon returning to his studio, Moran additionally used his sketches to paint approximately twelve scenes of the island.

Florida's hazy, semi-tropical atmosphere, so distinct from the arid West, inspired Moran to expand his artistic vocabulary, and in *Florida Scene*, he exchanged the hard-edged, linear style with which he had described the West, for a much softer application of paint. His suggestive, rather than detailed, treatment of the foreground vegetation, for example, represents a significant stylistic change for Moran and indicates his awareness of the French Barbizon style.[3]

Yet, in rendering this new environment, Moran retained at least one convention of his western canvases, that is the compositional device of a singular tree. Like Thomas Cole before him, Moran often anchored his compositions and symbolized the particular character of the scene with the prominent placement of a distinctive tree. The tall, gracefully curving palm featured in *Florida Scene* reappears in several of Moran's Florida paintings and is his southern version of the twisting pine that distinguishes several of his western canvases.[4]

Florida Scene's narrative content is particularly intriguing. The prominent, anchored ship and its disembarking passengers, which reappear in varying combinations in several of his other Florida paintings, are fairly uncharacteristic of Moran's landscapes and suggest that he may have been commenting on the South's post-Civil War society and economy for his predominantly Northern audience.

Visiting Fort George more than a decade after the Emancipation Proclamation, Moran painted former slaves as survivors of the South's devastation. The island's cotton and sugar industry, based on slave labor, had been destroyed by the war and many former slaves had left the island in search of work. Then, in 1869, a northerner purchased Fort George and revived its economy with a free-labor orange grove, attracting young African-Americans back to the island.[5] Thus, in *Florida Scene*, Moran depicts a recovering community, focusing on its lush vegetation and the freed slaves who, having endured much, return for a new beginning. AMB

NOTES

[1] The purchase price for this painting is given in G.W. Sheldon, *America Painters* (New York City, NY: Benjamin Blom, Inc., 1972, reprint of 1881 edition), 122.

[2] Julia E. Dodge, "An Island of the Sea," *Scribner's Monthly*, vol. XIV, no. 5 (September 1877): 652–61. Six of Moran's sketches illustrate the article.

[3] At about the time he was painting *Florida Scene*, Moran dismissed the Barbizon School as being limited in its invention and ideas. He was, however, periodically influenced by the School's atmospheric effects and comparatively free application of paint. For Moran's thoughts on contemporary French painting, see Sheldon, 126–28.

[4] The recurrence of the palm in Moran's Florida paintings was brought to my attention by Christina Orr-Cahall, director of the Norton Gallery. The pine motif is discussed in Joni Louis Kinsey, *Thomas Moran and the Surveying of the American West* (Washington, D.C.: Smithsonian Institution Press, 1992), 36.

[5] The history of the island is given by Dodge, 653–54.

PROVENANCE

Will Richeson, Jr., San Marino, CA; Christie, Manson and Woods, International, 1979 (listed as *Florida Landscape*); Norton Gallery, 1979.

EXHIBITION HISTORY

Virginia Museum of Art, Richmond, VA, *Painting in the South: 1564–1980*, travelling exhibition, September 14, 1983–February 3, 1985, no. 94.

The Deland Museum of Art, Deland, FL, *Early Florida Portrayed*, November 26, 1988–January 15, 1989.

Tampa Museum of Art, Tampa, FL, *At the Water's Edge, 19th and 20th Century American Beach Scenes*, travelling exhibition, December 9, 1989–January 6, 1991, p. 124.

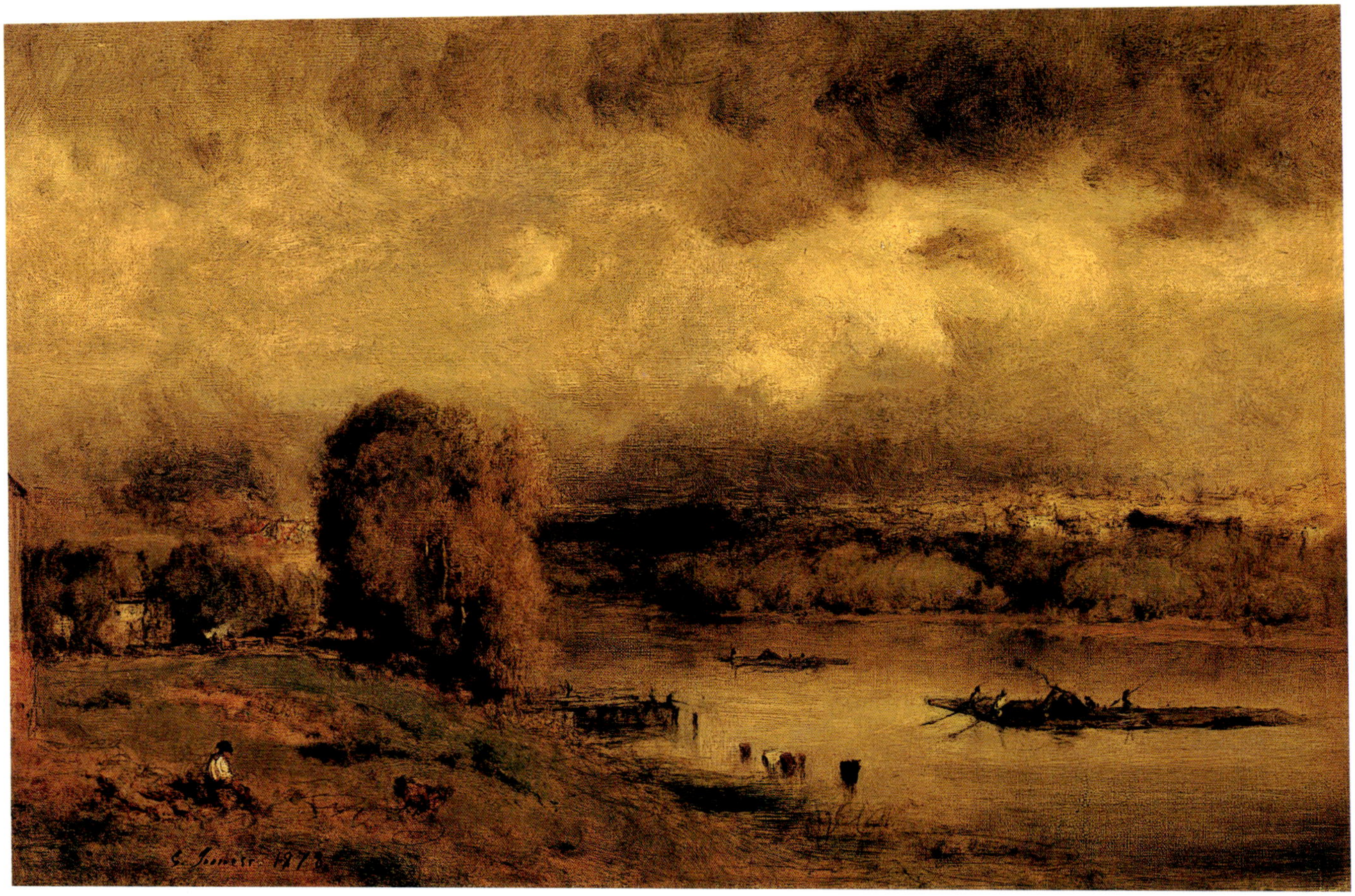

Along the Delaware, 1878
Oil on canvas
16 x 24 in.
Bequest of R. H. Norton

George Inness

1825–1894

In the final decades of the nineteenth century, George Inness substantially changed the concept and style of landscape painting in America. His personal, spiritual vision of nature prompted him to develop a more expressive artistic vocabulary, and in his mature works, Inness demonstrated landscape painting's potential to convey human sentiment and abstract truths.

Essentially self-taught, Inness studied briefly with an itinerant painter in Newark, New Jersey, before going to New York City in 1841. There he served a two-year apprenticeship as an engraver with a map-making firm and received some instruction from Regis Gignoux, a French-born landscape painter. Inness' subsequent education consisted of studying the work of his compatriots and copying prints of European paintings. In 1844, he made his professional debut at the annual exhibition of the National Academy of Design.

In New York, Inness had ample opportunity to see the works of the Hudson River School artists, and his early landscapes reflect their tight brushwork and descriptive style. After his second trip to Europe in 1853–1854, however, Inness began to assimilate aspects of the French Barbizon School into his work, particularly its looser, more suggestive brushwork, informal composition, and brighter range of color. Moreover, whereas other Americans such as Frederic Church, Albert Bierstadt and Thomas Moran were focusing on dramatic, unfamiliar scenery, Inness, like the Barbizon painters, preferred the cultivated landscape.

In 1863, Inness met the painter William Page who introduced him to the religious philosophy of the Swedish mystic Emanuel

Swedenborg. Inspired by Swedenborg's assertion that correspondences exist between the natural and spiritual worlds, Inness began to paint with increasing expression, creating landscapes in which objects appear halfway between the sharply defined, seen world and the more abstract, heavenly realm. From the mid-1880s until his death, Inness painted with an increasingly spiritual vision. His landscapes became almost otherworldly, characterized by simplified composition, palpable atmosphere, and blurred details.

Although Inness taught several students over the course of his career, among them Louis Comfort Tiffany, his greatest influence on American painting was made through the example of his work. As prominent contributions to the annual exhibitions of the National Academy of Design and the Society of American Artists, Inness' paintings were well known to his contemporaries and had a significant impact on the works of Alexander Wyant, Homer Martin, Dwight W. Tryon, Elliott Daingerfield and J. Francis Murphy.[1] In 1884, a major exhibition of his work, organized by the American Art Association, established Inness as America's leading landscape painter, a reputation he enjoyed for the remainder of his life.

Along the Delaware, 1878
Oil on canvas
16 x 24 in.
(l.l.: "G. Inness, 1878")
Bequest of R. H. Norton 53.88

Inness believed that the purpose of a work of art was not to instruct, but to "awaken emotion."[2] *In Along the Delaware*, this objective is clearly seen in Inness' deliberate subordination of the particular to the universal, and of detail to atmosphere. Moreover, this painting is especially interesting for what it reveals about Inness' experiments with the psychological effects of color.

Inness' landscapes are subjective compositions rather than literal transcriptions of a specific place. In his numerous paintings of the Delaware River, for example, he repeatedly uses certain motifs to convey his sense of the picturesque, cultivated landscape. Thus, the house in the woods, the steaming locomotive, the scattered figures, and floating barges of *Along the Delaware* all appeared, with slight variations, twelve years earlier in his *Delaware Water Gap*, 1857 (Metropolitan Museum of Art).

Yet, although the compositional conventions of *Along the Delaware* were established quite early, its style reflects a much more gradual progression toward greater abstraction and subjectivity. Painted in 1878, *Along the Delaware* represents a mid-point between the crisply descriptive paintings of his youth and the more symbolic landscapes of his later years.

Throughout the 1870s, Inness was experimenting with the effects of color, and by the time he painted *Along the Delaware*, he was being described in the press as "essentially a colorist, a luminarist."[3] That this painting is, in fact, a study in the expressive potential of color, is demonstrated by comparing it with his nearly identical canvas of the same year and title, now in the collection of the Smith College Museum of Art.[4]

Distinguished almost exclusively by their palettes, these paintings, nevertheless, convey very different moods. In both paintings, Inness presents one of his favorite themes, the approach of a storm. In the Norton's version, however, the storm's disturbance of the cultivated landscape's serenity is subtle. Smoothly blending his soft, autumnal palette, Inness unites the composition's psychologically disparate elements into a complex whole. The Smith canvas, on the other hand, is characterized by strong contrasts of dark and light, making the storm more prominent and the overall effect more ominous. In this context, *Along the Delaware* can be viewed as a vehicle for Inness' innovative investigations into the psychological significance of color and as a reflection of his remarkable ability to infuse his landscapes with emotion. AMB

NOTES

[1] Nicolai Cikovsky Jr., *George Inness* (New York City, NY: Praeger Publishers, 1971), 33.

[2] George Inness, "A Painter on Painting," *Harper's New Monthly Magazine* 56 (February 1878): 458. Reprinted in Nicolai Cikovsky Jr. and Michael Quick, *George Inness* (Los Angeles, CA: Los Angeles County Museum of Art, 1985), 205.

[3] *The Independent*, April 25, 1878 as quoted in Cikovsky, 43.

[4] Bruce Weber and William H. Gerdts, *In Nature's Ways: American Landscape Painting of the Late Nineteenth Century* (West Palm Beach, FL: Norton Gallery of Art, 1987), 9.

PROVENANCE

Marshall Field & Company, Chicago, IL; Ralph Norton, 1936; Norton Gallery, 1953.

EXHIBITION HISTORY

University Art Museum, Austin, TX, *The Paintings of George Inness*, December 12, 1965–January 30, 1966, no. 72.

The Lowe Art Museum, University of Miami, Coral Gables, FL, *Nineteenth Century American Topographic Painters*, November 21, 1974–January 5, 1975, no. 77.

Hunter Museum of Art, Chattanooga, TN, *An American Sampler: American Paintings in Southern Museums*, September 21–October 31, 1975, no. 9.

New Jersey's State Museum, Trenton, NJ, *Nineteenth Century Painters of the Delaware Valley*, travelling exhibition, January 21–April 24, 1983, no. 25.

Norton Gallery and School of Art, West Palm Beach, FL, *In Nature's Ways: American Landscape Painting of the Late Nineteenth Century*, February 21–April 12, 1987, no. 34.

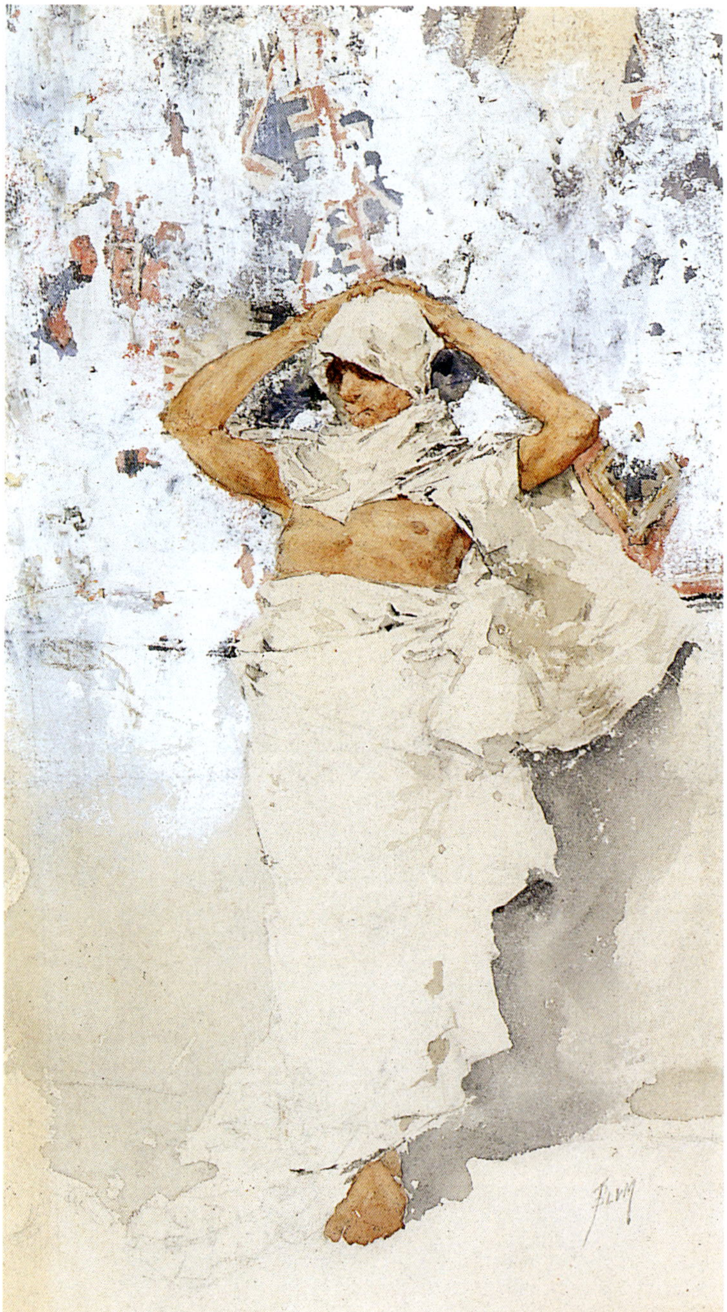

Figure of a Man in a Middle Eastern Costume, ca. 1879
Watercolor and gouache drawing on paper, mounted on paper
14 5/8 x 9 5/8 in.
Purchased through the D. Lorraine Yerkes Fund

Robert Frederick Blum

1857–1903

Robert Blum played a dual role in American art as both a conservative academic and a struggling innovator. While he worked with traditional subjects and stylistic concerns, Blum fought for the acceptance of watercolors, pastels and other media, as significant art forms.

Blum's early education in Cincinnati, his hometown, included a brief study with Frank Duveneck, an artist associated with the Munich school of realism. After moving to Philadelphia, Blum took traditional art classes from 1876 to 1877 at the Pennsylvania Academy of the Fine Arts. During the Centennial Exhibition of 1876, Blum saw the work of the Spanish artist Mariano Fortuny which he had earlier admired through the widespread photogravures of his paintings and graphic works. Fortuny's subjects included elegant eighteenth-century interiors and Middle Eastern scenes, elements which would find their way into Blum's own oeuvre.[1]

Also on display at the Centennial Exhibition were exhibits on Japanese culture and art. Blum became interested in Japanese art forms at this time, and he especially admired the asymmetrical compositions and flattened, ambiguous space of Japanese prints. Such non-Western stylistic elements began to enter Blum's own work to a great extent during the 1880s, and they played an important role in the development of his mature style.

In the 1880s, as an illustrator for *Scribner's Monthly*, Blum travelled to Europe, where he was able to see more examples of Fortuny's virtuoso brushwork. While in Venice, Blum became acquainted with the internationally acclaimed American expatriate artist James Abbott McNeill Whistler, whose fluid, painterly techniques and decorative motifs had a significant impact on the younger artist's work. Based on Whistler's influence, Blum's graphic work of this period became more atmospheric, and Whistler's love of Japanese prints strengthened the importance of that Japanese art form for Blum. During the mid-1880s, Blum executed several important oil paintings of the working women of Venice, and these paved the way for his election as an associate member of the National Academy of Design.

While he was relatively conservative in his education and stylistic approaches, Blum used an unusually wide variety of media for his art. These media included oils, pastels, watercolors, pen-and-ink drawings, etchings, drypoints, murals and stained glass. As early as the late 1870s, Blum became known for his illustrations and watercolors exhibited at the American Water Color Society in New York. Blum's innovations included a technique for applying watercolor in thin layers with modulations of color, whereas previous painters had attempted to imitate the consistency of oils. He worked in pastels as well, and together with his friend, the internationally known William Merritt Chase, he participated in the founding of New York's Society of Painters of Pastel in 1882. Although Blum's pastels and watercolors were somewhat unconventional in their experimental techniques, the conservative Chase admired his colleague's work greatly and had many of them in his own collection.[2]

Blum championed graphic work as well, returning to his work as an illustrator in 1890 with a commission from *Scribner's Magazine* to travel to Japan. There, Blum illustrated articles that were being written on the customs and people of Japan by Sir Edwin Arnold, later collected into the book *Japonica*. After his return to the U.S. in 1893, Blum continued to expand his forms of artistic expression by working on mural commissions, such as those for the Mendelssohn Glee Club's auditorium in New York. Soon after the completion of these murals, the artist became ill, and he was able to execute only a few additional works before his death in 1903.

Figure of a Man in a Middle Eastern Costume
ca. 1879
Watercolor and gouache drawing on paper, mounted on paper
14 5/8 x 9 5/8 in.
(l.r.: "Blum")
Purchased through the D. Lorraine Yerkes Fund 81.19

Figure of a Man in a Middle Eastern Costume is perhaps the first instance in which Blum used both watercolor and gouache together, and the combination of the two media exemplifies the innovations in technique characteristic of Blum s work. In *Figure of a Man*, the top of the wall is painted in gouache while the rest of the image is in watercolor. Different types of watercolor are used, both thin and thick, transparent and opaque. Blum began to exhibit watercolors at the American Water Color Society at the beginning of his career, and *Figure of a Man* belongs to this early period of innovation and experimentation. Blum's new techniques in watercolor, allied with those of his colleagues Winslow Homer and Frank Currier, rejected the conventional use of that medium to imitate oil paints. Instead, he used washes of paint that had less solid color. Blum utilized the inherent fluidity in watercolor paints to create artistic effects unique to the medium.[3]

Figure of a Man presents an image that is full of potential movement. The figure's cloaks seem to sway with energy, and the subject appears to be arrested in an instantaneous pose, as if leaning against the wall for a moment of rest. While Blum does model and shade the figure's contoured body, a pervasive sense of weightlessness results from Blum's fluid handling of the watercolor medium.

Under the influence of Fortuny, Blum became interested in depicting the exotic peoples of foreign cultures, such as those of the Middle East, even though he probably had never visited that region. Blum's depictions of peoples different from himself are dealt with quite sensitively. Although his representations are not portraits, they do present images of individuals and not perpetuations of negative stereotypes. In *Figure of a Man* the man leaning against the wall appears in a natural, calm pose, unaware of his status as an exotic object for both the artist and the viewer.

In many of his works, Blum was interested in abstract, decorative designs, such as the textile pattern on the wall in the background of this image. Like the figure, the textile pattern, itself, is somewhat exotic, and its inclusion suggests its significance as a decorative element of Middle Eastern culture. The background wall and the patterned fabric design lend a flattened quality to the overall composition that may derive, in part, from Blum's admiration for Japanese prints and other non-Western art forms. LTJ

NOTES

[1] Bruce Weber, "Robert Frederick Blum (1857–1903) and His Milieu" (Ph.D. diss., City University of New York, 1985), 18–47. Richard J. Boyle, *A Retrospective Exhibition: Robert F. Blum, 1857–1903* (Cincinnati, OH: Cincinnati Art Museum, 1966), 3.

[2] Margaretta Lovell, *Venice: The American View, 1860–1920* (San Francisco, CA: Fine Arts Museum of San Francisco, 1985), 24. For information on Blum's participation in the Society of Painters in Pastel, see Dianne H. Pilgrim, "The Revival of Pastels in Nineteenth-Century America," *American Art Journal* 10 (November 1978): 43–62. For Blum's watercolors and pastels, see Weber, 65, 74–75, 145, 169.

[3] Bruce Weber, *Master Watercolors and Drawings from the Norton Gallery of Art* (Washington, D.C.: Smithsonian Institution Press, 1988), 36–37; Weber, Blum, 145.

PROVENANCE

Norton Gallery, 1981.

EXHIBITION HISTORY

Smithsonian Institution, *Master Watercolors and Drawings from the Norton Gallery of Art*, travelling exhibition, February 11, 1988–September 24, 1989.

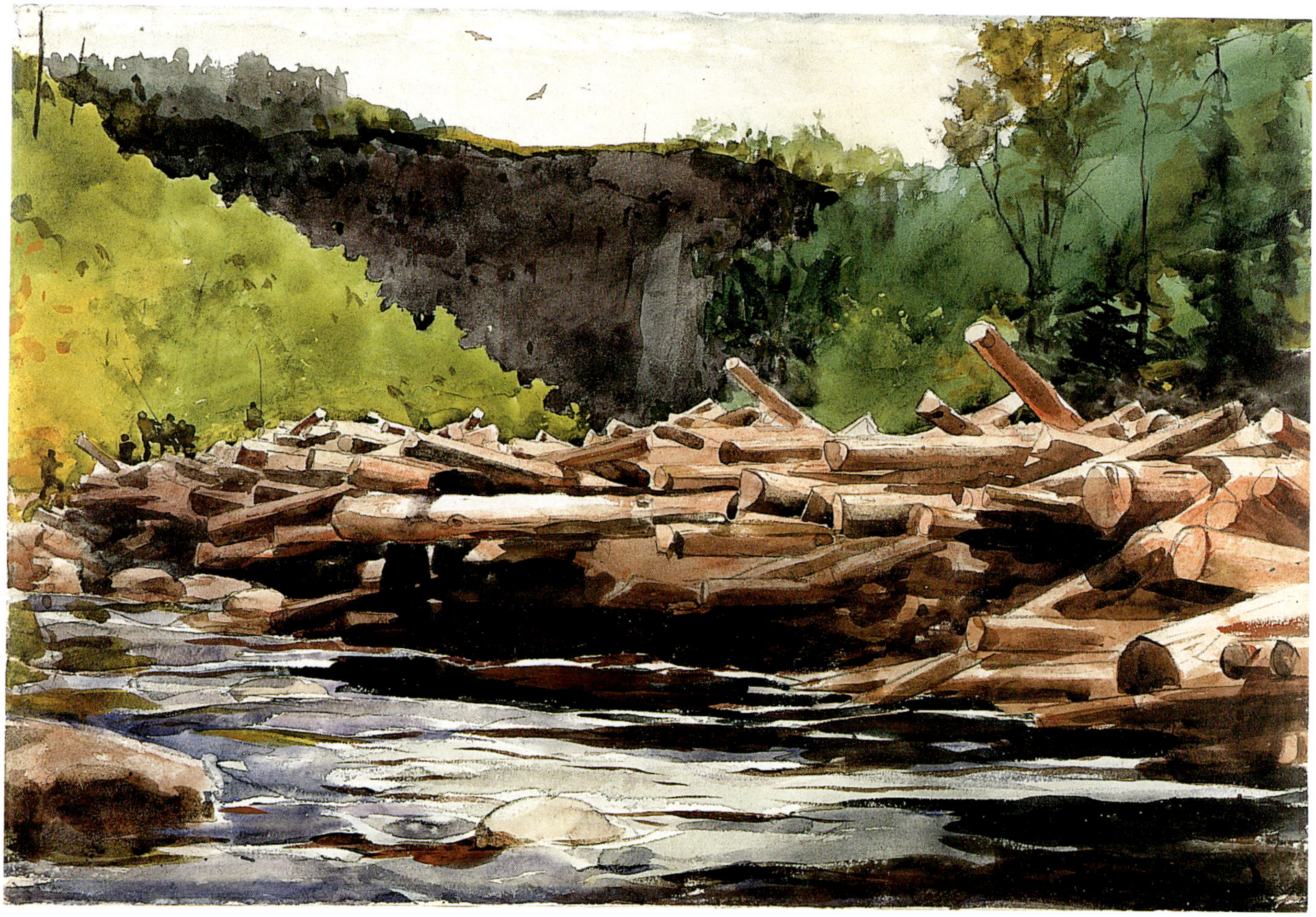

The Hudson River at Blue Ledge,
Essex County (The Log Jam), 1889
Watercolor on paper
14 1/2 x 21 in.
Bequest of R. H. Norton

Winslow Homer

1836–1910

Among the most renowned of American artists, Winslow Homer was an extraordinary illustrator, oil painter and watercolorist. In a career that lasted more than fifty years, Homer examined the many facets of life in nineteenth-century America and presented the power of nature with exceptional acumen.

Born in Boston and reared in Cambridge, Massachusetts, Homer began his limited formal training in 1855 when he was apprenticed to the lithographer J. H. Bufford. His career as an illustrator began two years later when he started drawing for *Ballou's Pictorial* in Boston. Within two years, Homer was also working as a freelance illustrator for *Harper's Weekly* in New York and in 1859, he moved there and began attending drawing classes at the National Academy of Design. With the outbreak of the Civil War, *Harper's* sent Homer to the front. His straight-forward, unromanticized drawings of the war quickly established him as one of the most respected illustrators in America.

During this period, Homer began his first professional paintings. After studying briefly with the little-known painter Frederick Rondel, Homer translated several of his war drawings into critically acclaimed oil paintings. Prominent among these was *Prisoners From the Front*, 1866 (Metropolitan Museum of Art) which secured Homer's election to the National Academy of Design. With the success of these first canvases, Homer increasingly viewed himself as a painter but continued working as an illustrator until 1875.

At the end of the war, Homer turned to chronicling the leisure activities of peacetime America. His sun-dappled, idyllic scenes of country life and seaside recreation owed much to the influence of the French Impressionists, whose work he had seen in Paris in 1866.

Homer's work changed dramatically in the early 1880s when he spent nearly two years in England, painting the rugged North Sea coast. Here, his earlier fair-weather leisure subjects were replaced by stormy scenes of fishermen struggling against turbulent seas. Visiting London frequently during this time, Homer undoubtedly saw Joseph M. W. Turner's watercolors which seem reflected in the newly emotional content of Homer's British seascapes.

Returning to America in 1882, Homer settled in Prout's Neck, on the coast of Maine, and continued to paint scenes of the struggle for survival in the face of elemental danger. Although Maine remained his home to the end of his life, Homer continued to travel, periodically seeking a change of scenery in the Adirondacks, the Caribbean, or Canada. His *View From Cape Diamond, Levis, Quebec*, also in the Norton Museum of Art collection, was painted during this period.

In the final years of his life, Homer became a virtual recluse, seemingly indifferent to his reputation as the foremost artist of the day. He remained active as a painter, however, creating provocative scenes of nature's power and the challenges faced by those who choose to confront it.

The Hudson River at Blue Ledge, Essex County (The Log Jam), 1889
Watercolor on paper
14 1/2 x 21 in.
(l.r.: "Homer," inscribed on original backing board: "The Hudson River at Blue Ledge, Essex County, New York. About 17 miles from North Creek dated 1889")
Bequest of R. H. Norton 53.83

Perhaps more than any other American artist, Homer established watercolor as an acceptable medium for professional artists by demonstrating that its expressive possibilities rivaled those of oil paint. Painted sixteen years after he had first started using watercolor, *The Hudson River at Blue Ledge*, familiarly known as "The Log Jam," illustrates Homer's fluid and brilliant handling of this medium.

Homer first visited the Adirondack area in 1870 and returned often to paint the natural beauty of the wilderness. In 1888, he became a member of the North Wood's Club, a private preserve which became his Adirondack base. During a two-month stay at the Club in 1889, Homer traveled a mile south to Blue Ledge and painted this scene of loggers struggling to free their "harvest," which has become jammed on its way down the river.

The specificity of Homer's inscription on the back of this watercolor, in which he clearly identifies the subject's location, is reminiscent of his detailed notations on wartime drawings and suggests that he was recording an actual scene.[1] In fact, Homer painted several images which detail the effects of logging in the area, causing some scholars to speculate on his possible environmental concerns.[2] This theory is discredited, however, when the logging scenes are viewed in the context of Homer's entire Adirondack oeuvre, in which he respectfully depicts woodsmen as a natural part of their environment.[3] Moreover, in its focus on the struggle between man and nature, *The Hudson River at Blue Ledge* is clearly thematically related to Homer's seafaring paintings. Finally, the loggers appear significantly minute in proportion to their surroundings, and the composition is dominated by the logs themselves.

The Hudson River at Blue Ledge reveals Homer's remarkable ability to depict a potentially mundane subject with forceful drama. The striking diagonals of the individual and tilting logs are echoed by those of the entire log jam and the mountains behind, giving the scene an overall dynamism which is reinforced by Homer's masterful handling of his medium. Broad, confident washes of color in the background, for example, meet along surprisingly delicate, undulating lines. Moreover, this bold handling of the background contrasts starkly with the more precisely painted foreground which is, in turn, animated by the varied effects of the brilliant spring sunlight. In all, *The Hudson River at Blue Ledge* represents an impressive balance of contrasts and reveals Homer's singular vision of nature and mastery of his art. AMB

NOTES

[1] For example, an undated drawing of Fort Lyon was inscribed by Homer: "Covers 36 acres. Sketched from Hunting Creek/This is the largest fort south of the Potomac/Near Alexandria." Reprinted in Sally Mills, "A Chronology of Homer's Early Career, 1859–1866," in Marc Simpson, ed., *Winslow Homer Paintings of the Civil War* (San Francisco, CA: The Fine Arts Museums of San Francisco, 1988), 18.

[2] See Matthew Zbornik, *Winslow Homer: Water and Light, Selected Watercolors 1873–1908* (Miami, FL: Center for the Arts, 1991), 19; Helen A. Cooper, "Old Friends," in Susan E. Strickler, ed., *American Traditions in Watercolor* (New York City, NY: Abbeville Press, 1987), 96; and Donelson F. Hoopes, *Winslow Homer Watercolors* (New York City, NY: Watson-Guptill Publications, 1978), 68.

[3] Homer's views on environmental issues were not recorded, and all speculations on this issue are therefore based on his paintings. For thorough discussions of his Adirondack work, see James Fosburgh, "Homer in the Adirondacks," *Portfolio* (Winter 1963): 72–87, 111–12; and David Tatham, "Winslow Homer at the North Woods Club," in Nicolai Cikovsky Jr., ed., *Winslow Homer, A Symposium*, Studies in the History of Art 26 (Hanover, NH: The University Press of New England, 1990), 115–132.

PROVENANCE

Artist; Doll and Richards Gallery; George H. Webster, Haverhill, MA; M. Knoedler and Company, Inc.; Ralph Norton, 1950; Norton Gallery, 1953.

EXHIBITION HISTORY

Pennsylvania Academy of the Fine Arts, Philadelphia, PA, *Third Annual Philadelphia Watercolor Exhibition*, March 26–April 21, 1906, no. 333.

Brooks Memorial Art Gallery, Memphis, TN, *A Loan Exhibition of American Painting*, October 5–29, 1945, no. 26.

North Carolina State Art Society, Raleigh, NC, *The American Scene from 1750*, December 12, 1945–January 3, 1946, no. 29.

Atlanta Art Association Galleries, Atlanta, GA, *Landscape into Art*, February 6–25, 1962, no. 42.

Storm King Art Center, Mountainville, NY, *Winslow Homer in New York State*, June 29–August 22, 1963, no. 45.

The Lowe Art Museum, University of Miami, Coral Gables, FL, *Nineteenth Century American Topographic Painters*, November 21, 1974–January 5, 1975, no. 77.

Hunter Museum of Art, Chattanooga, TN, *A Southern Sampler: American Paintings in Southern Museums*, September 21–October 31, 1975, no. 8.

Pensacola Museum of Art, Pensacola, FL, *American and European Masterpieces of the Nineteenth and Twentieth Centuries*, September 22–November 16, 1984.

Smithsonian Institution, Washington, D.C., *Master Watercolors and Drawings from the Norton Gallery of Art*, travelling exhibition, February 11, 1988–September 24, 1989, p. 10.

Center for the Fine Arts, Miami, FL, *Winslow Homer: Water and Light, Selected Watercolors 1873–1908*, November 2, 1991–February 15, 1992, p. 19.

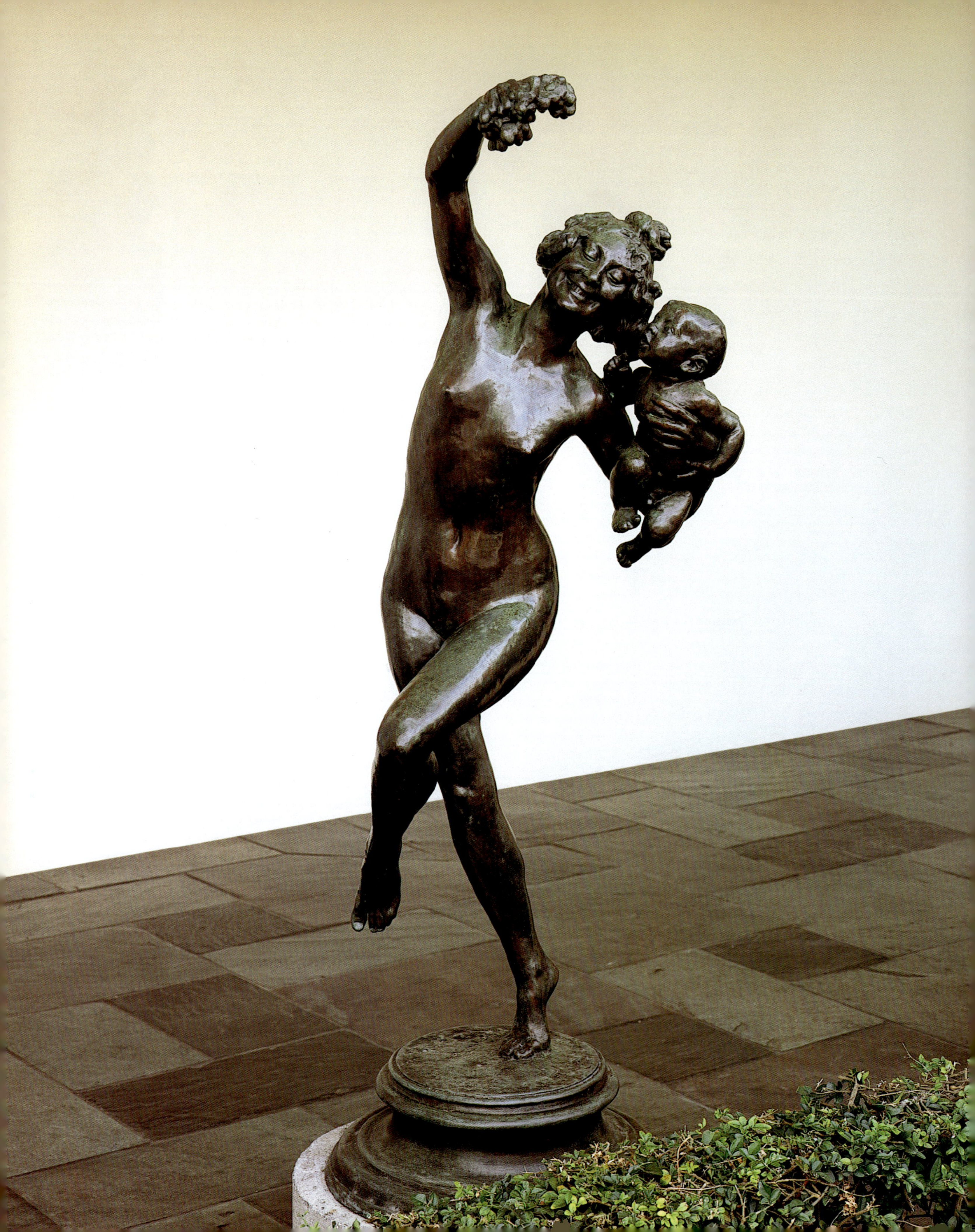

Frederick William MacMonnies

1863–1937

Frederick MacMonnies was one of the most successful American sculptors of the late nineteenth century. With his fluid style and technical virtuosity, he secured numerous public commissions and enjoyed critical acclaim both in the United States and Europe.

Born in Brooklyn Heights, New York, MacMonnies became an assistant to Augustus Saint-Gaudens, a highly regarded academic sculptor, in 1881. For the next four years, MacMonnies worked in Saint-Gaudens' studio and attended evening courses at the Art Students League, the National Academy of Design, and Cooper Union in New York City.

MacMonnies left for Paris in 1884, intending to study at the Ecole des Beaux-Arts, one of the most prestigious art schools in Europe. An outbreak of cholera forced MacMonnies to flee Paris shortly after his arrival, however, and his European studies thus began at the Royal Academy of Fine Arts in Munich. Returning to Paris two years later, MacMonnies began studying sculpture with Alexandre Falguiere at the Ecole. Adopting the sensual, decorative style of Falguiere in favor of the more restrained, didactic style of Saint-Gaudens, MacMonnies advanced quickly. In 1887, and again in 1888, he won the premier prix d'atelier in Falguiere's class, the highest award given to foreign students. His success continued at the Paris Salon, where he soon won numerous awards.

Bacchante and Infant Faun, 1893
Bronze
67 x 22 x 22 in.
Bequest of R. H. Norton

In 1893, MacMonnies was awarded the most prestigious sculptural commission of the World's Columbian Exposition in Chicago: the fountain for the central Grand Basin. His massive allegory, *Triumph of Columbia*, was a sensation. Seen by the millions who visited the Fair, and praised by his peers, the fountain firmly established MacMonnies' reputation as a leading American sculptor.

MacMonnies remained one of America's most honored and prolific sculptors up to the turn of the century when he temporarily gave up sculpture in favor of painting.[1] His canvases never received the critical acclaim his sculpture had enjoyed, however, and in 1904, he returned to sculpting. Yet, despite his receipt of several substantial commissions during this period, MacMonnies never regained primacy in his field. Failing to acknowledge the radical changes which were redefining modern sculpture, MacMonnies adhered to the Beaux-Arts style with which he had achieved his success, and his reputation as a progressive sculptor was gradually superseded by that of the modernists.

Bacchante and Infant Faun, 1893
Bronze
67 x 22 x 22 in.
(inscribed on base: "F. MacMonnies and JABOEUF & ROUARD, FONDEURS")
Bequest of R. H. Norton 53.116

MacMonnies' *Bacchante and Infant Faun* was perhaps the most notorious public sculpture of the late nineteenth century. Executed in the exalted Beaux-Arts style, the statue depicts a follower of Bacchus, the Roman god of wine, as she dances with a faun, or satyr, in a drunken celebration. The wanton inebriety of the figure offended American sensibilities, however, and when she was installed as the centerpiece of the Boston Public Library's courtyard in 1896, the *Bacchante* drew fire from numerous religious, temperance and social groups.[2]

Ironically, this sculpture exemplifies precisely those qualities that had previously made MacMonnies' work so celebrated in Paris. For example, although the sculpture's subject is classical, its style is not. Eschewing the massive female proportions favored in antique sculpture, MacMonnies created a svelte, lively figure which reflects the more naturalistic, albeit decorative, female nude that was then coming into fashion at the Ecole. Moreover, MacMonnies instilled his work with even greater naturalism by electing to give the *Bacchante* his model's face instead of an idealized, anonymous one. Finally, the figure's sprightly stance exudes a remarkable vitality which demonstrates MacMonnies' extraordinary technical skill.

In the Boston scandal of 1896, however, the *Bacchante*'s artistic merits were overshadowed by its social implications. Deeming the spirit of *Bacchante and Infant Faun* as inappropriate for a public setting, the Boston Library's trustees removed the statue from the courtyard only a few months after its installation.

Far from damaging MacMonnies' career, the *Bacchante* scandal only increased his fame and, in the end, Boston's rejection of the *Bacchante and Infant Faun* is perhaps most properly seen as a compliment. In believing that the sculpture was capable of corrupting its audience, critics of the *Bacchante* were acknowledging the thoroughly convincing exuberance with which MacMonnies had animated his figure.

The *Bacchante* was, in fact, popular enough to warrant numerous castings during MacMonnies' lifetime. Significantly, most of these succeeding casts were reduced in scale, making them more practical for private display. The Norton Museum of Art's *Bacchante*, for instance, is one of four known to have been cast in three-quarter scale, specifically to complement small gardens or courtyards.[3] AMB

NOTES

[1] In 1927, MacMonnies explained that this decision was based on his "suffering so from indigestion of sculpture and hard work." MacMonnies in an interview with DeWitt M. Lockman, quoted in Janis Conner and Joel Rosenkranz, *Rediscoveries in America Sculpture* (Austin, TX: University of Texas Press, 1989), 130.

[2] The most thorough account of the Boston scandal is given in Walter Muir Whitehill, "The Vicissitudes of Bacchante in Boston," *The New England Quarterly* (December 1954): 435–54.

[3] Susan E. Menconi, *Uncommon Spirit: Sculpture in America, 1800–1940* (New York City, NY: Hirschl & Adler Galleries, Inc. 1989), 44. Information on the provenance of each casting is given in E. Adina Gordon, "Frederick William MacMonnies: an American Sculptor," (Ph.D. diss., Institute of Fine Arts, New York University, forthcoming).

PROVENANCE

The Art Holding Company; Ralph Norton, 1941; Norton Gallery, 1953.

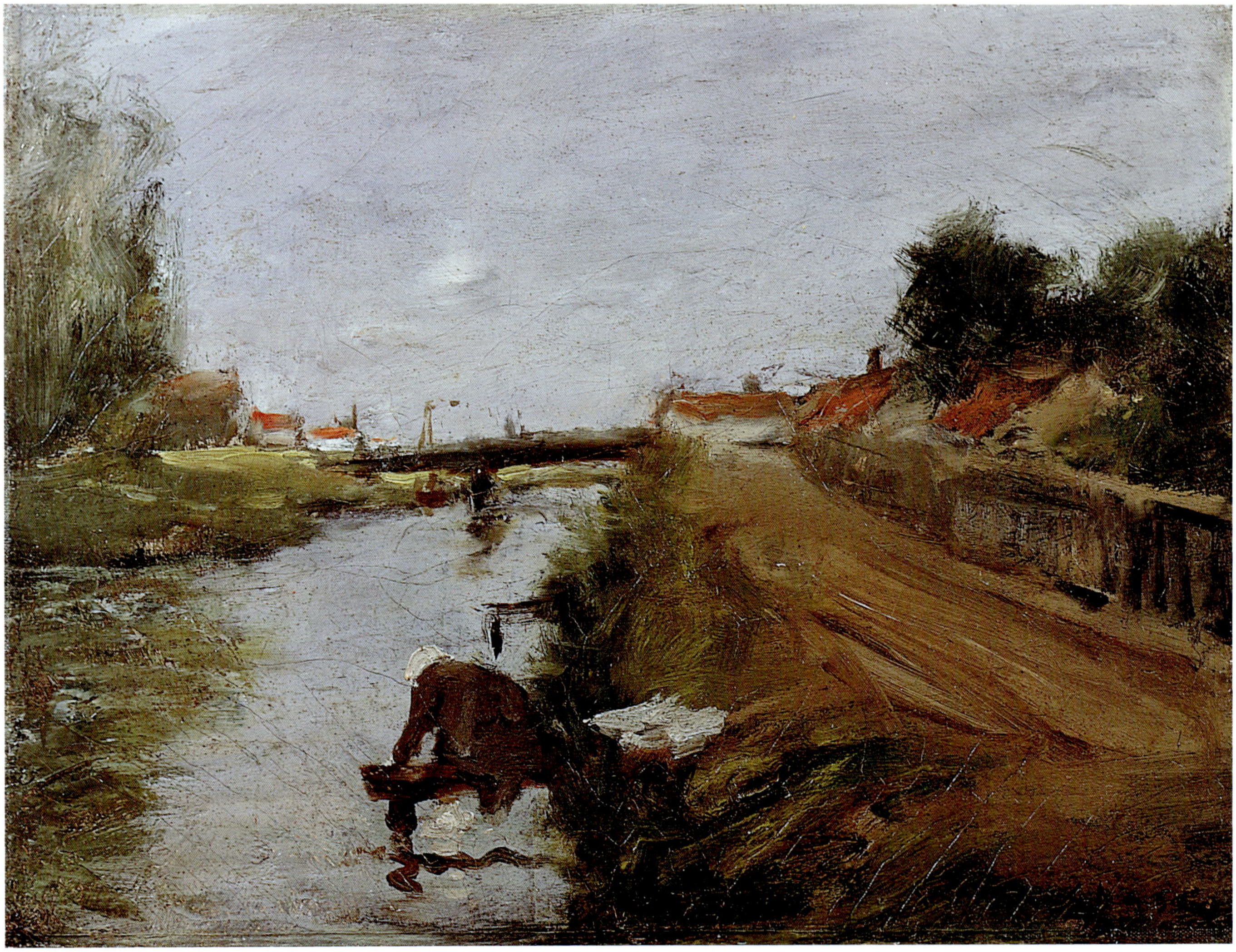

Untitled (Landscape), ca. 1912
Oil on canvas
9 1/2 x 12 1/2 in.
Acquired through deaccession

William Merritt Chase

1849–1916

After several attempts at other careers, William Merritt Chase decided to travel to New York in 1869, to pursue his artistic education at the National Academy of Design. With the donations of some wealthy patrons from St. Louis, Chase was able to travel in 1872, to Munich, a popular destination for aspiring young painters that rivaled Paris in its education of American artists. While at the Royal Academy in Munich, Chase studied the realist tradition that had been established by the circle of William Leibl. Adopting the darkened palette of the Munich painters, Chase shared their admiration for the work of the seventeenth-century masters Frans Hals and Diego Velázquez. The technical virtuosity and bravura brushwork of these painters and his Munich mentors, provided Chase with the basis of his own swiftly executed realist paintings. Combining these techniques with his own dynamic style, Chase became a successful painter of portraits, still lifes and landscapes soon after his return to the United States in 1878.

Having achieved a certain level of popularity in the United States, Chase returned to Europe in the 1880s, where he encountered the recent developments in French Impressionism. Chase admired the lightened palette and loose brushwork of the Impressionists, and he synthesized these with his own realist manner in a series of park scenes in New York City. In the 1890s, Chase adopted an even more thoroughly Impressionist style in his brilliantly lit landscapes painted on the New England coast. In these scenes, Chase shared with the French Impressionists a love of painting outdoors and a concern for light and atmospheric effects.

Chase was a popular artist, not just among American patrons of art, but also among his artistic colleagues. Chase's famous Tenth Street studio in New York City was a gathering place for artists in the 1880s and 1890s, and during that same period, Chase served as the President of the Society of American Artists and a member of the National Academy of Design. Although during the 1880s and 1890s Chase was internationally known as a leader in American art, by the end of his life, his popularity had begun to wane. During the last years of his life, Chase's work was greatly overshadowed by the recent developments in American modernism.

With his flair for the eccentric and his virtuoso style, Chase enthralled a generation of students at several institutions, including the Art Students League in New York City, where he taught for much of the period from 1878 to 1911. Chase eventually opened his own school of art in New York and a summer school at Shinnecock, near Long Island, which became the most important school for plein air painting in America. Several of his pupils were the painters who, a couple of decades later, would participate in the origins of American modernism: Georgia O'Keeffe, Alfred Maurer, Charles Demuth, and Marsden Hartley, among others. Although his students did not continue to work in Chase's realist style, their technical training proved essential for the early development of American abstraction.

Untitled (Landscape), ca. 1912
Oil on canvas
9 1/2 x 12 1/2 in.
(l.r.: "Wm. M. Chase")
Acquired through deaccession 83.194

Although Chase produced mainly portraits and still-life paintings during the last two decades of his life, he also painted outdoor scenes on his annual tours of Europe with American students. This untitled landscape could have been painted on such a trip because it is small and would have been easily portable. According to the leading scholar on Chase, Ronald G. Pisano, this painting may be a plein air work done in Holland or Belgium during Chase's visit to Europe in the summer of 1912.[1]

As in many of Chase's landscapes from his last journeys to Europe, his palette returned in this work to a significantly darker one. This change in Chase's palette may have resulted from his admiration for the dark colors of the Baroque masters, whom he would have seen once again with his students at the galleries of Europe. Chase encouraged his students to study the old masters who had been important influences for his own early artistic career.[2]

Many of Chase's landscapes present a horizon line at the middle of the canvas and a strong diagonal that recedes from the foreground to the background along a road or pathway. In this landscape, the strong diagonal of the road on the right suggests a conventional perspectival recession of space, while at the same time, the loosely rendered composition is filled with spatial ambiguities.

The placement of the solitary figure on the short pier in the foreground, creates a certain intimacy of space on the rather small canvas, but the figure's turned back forces the viewer to remain detached from the scene. Although the road on the right provides an entrance into the illusionistic space of the painting, it prevents that entry by wrapping around to the right side of the canvas. These compositional elements, though they appear throughout Chase's oeuvre, may in this painting signal an especially poignant feeling of alienation. Chase may have felt a similar detachment in his own life, as his popularity and status waned sharply in the final years of his lengthy career. LTJ

NOTES

[1] I am grateful to Ronald G. Pisano for his helpful comments on this painting's place within Chase's oeuvre.

[2] Ronald G. Pisano, *Summer Afternoons: Landscape Paintings of William Merritt Chase* (Boston, MA: Little, Brown, and Co., 1993), 15.

PROVENANCE

Norton Gallery, 1985.

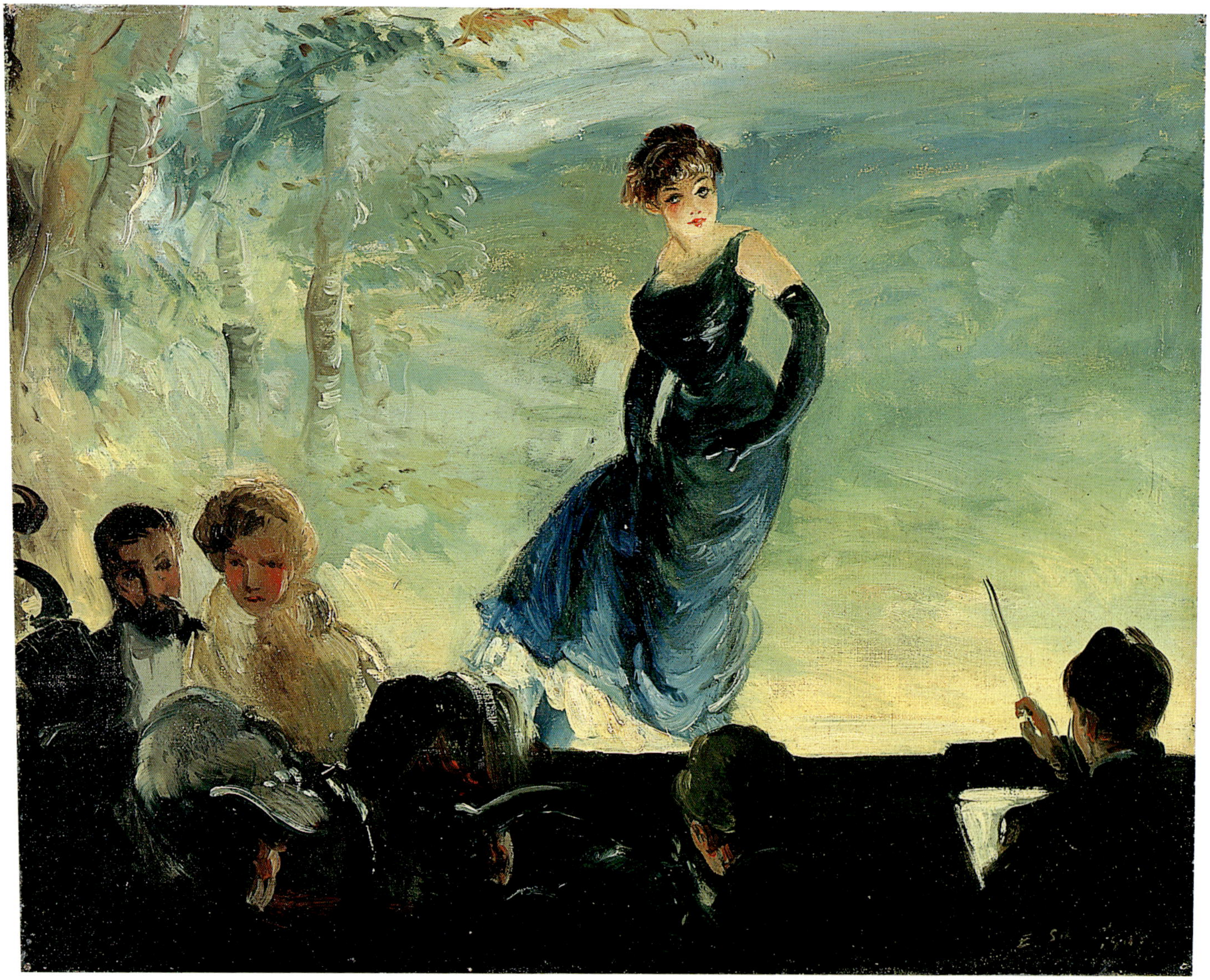

Concert Stage, 1905
Oil on canvas
16 1/2 x 20 in.
Bequest of R. H. Norton

Everett Shinn

1876–1953

Everett Shinn's formal artistic education began in Philadelphia in 1893 at the Pennsylvania Academy of the Fine Arts, and his occupation as a newspaper illustrator during the same decade, gave him the opportunity to develop his artistic talents. Working at the *Philadelphia Inquirer*, and then at the *Philadelphia Press*, Shinn met George Luks and other colleagues with whom he would continue to associate upon his move to New York in 1897. Shinn worked with Luks as well as William Glackens at the *New York World* at the turn of the century, drawing illustrations for newspaper stories from his notes and memories of the actual scenes. This practice gave Shinn the skill to depict crowds of bustling activity with great speed of execution, and soon, he extended his work to include color magazine illustrations for *Harper's Weekly*.

During the late 1890s, Shinn translated his reportage techniques into more formal art forms,such as pastels, while continuing to depict scenes of the life of New York. Shinn's use of pastels for urban images differed from the usual employment of this medium for more traditional subject matter. He considered pastels, as well as charcoal and watercolor as an appropriately flexible and direct media for depicting the bustling scenes of city life. Using a darker palette than was common at the time, Shinn developed a technique for executing his pastel works on a wet surface, a method that demanded the same swift drawing found in his newspaper illustrations.

After he returned from a trip to France and England in 1900, both Shinn's subjects and his medium underwent several changes.

Concert Stage, 1905
Oil on canvas
16 1/2 x 20 in.
(l.r.: "E. Shinn 1905")
Bequest of R. H. Norton 53.176

Although he did continue to depict scenes of the city streets, Shinn became increasingly devoted to the theater, and he began to record its stages and audiences in oil paintings. European influences that may have inspired these changes in Shinn's work include scenes of the theatre by the French painter Edgar Degas and the illustrator Jean-Louis Forain. By 1904, the theater had become Shinn's signature subject, and the *New York Times* could refer to the artist thus, "His great haunt is the open-air stage, the café chantant, or the small Parisian theatre." [1]

Shinn was the youngest of the group of The Eight, organized by his friend and colleague, Robert Henri. This group, who exhibited together at the Macbeth Galleries in 1908, included Shinn, Henri, Glackens, John Sloan, Ernest Lawson, Maurice Prendergast, George Luks and Arthur B. Davies. Shinn contributed mostly theatrical scenes to their exhibit at Macbeth Galleries. His images of the theater contain loose brushwork and a darkened palette that was shared by several other members of The Eight.

Shinn's love of the theatre was not limited to his paintings and drawings. He was commissioned to paint the murals for the Stuyvesant Theater in 1906, and he filled the walls of this Broadway institution with "neo-rococo" images of the dramatic passions. In 1912, following the first of a series of divorces, Shinn's career as an artist was superseded by his desire to work as an art director and set designer for movies. Repeating the theatrical motifs that had enchanted him in his youth, Shinn continued to paint until his death despite a declining audience for his work.

Although he could not remember who the performer was, Shinn described *Concert Stage* in a letter to Ralph Norton as "...one of our vaudeville theatres in those days of smothering skirts..." [2] Vaudeville was a popular form of middle-class entertainment around 1905, and most of Shinn's theaters were vaudeville ones, rather than the more exclusive uptown establishments. This painting depicts a female performer lit with bright stage spotlights and surrounded by a painted landscape set design in the background.

Watching and being watched became important themes in Shinn's early illustrations of dramatic city events, and this voyeuristic phenomenon functions more literally as a significant part of his theatrical scenes. Subjects such as vaudeville allowed Shinn to explore the roles of the audience and the performers as a microcosm of the theatricality of modern city life.[3] In *Concert Stage* the viewer's proximity to the stage positions him or her in the front rows of the theater as part of the audience looking at the performer, the orchestra, and the other members of the audience. Shinn's figures in this and other paintings display a keen awareness of their visual presence, as if conscious of their own positions as objects of display and as participants in the theatrical spectacle. The singer functions as the central object of attention for the audience, the orchestra and the viewer of the painting. At the same time, the singer is the most centrally positioned "viewer" herself, staring out at the onlookers from her position on the stage. The couple at the front left also gaze out at the viewer of the painting, while, ironically, turning their backs on the performer.

As contemporary critics noted, Shinn's theatrical images, such as *Concert Stage*, are indebted to a French tradition of theatrical scenes in the works of Edgar Degas and Jean-Louis Forain. Shinn utilized similar compositional elements as these earlier artists, such as an unusual point of view, often from a low position in or near orchestra pit. Other common stylistic elements include the arbitrary cropping of the subject at the edge of the canvas and the dramatic stage lighting of central figures. Despite these similarities, Shinn's swiftness of execution, combined with his loosened, painterly style, clearly separate his works from the often more tightly finished images of Degas. The sketchy presentation of the stage set and the thickly applied white highlights on the performer and the audience exemplify the gestural manner that Shinn shared with many of his American colleagues in The Eight. LTJ

NOTES

[1] Linda Ferber, "Stagestruck: The Theatre Subjects of Everett Shinn," *Studies in the History of Art* 37 (1990): 52–55, 64. Sylvia L. Yount, "Consuming Drama: Everett Shinn and the Spectacular City," *American Art* 6 (Fall 1992): 89–91, 99.

[2] Everett Shinn, letter to R. H. Norton, ca. 1940, Norton Gallery and School of Art, West Palm Beach, FL.

[3] Yount, 103–6.

PROVENANCE

Milch Galleries, 1940; Ralph H. Norton, 1940; Norton Gallery, 1953.

EXHIBITION HISTORY

The Art Institute of Chicago, Chicago, IL, *Half a Century of American Art*, November 16, 1939–January 7, 1940, no. 149.

Morse Gallery, Rollins College, Winter Park, FL, *The Eight and the American Scene*, December 3–24, 1960, no. 21.

Columbus Gallery of Fine Arts, Columbus, OH, *Art in the Homes of Columbus*, February15–March 15, 1963.

Museum of Fine Arts, St. Petersburg, FL, *Masters from the Norton Gallery*, April 16–May 21, 1978.

Visual Arts Gallery, Florida International University, Miami, FL, *Treasures from the Norton Gallery of Art*, September 28–October 21, 1982, no. 22.

Pensacola Museum of Art, Pensacola, FL, *American and European Masterpieces of the Nineteenth and Twentieth Centuries*, September 22–November 16, 1984.

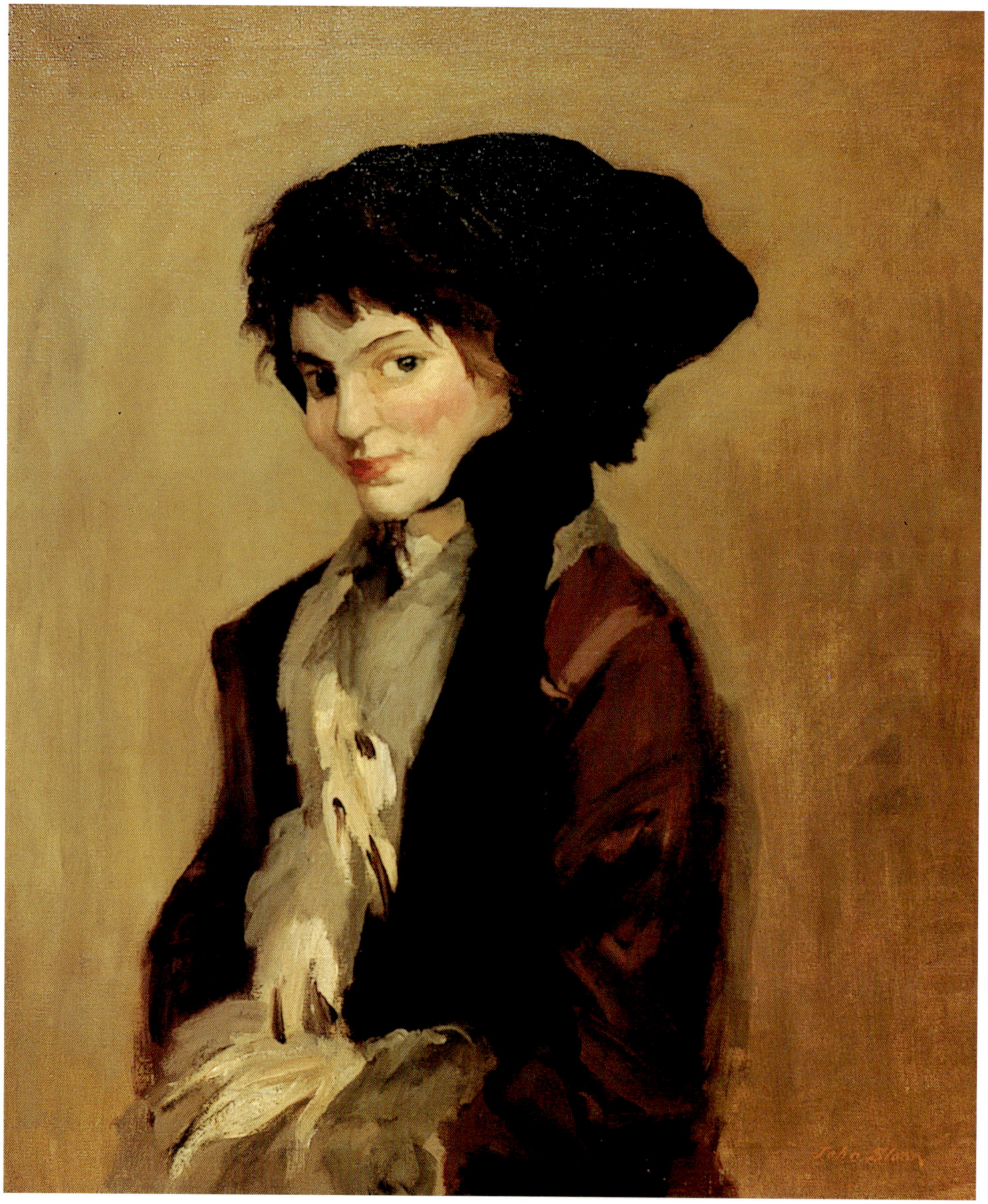

Yolande in Gray Tippet, 1909
Oil on canvas
32 x 26 in.
Bequest of R. H. Norton

John Sloan

1871–1951

John Sloan began his artistic career in the graphic arts, first as a book illustrator and then as a designer for the feature pages of the *Philadelphia Inquirer*. He had moved from his birthplace in Lock Haven, Pennsylvania, to Philadelphia at an early age, and his first job with Porter and Coates booksellers inspired him to become a graphic artist. In addition to the reportage illustrations of some of his colleagues in the Philadelphia press, Sloan created decorative illustrations for the *Inquirer* in the florid, linear, Art-Nouveau style popular during the 1890s. He continued to do book and magazine illustrations throughout much of his early career, including a 1905 series of etchings of life in New York City.[1]

Sloan had begun his formal artistic education under Thomas Anshutz at the Pennsylvania Academy of the Fine Arts in 1892, but perhaps the most important influence on Sloan's artistic development was that of Robert Henri and his colleagues in Philadelphia: George Luks, William Glackens, and Everett Shinn. Sloan shared with Henri and the others a darkened palette and swift application of brushwork, qualities that they all had admired in the seventeenth-century works of Frans Hals. Sloan's subjects included scenes of city life similar to those of Henri and his friends, as well as figural studies, portraits, and landscapes. When Henri and his colleagues left Philadelphia for New York at the turn of the century, Sloan joined them soon afterward, in 1904. He participated with them, together with Maurice Prendergast, Ernest Lawson, and Arthur B. Davies, in the 1908 *Exhibition of the Eight* at the Macbeth Galleries in New York as a protest against the rigid jury selection process of the National Academy of Design.

Sloan's paintings from New York often depict a type of urban realism focused on the life of the city around him, and especially the city's poor and lower classes. He rejected what he called the "sentimentality and artificial studio subject matter" that he found in much of the art of this period, and instead, he depicted the lives of the urban poor.[2] Although Sloan did have strong political convictions as a member of the Socialist Party from 1909–1916, his paintings often represent detached visions of city life, rather than a particular political agenda. Sloan's figures, though occasionally lonely and detached, often participate in cheerful leisure activities; indeed, a sense of optimism pervades even his most squalid scenes of the lives of the poor. Sloan described himself as a detached spectator watching the activities of modern New York society as a distanced voyeur, rather than a participant. In fact, he painted most of his scenes not in the midst of urban activity, but in his studio, from memory or sketches. In contrast to his paintings, Sloan's illustrations for the Socialist magazine *The Masses*, depict the injustices of contemporary social conditions in a propagandistic mode.

Portraiture played an important role in Sloan's oeuvre, from his earliest self-portrait attempts of the 1890s, through his later images of his artistic persona. Sloan's portrait subjects included both professional models, whom he often hired, as well as a few commissioned portraits, beginning in 1911.

The Armory Show of 1913 exposed Sloan to avant-garde European art and significantly affected his palette, subjects, and stylistic concerns. While many of his colleagues felt alienated from the contemporary art world after the Armory Show, Sloan returned to his work with a sense of renewal. In his later works, he extended his investigations into form and color relationships to images of female figures and nudes. He developed a new technique for these paintings in which he first created a monochrome drawing on the panel or canvas and then applied layers of color, often in cross-hatched markings, as in *Nude and Chief Blanket* in the Norton Gallery's collection.

Yolande in Gray Tippet, 1909
Oil on canvas
32 x 26 in.
(l.r.: "John Sloan"; verso: "Yoland in Gray Tippet / John Sloan")
Bequest of R. H. Norton 53.179

Sloan made a series of eight portraits of the model Yolande Bugbee throughout his life. The first four of the portraits were painted in November and December 1909, and they were followed by two in the next few years and two at Yolande's request, near the end of Sloan's life. The changes in Sloan's artistic style as it developed and matured are manifest in the eight paintings of Yolande, from the earliest image of her in the manner of Robert Henri's portraits, to the last painting in Sloan's unique cross-hatching style.

According to Rowland Elzea, author and compiler of Sloan's catalogue raisonné, Sloan began the Norton's portrait on the first day that Yolande modelled for him, on November 10, 1909, and he finished the work in the next three or four days. Sloan's endeavors to paint Yolande's portrait four times in the following month may have been an attempt to master this genre. Earlier in 1909, he had especially struggled with another portrait of a different model, entitled *Girl with Fur Hat*

(New Britain Museum of American Art).[3]

Sloan perhaps responded to his earlier frustrations with portraiture by adopting a different painterly manner. The loose brushwork of this painting resembles Sloan's style of this period in his city scenes and landscapes, rather than in his previous, more tightly delineated portraits. Finishing these first four portraits of Yolande within a few weeks, Sloan may have been attempting to apply the brushwork of his city scenes and the speedy manner of Henri's style to the genre of portraiture. Sloan's loosely applied brushwork in this painting also suggests the movement of the sitter, which Sloan himself mentioned in his description of Yolande. "[My portraits were] devoted to the attempt to catch and fix some of the lovely fire and spirit of this young girl. She worked hard and liked to pose, and yet she flitted about like a bird."[4] Yolande had a spirited personality, and it has also been suggested that she had a nervous twitch that made it difficult for her face to remain still for a period of time.

Yolande Bugbee was a model, about seventeen years old, whom Sloan hired for this week-long project, a luxury for a struggling painter. Yolande was probably a working class model who would have posed for Sloan as a means of increasing her income. Sloan's pictorial description of Yolande elevates her above class distinctions and attempts to place her as a timeless figure of beauty in a similar way that Henri's portraits depict ideal working class people and their children.

The detachment often found in Sloan's images of city life disappears in his attempts at portraiture and, especially, in this one of Yolande. In this painting, the sitter stares out of the canvas, giving the viewer a knowing gaze from her slightly cocked head. The simple background of Sloan's painting focuses the composition on the sitter's intense gaze and dramatizes her presence. Moreover, the immediacy of her gaze suggests her awareness of the artist's and the viewer's presence, an awareness that Sloan's women usually do not possess.[5]

Interestingly, the grays and browns of this painting do not seem to reveal the major change in Sloan's palette that had occurred a few months earlier. After Henri introduced him to Hardesty Maratta in the summer of 1909, Sloan began to use the Maratta color system, in which the colors were pre-mixed and organized according to chromatic relationships. These palettes allowed the artist to choose colors as one would a musical harmony, and once a certain "chord" was decided, other possible color combinations would be available for the artist to choose from. Maratta's colors were brighter than the ones that Sloan had used previously, and this allowed him to create paintings with a variety of intense colors that still retained a realistic effect. Sloan was perhaps not as experimental with Maratta's bright colors in *Yolande in Gray Tippet* as in his later paintings because the Yolande portraits were some of the first ones in which he may have used this system.[6] LTJ

NOTES

[1] David W. Scott and E. John Bullard, *John Sloan 1871–1951* (Boston, MA: Boston Book and Art, Publisher, 1971), 27–29.

[2] Rowland Elzea, *John Sloan's Oil Paintings : A Catalogue Raisonné* (Newark, NJ: University of Delaware Press, 1991), 21–2.

[3] Ibid., 95, 100–101.

[4] Ibid., 21, 76, 100, 102. See Sloan's version of the model in *John Sloan's New York Scene*, ed. Bruce St. John (New York City, NY: Harper and Row, 1965), 348–9.

[5] H. Barbara Weinberg et al., *American Impressionism and Realism: The Paintings of Modern Life, 1885–1915* (New York City, NY: Harry N. Abrams, 1994), 15, 265.

[6] Elzea, 22–23, 99.

PROVENANCE

John Sloan Inventory Number 376; Kraushaar Galleries, after 1925; Carson, Pirie, Scott, & Co.,Chicago, IL, until 1934; Ralph Norton, 1934; Norton Gallery, 1953.

EXHIBITION HISTORY

Pennsylvania Academy of the Fine Arts, Philadelphia, PA, *107th Annual Exhibition of the Pennsylvania Academy of the Fine Arts*, February 4–March 24, 1912, no. 13.

C. W. Kraushaar Art Galleries, New York City, NY, *Exhibition of Paintings by John Sloan*, January 26–February 8, 1925, no. 4.

The Art Institute of Chicago, Chicago, IL, *Exhibition of Paintings by John Sloan*, December 27, 1928–January 27, 1929, no. 7.

Albright Art Gallery, Buffalo, NY, *Twenty-Fourth Annual Exhibition of Selected Paintings by American Artists*, April 27–June 12, 1930, no. 134.

The Art Institute of Chicago, Chicago, IL, *Forty-Fifth Annual Exhibition of American Oil Paintings and Sculpture*, October 27, 1932–January 2, 1933, no. 182.

Worcester Art Museum, Worcester, MA, *Exhibition of American Paintings of Today*, December 1, 1933–January 15, 1934, no. 114.

The Art Gallery, McCormick Place, Chicago, IL, *Inaugural Exhibition*, November 18–December 23,1960, no. 22.

Society of the Four Arts, Palm Beach, FL, *Portraits: A Record of Changing Time*, February 1964, no. 37.

Fort Lauderdale Museum of Art, Fort Lauderdale, FL, *The Real Figure*, May 9–June 25,1978, no. 86.

Visual Arts Gallery, Florida International University, Miami, FL, *Treasures from the Norton Gallery of Art*, September 28–October 21, 1982.

Edward Middleton Manigault

1887–1922

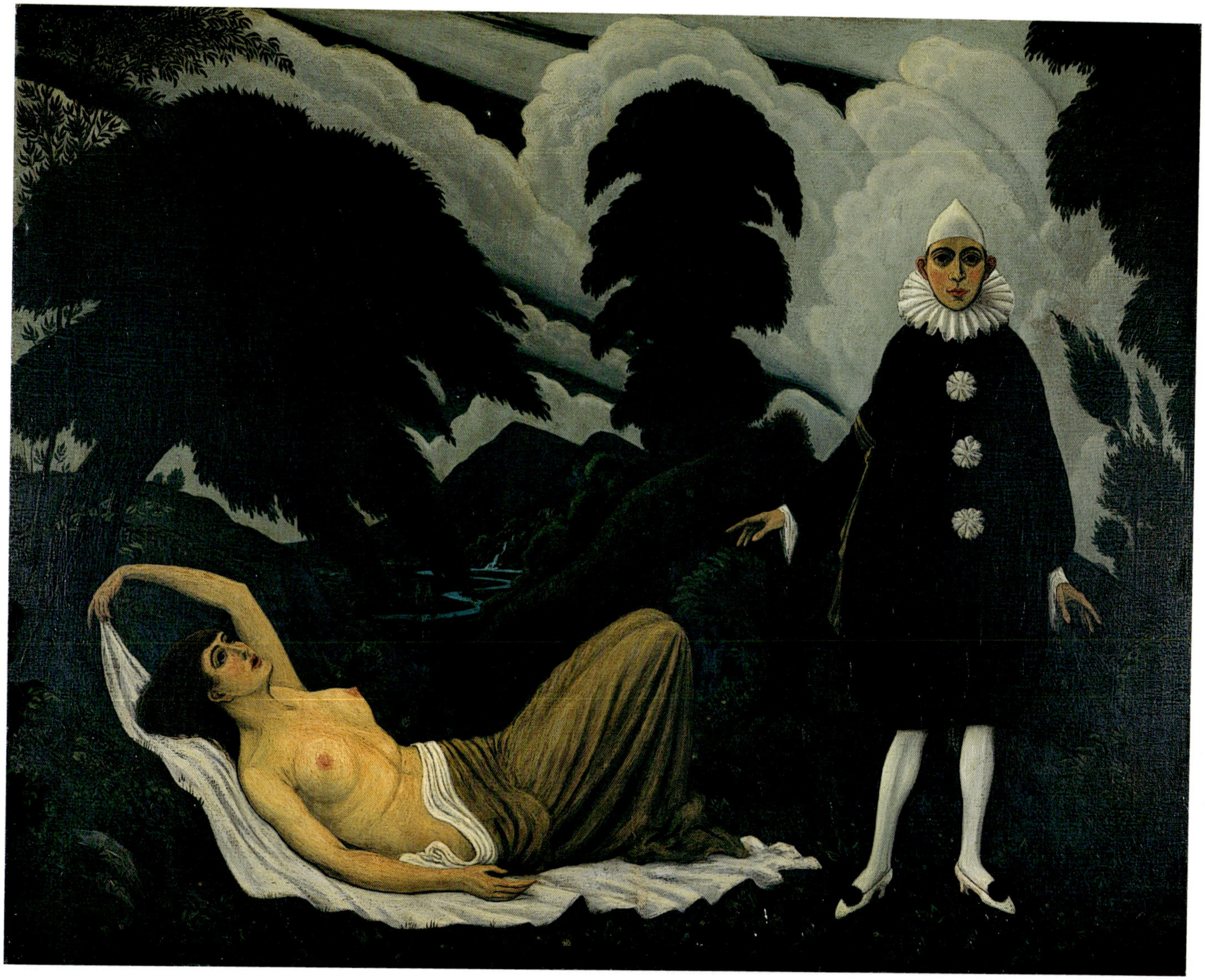

Nymph and Pierrot (Eyes of Morning), 1913
Oil on canvas
27 x 33 in.
Gift of Mr. and Mrs. E. Douglas Graydon

Edward Middleton Manigault, 1887–1922

Edward Middleton Manigault left few canvases for posterity due to his early death at the age of thirty-five and his habit of destroying works that dissatisfied him. Born in London, Ontario, to parents who were natives of Charleston, South Carolina, Manigault received art training in 1905 at the Art Students League in New York City. His teacher at this institution, who became a good friend, was painter Kenneth Hayes Miller. Manigault exhibited for the first time in 1909 and was included in Robert Henri's Exhibition of Independent Artists in 1910. In 1912 he travelled briefly in England and France. Manigault had his first one-person exhibition in 1914, but the acclaim that he experienced as a result of the show was short-lived due to the outbreak of World War I. During the year 1915, Manigault drove an ambulance for the British expeditionary forces in Flanders, but he was invalided and discharged in November.

Manigault's initial paintings are based on reality, but are executed in a style related to pointillism. These early works make use of short dashes and dots of pure colors chosen from a palette made up of mostly primary hues. Manigault fasted for periods of time because he believed that the activity helped him to attain a spiritual plane wherein he saw vivid colors not visible under normal circumstances. His subsequent paintings derive primarily from his imagination and exude a fantastic or visionary quality similar to the works of older painters like Arthur B. Davies, Albert Pinkham Ryder, and Ralph Albert Blakelock. After 1919, Manigault experimented with Cubism and abstraction, but he destroyed most of these canvases. His late works are, again, visionary and are influenced by Oriental art.

If little is known about Manigault's oeuvre, even less is known about his personal life. Manigault's death, brought about by the effects of his frequent fasting, caused his name to be associated with tragedy. As a result of this reputation, and due to the fact that Manigault left only a small number of paintings behind, few scholars have treated Manigault in a critical fashion. He is an artist who clearly deserves greater attention.

Nymph and Pierrot (Eyes of Morning), 1913
Oil on canvas
27 x 33 in.
(no inscription)
Gift of Mr. and Mrs. E. Douglas Graydon 62.36

Nymph and Pierrot (Eyes of Morning) belongs to a set of visionary landscapes executed by the artist before he joined the war effort. The painting portrays a reclining nude female watched over by a male figure known as Pierrot in French pantomime. Pierrot is characterized by a whitened face and loose ornate costumes. In Manigault's painting the figure engages the viewer with his eyes, and he gestures, almost imperceptibly, toward the nymph on his right, creating a sense of mystery and tension.

Formal characteristics contribute to the intrigue of *Nymph and Pierrot*. Most noticeably, fantastic mountains and trees in the work's background are echoed, abstractly, in the sky behind them. It is as if the foreground elements radiate an invisible substance which has repercussions in the cloud formations above them. In addition, the overall tonality of the piece is dark and vaguely threatening. The morning light is not sufficiently strong to illuminate details surrounding the figures, and one finds oneself straining to look for clues which may unveil the painting's meaning.

In the end, the content of the work remains elusive. If *Nymph and Pierrot* did have something specific to Manigault—and the piece may well have had only general symbolic meaning—the documentation does not exist to prove it. CMC

PROVENANCE

Amy Lyman Phillips; Mr. and Mrs. E. Douglas Graydon, 1962; Norton Gallery, 1962.

EXHIBITION HISTORY

Norton Gallery and School of Art, West Palm Beach, FL, *Paintings by E. Middleton Manigault*, November 29–December 8, 1963.

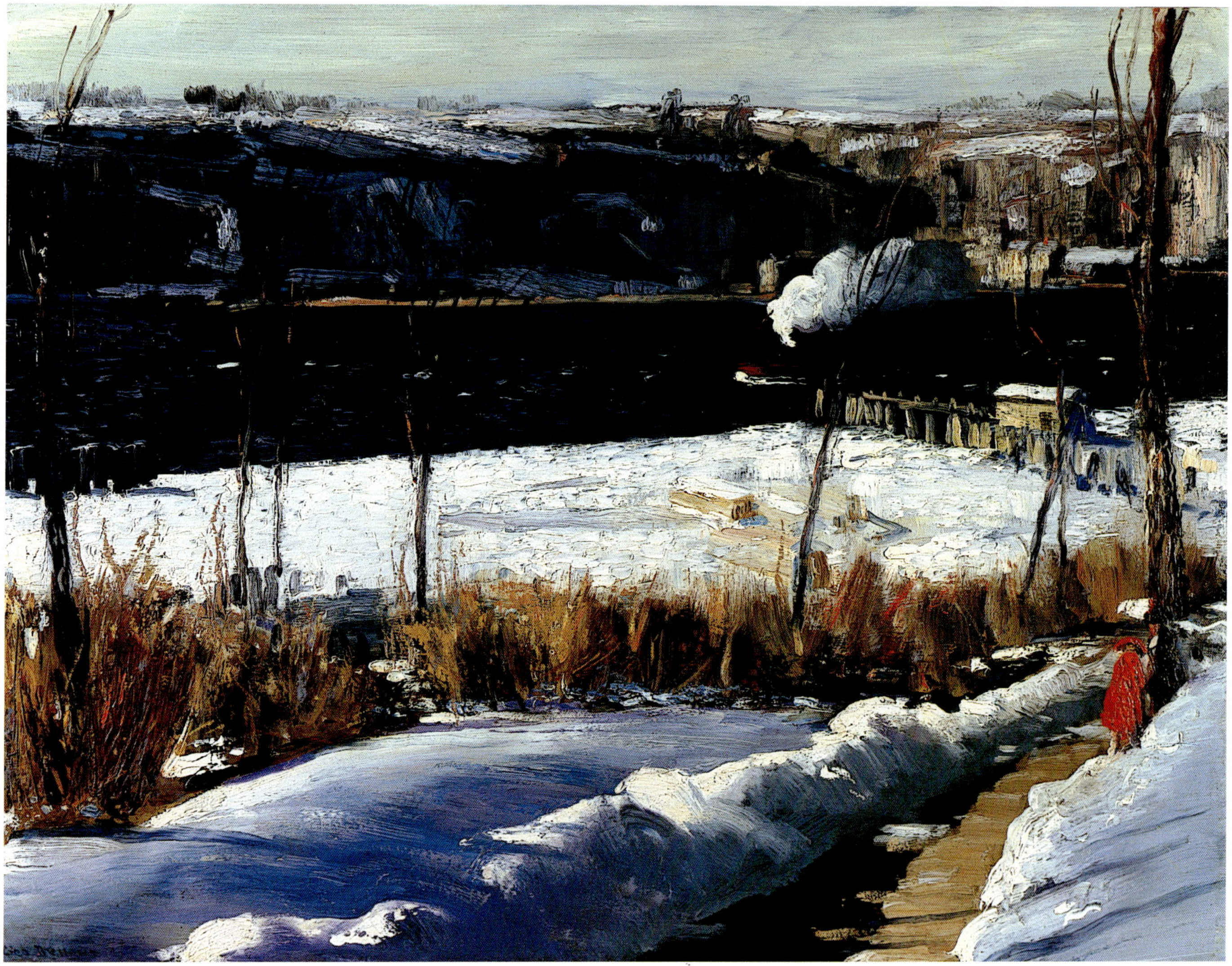

Winter Afternoon
(Riverside Park, New York City), 1909
Oil on canvas
30 x 38 in.
Gift of R. H. Norton

George Wesley Bellows

1882–1925

Though the career of George Wesley Bellows was cut short by his early death from appendicitis, the artist enjoyed a tremendous amount of success in his lifetime. In fact, Bellows' paintings are still regarded today as some of the most engaging depictions of American life. His achievement came in spite of the fact that he never went to Europe to acquire the training that most other painters at the time believed to be crucial to artistic refinement.

Born in Columbus, Ohio, Bellows attended Ohio State University from 1901–1904, then moved to New York City to study painting. He enrolled at the New York School of Art where he studied under Robert Henri, but took a studio after only two years in order to begin his career. Bellows garnered accolades almost immediately, and in 1909 he became the youngest person ever to be inducted into the National Academy of Design. His affiliation with the conservative Academy, however, did not stop him from moving in more radical circles. In 1913, Bellows helped to organize the revolutionary Armory Show, which brought works by avant-garde artists such as Gauguin, Cézanne, Matisse, Picasso, and Duchamp to America for the first time.

Bellows' early works, which are some of his finest, reflect his association with the Ashcan School, a loosely related group of artists who sought to capture the essence of urban living. The artist's scenes of New York City make use of the Ashcan School's dark palette, dramatic light and dark contrasts, and bold, slashing brushwork. Bellows' most well-known Ashcan-style works, however, are his depictions of boxing matches. Works such as *Stag at Sharkeys*, 1909, recall paintings of the same subject by the much older Thomas Eakins, an artist from whom the Ashcan painters drew inspiration.

Bellow's oeuvre was not limited to depictions of city life, however. His repertoire eventually expanded to include subject matter like river scenes, snow scenes, seascapes, and portraiture. With this broadening of subject matter came Bellows' usage of more modern modes of representation, and experimentation with various color theories. Bellows' interest in color theory led him to introduce more and brighter hues into his palette. Despite this interest and his forays into modernism, however, Bellows continued to paint in a realistic manner. His work never approached total abstraction as did the paintings of other artists at the time.

Winter Afternoon
(Riverside Park, New York City), 1909
Oil on canvas
30 x 38 in.
(l.l.: "Geo Bellows")
Gift of R. H. Norton 49.1

Winter Afternoon, one of Bellows' most commanding paintings, portrays Riverside Park, located on the west side of Manhattan, with the Hudson River and the New Jersey shore in the background. Bellows conceived the piece during a period when attention was focused on the park for the series of expansions and general improvements it was undergoing. Large sums of money had been allotted to extend Riverside Drive northward and to add promenades, a bridle path, and terraces. It was planned that the park would provide the primary vantage point for onlookers attending the much-publicized Hudson-Fulton Celebration Parade and other events, including a spectacular naval display intended to mark the three-hundredth anniversary of Henry Hudson's discovery of Delaware Bay and the eponymous river. Held in September 1909, the year that Bellows painted the piece, the events attracted hundreds of spectators, including the artist.[1]

Winter Afternoon reveals Bellows' relationship to the Ashcan School primarily in its subject matter. The picture does not portray a pastoral landscape, but rather a much used, urban park. While the scene does give the appearance of being calm and removed, the steamboat on the river and the suggestion of buildings in the painting's upper right corner inform the viewer that the city lurks nearby.

Not only did the urban character of the park scene interest Bellows, but also the snow that covered it. Bellows loved snow and wrote in 1913, "I must always paint the snow at least once a year."[2] With its lack of color, snow presented a particular challenge for Bellows. He used it as a neutral backdrop on which to experiment with color. Against the whiteness of the snow, Bellows splashed blues, reds, yellows, and greens. In *Winter Afternoon*, the bright red of the figure's coat immediately catches the eye, as do the blue shadows in the foreground.

Sources indicate that Bellows became interested in painting snow in 1909 during a visit to Zion, New Jersey. This trip was unusually productive for the artist, with most of the works that date from the trip depicting snow scenes. If such is the case, then records that indicate that *Winter Afternoon* was painted before the trip may be wrong. This painting is similar to, yet more masterful than, the Zion pictures, a fact that suggests that the work was created either during or after this sojourn. Indeed, *Winter Afternoon* is very similar in subject matter, composition, and palette to *The Palisades*, 1909 (Terra Museum of American Art, Chicago), a work that was created soon after the Zion visit.[3]

Formal qualities of note in *Winter Afternoon* include Bellows' use of horizontals, verticals, and diagonals. From top to bottom, horizontal strips which denote sky, background foliage, river, snow, and grass lend stability to the composition and add to the picture's sense of serenity. This stability is broken only by verticals provided by a group of evenly spaced trees in the foreground and by the diagonals formed by the pier and the path. The path, a typical motif of Bellows, invites the eye to wander through the composition and creates the illusion of distance.

Beyond the visual, *Winter Afternoon* is noteworthy for the manner in which it excites the other senses. One can almost feel the cold, crisp air, and smell the electrical charge of the winter air. In addition, Bellows has successfully captured the illusion of silence, broken only by the suggestion of a distant tugboat whistle or the scuffling of shoes on the sidewalk. CMC

NOTES

[1] Marianne Doezema, *George Bellows and Urban America* (New Haven, CT: Yale University Press, 1992), 62–63.

[2] John Wilmerding et al., *The Paintings of George Bellows* (New York City, NY: Harry N. Abrams, 1992), 47.

[3] Ibid., 18–19.

PROVENANCE

Artist, New York City, NY; The Milch Galleries, New York City, NY, 1946; R. H. Norton, 1949; Norton Gallery, 1949.

EXHIBITION HISTORY

National Gallery of Art, Washington, D.C., *George Bellows, A Retrospective Exhibition*, January 19–February 24, 1957.

Birmingham Museum of Art, Birmingham, AL, *Works of Art Lent by Southern Museums*, May 1–June 15, 1959.

The Art Gallery, McCormick Place, Chicago, IL, *Inaugural Exhibition*, November 18–December 23, 1960.

Museum of Fine Arts, St. Petersburg, FL, *The New Vision*, January 13–February 15, 1976.

Norton Gallery and School of Art, West Palm Beach, FL, *Masters from the Norton Gallery*, April 16–May 21, 1978.

Columbus Museum of Art, Columbus, OH, *George Wesley Bellows: Paintings, Drawings, Prints*, April 1–May 8, 1979.

Cleveland Museum of Art, Cleveland, OH, *Reckoning with Winslow Homer: His Late Paintings and Their Influence*, September 19–November 18, 1990.

Los Angeles County Museum of Art, Los Angeles, CA, *The Paintings of George Bellows*, February 16–May 9, 1992.

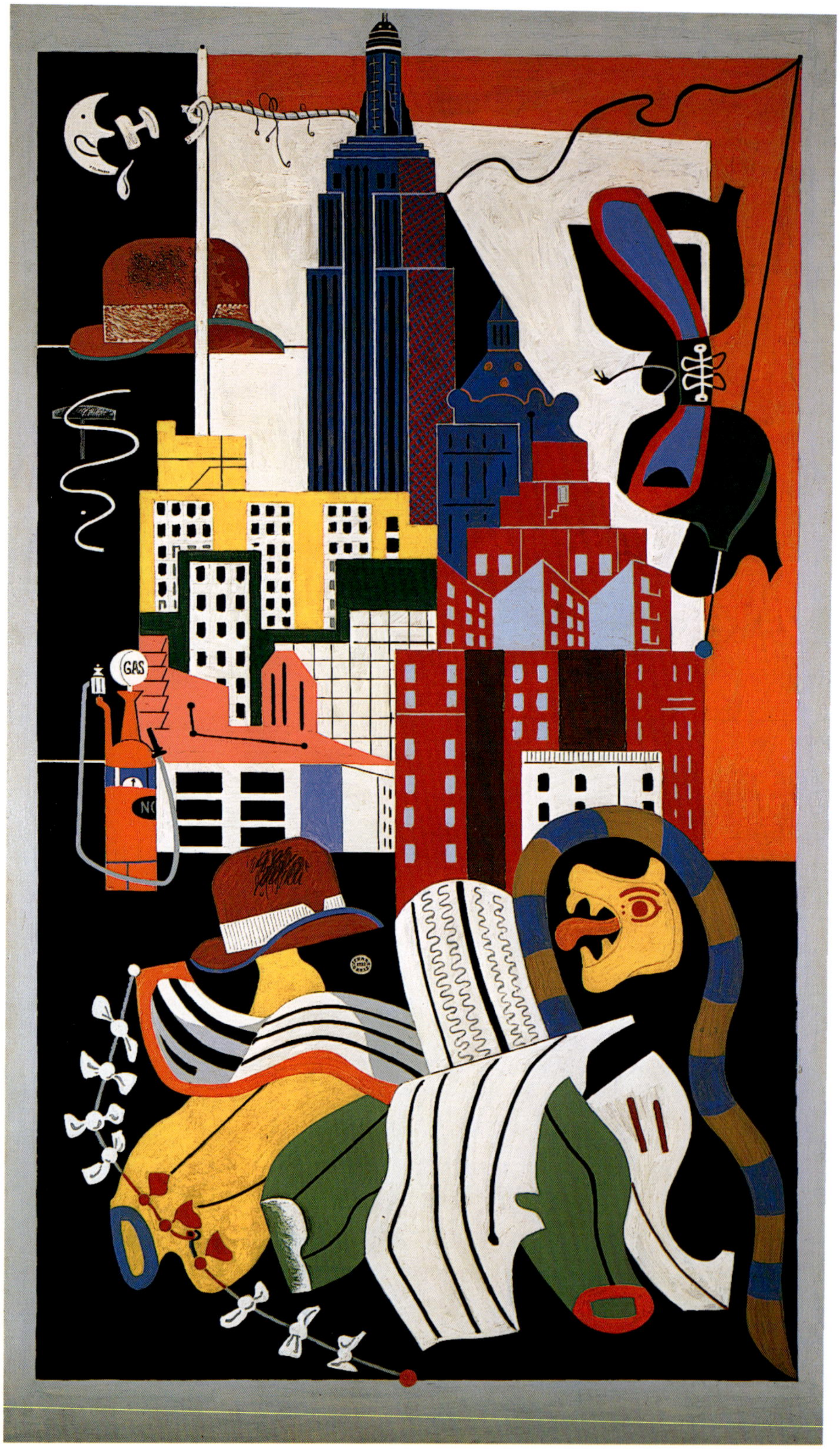

New York Mural, 1932
Oil on canvas
84 x 48 in.
Purchased through the R. H. Norton Fund

Stuart Davis

1894–1964

Stuart Davis is noteworthy for his commitment to modernist abstraction, even during periods when others painted subject matter that was easily recognizable. Born in Philadelphia, Pennsylvania, however, his first exposure to art was to the group that eventually constituted the Ashcan School. Davis' father worked as art editor of the *Philadelphia Press*, a publication to which John Sloan, William Glackens, George Luks, and Everett Shinn—artists who associated with Robert Henri, the Ashcan School's spiritual leader—contributed drawings during the 1890s. Later, Davis' only formal art training brought him into contact with the mature ideologies of this group. He learned to paint sympathetic scenes of urban life at the Robert Henri School of Art in New York City from 1909–1912, then took a job with John Sloan as a cartoonist and an illustrator for the left-wing journal *The Masses* from 1913–1916.

Davis began experimenting with modernism in 1913 after visiting the Armory Show. He claimed that this exhibit, the first major presentation of American and European avant-garde art in America, was the single greatest influence on his stylistic development. He viewed "radical" works by Cézanne, van Gogh, Gauguin, Matisse, Braque, Picasso, Duchamp, and others, for the first time, and subsequently, began to experiment with a variety of post-Impressionist styles. Davis did not go to Europe himself until 1928, at the age of 35, when he spent 13 months in Paris. There, he came to know American expatriates Isamu Noguchi, Alexander Calder, Niles Spencer, Marsden Hartley, and Gertrude Stein, as well as the French artist Fernand Léger.

Synthetic Cubism, which was concerned with the building up of form from a variety of angles, especially intrigued Davis, and he explored the possibilities inherent to this approach throughout the 1920s. Works such as *Lucky Strike*, 1921 (Museum of Modern Art, New York), reveal Davis' humorous commenting on the Cubist innovation of collage, incorporating bits of paper and found-objects into a work of art, by painting an *imitation* collage. Works in the famous *Egg Beater Series*, c. 1927, demonstrate his commitment to synthesizing common, elemental shapes from unrelated objects—here an eggbeater, a fan, and a pair of rubber gloves—to create an artistic product.

During the 1930s, artists such as Grant Wood and Thomas Hart Benton rejected European modes of representation because they believed that more realistic styles could better portray the American Scene. Though Davis, too, wished to capture American life, he did not espouse theories that endorsed realism as the only means to achieve this end. Maintaining a modernist orientation throughout his career, Davis responded to critics like Thomas Craven, who condemned Cubism and its American imitators, by saying, "I am an American, born in Philadelphia of American stock. I studied art in America. I paint what I see in America, in other words, I paint the American scene."[1] Works like the well-known *House and Street*, 1931, that depicts a variety of architectural forms in a distinctly American city setting, testify to this assertion. The artist carried out this work in his mature, Cubist style, which unlike his early style, emphasized color and pattern over synthesizing varying viewpoints.

New York Mural, 1932
Oil on canvas
84 x 48 in.
(l.c.: "STUART DAVIS 1932"; verso stretcher bar: "Stuart Davis March 1932")
Purchased through the R. H. Norton Fund 64.17

New York Mural is one of Davis' finest paintings. Originally titled *Abstract Vision of New York; a building, a derby hat, a tiger's head, and other symbols*, the piece was created for a show intended to bring American artists to the attention of the administrators of the new Rockefeller Center. It was hoped that artists participating in the exhibit would be commissioned to decorate the building. While the show failed to achieve its purpose, Davis' painting was singled out for praise, and he was asked to paint a mural for Radio City Music Hall.[2]

Like the other works in the exhibit, Davis' piece measured eighty-four by forty-eight inches. These dimensions were set by the organizers of the show to approximate the conditions of creating works for commissions. The artists were also asked to paint studies for their pieces that were to consist of three works to be contained within a single, twenty-one-by-forty-two-inch canvas. But Davis' highly abstract studies *Gaspump, Pre-Wall, and T-Scape*, do not strongly resemble *New York Mural*, which is much more realistic. Rather, they have the appearance of finished works in their own right.

New York Mural is loaded with symbolism that refers to both the city of New York, in general, and to the politics of the time. The white sail and mast behind the image of the Empire State

Building, for instance, cleverly alludes to New York's status as a major port city. (The Empire State Building acted as a mooring mast for dirigibles at the time.) But the sail's rope, along with the half moon next to it in the upper left corner of the work, also refers to the smuggling, by ship, of alcohol ("moonshine") into the city during the prohibition period of 1919–1933. A drop of alcohol falls from a cocktail glass next to the moon, which also resembles an anchor, in the direction of a brown derby hat, or the symbol for Al Smith's 1928 presidential campaign. Smith was a major advocate for the repeal of prohibition. When the election was lost to Herbert Hoover, John Jacob Raskob, who was Vice President of General Motors, a supporter of Smith, and one of the backers of the Empire State Building, employed the failed candidate. Other symbols include the bananas that refer to the tune to which one of Smith's campaign songs was set ("Yes! We Have No Bananas"), and the tiger's head and tail. The tiger was the mascot for Tammany Hall, the executive committee for New York's Democratic Party, and the tiger's tail, shaped like a shepherd's crook, probably alludes to the recently exposed "crookedness" of the party.

New York Mural reflects Davis' interest in synthetic Cubism primarily for its resemblance to collage and for its color scheme. The various compositional elements consist of simplified shapes which resemble cut-outs and give the appearance of being pasted onto the canvas. The colors are bright, primary and secondary colors that Picasso used in synthetic works like *Three Musicians*, 1921. Unlike Picasso's work, however, the colors are organized in such a way that they form a decorative allover pattern, and the picture does not have a central focus. CMC

NOTES

[1] Lowery Stokes Sims, *Stuart Davis: American Painter* (New York City, NY: The Metropolitan Museum of Art and Harry N. Abrams, 1991), 26.

[2] Bruce Weber, *Stuart Davis' New York* (West Palm Beach, FL: Norton Gallery and School of Art, 1985), 12–16.

PROVENANCE

The Downtown Gallery, New York City, NY, 1964; Norton Gallery, 1964.

EXHIBITION HISTORY

Walker Art Center, Minneapolis, MN, *Stuart Davis*, March 30–November 17, 1957.

Brandeis University, Waltham, MA, *American Modernism: The First Wave Painting from 1903 to 1933*, October 4–November 10, 1963.

Norton Gallery and School of Art, West Palm Beach, FL, *Stuart Davis' New York*, October 26–December 8, 1985.

The Brooklyn Museum, New York City, NY, *The Machine Age: The Americanization of Art 1920–1941*, October 16, 1986–February 15, 1987.

The Metropolitan Museum of Art, New York City, NY, *Stuart Davis, American Painter*, November 23, 1991–February 16, 1992.

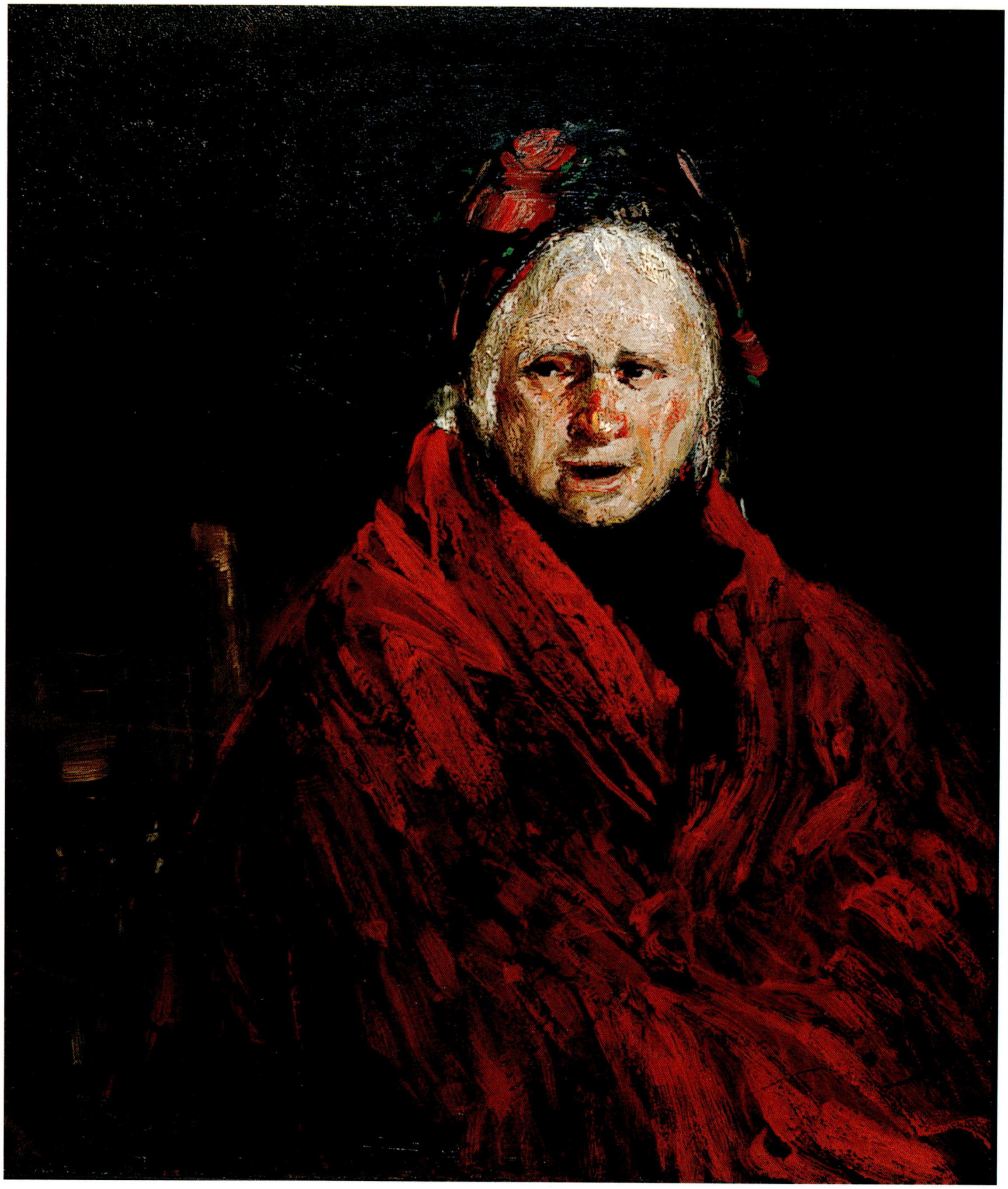

An Old Pal, ca. 1915
Oil on canvas mounted on masonite
30 x 25 in.
Bequest of R. H. Norton

George Benjamin Luks

1867–1933

Like other members of The Eight—a group of artists who banded together to protest the conservatism of the established art world—George Luks began his career as a reporter and illustrator for several daily newspapers. The journalistic approach to life he learned in this capacity affected his view of the world and carried over into his painting. Along with artists such as Robert Henri, Everett Shinn, and John Sloan, Luks painted all aspects of modern urban life, including its seamier or less genteel sides. Though critics initially responded harshly to Luks, they eventually came to understand him and to support his radical approach.

The son of well-to-do parents, George Luks was born in Williamsport, Pennsylvania. He enrolled at the Pennsylvania Academy of the Fine Arts in 1884, but left, after only a brief period, to tour in a vaudeville comedy act with his brother. The show met with little success, however, and the two soon turned to other endeavors. Luks indulged in his passion for art by travelling to Europe several times during the 1880s, where he studied at various art academies, including the Düsseldorf Academy in Germany. In 1894 he took a job in the art department of the *Philadelphia Press*, where he met and befriended William Glackens, Everett Shinn, and their mentor Robert Henri, who were three of the artists that eventually constituted The Eight.[1] Luks worked for the Philadelphia *Evening Bulletin* in 1895, and took a job as a cartoonist with the *New York World* in 1896.

Glackens and Shinn joined Luks on the staff of the *World* in 1897 and encouraged their friend to paint seriously. Luks responded by visiting the poorer sections of New York City and zealously painting the portraits of individuals he described as having an "edge." [2] These subjects included dock workers, street children, and all manner of social outcasts—people often overlooked by artists in favor of middle-and upper-class subjects. Luks soon developed a portraiture style marked by dark tones and bold, slashing brushwork which was similar to Glackens' and Henri's, but more influenced by the Dutch realists. Luks especially admired Frans Hals. Unabashedly egotistical, he often stated, "There are only two great artists in the world—Frans Hals and little old George Luks!" [3] Notable works from Luks' early period include *The Spielers*, 1905 (Addison Gallery of American Art), which portrays two young girls dancing, and *The Wrestlers*, 1905 (Museum of Fine Arts, Boston). By the time that The Eight exhibited together in 1908, Luks was the group's most powerful realist.

Luks contributed drawings and paintings to the Armory Show in 1913, an exhibition noted primarily for its introduction of European moderns, such as Pablo Picasso and Henri Matisse, to the American public, and he also began to exhibit on his own. His later work is marked by a lighter and more colorful palette and by a broader range of subjects. However, Luks never ceased to create the character studies that so interested him.

Luks taught at the Art Students League in New York City, and then at a small school that he operated himself. But by the late 1920s, alcoholism began to interfere with his professional life. Luks was notorious for the rambunctious behavior that accompanied his frequent drinking binges. He died on the street in 1933, at the age of 66, the victim of a barroom brawl.

An Old Pal, ca. 1915
Oil on canvas mounted on masonite
30 x 25 in.
(u.l.: "George Luks")
Bequest of R. H. Norton 53.114

An Old Pal depicts an elderly woman wrapped in a shawl, wearing a hat adorned with flowers. Luks portrays her against a rich, dark background which probably represents urban forms, as most of Luks' sitters lived in New York City. One senses that she is not well off, for she clutches her thin shawl about her as if it is not enough to keep her warm. In addition, she gazes wearily out at the viewer, mouth slightly open, and appears to be aware that she is regarded as a "character." In his usual manner, however, Luks does not look down upon his subject. Instead, he portrays her empathetically. It is evident that Luks respected the woman, despite her station, who, if we are to believe the title of the work, was his friend.

Conceptually, the picture typifies works by certain members of The Eight, in that it does not portray lofty subject matter. Rather, it depicts an ordinary person in an ordinary manner, for the picture is devoid of added poetic overtones. Luks makes no attempt to glorify the woman's impoverished state, as does Millet in his nineteenth-century portrayals of peasants, or to make a moral statement. Nor does he idealize her physical appearance by employing tactics intended to make her more attractive than she is. The work is instead conceived in the manner of Frans Hals' seventeenth-century portraits, which are noted for their realism. In fact, Luks may have been directly inspired by Hals' *Malle Babba* (insane woman), ca. 1650 (State Museum, Berlin-Dahlem), which also depicts a rough-looking woman with a distracted look in her eyes and a half-opened mouth. One might even say that certain of the two figures' features, like their large noses, are identical. Luks' paintings in this vein resemble those of Robert Henri more so than works by the other members of The Eight, several of whom did not concern themselves with the lower classes. Like Luks, Henri favored the portrait format. CMC

NOTES

[1] In addition to Luks, the other members of The Eight were John Sloan, Arthur B. Davies, Ernest Lawson, Maurice Prendergast, William Glackens, Robert Henri, and Everett Shinn.

[2] Ira Glackens et al., *George Luks 1866–1933* (Utica, NY: Munson-Williams-Proctor Institute, 1973), 18.

[3] Ibid., 6.

PROVENANCE

Carson, Pirie, Scott & Co., Chicago, IL, 1934; Ralph Norton, until 1953; Norton Gallery, 1953.

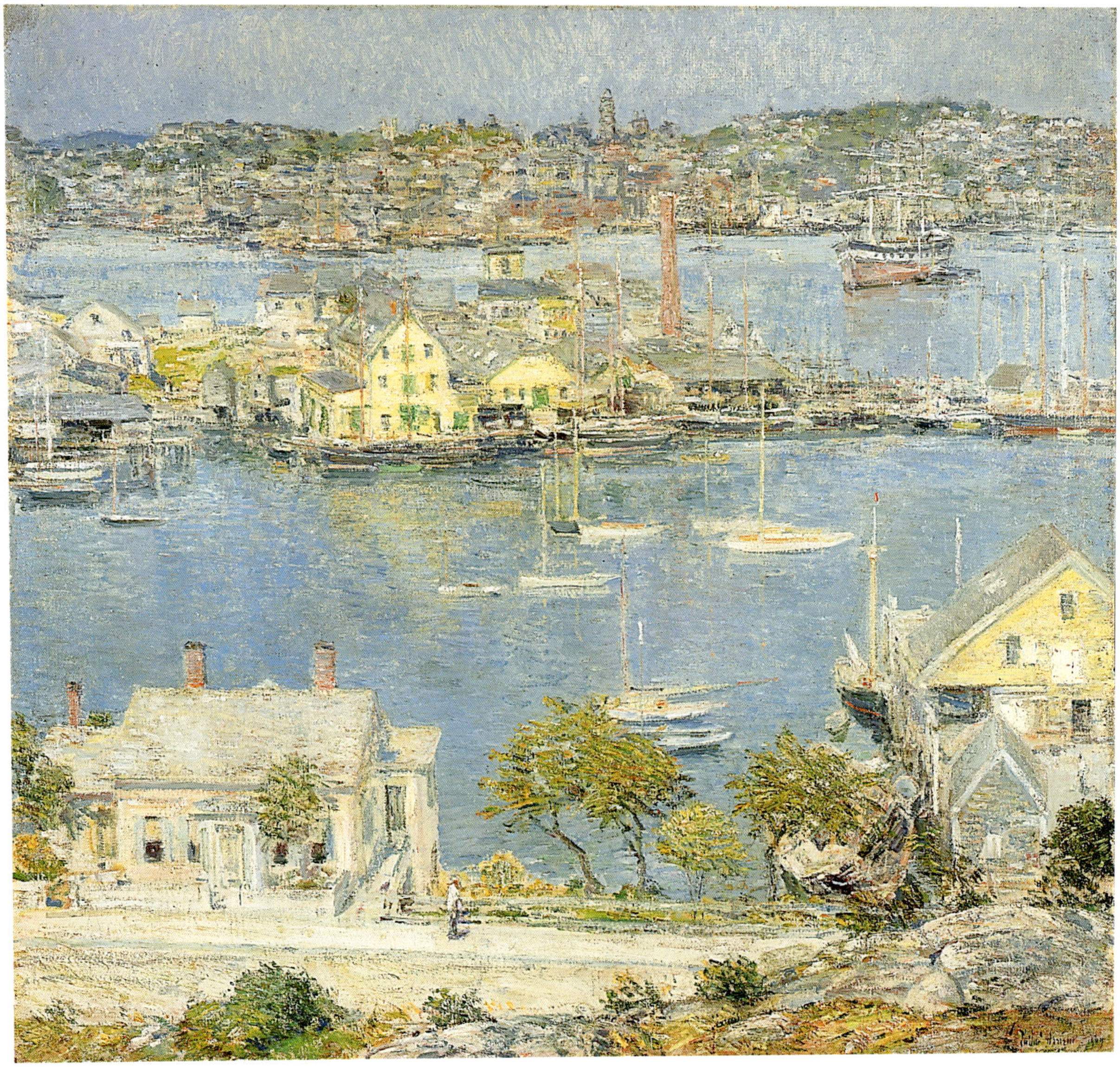

Gloucester Harbor, 1909
Oil on canvas
25 x 26 in.
Bequest of R. H. Norton

Childe Hassam

1859–1935

Acquiring an understanding of French Impressionism from his many European travels, Childe Hassam played a significant role in the development of Impressionism in the United States. After taking classes at the Boston Arts Club and the Lowell Institute, Hassam travelled to Paris in 1886 to study at the Académie Julian, an internationally renowned center of traditional training. During his travels, he encountered a wide range of work by the French Impressionists: sketchy images of modern landscapes and city streets, which lacked the usual, painterly "finish." Hassam gradually adopted some of the Impressionist techniques for depicting the light and atmosphere of the Parisian boulevards, using short, sometimes choppy, brush strokes and bright hues. Returning to New York around 1889, Hassam even more fully assimilated this style, so much so that several critics misunderstood him to be a devoted follower of the father of French Impressionism, Claude Monet.[1] Throughout his career, Hassam continued to paint in a style based on his understanding of the French movement, juxtaposing high-key, often complementary colors to create varying effects of light, atmosphere, and weather.

Hassam's paintings synthesized his understanding of French Impressionism with uniquely American subjects to create a national style of Impressionism that gained great popularity at the turn of the century. While later trends in the French Impressionism of Monet and others led to a focus on pure landscape imagery, Hassam and many American Impressionists continued to depict the human figure in much of their work, including their landscapes. Hassam's American subjects included scenes of Boston and New York's elegant boulevards, as well as the developing, artists' colonies along the New England coast, such as Gloucester, Cos Cob, Old Lyme, and Isle of Shoals. It was in Paris that Hassam created his first "flag" paintings, images of Bastille Day, and he transformed this motif, later in his career, into a banner of American Impressionism. From 1916 to 1919, Hassam painted a series of images of boulevards lined with American flags, including the display of the flags of the Allied Nations on Fifth Avenue in New York. The artist described his preference for the depictions of modern American life thus, "I believe the man who will go down to posterity is the man who paints his own time and the scenes of every-day life around him.... There is nothing so interesting to me as people. I am never tired of observing them in every-day life, as they hurry through the streets on business or saunter down the promenade on pleasure."[2]

Hassam's membership in several important artistic organizations, including the Ten American Painters, which he joined at their founding in 1897, allowed him to foster the spread of American Impressionism among his colleagues and aspiring students. Even though his work remained conservative in comparison to the beginnings of American modernism, Hassam continued to work successfully throughout his life and to exhibit his work frequently.

After 1915, Hassam returned to the print media with which he had first worked as a young artist. Using lithography, drypoint, and etching, Hassam recaptured, in his graphic works, the beloved boulevards and crowds of people that had filled his earlier canvases.

Gloucester Harbor, 1909
Oil on canvas
25 x 26 in.
(l.r.: "Childe Hassam 1909")
Bequest of R. H. Norton 53.77

Gloucester, Massachusetts, served as an important artistic inspiration for Hassam, as well as for many artists at the turn of the century, including his fellow American Impressionist John Twatchman. Hassam first visited Gloucester in 1882, and he spent the summer there in 1890. Returning around 1899, Hassam painted at least a couple of images of the harbor which are comparable in subject and palette to this *Gloucester Harbor*. According to Stuart Feld, the pre-eminent scholar on Hassam's oeuvre, the Norton's *Gloucester Harbor* may have been painted during Hassam's 1899 sojourn in Gloucester, and it may have remained in his studio until it was exhibited for the first time in 1911. Because the signature and the date appear to be in slightly different colors, the date of "1909" may have been inserted during a supposed repair to the painting made by Hassam sometime prior to its exhibition in 1911.[3]

Hassam continued to depict Gloucester through much of his career, even in a series of lithographs of the town from 1918. The site from which Hassam executed the Norton's painting was somewhere near the Hawthorne Inn where Hassam often stayed. This scene depicts a view of the harbor from Banner Hill, with the east part of the town in the foreground, overlooking Smith's Cove. By travelling often to several of these budding, artists' colonies on the New England coast, Hassam supported their development and the identification of painters with specific American locales.

Gloucester Harbor exemplifies Hassam's American Impressionist style as it had developed from French influences. The bright sunshine reflecting on the water of the harbor allowed Hassam to explore the effects of intense light as Monet had done in his views of water. Hassam's painting further shares with those of his French counterparts the use of complementary colors, such as the pinks and the greens of his palette, and the seemingly arbitrary cropping of the scene, as in the partially depicted houses in the foreground.

Like other American Impressionists transforming the French style into their own, Hassam presents a distinctly American scene within a somewhat flattened composition. Hassam's harbor scene depicts activity in an identifiably American town sprinkled with Colonial architecture. The atmospheric perspective of the scene clearly suggests its placement within an illusionistic space, but at the same time, Hassam's painting shares with those of his colleague Twatchman, a compositional flatness. This two-dimensionality, in part, derives from the high horizon line, favored by both artists, which focuses the viewer's attention on the materiality of the scene, rather than on the illusionistic recession of space. In *Gloucester Harbor*, as the viewer looks out over the harbor, the composition's strong horizontals seem to emphasize a reading across the canvas, rather than into its illusionistic depth. In choosing the (almost) square format of the canvas of *Gloucester Harbor* and other paintings of this period, Hassam rejected the window-view of traditional canvases in favor of the surface design of the composition.[4] LTJ

NOTES

[1] Julia Alexander, *A Private View: American Paintings from the Manoogian Collection* (New Haven, CT: Yale University Art Gallery, 1993), 12, fn. 1.

[2] William H. Gerdts, *American Impressionism* (New York City, NY: Artabras, 1984), 96.

[3] I am grateful to Stuart Feld for sharing his valuable opinion on this painting's date, exhibition history, and provenance. I am also indebted to the prior research of Kathleen Burnside and Bruce Weber. Donelson Hoopes, *Childe Hassam* (New York City, NY: Watson-Gupthill, 1979), 6, 11.

[4] Gerdts, 187–189. William H. Gerdts, *American Impressionism* (Seattle, WA: Henry Art Gallery, 1979), 58–60. For further reading, see William H. Gerdts, "The Square Format and Proto-Modernism in American Painting," *Arts Magazine* 50 (June 1976): 70–75.

PROVENANCE

Artist to Montross Gallery, New York City, NY, before 1911; Charles V. Wheeler, Washington, D.C., 1913; Montross Gallery, 1925; Hersey Eggington, New York City, NY, through 1929; Milch Gallery, 1929–1941; Ralph Norton, 1941; Norton Gallery, 1953.

EXHIBITION HISTORY

Montross Gallery, New York City, NY, *Fourteenth Annual Exhibition: Ten American Painters*, March 17–April 8, 1911, no. 9.

Corcoran Gallery, Washington, D.C., *A Loan Collection of Paintings Mostly by American Artists Selected by the Owner for the Summer Exhibition*, June–August 1923, no. 14.

Albright Art Gallery, Buffalo, NY, *Exhibition of a Retrospective Group of Paintings Representative of the Life Work of Childe Hassam*, N.A., March 9–April 8, 1929, no. 27.

Dallas Museum of Fine Arts, Dallas, TX, *Texas Centennial Exposition*, June 6–November 29, 1936.

Brooklyn Museum, Brooklyn, NY, *Leaders of American Impressionism: J. H. Twatchman, J. Alden Weir, Mary Cassatt, Childe Hassam*, October 1937, no. 51.

M. Knoedler & Co., New York City, NY, *Loan Exhibition in Honour of Royal Cortissoz*, December 1–20, 1941, no. 35.

The Art Gallery, McCormick Place, Chicago, IL, *Inaugural Exhibition*, November 18–December 23, 1960, no. 10.

Museum of Fine Arts, St. Petersburg, FL, *Masters from the Norton Gallery*, April 16–May 21, 1978.

Visual Arts Gallery, Florida International University, Miami, FL, *Treasures from the Norton Gallery of Art*, September 28 – October 21, 1982, no. 7.

Norton Gallery and School of Art, West Palm Beach, FL, *In Nature's Ways: American Landscape Painting of the Late Nineteenth Century*, February 21–April 12, 1987, no. 29.

Alfred Henry Maurer

1868–1932

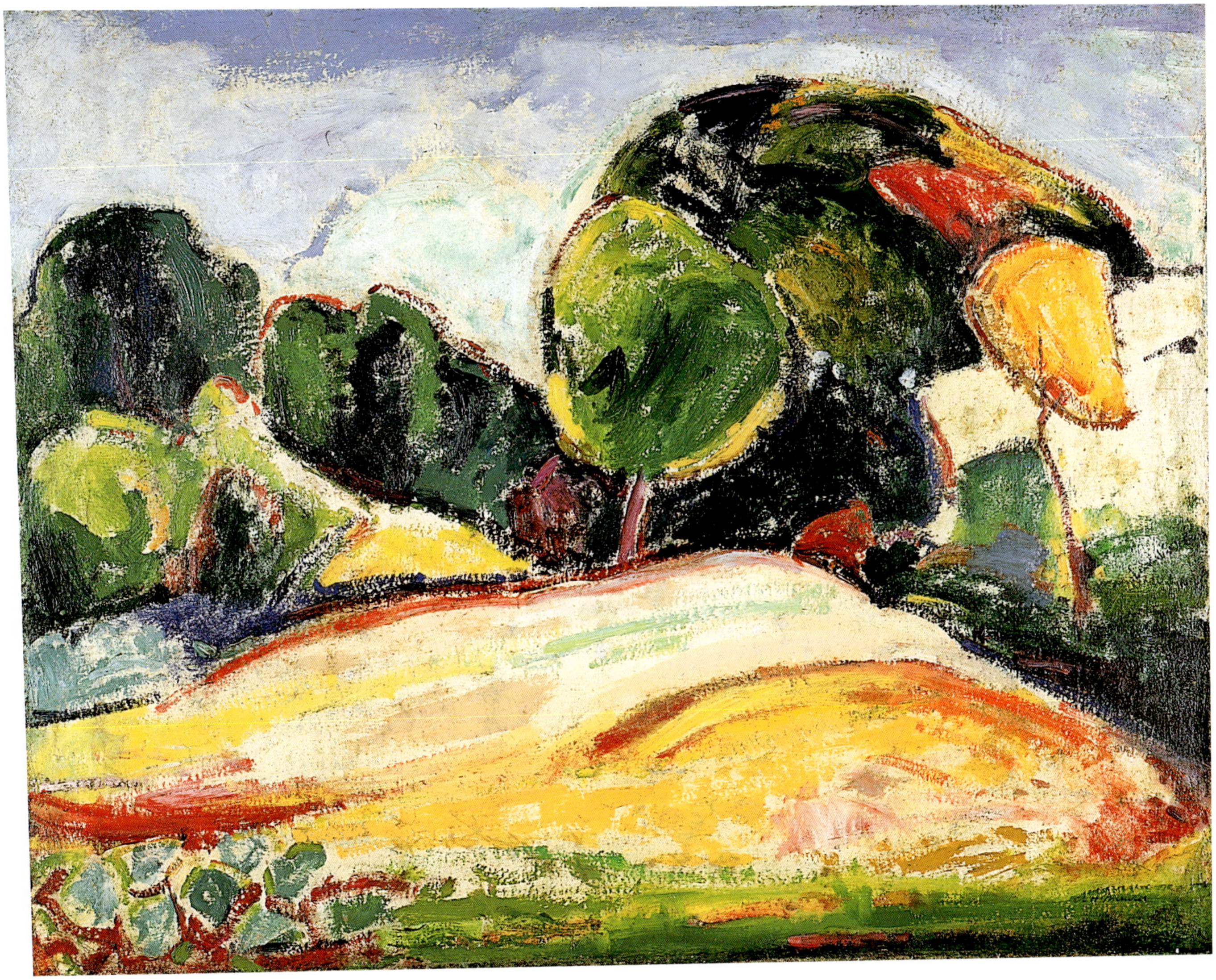

Paysage, 1906
Oil and egg white on canvas
25 x 31 1/2 in.
Purchased through the R. H. Norton Fund

Alfred Henry Maurer, 1868–1932

Alfred Maurer was so impressed with European modernism that he forfeited a successful career in his mid-thirties as a traditional artist and converted to avant-garde expression. Though he was committed to modernism, many disliked his new work and withdrew their patronage. Maurer's father, a well-known lithographer for Currier and Ives, especially disapproved of his son's transformation. Eventually, the lack of encouragement wore on the artist, and in 1932, soon after his father's death, Maurer took his own life. Though he did not garner praise in his own time, today we appreciate the originality of Maurer's vision and recognize him as a leading American modernist.

Alfred Maurer was born in New York City in 1868. After working as a lithographer and attending night classes at the National Academy of Design, he sailed for Paris in 1897. There, he studied at the Académie Julian for a period, then began painting on his own. Stylistically, work from this early period is grounded in the genteel late-nineteenth-century tradition reminiscent of James A. M. Whistler. Pictures such as *An Arrangement*, 1901 (Whitney Museum of American Art), which won first place at the prestigious Carnegie International in 1901, demonstrate his debt to this artist. Like many of Whistler's works, the painting depicts a woman in an interior decorated with Japanese objects, but the muted tones and poetic distribution of formal elements, such as shapes and lines, take precedence over subject matter.

Maurer befriended expatriates Gertrude and Leo Stein in Paris in 1904, however, and through their regular gatherings of literary and artistic elites, he was introduced to modernism. He ceased showing at the official Paris Salon, and instead, sent work to the revolutionary Salon d'Automne, organized primarily by Matisse and the Fauves. A visually startling idiom, Fauvism employed dazzling colors and wild, slashing brush-work to record the artists' emotive responses to nature.

Maurer was impressed by the ideology and the formal approach of Fauvism, as well as by the structural investigations of form found in the oeuvre of Paul Cézanne, who was honored with a retrospective at the 1904 Salon d'Automne. Consequently, during the period 1905–1907, he changed stylistically to create a personal visual language which incorporated elements from these sources. Maurer worked in this vein, approaching almost total abstraction at times, until the 1920s, when he began to portray the female form almost exclusively. These figurative works are Picassoesque for their distorted facial features, and expressionist for the sense of gloom that many of them exude.

Maurer returned to the United States, permanently, with the outbreak of World War I. Deeply saddened by the loss of his Paris lifestyle, he continued to work in a modern mode. Alfred Stieglitz, the major American patron of avant-garde art and the first to show both Matisse and Cézanne on this side of the Atlantic, exhibited Maurer's work in 1909 and 1910. In addition, Maurer sent four paintings to the ground-breaking Armory Show, which brought works by European and American moderns to the attention of the New York public in 1913.

But few other opportunities arose for Maurer. From 1914 until his death in 1932, and throughout the period when he painted figurative works,

Maurer sold few canvases and received little critical acclaim. His story, while tragic, is unfortunately the story of numerous avant-garde artists who struggled for acceptance during the early decades of the twentieth century.

Paysage, 1906
Oil and egg white on canvas
25 x 31 1/2 in.
(no inscription)
Purchased through the R. H. Norton Fund 82.41

Paysage belongs to the large group of paintings that Maurer created during the seventeen-year period that he lived and worked in Paris. In 1914, when the artist returned to the United States, he was financially unable to bring his canvases with him. Maurer's father, infuriated by his son's turn to modernism, refused to lend him money to ship the works to New York City. Though the early traditional paintings would have sold easily, all of the works, including the modern ones, remained in Maurer's studio for eleven years, until his landlord was forced to auction them in 1925 for back rent. The dispersal of Maurer's works, which included *Paysage*, was a great loss to the artist, and it contributed, understandably, to his sense of despondency.

Though the artist's mental state deteriorated upon his return to the United States, his Paris years were satisfying in comparison. Correspondingly, the works from this period exude a joie de vivre that the later works lack. In consonance with Matisse's belief that good art should relax the viewer and entice the eye, Maurer's Paris works, with their vibrant colors and lyrical lines, are a pleasure to view. The Cubist-inspired figurative studies executed in America, on the other hand, are somber in tone and symptomatic of Maurer's melancholia.

Paysage is an exemplary piece from Maurer's early Fauve period. Upbeat and colorful, the painting clearly shows the influence of Matisse's bright palette in its utilization of pure reds, yellows, greens, and other hues. Yet the way in which the colors are applied is peculiar to Maurer. Instead of Matisse's broad flat areas of color, Maurer's compositions are busier and make use of dryer, scumbling brushwork.

Compositionally, landscapes such as *Paysage* are some of Maurer's most successful Fauve paintings. Here, dark greens cut diagonally across the picture plane to dominate the upper portion of the canvas. A variety of lighter hues balances this weight below and emphasizes the piece's foreground. The horizontals of the pale blue sky at the top of the picture, and the strip of green grass at the bottom, complement these diagonals and serve to stabilize the work.

Because few understood Fauvism, works such as *Paysage* consistently received negative criticism. But such is often the case with radical art, or even with art that is simply not wholly realistic, and thus easily understood. In the aftermath of modernism, we are able to appreciate a variety of approaches to painting. CMC

PROVENANCE

Bernard Danenburg Galleries; Jordan Volpe Gallery, New York City, NY, 1982; Norton Gallery, 1982.

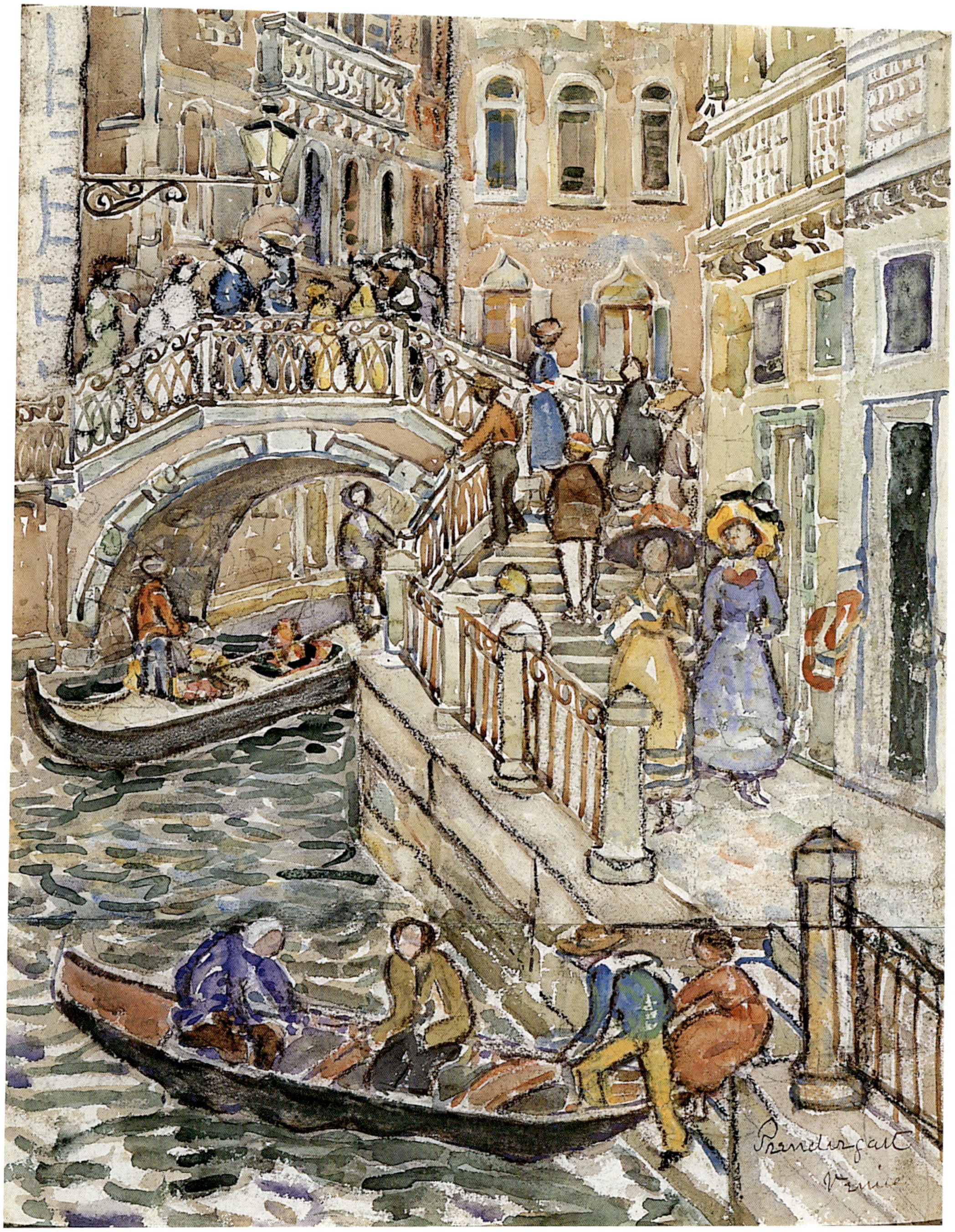

Bridge and Steps, Venice, ca. 1911–1912
Watercolor, pastel, gouache, charcoal, and pencil on paper
20 3/8 x 15 1/4 in.
Bequest of R. H. Norton

Maurice Prendergast

1858–1924

Maurice Brazil Prendergast began his career as a commercial artist in Boston, and his subsequent European travels inspired him to pursue serious artistic endeavors. Relatively late in his life, after years spent creating illustrations in a florid Art-Nouveau style, Prendergast decided to travel to Europe in 1891, with his brother, to study art at the internationally known Parisian academies of Julian and Colarossi. While there, Prendergast befriended two fellow artists who would exert a greater influence on his artistic development than his traditional academic training: Charles Wilson Morrice and Charles Conder. Together, they introduced Prendergast to the avant-garde art of Europe in the 1890s and, perhaps, even to an American colleague, the organizer of the *Exhibition of the Eight*, Robert Henri.

Prendergast's early Art-Nouveau style soon collided with the Post-Impressionism of European art, the style to which the artist is most often linked. The saturated colors of Post-Impressionist paintings, such as those he saw at the Champs de Mars Salon in 1907, exerted, perhaps, the most significant influence on him, as the artist himself noted.[1] In many of Prendergast's oils and watercolors, this influence is manifest through a type of pointillism in which vibrant colors are applied in multiple short brush strokes to create a mosaic, or tapestry, effect. The variety and application of these rich colors in Prendergast's works generated much attention in the United States, including criticisms that described his works as "an explosion in a color factory."[2]

Although often viewed as an outsider to the developments in early American modernism, Prendergast, in fact, played a significant role in exposing Americans to a synthesis of current trends in European modernism at the beginning of the twentieth century. Among other European artists, Prendergast especially admired Paul Cézanne and Henri Matisse. In combining the subjects and styles of these artists with his own understanding of Post-Impressionist color, Prendergast created a unique blend of European influences that he then exhibited to an American audience.

Certain American critics, and even historians, have interpreted Prendergast's synthetic style and his lack of sociability to signify his distance from the art world and contemporary styles in America. In relation to the other members of The Eight with whom he exhibited in 1908, such as Robert Henri and John Sloan, Prendergast, indeed, stood quite apart, but it was because he represented more European than American artistic developments. His paintings depict scenes of crowds at leisure in the park and on the beach rather than individuals of the urban working class. Moreover, he utilized much brighter, more jewel-like colors than others in The Eight, and his flattened compositions seem to have less concern for figural realism or perspectival illusionism than do those of his American colleagues.[3]

Although he worked for short periods in many different media, including monotypes and mural projects, Prendergast continued to paint in oils and watercolors throughout his career. During the 1910s, he began to experiment with the medium of watercolors, combining them with pastels and other media.

In his works after 1913, Prendergast combined his developed sense of Post-Impressionism with a newly awakened interest in ancient art historical sources. He continued to paint and to receive awards for his exhibited works until his death in 1924.

Bridge and Steps, Venice, ca. 1911–1912
Watercolor, pastel, gouache, charcoal, and pencil on paper
20 3/8 x 15 1/4 in.
(l.r.: "Prendergast/Venice")
Bequest of R. H. Norton 53.155

During his second stay in Venice, Prendergast completed a series of approximately twenty-seven watercolor sketches, including *Bridge and Steps, Venice*. This trip to Venice, however, proved to be somewhat of a disappointment for the artist. He had arrived in Italy in August 1911 and soon became disenchanted with the city that he had previously idealized. Shortly after his arrival, Prendergast became ill, and by the fall, he entered the Cosmopolitan Hospital for surgery, finally leaving Europe on January 31 of the next year.[4]

As in this mixed-media watercolor, Prendergast often portrayed crowd scenes, groups of people in the city streets or parks who may represent society as a whole. Even within his cheery and delightful scenes, however, a level of impersonality pervades the images and distances the viewer from the crowd depicted. In *Bridge and Steps, Venice*, the people remain detached from the artist and the viewer, wandering with expressionless faces through the crowded city streets. As in other works from this period, *Bridge and Steps, Venice* organizes the composition into figural groups as a means to perspectival illusionism. Prendergast separates the composition into sections of people, such as those in the foreground gondola, the middle ground gondola and steps, and the background bridge.[5]

In the 1911–1912 Venetian views, such as this one, architecture plays an unusually predominant role over the figural groupings. Canals, especially, became important as Prendergast's subjects during this trip, and the architecture of each canal has been so specifically depicted that, in many cases, their exact locations are identifiable. The buildings on this canal in Venice are abruptly cropped at the top and sides of the image. The scene in *Bridge and Steps, Venice* is depicted from a high angle that completely eliminates a view of the sky, thus promulgating a sense of entrapment within the composition. The enclosed spaces of Venetian scenes, such as this one, may in some way relate to Prendergast's own feelings of confinement during this period of prolonged hospitalization.

Another unusual element which appears in this series of Venetian images is the dark outlining of figures and architecture. Prendergast's sudden affinity for the solid definition of figural forms coincided with his awakening interest in art history. During the period of his hospitalization, Prendergast spent much of his time studying reproduced images of art historical masterpieces, and the artist's own statements indicate the important influence of Italian masters on his work, including the early Renaissance Italian painter Giotto. The solidly outlined forms in *Bridge and Steps, Venice* and other works may derive, in part, from Prendergast's growing admiration for the depictions of volumetric form and three-dimensional illusionism found in the work of Giotto and other Italian painters.[6]

In his later works on paper, Prendergast often combined pastels and other media with watercolors. For *Bridge and Steps, Venice*, he sketched the image first in graphite pencil and then applied the watercolor paint. Later additions were made in charcoal and gouache, as well as pastel. The combination of these media with the watercolor allowed Prendergast to outline his forms and to create a luminous effect in which the original watercolor paint becomes visible underneath the layers of other media.[7] LTJ

NOTES

[1] Nancy Mowell Mathews, *Maurice Prendergast* (Williamstown, MA: Williams College Museum of Art, 1990), 12–13, 23. Prendergast's description of the 1907 exhibition included the following statement: "One thing [that] made a great impression on me were the beautiful colors..."

[2] Ibid., 26.

[3] Nancy Mowell Mathews, "Maurice Prendergast and the Influence of European Modernism," in Carol Clark et al., *Maurice Brazil Prendergast, Charles Prendergast: a Catalogue Raisonné* (Williamstown, MA: Williams College Museum of Art, 1990), 35.

[4] Clark, 728. Eleanor Green, *Maurice Prendergast: Art of Impulse and Color* (College Park, MD: University of Maryland Art Gallery, 1976), 62.

[5] Milton Brown, "Maurice B. Prendergast," in Clark, 16–17. Brown has described Prendergast's compositional methods as "banding" and "climbing perspective."

[6] Eleanor Green, *Maurice Prendergast: Art of Impulse and Color* (College Park, MD: University of Maryland Art Gallery, 1976), 132. Mathews, *Maurice Prendergast*, 31–32.

[7] Bruce Weber, *Master Watercolors and Drawings from the Norton Gallery of Art* (Washington, D.C.: Smithsonian Institution Press, 1988), 13.

PROVENANCE

Charles Prendergast, 1924; Kraushaar Galleries; Mr. and Mrs. William F. Laporte; Kraushaar Galleries, 1950; Ralph Norton, 1950; Norton Gallery, 1953.

EXHIBITION HISTORY

Cleveland Museum of Art, Cleveland, OH, *The Maurice Prendergast Memorial Exhibition*, January 15–February 15, 1926, unpublished checklist, no. 41 as *Rio di San Severo.*

Kraushaar Galleries, New York City, NY, *Maurice Prendergast: Retrospective Exhibition of Paintings, Water Colors and Monotypes*, January 3–28, 1950, no. 30.

Norton Gallery and School of Art, West Palm Beach, FL, *Masters of Watercolor: Marin, Demuth, Prendergast*, February 3–26, 1950, no. 22.

All India Fine Arts and Crafts Society, New Dehli (sponsored by the American Federation of Arts), *American Watercolor Exhibition*, October 11–21, 1954, no. 5.

Morse Gallery of Art, Rollins College, Winter Park, FL, *"The Eight" and the American Scene*, December 3–24, 1960, no. 21.

Lakeview Center for the Arts and Sciences, Peoria, IL, *A Revolt: The 12345678*, September 12–November 9, 1969, no. 28.

Visual Arts Gallery, Florida International University, Miami, FL, *Treasures from the Norton Gallery of Art*, September 28–October 21, 1982, no. 19.

Pensacola Museum of Art, Pensacola, FL, *American and European Masterpieces of the Nineteenth and Twentieth Centuries*, September 22–November 16, 1984.

Smithsonian Institution, Washington, D.C., *Master Watercolors and Drawings from the Norton Gallery of Art*, travelling exhibition, February 11, 1988–September 24, 1989, no. 42.

Hayley Lever

1876–1958

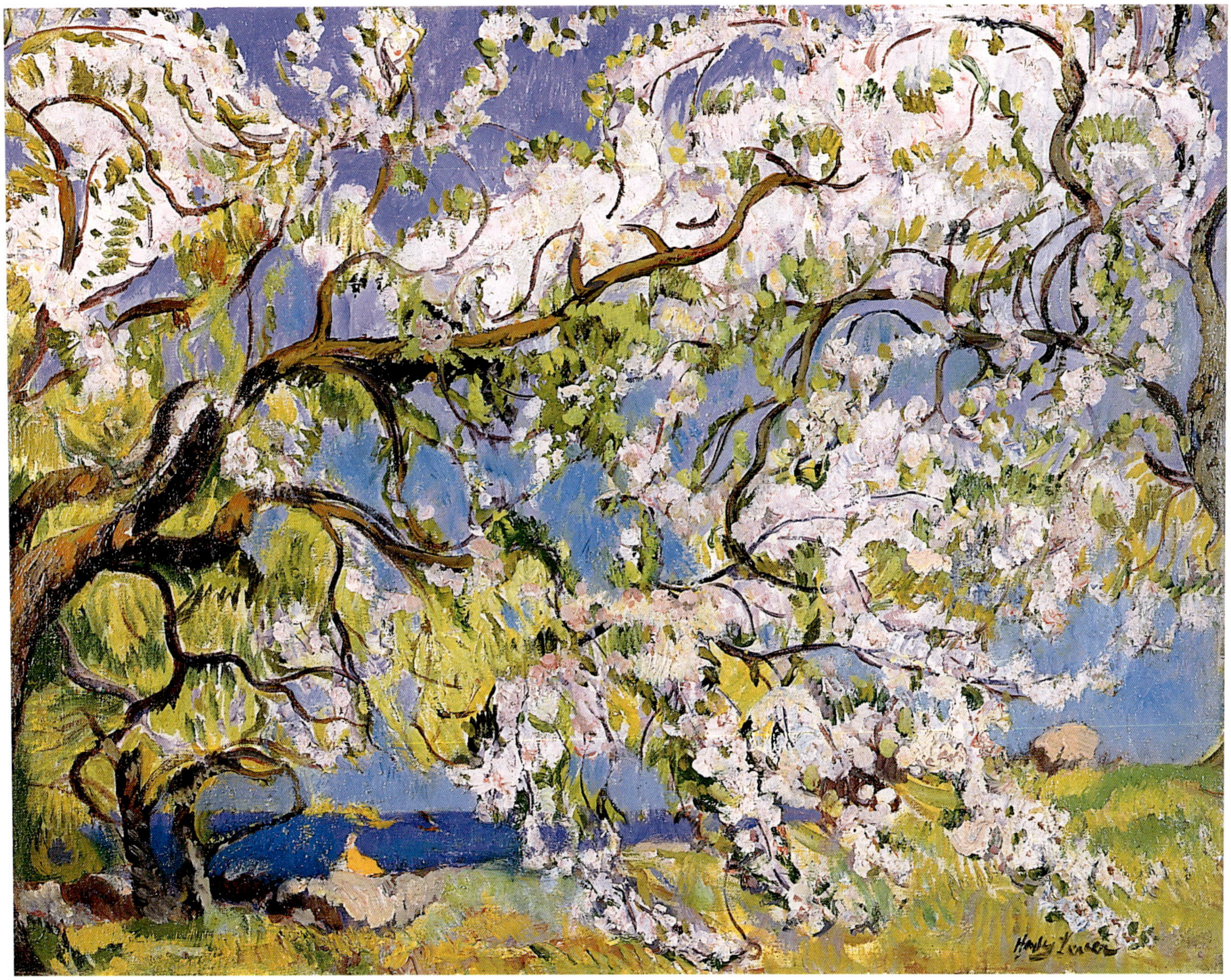

Summer in Gloucester, ca. 1915–1930
Oil on canvas
16 x 19 1/2 in.
Gift of Dr. and Mrs. George A. Hyman

Hayley Lever, 1876–1958

From his formative years at the international artists' colony at St. Ives to the end of his life, Hayley Lever remained captivated by views of the sea. Although Australian by birth, Lever first studied at St. Ives, Cornwall, on the English coast, under the tutelage of Julius Olsson and A. M. Talmadge. From these two artists known for their seascapes, Lever learned a gestural, painterly technique for depicting marine scenes. While at St. Ives, Lever met the American artist Ernest Lawson, who may have convinced him to move to the United States.[1] Once in America in 1911, Lever continued to paint seascapes in his summers spent at artists' colonies, such as Gloucester, on the New England coast. He also expanded his oeuvre at this time to include scenes of New York, landscapes, and still lifes. Near the end of his life, though crippled with arthritis, Lever still continued to paint his famous views of the sea, but his most well-known pieces from this period are a series of still-life flower arrangements.

The work of Vincent van Gogh exerted perhaps the most important influence on Lever's development as an artist. Lever greatly admired van Gogh's paintings when he saw them on a trip around Europe in 1908, and during that same period, he did a series of paintings entitled *Van Gogh's Hospital, Holland.* Lever's works, like van Gogh's, make use of a repetition of parallel brush strokes and a linearity of composition that tends to flatten the scene depicted. Lever's admiration for Japanese prints, which van Gogh himself appreciated, may have also contributed to the strong outlining of forms in Lever's work.[2] Early reviews of Lever's paintings occasionally noted his debt to van Gogh and, at the same time, most praised Lever's work, primarily for its superb coloration.[3] Lever's use of bright, often complementary colors expresses an intensity of feeling that pervades much of his work.

Lever achieved some level of notoriety in his day, including a Presidential commission, and his works were widely collected by museums during the early part of the century. He outlived his popularity as an artist by many years, however, and died in poverty and obscurity. Because he continued to paint representational compositions, rather than participating in the dramatic innovations of the art world in the twentieth century, Lever's work was judged by most to be quite conservative. The artist admitted a similar assessment of his work when he said, in 1936, "One thing that amuses me, is being called a modernist. Why, I'm one of the old fellows." [4]

Summer in Gloucester, ca. 1915–1930
Oil on canvas
16 x 19 1/2 in.
(l.r.: "Hayley Lever")
Gift of Dr. and Mrs. George A. Hyman 75.78

Lever painted this canvas during one of his summers spent in the small community of Gloucester, Massachusetts. After his first visit there in 1915, the New England coastal town immediately captured his love and imagination, as it did for many artists during this period. The artists' colony there reminded Lever of his years in St. Ives and, perhaps, of his home in Australia. For much of the 1920s, Lever spent his winters teaching at the Art Students League in New York City and his summers painting and teaching in Gloucester.

Summer in Gloucester dates to one of these sojourns from 1915 to 1930. More precise dating of this painting is problematic because most of Lever's oeuvre remains undated.

In *Summer in Gloucester*, Lever depicted a landscape as if it were a still-life bouquet of flowers. By combining two of his prominent subjects, still-life floral arrangements and coastal scenes, Lever produced in this painting a unique synthesis of his pictorial concerns. The flatness of a decorative floral design and the three-dimensional, illusionistic space of a seascape seem to collide in this image, which may represent a view out of Lever's own studio window in Gloucester.[5] The dogwood buds seem to spiral out of control as the viewer's eyes wander over the canvas, which has no strong compositional center. At the same time, the seascape just beyond our view suggests the solid geometric forms of Lever's coastal scenes.

The flatness of the tree limbs against the surface of the canvas, the agitated quality of the swirling lines of paint, and the decentralization of the painting's composition exemplify the influence of van Gogh on Lever's work. Interestingly, Lever's *Van Gogh's Hospital, Holland*, ca.1908 (location unknown) presents a depiction of similar blossoming trees outside of the artist's hospital residence. The vibrancy of the compositional forms in *Summer in Gloucester* derives from Lever's use of bright, complementary colors; for example, the pink and green of the trees' flowers and leaves intensify each other and add vibrancy to the entire painting.

As a whole, the composition of this painting creates a harmonious arrangement of color and form for its own sake. Bathed in rich sunlight, without creating any shadows, the trees of Lever's painting fill the canvas with their sprawling limbs and bursting pink buds as they meet together in an almost abstract composition of color and form. LTJ

NOTES

1 Cheryl A. Kempler, *Hayley Lever (1876–1958): Works in Various Media* (Wilmington, DE: Delaware Art Museum, 1978), 2, 6.

2 Ibid., 5.

3 Kennedy Galleries, *Hayley Lever, N.A. (1876–1958): Paintings and Watercolors* (New York City, NY: Kennedy Galleries, 1965), n.p. Helen Wright, "A Visit of Hayley Lever's Studio," *International Studio* 70 (May 1920): lxx.

4 George Parret, *Hayley Lever* (Bridgehampton, NY: Clayton and Liberatore Art Galleries, 1969), n.p.

5 The flatness of the tree limbs on the canvas surface, their proximity to the front of the canvas space, and the relatively high viewpoint of the artist, may indicate that this is a view out of an upper window of Lever's studio. Another painting, *My Studio and My Wife's Garden, Gloucester, Massachusetts*, shows that his house in Gloucester was, indeed, surrounded by somewhat similar trees. Even if it is not a view from the artist's window, however, this scene does represent a similarly high viewpoint from a hilly area near the coast.

PROVENANCE

Dr. and Mrs. George A. Hyman; Norton Gallery, 1975.

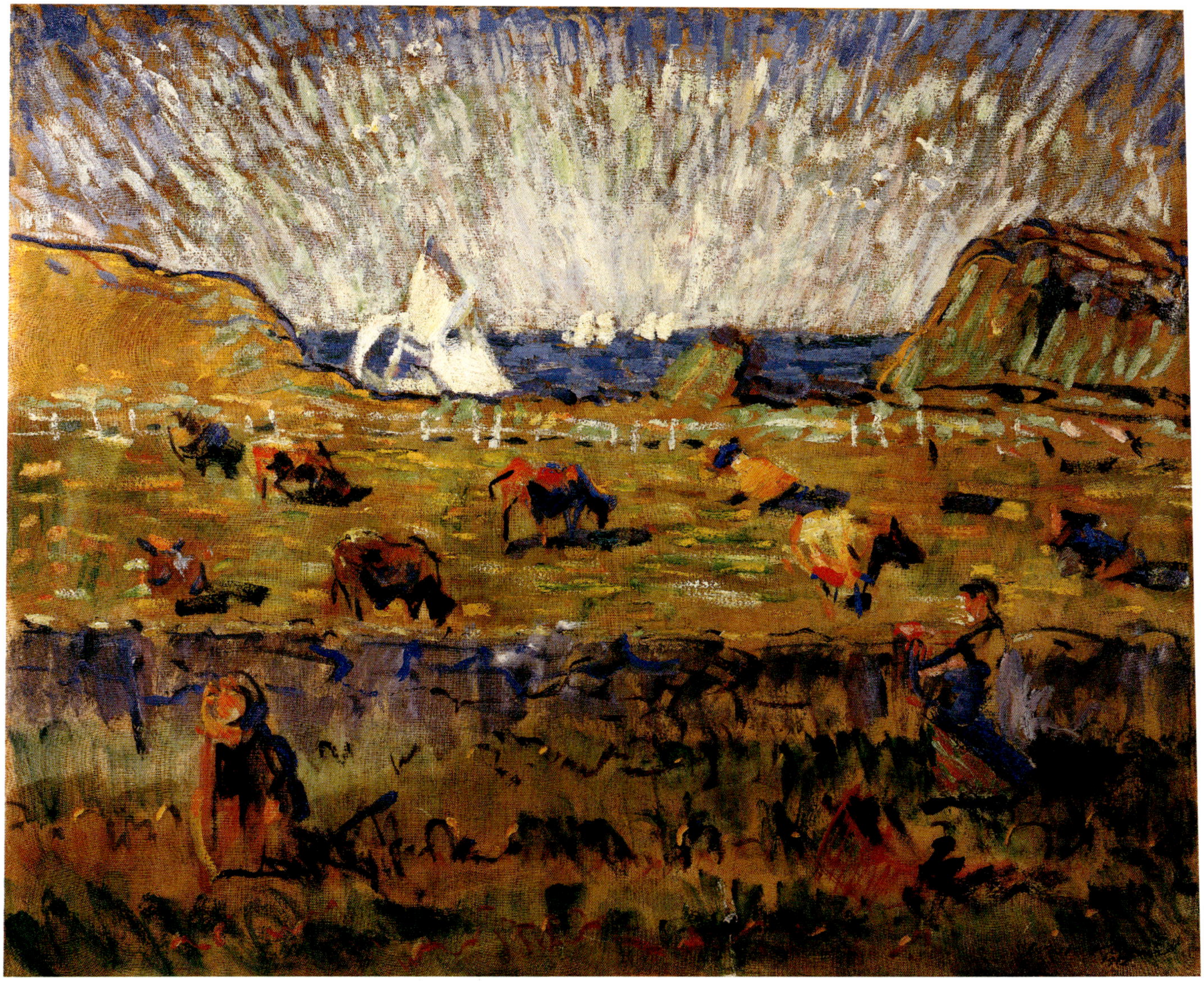

Morning, 1912
Oil on canvas
33 x 40 in.
Gift of R. H. Norton

Walt Kuhn

WILLIAM "WALTER FRANCIS" KUHN, 1877–1949

A painter best known for his romantic portraits of circus performers, Walt Kuhn was, nonetheless, a believer in the cause of modern art. He was a principal organizer of The Armory Show, the famed 1913 exhibition which opened in New York City and exposed American audiences to European avant-garde art. Although his own experiments in modernist styles were cautious, they provide a broader understanding of the influence of twentieth-century European styles on a determinedly independent American artist.

Like many American artists who came of age at the turn of the century, Kuhn was academically trained in the United States and Europe. The Brooklyn native studied art, first at the Brooklyn Polytechnic Institute, and then, briefly in Paris, before attending the Royal Academy in Munich, Germany, from 1901 to 1903. During this period, Kuhn absorbed the dark palette and impasto style of nineteenth-century, German academicians. Only later, following subsequent trips to Paris, did the artist begin to use lighter, Impressionist colors and the thick, post-Impressionist brush stroke evident in the Norton's painting *Morning*.

While Kuhn did not consistently paint in a progressive manner throughout his career, he disapproved of academic conservatism and elitism, and he championed post-Impressionism and Fauvism. He returned to New York City to live and work as an illustrator in 1903. He lived in New York for the rest of his life, yet from 1904 onward, he regularly travelled to Europe, visiting his artist friends, such as Constantin Brancusi and André Derain, and attending modern art exhibitions.

In 1911, Kuhn formed the Association of American Painters and Sculptors, a group dedicated to organizing exhibitions for progressive American painters and exposing the American public to modern art.[1] The Association was short-lived, dissolving in 1914, yet its achievement in the history of art is significant. Led by its president Arthur B. Davies and its secretary Kuhn, the Association organized The Armory Show, an exhibition of more than 2,000 works of painting and sculpture which travelled from New York to Chicago and Boston. American art outnumbered European works, but the latter, selected from European galleries and dealers by Kuhn, Davies, and the artist-critic Walter Pach, generated the most interest and controversy. Thousands of viewers saw works by Pablo Picasso, Henri Matisse and Marcel Duchamp, as well as Kuhn's *Morning*. The variety of radical and nonrepresentational styles both puzzled and excited American audiences. Many American collections in modern art were begun with purchases from the Armory Show, and in subsequent years, several new galleries opened specializing in this area. Kuhn influenced several New York institutions and collectors, most notably, John Quinn; Lilly P. Bliss, a major donor to the Museum of Modern Art and its first vice president; Marie and W. Averell Harriman, who ran a gallery during the 1930s; and the Montross Gallery.[2]

After the Armory Show, Kuhn continued to explore post-Impressionist and Fauvist techniques, and simplified, flattened forms. He also showed an interest in Synthetic Cubism and its juxtapositions of colorful pattern and design, and varied paint textures. Along with his modernist investigations, Kuhn maintained a steadfast interest in expressive realism throughout his lengthy career.

In his last, active years of painting, Kuhn enjoyed the reputation of a master. Reviewers praised Kuhn's exhibited works and deemed them appropriate continuations of Realist still-life and portrait traditions. The public clearly appreciated his work because, in 1946, his painting *Roberto* brought a record price for a contemporary American art work. Kuhn's commercial and critical success, however, failed to allay his personal difficulties. The artist's increasingly eccentric behavior led to his institutionalization at a New York state hospital in 1948, where he died in July 1949, from a perforated ulcer.

Morning, 1912
Oil on canvas
33 x 40 in.
(l.r.: "Kuhn")
Gift of R. H. Norton 46.13

Morning shows the influence of neo-Impressionism and Fauvism, and yet its presentation of forms in measured space make it a cautious foray into modernism. According to the artist's papers, the painting was more a sketch than a finished product. Considering his habit of destroying work he believed did not positively represent him, Morning is a rare document of Kuhn's artistic development.[3]

Painted during a summer trip to Nova Scotia, *Morning* is the artist's celebration of an idyllic coastline at sunrise. The sailboat, which may be a pleasure craft or a fishing vessel, is an ambiguous symbol in the picture, harder to decipher than the foreground scene of backbreaking, agrarian labor. Yet social commentary is not a factor in this painting. More germane to its success is the artist's determination to retain the fresh and quickly executed look of a plein air work, and indeed, the painting may have been painted outdoors.

Morning gathers much of its dynamism from the quickly applied brush strokes of color. Kuhn uses pigment both in a descriptive and expressionistic manner. For instance, the sea is predictably colored blue and the boat's sail white, but other simplified forms are unconventionally sparked with aggressive dashes of color. Human faces, animals, grasses, and harvest baskets are intensely red; the hills and meadow are heavily lined with green; and the sky, though predominantly white, is a neo-Impressionist mélange of brown and blue underpainting. Pigment is expressively applied to the canvas and does not rigidly remain within the boundaries of the depicted forms. Clearly informed by Van Gogh's post-Impressionism and by Fauvism, the painting excites the eye.

Morning was part of the large, art collection amassed by John Quinn in the years following the Armory Show of 1913. Quinn purchased *Morning*, and until the time of his death in 1925, he was an important patron of the artist. In turn, Kuhn advised Quinn, who purchased a range of European and American art, from works by Constantin Brancusi, Henri Matisse, and the Italian Futurists, to those done by Americans, such as Marsden Hartley, John Marin, Charles Sheeler, and Joseph Stella. JF

NOTES

[1] Walt Kuhn, "The Story of the Armory Show," *Art News Annual* 37 (1939): 163.

[2] Barbara Rose, *American Art Since 1900* (New York City, NY: Praeger, 1975), 49–64; Judith Zilczer, "Walt Kuhn," in *The Advent of Modernism: Post Impressionism in North American Art* (Atlanta, GA: High Museum of Art, 1986), 107.

[3] Zilczer, 107.

PROVENANCE

John Quinn, New York City, NY, 1913–27; Samuel Lustgarten, Chicago, IL, until 1946; Ralph Norton, 1946; Norton Gallery, 1946.

EXHIBITION HISTORY

The Armory of the Sixty-ninth Regiment, National Guard of New York, *International Exhibition of Modern Art given under the auspices of the Association of American Painters and Sculptors (The Armory Show)*, February 17–March 15, 1913, no. 862.

Art Center, New York City, NY, *Memorial Exhibition of Representative Works from The John Quinn Collection*, January 7–30, 1926, no. 16.

Cincinnati Art Museum, Cincinnati, OH, *Pictures for Peace: A Retrospective Exhibition Organized from the Armory Show of 1913*, March 18–April 16, 1944, no. 16.

Amherst College, Amherst, MA, *The 1913 Armory Show in Retrospect*, February 16–March 17, 1958, no. 27.

Lowe Art Museum, University of Miami, Coral Gables, FL, *In Search of the Present:American Prophets*, February 22–March 25, 1973, no. 29.

Munson-Williams-Proctor Institute, Utica, NY, *The Armory Show Fiftieth Anniversary Exhibition*, February 17–March 31, 1973, no. 862.

Hirshhorn Museum and Sculpture Garden, Smithsonian Institution, Washington, D.C., *John Quinn, Patron of the Avant-Garde*, June 15–September 4, 1978, no. 38.

Visual Arts Gallery, Florida International University, Miami, FL, *Treasures from the Norton Gallery of Art*, September 28–October 21, 1982, no. 11.

Pensacola Museum of Art, FL, *American and European Masterpieces of the Nineteenth and Twentieth Centuries*, September 22–November 16, 1984.

High Museum of Art, Atlanta, GA, *The Advent of Modernism: Post-Impressionism in North American Art*, March 4–May 11, 1986.

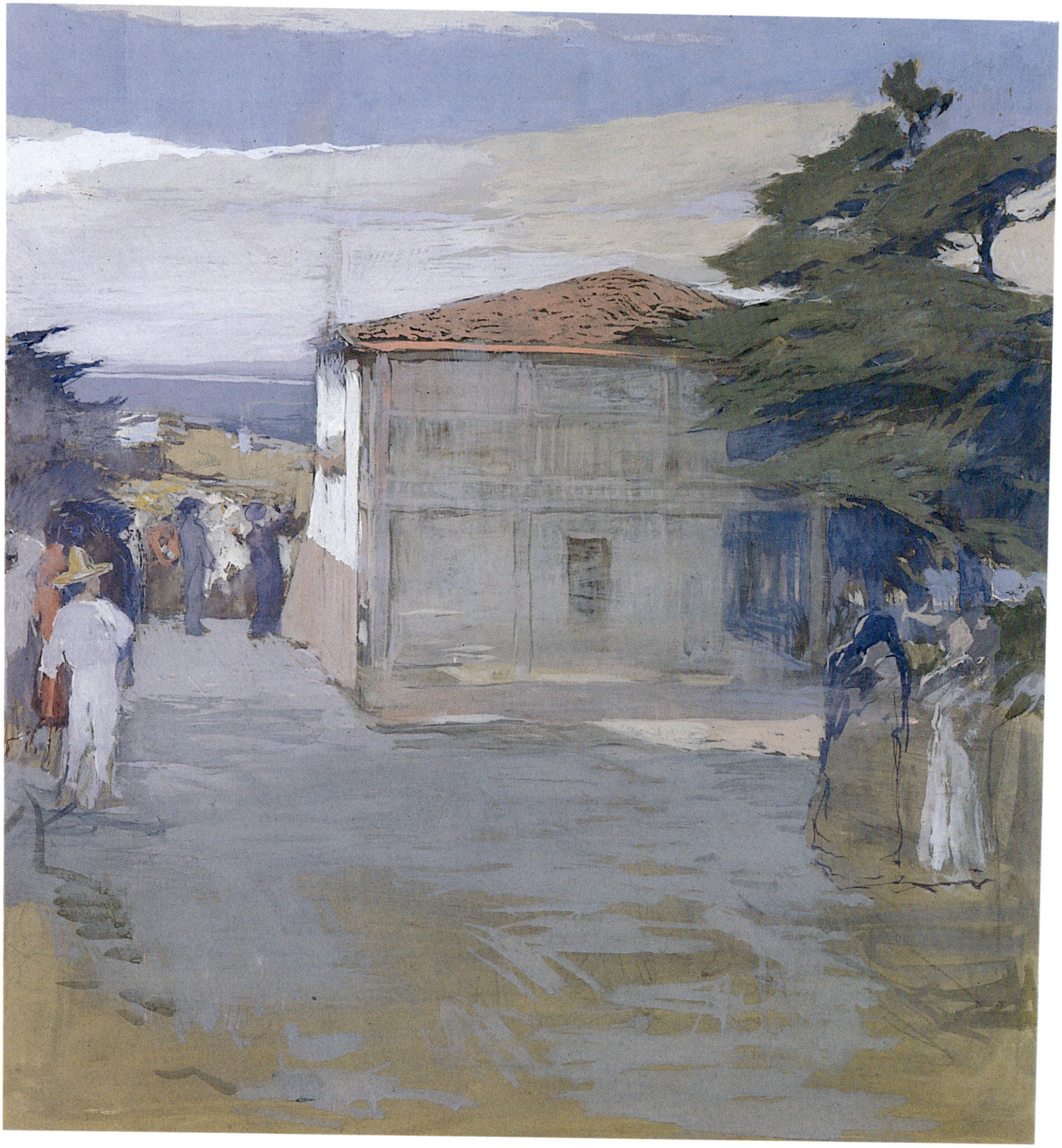

Gathering in Monterey, California, ca. 1913
Gouache and graphite on paper
23 x 21 1/2 in.
Purchased through the R. H. Norton Fund

Arthur Frank Mathews

1860–1945

An equally accomplished painter, decorator, and teacher, Arthur Mathews, along with his wife Lucia, is best known today for founding the California Decorative Style. Yet, through his teaching, Mathews also introduced a generation of California artists to the latest European movements and, through his own work, demonstrated how these stylistic innovations could be applied to distinctly American subject matter.

Born in Wisconsin, Mathews moved with his family to California at age seven. After training as an architectural draftsman in his father's office, Mathews went to Paris in 1885 and studied painting at the Académie Julian.

Returning to California in 1889, Mathews became an instructor at the School of Design of the Mark Hopkins Institute, San Francisco's art academy. He then served as Dean of the Institute from 1890 until 1906, the year of San Francisco's major earthquake and fire.

Mathews immediately took a leading role in rebuilding the devastated city. In 1906, he and Lucia, who had been his student, established the Furniture Shop and through it, founded the California Decorative Style. Philosophically related to the late-nineteenth-century Arts and Crafts Movement, the California Decorative Style advocated improved standards of design and craftsmanship in the decorative arts, and treated interiors as unified, artistic wholes. In its fourteen-year existence, the Furniture Shop produced a number of custom-designed interiors, as well as a wide range of separate furnishings. The Furniture Shop's designs incorporated modern adaptations of historical decorative styles and were particularly distinguished by their specifically Californian motifs, especially the California poppy, which became a virtual trademark.[1] Also during this period, Mathews began publishing *Philopolis*, a magazine through which he promoted aesthetic principles and rational, urban planning.

During his lifetime, Mathews rarely exhibited his work outside of California; consequently, his reputation was predominantly regional. In recent years, however, Mathews' paintings and decorative designs have attracted broader audiences, and he is now generally acknowledged as an inspired leader of the California art scene at the beginning of the century.

Gathering in Monterey, California, ca. 1913
Gouache and graphite on paper
23 x 21 1/2 in.
(no inscription)
Purchased through the R. H. Norton Fund 91.3

In *Gathering in Monterey*, Mathews reveals an extraordinarily fresh approach to the traditionally conservative genre of history painting. This intimate and luminous gouache is actually a preparatory sketch for a mural depicting the history of California which Mathews painted for the State Capitol in Sacramento. Installed in the rotunda in 1914, the mural was Mathews' most important public commission.

Mathews' twelve-panel mural is organized into four triptychs, each dealing with a separate aspect of the state's development. *Gathering in Monterey* belongs to the second of these, which describes "The Mission Period and the Picturesqueness of the California Landscape." According to the original description that accompanied the mural, the third panel of this triptych depicts the arrival in Monterey Bay of Commodore John Sloat of the United States Navy, the event which signaled the end of Mexican rule in California. Mathews tells this patriotic narrative with remarkable subtlety, emphasizing not the hero, but the beautiful landscape and local inhabitants that greet him.

Executed in his mature style, *Gathering in Monterey* reflects a synthesis of Mathews' European training and American sensibilities. Gracefully placing his figures along a gentle curve from the right foreground to the left background, Mathews creates a timeless, serene quality reminiscent of Puvis de Chavannes' carefully composed, murals which Mathews had admired in France. The loose application of paint, while less formal, is similarly derived from his student days in Paris and suggests the influence of James McNeill Whistler's tonalist paintings. Yet, the scene is undeniably Californian. With the eye of a native, Mathews frames his composition with indigenous cypress trees and makes the peculiarly bright, but hazy, California light a focal point of *Gathering in Monterey*.

In his final design for the mural, Mathews significantly altered the composition of *Gathering in Monterey*, while retaining its general emphasis and style. The building and most of the figures in the Norton's sketch were shifted to the far left of the mural, giving the center of the composition to the bay and Commodore Sloat's ships. Yet, despite their prominent placement,the ships are small and distantly viewed and, thus, remain subordinate to the California landscape and its inhabitants. AMB

NOTES

[1] Harvey L. Jones, *Arthur and Lucia Mathews, Masterpieces of the California Decorative Style* (Oakland, CA: The Oakland Museum, 1972).

PROVENANCE

Anthony White, Hillsborough, CA; North Point Gallery, San Francisco, CA; James L. Coran and Walter A. Nelson-Ries, Oakland, CA; Miller Parker, Merced, CA; Spanierman Drawings, New York City, NY; Norton Gallery, 1990.

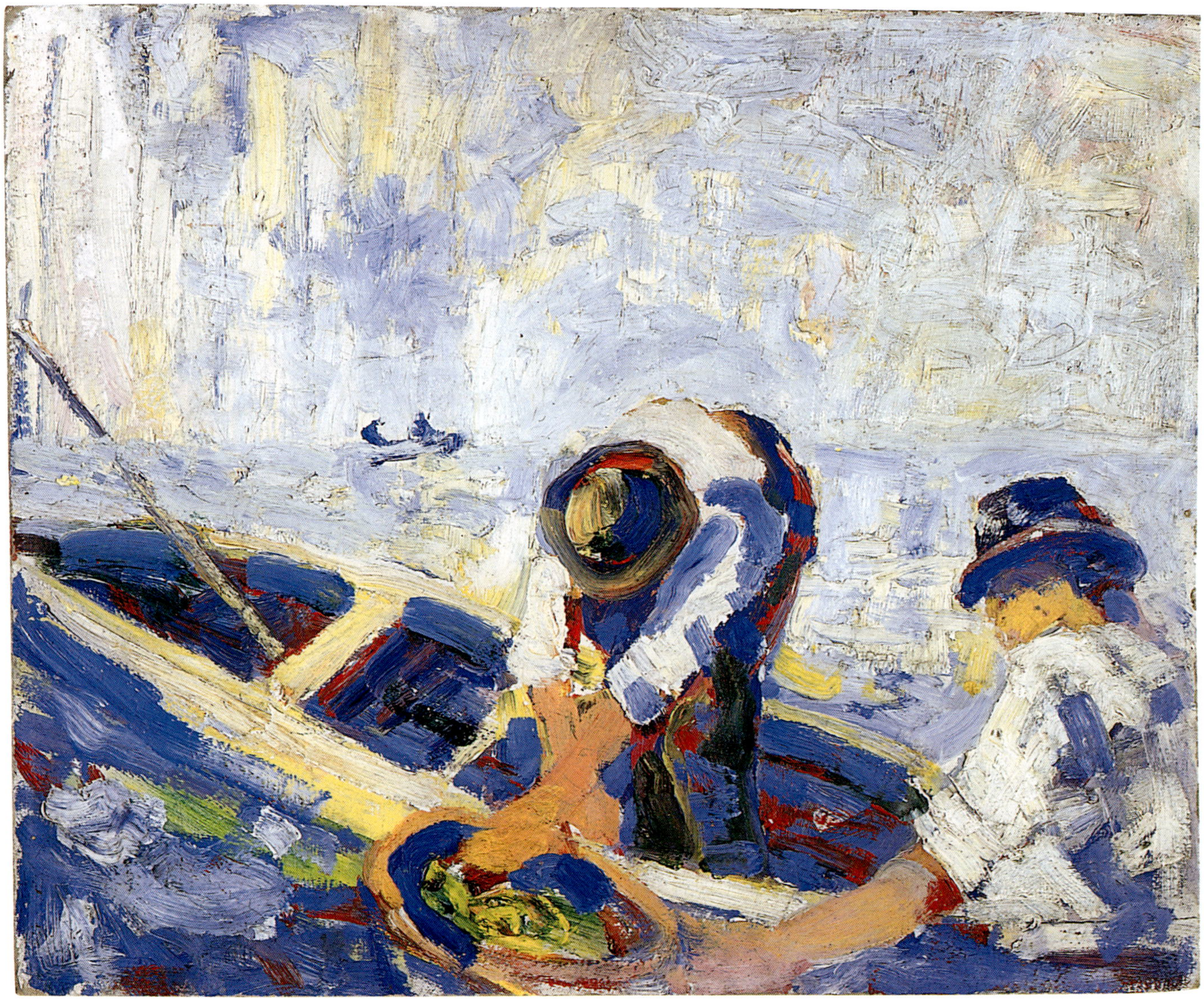

Two Fishermen and a Boat, ca. 1917
Oil on panel
15 x 18 in.
Purchased through the R. H. Norton Fund

Selden Connor Gile

1877–1947

Selden Connor Gile's formal artistic education consisted of a few classes at the California School of Arts and Crafts in Berkeley, which he may have unofficially attended. While working as a business manager and an accountant in Oakland, California, at the beginning of the century, Gile began to paint the California landscape in the traditional manner that had been established by the tonalist landscapist William Keith. Soon afterward, Gile began to develop his own style. He befriended several artists from the Oakland area who shared his artistic concerns and would meet regularly at his residence.

Gile served as the leader of this group of friends, which included William Clapp, August Gay, Maurice Logan, Louis Siegriest, and Bernard von Eichman. They became known as the Society of Six when they began to exhibit together in 1923. Gile and his colleagues utilized a palette of intense hues in their thickly painted, plein air compositions. In a statement of the group's beliefs from 1923, one member noted, "All great art is founded upon the use of visual abstractions to express beauty.... we are not trying to illustrate a thought or write a catalogue, but to produce joy through the use of the eyes. We have much to express, but nothing to say."[1] In their unconventional support of the abstractions of landscapes and figures for their own sake, the Society of Six differed from the more naturalistic California Impressionists of the period and from the avant-garde, nonrepresentational artists of the East Coast. Because they have not been easily categorized, the Society of Six have, until recently, been somewhat overlooked as a part of American art history.

The group's most important artistic influences stem from several important exhibitions in California, including the 1915 Panama-Pacific International Exposition in San Francisco, which included a handful of the works shown in the famous Armory Show of 1913 in New York. The Panama-Pacific Exposition showcased European Impressionist and Post-Impressionist works, as well as those of the Italian Futurists, amidst an abundance of American Impressionism, including the work of several California artists. After this exhibition, Gile's colors brightened as his compositions became more flattened, perhaps in response to the Impressionism which he and his colleagues admired.[2]

Other significant exhibitions in the area during the 1920s exposed the Society of Six to Post-Impressionism in the Fauvist works of Henri Matisse, Edouard Vuillard, and André Derain. These European painters' use of intense, nonlocal colors contributed to Gile's and his colleagues broad application of similarly strong hues in a painterly, gestural manner.

After he had exhibited with the Society of Six for several years, Gile left his job in Oakland and devoted himself to painting on a full-time basis. At this period in his life, in the late 1920s and the early 1930s, he began to paint on much larger canvases. He also experimented with watercolors, continuing to paint abstracted landscape scenes in a Fauvist-derived style. With the difficulties in the art market as a result of the Depression, Gile suffered serious financial setbacks for the latter part of his life. Unfortunately, many paintings from his large oeuvre were destroyed during this difficult period.

Two Fishermen and a Boat, ca. 1917
Oil on panel
15 x 18 in.
(no inscription)
Purchased through the R. H. Norton Fund 91.24

Many of Gile's images take their inspiration from landscape scenes which the artist studied while working outdoors. Gile would often paint outdoors with his colleagues, either in the landscape of Oakland Bay or on excursions to nearby locales. *Two Fishermen and a Boat* depicts the actions of two figures on the water, a scene which Gile could have seen on his plein air painting trips. The small size of this canvas further indicates that Gile probably painted this scene outdoors. Gile depicted, in this painting, two men absorbed in a fishing-related activity, in a similar way that which he occasionally represented his colleagues intensely at work on their artistic projects. Notably, these fishermen partake of a simple life unchanged by modern technology, a vision of rural life that pervades Gile's work.[3]

Despite its natural subject, however, a powerful sense of abstracted design arises in *Two Fishermen and a Boat*, as in many of Gile's paintings. The seemingly arbitrary cropping of the figure on the right and the placement of both figures in the bottom half of the composition push them into the viewer's space and deny their illusionistic presence. The ambiguous positions of the two men and the boat are heightened by the unstable point of view provided by the artist. The bright sunlight of the scene, which does not cast consistent shadows on the figures, further emphasizes the surface design of the composition, rather than its illusionistic depth.

The intense colors of this painting are characteristic of Gile's work, typically excluding black. The Fauvist works which Gile saw exhibited in California, and, perhaps, those of the early American modernist John Marin, may have given Gile a precedent for his own intense palette.[4] The vivid hues of blue and yellow in *Two Fishermen and a Boat*, and its small size, support the traditional dating of this painting as the early period of Gile's career, around 1917.

Gile's technique, like that of several of his colleagues, was to paint in layers of color on the canvas, itself, mixing them while he worked, rather than on his palette. Gile would, sometimes, even paint the whole canvas with red or yellow and then layer other colors on top. His colors were what critics most often noted and praised about Gile's work; for example, one critic in 1924 described Gile's painting thus, "He certainly riots in color. As a matter of fact, he lives it. It lights up his garden, his house, his heart."[5] LTJ

NOTES

[1] Terry St. John, *Society of Six* (Oakland, CA: The Oakland Museum, 1972), 15.

[2] Nancy Boas, *The Society of Six: California Colorists* (San Francisco, CA: Bedford Arts, 1988), 60–61, 69, 71, 84–85. Past scholarship has mistakenly dubbed the Panama-Pacific Exposition as the California Armory Show. Boas' recent investigations have shown that no more than thirty of the almost 14,000 works at the Exposition were also shown at the Armory Show of 1913.

[3] Ibid., 80, 87.

[4] Joseph Armstrong Barid, ed., *From Exposition to Exposition: Progressive and Conservative Northern California Painting 1915–1939* (Sacramento, CA: Crocker Art Museum, 1981), 26. Boas, 69.

[5] Boas, 90, 115.

PROVENANCE

Louis Bassi Siegriest; Campbell-Thiebaud, San Francisco, CA, until 1991; Norton Gallery, 1991.

EXHIBITION HISTORY

Charles Campbell Gallery, San Francisco, CA, *Selden Gile (1877–1947): Oils and Watercolors*, May 19–June 26, 1976.

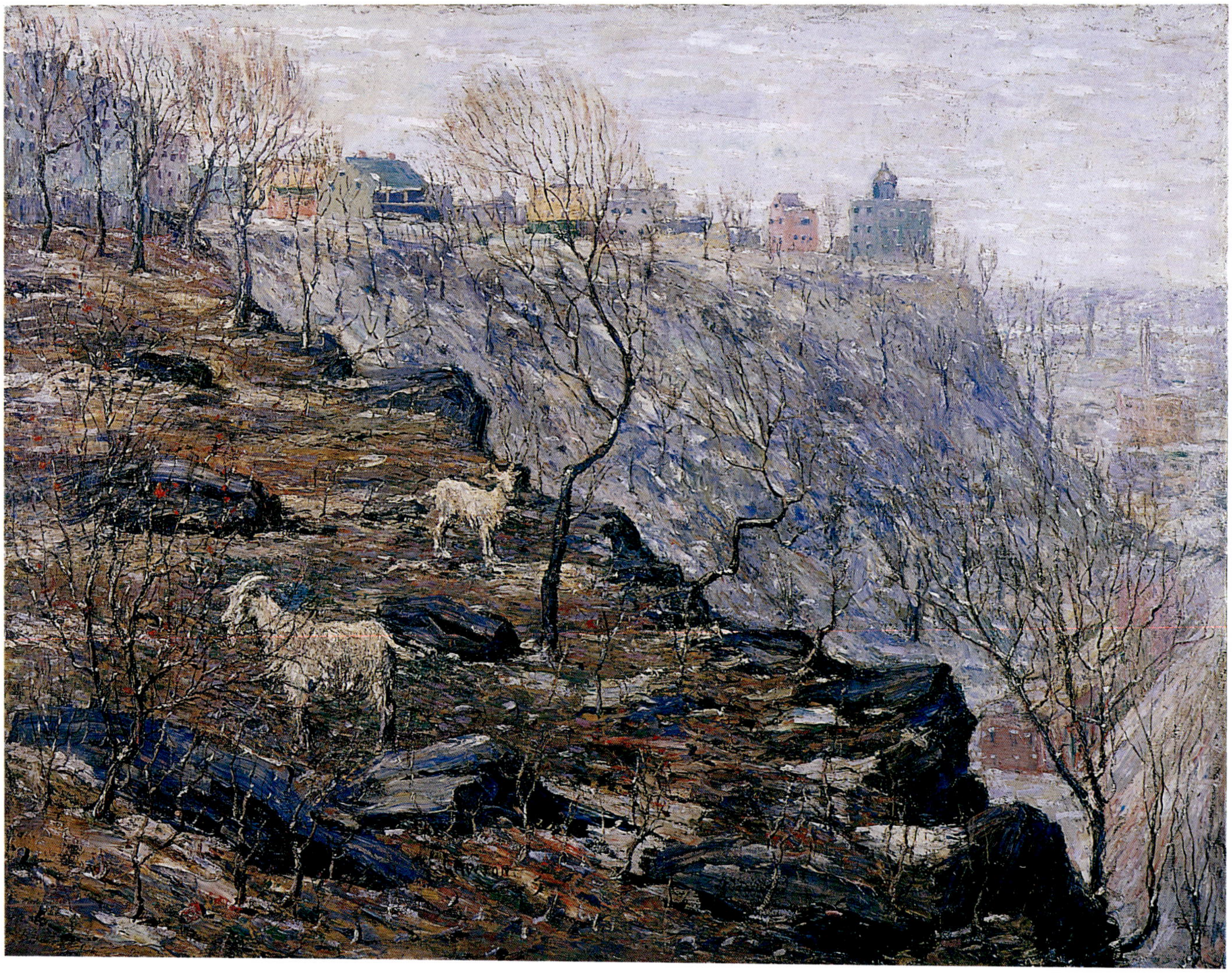

Hoboken Heights, ca. 1900–1910
Oil on canvas
37 1/2 x 47 1/4 in.
Bequest of R. H. Norton

Ernest Lawson

1873–1939

Ernest Lawson lived and worked in France during the 1890s, when many Americans began to adopt Impressionism, and he synthesized this French style with the teachings of the American artists John Twatchman and J. Alden Weir. Lawson's years in France included a brief period of study at the internationally renowned Académie Julian in Paris, in 1893, as well as trips to the countryside to paint *en plein air*. During one of these outings, he, by chance, met Alfred Sisley, whose Impressionist landscapes may have inspired the young Lawson in his own artistic projects. Lawson's formal education under Twatchman, however, was the primary catalyst for his outdoor painting and Impressionist manner. Admired by many aspiring young American artists, Twatchman had taught at the Art Students League of New York during Lawson's year there, in 1891. The following year, Lawson left the Art Students League to join the new program of plein air painting in Cos Cob, Connecticut, which was taught by Twatchman and Weir. Lawson remained close to Twatchman until the older man's death in 1902, and although Lawson's style did undergo slight variations throughout the years, it retained its basis in the artist's early Impressionist training.

As in much of French Impressionism, Lawson's paintings contain a thick application of paint which often asserts the very surface of the painting. The high horizon lines of the American Impressionists further focused their compositions on the materiality of their painted surfaces, rather than on perspectival illusionism. Their occasional use of square, or almost square, canvases, also suggests a denial of illusionism, in favor of two-dimensional designs. Unlike his French predecessors, however, Lawson did not focus on color theory for its own sake, or on serial depictions of the changes in light or seasons. His paintings depict emotive and personal expressions of the beauty of nature, rather than scientific or optical investigations into the effects of light and atmosphere.[1]

As one of the few American Impressionists to depict city scenes as landscapes, Lawson's unusual choice of subjects and his conservative style placed him in both unconventional and academic artistic circles. The annual exhibitions of the conservative National Academy of Design included Lawson's idyllic landscapes for most of the artist's career, and he became an associate member of the Academy at the beginning of the century. At the same time, however, he participated in independent exhibits, such as the 1908 Macbeth Galleries *Exhibition of the Eight*, which Lawson had joined through his close friend William Glackens. Lawson exhibited similar Impressionist New York landscapes at the significantly more avant-garde Armory Show of 1913.

The works of Paul Cézanne and the Cubists, as well as others at the Armory Show, may have inspired the geometric solidity that begins to appear in Lawson's paintings after 1913. These same influences may have also inspired a darkening of Lawson's palette in his later works, such as those from his trip to Spain in 1916.

Throughout his career Lawson continued to paint in his Impressionist mode, depicting not only the New York landscape, but also, other places where he lived. At the end of his life, Lawson's style lost much of its audience, and even though he continued to paint with arthritis, he became dependent on friends and colleagues for financial support. On a beach in Miami, he died a mysterious death that was widely rumored to be a suicide.[2]

Hoboken Heights, ca. 1900–1910
Oil on canvas
37 1/2 x 47 1/4 in.
(l.l.: "E. Lawson")
Bequest of R. H. Norton 53.105

Lawson devoted himself to landscape painting, and his chosen scenery was the area around New York City. Lawson settled in the Washington Heights area of New York in 1898, and he painted that area of the Hudson, as well as scenes of the Harlem River and of Hoboken, New Jersey, until the mid-1920s. *Hoboken Heights* depicts a scene of the cliffs at Hoboken with the Hudson River in the far distance. The inclusion of goats in the foreground makes it a rare example of Lawson's landscapes, which are usually uninhabited.

The rural cliffs and the goats blend with the encroaching factories of the city into a harmonious whole as do many of Lawson's images of the changing modern landscape. Lawson discovered a poetic beauty in his views of the New York area, and he translated this into visions of color and forms on his canvases. The artist described his method of transforming the natural landscape into a unified composition: "Impressions in nature are merely jumping-off points for artistic creations."[3] Eliminating the details of the scene in favor of its overall effect, Lawson elegantly applied thick, impasto strokes of paint to the goats in *Hoboken Heights*, and he covered the background in a dazzling mist that veils the factory buildings in the distance.

Lawson's colors, called by critics a palette of

"crushed jewels," transform the scene into a harmony of whites and dark greys, complemented by the intense red leaves of the trees and the light pastels of the city buildings. White was an essential color for Lawson, as it was for Twatchman, and many of Lawson's paintings, such as *Hoboken Heights*, depict snowy, wintry scenes that allowed him to use white as a predominant color.

Despite its painterly assertion of two-dimensionality, *Hoboken Heights* hints at a geometrical firmness and a concern for perspectival illusionism which appeared more pervasively in Lawson's works after 1913. The strong recessional diagonal into the left of the scene, along the cliff, recalls similar diagonal elements that Lawson used to structure his compositions throughout his career. LTJ

NOTES

[1] William H. Gerdts, "The Square Format and Proto-Modernism in American Painting," *Arts Magazine* 50 (June 1976): 70–75. William Gerdts, *American Impressionism* (New York City, NY: Artabras, 1984), 113, 159, 275–76.

[2] Dennis Anderson, *Ernest Lawson: Retrospective* (New York City, NY: ACA Galleries, 1976), 8–9. The rumor of Lawson's suicide has no factual basis, and several writers, including D. Anderson, have suggested much more plausible, but still unprovable, accounts. Anderson asserts that Lawson's death was probably the result of one of a series of muggings in the area.

[3] Gerdts, *American Impressionism*, 278; H. Barbara Weinberg et al., *American Impressionism and Realism: The Painting of Modern Life, 1885–1915* (New York City, NY: Harry N. Abrams, 1994), 165.

PROVENANCE

Artist to John Quinn, 1910; John Quinn collection sale at the American Art Association, 1927; Samuel A. Lustgarten, Chicago, IL, 1927; Ralph Norton, 1940; Norton Gallery, 1953.

EXHIBITION HISTORY

The Art Gallery, McCormick Place, Chicago, IL, *Inaugural Exhibition*, November 18–December 23,1960, no. 15.

Columbus Gallery of Fine Arts, Columbus, OH, *Art in the Homes of Columbus*, February 15–March 15, 1963.

Museum of Fine Arts, St. Petersburg, FL, *Masters from the Norton Gallery*, April 16–May 21, 1978.

Huntsville Museum of Art, Huntsville, AL, *American Impressionist Painters*, December 3, 1978–January 14, 1979, no. 23.

Henry Art Gallery, University of Washington, Seattle, WA, *American Impressionism*, January 3–March 2, 1980.

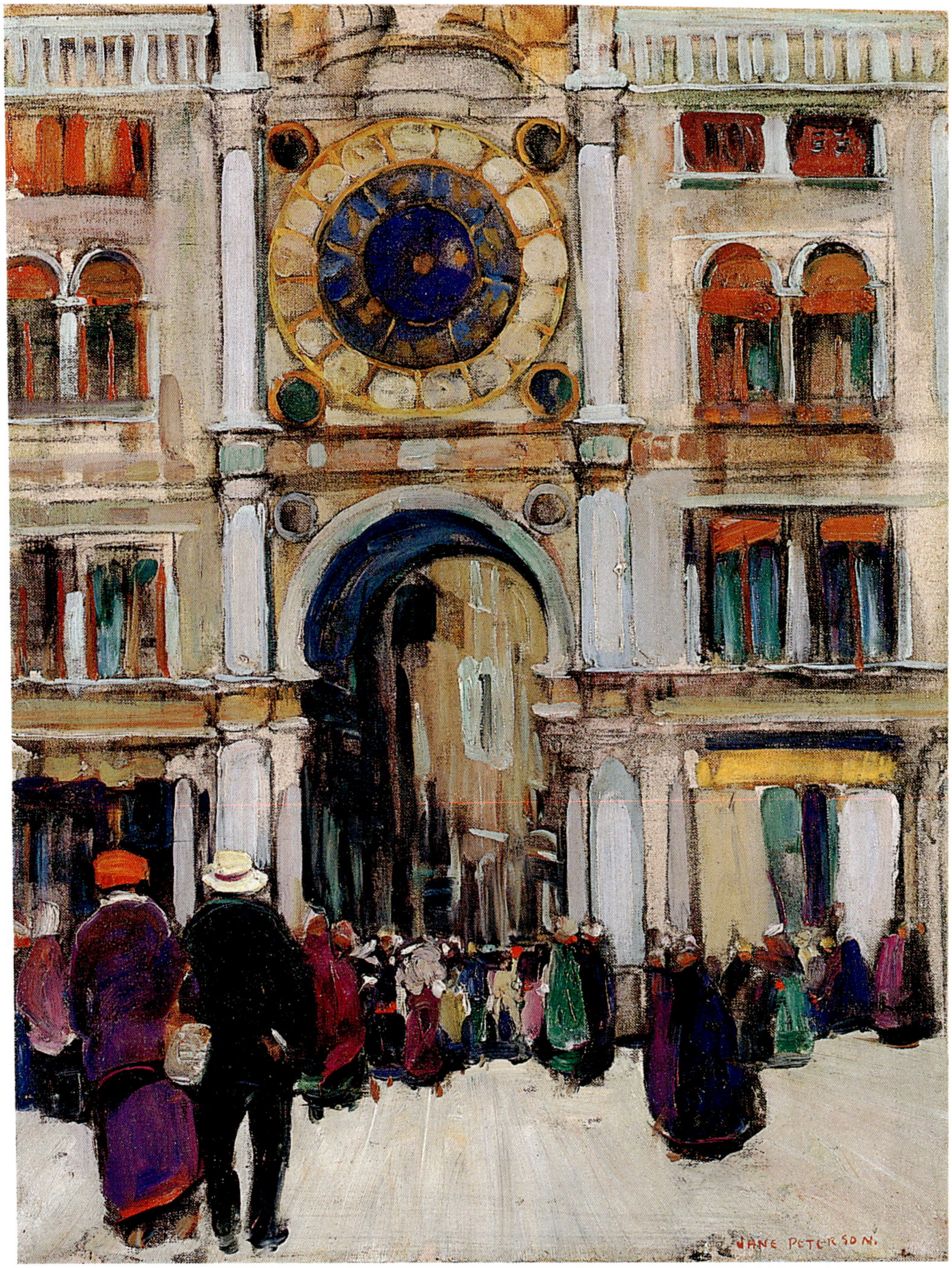

St. Mark's, Venice, ca. 1920
Oil on canvas
23 1/2 x 17 1/2 in.
Gift of Dr. and Mrs. Julian Hyman

Jane Peterson

1876–1965

Jane Peterson led a life of international travel and independence unusual for a woman of the early twentieth century, studying with artists in New York and all over Europe. Peterson first studied at the Pratt Institute in Brooklyn and then at the Art Students League, under the well-known landscapists Frank Du Mond and Birge Harrison. Soon afterward, she began her extensive European travels in London, where she studied with Frank Brangwyn from 1907–1908. Impressed by her talent, Brangwyn suggested that Peterson next travel to Paris, in 1908, to study with the famed portraitist Jacques-Emile Blanche. During this same year, her paintings gained their first critical prominence, and a one-woman exhibition of her work was scheduled in the United States. Peterson's last European mentor was perhaps the most influential: Joaquin Sorolla y Bastida. Peterson studied with Sorolla in Madrid from 1909–1910, and his Impressionist style, utilizing bright colors applied broadly and quickly, inspired Peterson in the development of her own gestural artistic manner.

The work of the Post-Impressionists that surrounded Peterson on her travels also contributed significantly to her style. On exhibit during her stay in Paris were the Fauve works of Henri Matisse and André Derain, and although she did not associate with these artists as a group, she did adopt their intense coloration and broadly rendered compositional method. Working with a palette of unusual hues, Peterson combined large areas of flat color and thick outlining in her compositions, but unlike some of the Fauvist artists, Peterson did not usually apply color arbitrarily. In her travels in America, Peterson may have seen the

Post-Impressionist works of Maurice Prendergast, to whom she is often compared. Peterson often shared Prendergast's varied palette and his interest in depicting European locales crowded with people. Also, like Prendergast, Peterson combined European Post-Impressionist styles with traditional artistic training to produce her own unique manner. Peterson's work was overshadowed during her lifetime, however, by the avant-garde experiments in early modernist abstraction that were taking place in America and abroad.

Cityscapes of the many locales which she visited dominate Peterson's oeuvre, and her destinations include a wide variety of places: Venice, London, Paris, and Madrid, as well as cities in Egypt and Canada. Later in her artistic career, Peterson decided to work out of a studio in New York, where she created an entire series of still-life flower arrangements. Stylistically, these paintings remain similar to her landscapes in color and composition. Peterson's flower arrangements seem to have a great depth not often achieved in the still-life genre, and the artist referred to these works as "flower portraits." [1]

St. Mark's, Venice, ca. 1920
Oil on canvas
23 1/2 x 17 1/2 in.
(l.r.: "Jane Peterson")
Gift of Dr. and Mrs. Julian Hyman 75.84

Peterson's first trip to Venice was in 1907, and she made many subsequent journeys there during the years before World War I and in the years immediately following.[2] She did not usually date her paintings, and this work, though it may date to Peterson's early trips to Venice between 1907 and 1914, probably dates from her later trips to that city, around 1920, when she painted several other images of St. Mark's. As do many of Peterson's travel paintings, this scene depicts a popular tourist spot, St. Mark's Square. The central structure in the image is the clock tower of the Byzantine church complex, an architectural group that had been depicted by many artists at the turn of the century, including Maurice Prendergast and James Abbott McNeill Whistler.

Unlike other views of the tower, however, Peterson's focuses on a detail of the building's lower register. Peterson avoids the symbolic sculptural details, such as the monumental lion which stands guard above the astrological clock, in favor of the simple, geometric forms of the façade. The details of the clock do not even interest Peterson as much as the harmonious design of the complementary parts of its face. The clock is transformed by her brush into variations in blue, gold, and white that almost resemble a rose window. The vivid, rich tones of blues and golds of Peterson's palette seem especially appropriate for this image because of the medieval mosaics of similar colors that fill the interior of St. Mark's. Indeed, it may have been the stunning colors of both the interior and the exterior of this building complex that initially attracted Peterson to it as a subject.

In contrast to the geometrically simplified architectural forms, *St. Mark's, Venice* does retain a sense of perspectival illusionism. Despite its otherwise flattened composition, this painting allows for a recession of space indicated by the street of the square, the people of the scene, and the archway underneath the tower. The movement of the two figures on the left toward the tower also suggests a possible three-dimensional space within this composition. A dynamic quality also results from the cropped edges that cutoff part of the left façade, leaving the image slightly off center.

As in *St. Mark's, Venice*, many of Peterson's paintings from Europe depicted popular tourist destinations, and these scenes enjoyed a limited amount of popularity in the early decades of the twentieth century in America. Peterson's position outside of the formalist developments in modern art during this period precipitated her short-lived fame as one of the first well-known American women artists. LTJ

NOTES

[1] Jonathan J. Joseph, *Jane Peterson: An American Artist* (Boston, MA: privately printed, 1981), 39.

[2] Ibid., 16–17, 23–29, 34. Joseph often dates the Venice paintings to either ca. 1908, ca. 1912, or ca. 1920.

PROVENANCE

Dr. and Mrs. Julian Hyman; Norton Gallery, 1975.

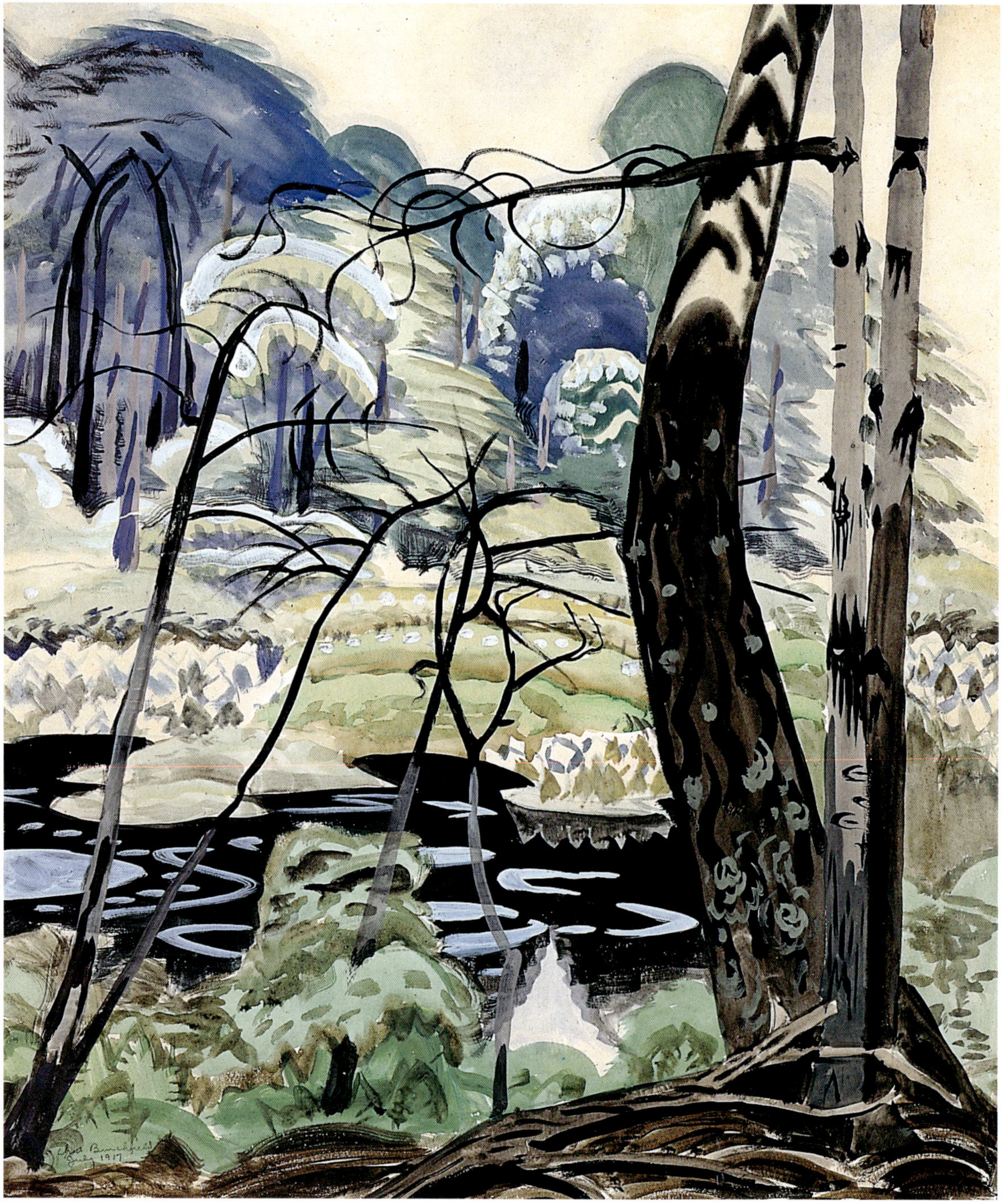

In the Swamp, 1917
Gouache on paper
21 7/8 x 18 in.
Bequest of Elizabeth C. Norton

Charles Ephraim Burchfield

1893–1967

One of America's most distinctive and original artists, Charles Burchfield painted nature in all its vitality. In hundreds of poetic watercolors, Burchfield captured the sounds, movements, and mysteries of the natural world.

Burchfield's career is traditionally divided into three periods. The first of these, 1915–1921,was principally devoted to the recreation of childhood impressions of nature. In his second period, 1921–1943, Burchfield's focus shifted to the farms, villages, and cities of the Midwest. Finally, from 1943 until his death, Burchfield deliberately returned to the nature fantasies of his youth.

Raised in Salem, Ohio, Burchfield spent much of his adolescence sketching local wildflowers and in 1912, entered the Cleveland School of Art. During this period, he became acquainted with Eastern art and philosophy and deeply identified with its personification of natural phenomena.

In 1916, a scholarship from the National Academy of Design lured him to New York. Never a figure painter, Burchfield left the Academy after one day in life-drawing class, but remained in the city, attempting to launch his career as a painter. Yet, despite encouragement from the art critic Walter Pach and the enthusiastic representation of the dealer Mary Mowbray-Clarke, Burchfield soon moved back to Salem.

With his return to his childhood haunts in 1917, Burchfield entered his self-proclaimed "golden year." In a virtual explosion of creative energy, Burchfield produced at least 165 watercolors of unprecedented expressiveness, as his former decorative style gave way to a highly personal vision of nature.[1] Tapping into childhood fantasies and his subconscious, Burchfield painted extraordinary visions of enchanted forests and fields where flowers have faces, and choruses of insects produce visible sound waves.

In 1920, Burchfield lost the office position with which he had been supporting himself and, the following year, moved to Buffalo, New York, where he secured a position as a wallpaper designer. This move marked the beginning of Burchfield's middle period, characterized by changes in both subject matter and style. Comparatively few in number, Burchfield's paintings now described the man-made environment of Buffalo—its houses, factories and streets—and were executed with far more realism.

In 1943, while reviewing his earlier work, Burchfield was struck by its comparative freedom and realized that in his subsequent pursuit of form and solidity, he had lost much of his spontaneity. Reworking and elaborating on these earlier paintings, Burchfield consciously summoned the romantic vision of his youth and, in this final stage of his career, produced remarkable landscapes which unite youthful fantasy with mature technical proficiency.

In the Swamp, 1917
Gouache on paper
21 7/8 x 18 in.
(l.l.: "Chas Burchfield July 1917")
Bequest of Elizabeth C. Norton 47.4

"July 18, 1917—The bottomless swamp, black evil pool, surrounded by the haunting deceptive beauty of nature." This notation which Burchfield made on the back of *In the Swamp* is especially revealing. Such precise dating is unusual in the history of art, but typical for Burchfield, and it reflects the intensity with which he observed natural phenomena. In copious notebooks and journals, he recorded his almost daily sojourns into the woods and fields, noting seasonal peculiarities and precise weather conditions. As his poetic caption for *In the Swamp* suggests, however, Burchfield was equally concerned with the changing moods of nature, and the inspiration for the menacing mood that prompted, and pervades, this romantic watercolor may actually have been a dream.

Burchfield's journal entry for the day prior to this painting's execution describes, in language reminiscent of his caption for *In the Swamp*, his "half sleep" visit to an unnamed lake where he had actually been earlier that day.[2] "All at once strange hideous shapes loomed out of the tree... ; the water became inky black... ; the air grey dark; the waters parted to a bottomless blackpit...."[3] Such dreams fascinated Burchfield, not for their Freudian significance, but for what they revealed about buried memories and their relationship to his imagination. In some cases, such as *Memory of a Dream*, 1919 (Burchfield Art Center), Burchfield recorded his dream imagery directly. In others, such as *In the Swamp*, Burchfield's dream world seems to have inspired a particular mood.

Painted in his "golden year," *In the Swamp* is animated by the whiplash, calligraphic line which Burchfield had borrowed from Chinese painting and developed to express nature's energy. Yet, in contrast to its lively execution, the composition is dominated by a predominantly dark and leafless cluster of trees in the foreground which, through their animated, gesturing branches, become the protagonists of Burchfield's enchanted swamp.

Burchfield was working full time in 1917 and, therefore, painted in his studio during lunch breaks and evenings, using sketches he had made on his walks to and from work. Since he had sold *In the Swamp* prior to 1943, the year he began reworking the images of his "golden year," it remains in its original condition and is a fine example of the mystical appreciation of nature which distinguished his most creative year. AMB

NOTES

[1] Joseph S. Trovato, *Charles Burchfield, Catalogue of Paintings in Public and Private Collections* (Utica, NY: Munson-Williams-Proctor Institute, 1970), 56–72. Baur asserts that there were "actually many more" paintings produced in 1917, but provides neither documentation nor specific numbers. John I. H. Baur, *The Inlander, Life and Work of Charles Burchfield, 1893–1967* (Newark, NJ: University of Delaware Press, 1982), 58. The 165 count is accepted by Townsend in J. Benjamin Townsend, ed., *Charles Burchfield's Journals, The Poetry of Place* (Albany, NY: State University of New York Press, 1993), 436. Finally, Richard Wooten states that Burchfield created 400 artworks that year, but provides no documentation. Richard Wooten, "Paint the Town, Charles Burchfield: The Salem Years," *American Art Review* 5 (Spring 1993): 108.

[2] Townsend states that the lake Burchfield visited on July 17, 1917 was "probably Lake Westville, 5 miles west of Salem." He provides no other support for this attribution, however. Townsend, 671. Trovato Associates *In the Swamp* with Turkeyfoot Lake, Barberton, OH, similarly without documentation. Trovato, 62.

[3] Burchfield's journal entry for July 17, 1917. Reprinted in Townsend, 111.

PROVENANCE

Frank K. M. Rehn, Inc., New York City, NY; Elizabeth C. Norton, West Palm Beach, FL, 1937; Norton Gallery, 1947.

EXHIBITION HISTORY

Boston Museum of Modern Art (Institute of Contemporary Art), Boston, MA, *Contemporary American Watercolors*, December 8–26, 1936.

The Cleveland Museum of Art, Cleveland, OH, *American Painting from 1860 until Today*, June 22–October 4, 1937.

The Art Gallery, McCormick Place, Chicago, IL, *Inaugural Exhibition*, November 18–December 23, 1960, no. 4.

University of Arizona Art Gallery, Tucson, AZ, *Charles Burchfield: His Golden Year: A Retrospective Exhibition of Watercolors, Oils and Graphics*, November 14, 1965 January 9, 1966, no 92.

Visual Arts Gallery, Florida International University, Miami, FL, *Treasures from the Norton Gallery of Art*, September 28–October 21, 1982, no. 3.

Pensacola Museum of Art, FL, *American and European Masterpieces of the Nineteenth and Twentieth Centuries*, September 22–November 16, 1984.

Smithsonian Institution, Washington, D.C., *Master Watercolors and Drawings from the Norton Gallery of Art*, travelling exhibition, February 11, 1988–September 24, 1989, no. 4.

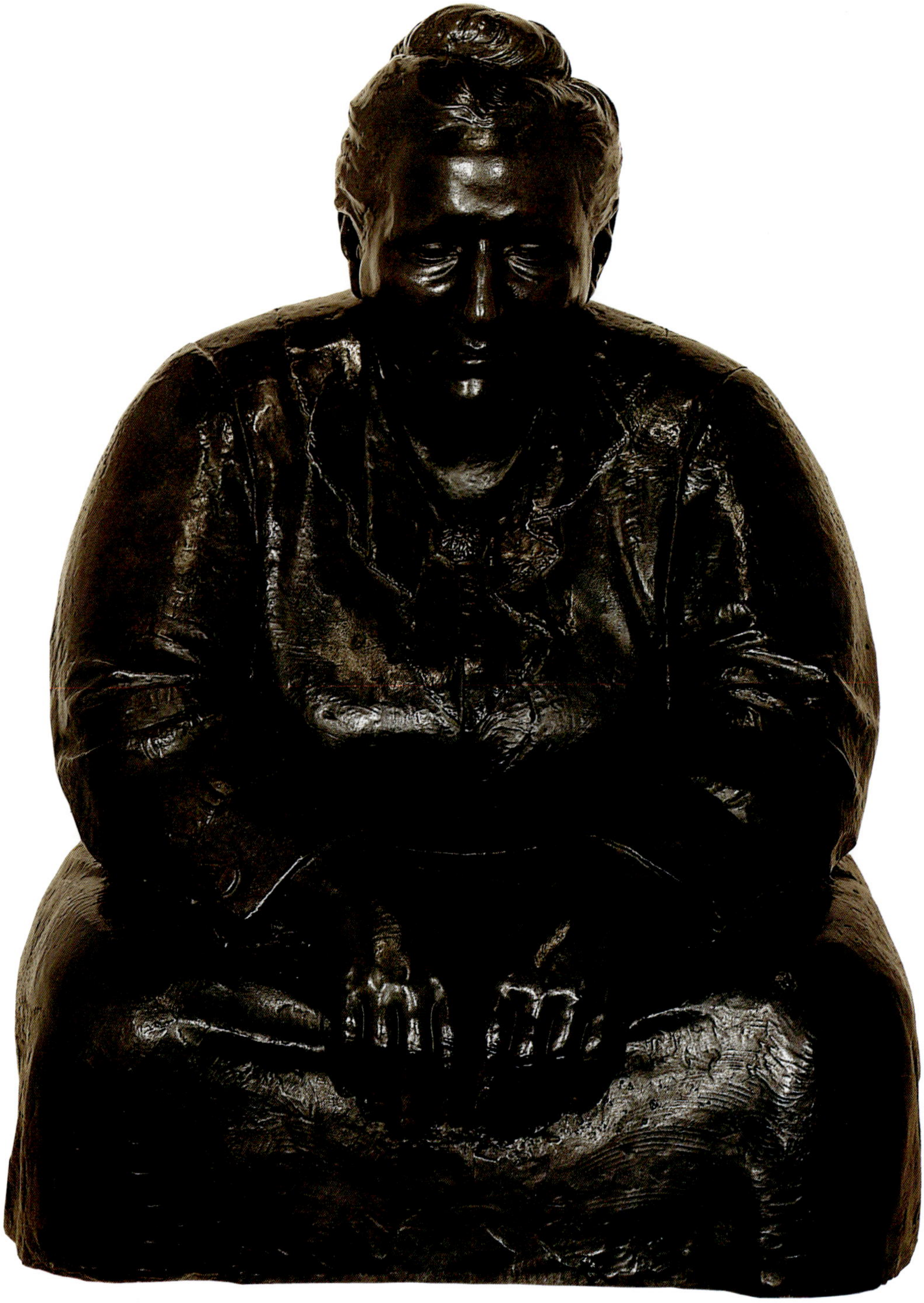

Jo Davidson

1883–1952

Jo Davidson fused new life into the tradition of naturalistic portraiture at a time when many sculptors chose to experiment with modernism. Stylistically, the bulk of Davidson's art belongs to a late-nineteenth-century, Beaux-Arts style, due to its fluid lines and rough surface treatment. Born in New York City, Davidson studied informally under George de Forest Brush at the Art Students League in 1899, then took time off to prepare for medical school. He decided against becoming a physician, however, when he visited the art studios at Yale University and began working with clay. From 1901–1904, Davidson assisted Yale's resident sculptor Hermon Atkins MacNeil and in 1907 he sailed for Paris, where he briefly enrolled at the Ecole des Beaux Arts. Except for periodic visits to the United States, Davidson lived and worked in France for the rest of his life.

Davidson specialized in bronze portrait busts of political leaders and other celebrities because he was fascinated with the personalities that shaped the world. "Portraiture became an obsession," he reminisced. "Meeting and knowing people meant becoming acquainted with their thinking."[1] After successfully sculpting a bust of President Woodrow Wilson at the outset of World War I, dignitaries in Washington granted Davidson permission to create likenesses of prominent wartime figures, a project that resulted in busts of General Pershing, Marshal Foch, and others. When Davidson finished the bust of Foch, the leader established a precedent that Davidson followed in subsequent works—placing his signature next to the artist's.

Gertrude Stein, ca. 1920
33 x 24 x 24 in.
Bronze
Gift of Dr. Maury P. Leibovitz

Davidson modeled many important figures during his lifetime. He created likenesses of writers James Joyce and Walt Whitman, for instance, and of art patrons Gertrude Vanderbilt Whitney and Gertrude Stein. Other important works by Davidson include: those of physicist Albert Einstein; actor and humorist Will Rogers; and Helen Keller, who overcame severe handicaps to become an advocate for the blind. In addition to the portrait of Gertrude Stein, the Norton owns bronzes of industrialist and philanthropist John D. Rockefeller, Israeli politicians Golda Meir and David Ben-Gurion, United States President Herbert Hoover, and British playwright George Bernard Shaw. Davidson also occasionally sculpted ideal subjects, such as the nude, but these works have not received the attention of his portraits.

Although Davidson exhibited several pieces at the 1913 Armory Show, his work appeared increasingly more conservative than of his contemporaries. Artists, such as Constantin Brancusi, Henry Moore, and Alexander Calder, experimented with abstract approaches to representation, fostered by the modern movement. Nonetheless Davidson continued to work in a traditional style with no loss to his reputation. Today, he is remembered as one of America's most important portraitists.

Gertrude Stein, ca. 1920
33 x 24 x 24 in.
Bronze
(on base: "Gertrude Stein/by/Jo Davidson/
Paris, 19 [illeg.]")
Gift of Dr. Maury P. Leibovitz 86.80

Expatriated Gertrude Stein, whose apartment at 27 rue de Fleurus, Paris, was home to a progressive salon for avant-garde artists and writers, intrigued Davidson, perhaps more so than many of his other sitters. Davidson sculpted Stein, who was, herself, a noted modernist writer, on more than one occasion. His pieces of the well-known arts patron portray her in a variety of formats. Institutions, such as the Whitney Museum of American Art, the National Portrait Gallery, the Los Angeles County Museum of Art, the Carnegie Museum of Art, and Yale University, own portraits of Gertrude Stein which differ in both overall conception and size.[2]

Works created in the same vein as the Norton's piece stand out within Davidson's oeuvre because they deviate from the artist's usual practice of depicting only the head and shoulders of his sitters. Davidson believed that the bust format he generally used for his portraits would not adequately capture the likeness of Stein, who posed for several portraits, including one by Pablo Picasso. In order to better convey the compactness of Stein's body, Davidson deviated from his usual formate and sculpted her entire form. "To do a head of Gertrude Stein was not enough," Davidson commented, "there was so much more to her than that. So I did a seated figure of her—a sort of modern Buddha."[3]

The Norton's portrait of Stein also differs from Davidson's other pieces, in that the surface is treated relatively smoothly. To execute the piece in his usual manner, which is, at once, rougher and more fluid, would detract from the overall sense of volume. Only a few elements are described in detail. These include Stein's brooch, collar, and hair. Her face, on the other hand, is almost completely smooth, and the texture of her clothing is only suggested.

Most portraits of notable personalities are signed only by the artist who conceives them, the physical representation of the sitter being enough to evoke his or her personality. However, like many of Davidson's famous sitters, Stein provided further insight into her personality by inscribing her name in scrawling letters next to Davidson's. CMC

NOTES

[1] Wayne Crave, *Sculpture in America* (Newark, NJ: University of Delaware Press, 1984), 558.

[2] Works that differ only slightly in dimensions may be casts from the same mold.

[3] Craven, 559.

PROVENANCE

Norton Gallery, 1986.

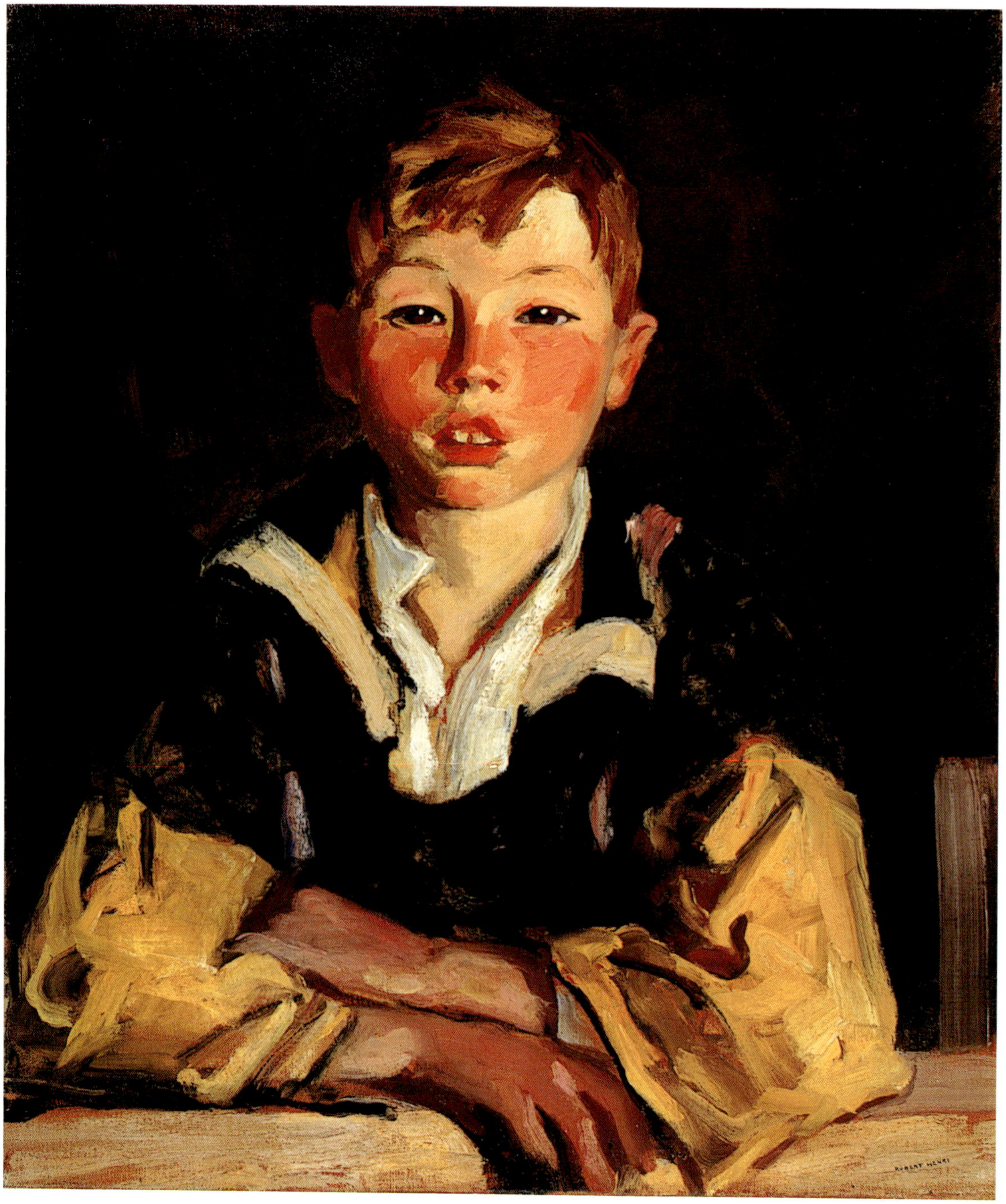

Portrait of a Boy (Sonny Mac), 1926
Oil on canvas
24 x 20 in.
Bequest of R. H. Norton

Robert Henri

1865–1929

Robert Henri's childhood as the son of a riverboat gambler may have prepared him for the role of an artistic rebel, a role which would later bring him much publicity and fame. He was born Robert Henry Cozad, in Cincinnati. His family founded several towns in the American West, but they were forced to move to the East under assumed names after Henri's father was involved in the death of one of his employees. Having settled in New Jersey in 1884, Henri made his way successfully through academically artistic circles, first as a student at the Pennsylvania Academy of the Fine Arts in Philadelphia from 1886–1888, and then in Paris, at the Académie Julian from 1888–1890.

Henri worked within a vocabulary of American Impressionism in his paintings of the early 1890s, using a pastel palette to depict pleasant seaside and landscape scenes. During his travels in Europe later in that same decade, however, he came to admire the dark greys, browns, and blacks used by the seventeenth-century artists Diego Velázquez and Frans Hals. Henri's palette was also influenced by a modern French artist indebted to these same old masters, Edouard Manet. In the late 1890s, while Henri was adopting a much darker palette, he also began to change his subject matter to include the urban street scenes of Paris and New York. His painting of a Parisian street in the snow, *La Neige*, was purchased in 1899, from the Paris Salon by the French government and hung in the Palais de Luxembourg.

After having settled in New York in 1900, Henri began to focus increasingly on portraiture, and his sitters ranged from family and friends to people on the streets of New York. In 1905, Henri was elected to the National Academy of Design in New York as an associate member, but he soon became dissatisfied with his academic accomplishments. Disagreements over the selection and hanging process for the Academy's annual exhibition sparked Henri's decision to hold an independent exhibition in 1908. Through the press, with which many of his New York friends were associated, Henri orchestrated the sensational publicity for this exhibition, called the *Exhibition of the Eight*. Under Henri's guidance, these eight painters, including John Sloan, William Glackens, Maurice Prendergast, George Luks, Arthur B. Davies, Everett Shinn, and Ernest Lawson, joined together in a revolt against the National Academy's jury selection system and in support of wider exhibition opportunities for all artists. Although several of these artists shared similar urban subject matter and darker palettes, their representative works in the Norton's collection, alone, indicate the diversity of their styles and subjects.[1]

In his rather conservative realistic portraiture, Henri's art fell somewhat short of his controversial ideals of artistic freedom and rebellious originality promoted in the *Exhibition of the Eight*. After the 1913 exhibition of the work of the European avant-garde at the Armory Show, he irretrievably lost his position as the leading rebel in American art. Henri's teachings, rather than his art, exerted a significant influence over many of the younger artists who began to shape early American modernism. Ever since his first teaching position at the New York School of Art, Henri had been popular as an innovator in art education, who encouraged the individuality of his students, rather than any dogmatic artistic principles. Henri described his methods as, "I do not teach my students to lean on what I say or what I see. I want them to see for themselves."[2] In 1923, one of his admiring students, Margery Ryerson, compiled Henri's teachings into an anthology entitled *The Art Spirit*.

Henri continued to paint for the remaining years of his life, spending much of his time at his estate in Corrymore, Ireland, with his wife Marjorie. Henri died of cancer in a New York hospital in 1929.

Portrait of a Boy (Sonny Mac), 1926
Oil on canvas
24 x 20 in.
(l.r.: "Robert Henri"; verso: "N 63/ Sonny Mac")
Bequest of R. H. Norton 53.79

Ralph Norton purchased this painting, one of his personal favorites, in 1929, the year of Henri's death. It had been painted only three years earlier, sometime between July and November of 1926, at Henri's house in Corrymore, on Achill Island, County Mayo, on the west coast of Ireland. Henri's first visit to Ireland had been in 1913 with his wife Marjorie, and they enjoyed their visit there, if only as an escape from Henri's feelings of depression and alienation after the 1913 Armory Show.[3] Henri painted a few landscapes on this first visit, but he especially enjoyed painting the people there and, most of all, the children. The Henris enjoyed their time in Ireland so much that they bought a house in Corrymore in 1924. Perhaps because they did not have any children, the Henris delighted in entertaining those from the Irish countryside who would come to sit for Henri's paintings, such as the subject of this portrait, Sonny Mac. Between 1927 and 1928, Henri painted almost 140 portraits of Irish children.[4]

By this late point in his career, Henri had become disenchanted with the Maratta color system, a technical system of color harmonies which he had strongly advocated in the 1910s. Nevertheless, in these portraits, Henri was able to achieve similar harmonious contrasts between vivid colors without using Maratta's premixed pigments.[5] In *Sonny Mac*, Henri presents an image of a robust young Irish boy with pale skin and ruddy cheeks. The color contrasts between his skin and cheeks typify Henri's portraits of this period, as do the dominant black and white tonalities in this painting. At the same time, the yellow of the boy's sleeves and hair provides a characteristically vivid, colorful foil to the portrait's black and white contrasts.

Henri's portraits dominated his oeuvre after the turn of the century and served as his primary contribution to the *Exhibition of the Eight*. Like many of his American colleagues, Henri did produce commissioned portraits, but most of his sitters were people whom he saw on his trips around the U.S. and Europe. He admired the Irish immigrant children in New York, as well as those in Ireland itself, and he became more interested in depicting peoples of all races as the years passed, including those of Hispanic, Asian, and Native-American descent. He once observed: "The people I like to paint are 'my people,' whoever they may be, wherever they may exist.... wherever I find them,... my interest is awakened and my impulse immediately is to tell about them through my own language—drawing and painting in color."[6]

Henri aimed to depict individuals as representations of their race, age, or social status, which he considered the essence of their identity. At the same time that he attempted to represent different types of people, however, Henri believed strongly in equality and individual rights. He instilled his figures with a certain indomitable, individual spirit, and not a stereotypical identity. In this painting, the figure of Sonny Mac presents the forceful spirit of a distinct individual, as well as a facial type of a young Irish boy. Sonny Mac's dominating presence extends to the outer edges of the composition, while his commanding, but calm expression suggests the simple life of rural Ireland. CMC

NOTES

[1] Although often referred to as the Ashcan School, this title is a misnomer for the Eight as a whole. It is a term that was used by Holger Cahill and Alfred Barr, in the 1930s, to describe the artists depicting urban scenes in the early twentieth century. The Eight's subjects were by no means limited to "urban realism," but included a wide variety of individual concerns. See Elizabeth Milroy, *Painters of a New Century: The Eight and American Art* (Milwaukee, WI: Milwaukee Art Museum, 1991), 15–16.

[2] Ibid., 26.

[3] Bennard Perlman, *Robert Henri: His Life and Art* (New York City, NY: Dover, 1991), 110–11.

[4] Ibid., 112, 134. Sonny Mac is most likely the nickname for Michael McNamara, whose relatives still reside on Achill Island, Ireland. I gratefully acknowledge that this information is the result of research by Tom McNamara.

[5] Perlman, 130.

[6] William Inness Homer, *Robert Henri and His Circle* (New York City, NY: Hacker Art Books, 1988), 252.

PROVENANCE

Artist; Macbeth Gallery, until 1929; Ralph Norton, 1929; Norton Gallery, 1953.

EXHIBITION HISTORY

Art and Culture Center of Hollywood, FL, *American Portraits*, September 10–October 20, 1978, no. 23.

Visual Arts Gallery, Florida International University, Miami, FL, *Treasures from the Norton Gallery of Art*, September 28–October 21, 1982, no. 8.

Center for the Arts, Inc., Vero Beach, FL, *William Merritt Chase and Robert Henri: American Master Painters*, January 31–March 16, 1986, no. 46.

Polk Museum of Art, Lakeland, FL, *A Century of American Painting*, December 2, 1988–January 15, 1989.

George Grosz

1893–1959

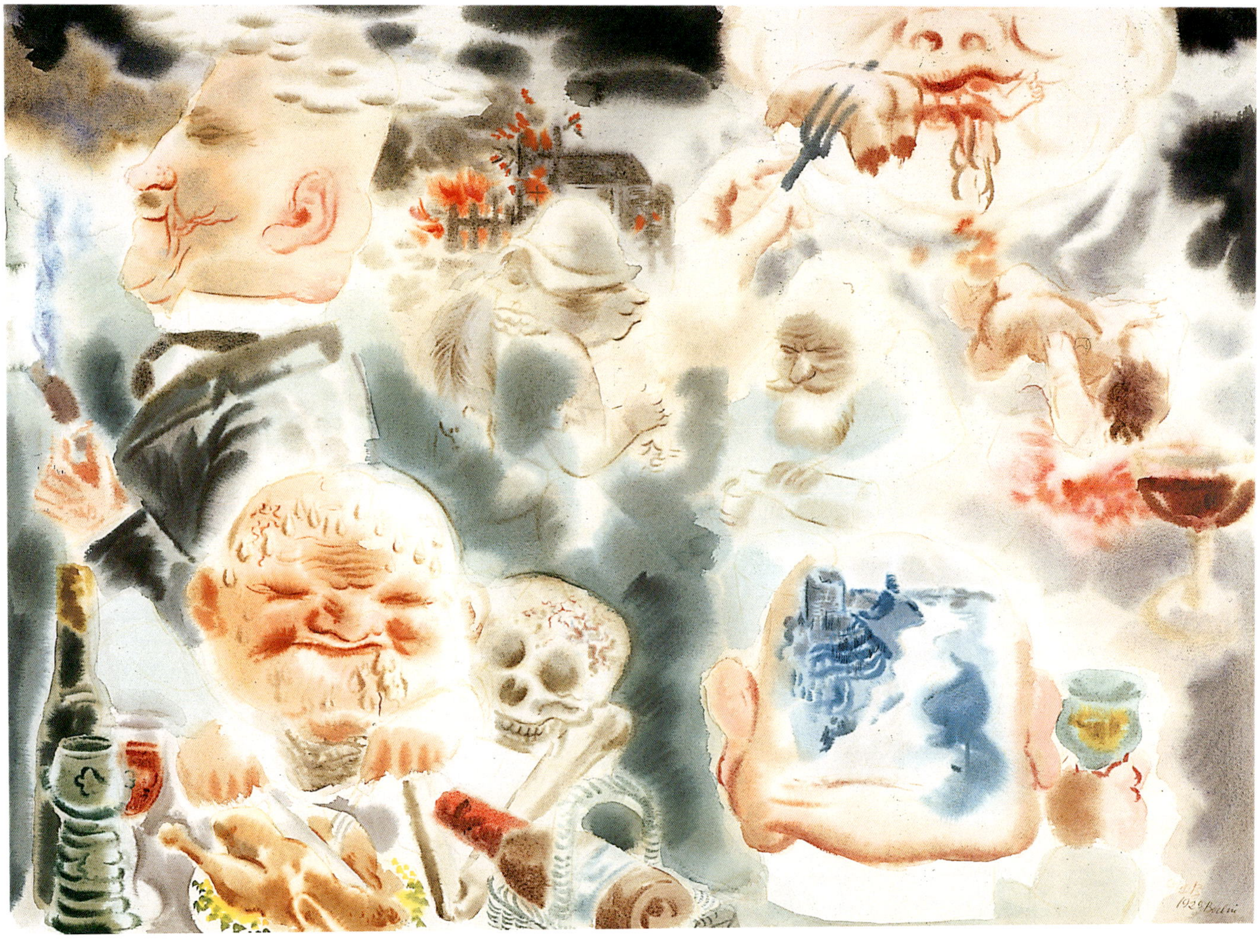

Eaten and to be Eaten, 1929
Watercolor on paper
20 x 27 in.
Bequest of R. H. Norton

George Grosz, 1893–1959

Born in Berlin, Germany, George Grosz emigrated to America in 1933 in the wake of government censure. Although he had been academically trained and, initially, had intended to become a traditional history painter, Grosz discovered satire as a more assured source of income and, from 1914 until his death, devoted his considerable talents as a draftsman to depicting the darker side of human nature.

Grosz studied at the Royal Saxon Academy of the Fine Arts in Dresden, the Royal Arts and Crafts School in Berlin, and the Academie Colarossi in Paris. In 1910, while still a student, he began selling line drawings to popular magazines, and by 1913, his satirical illustrations of German life were being widely published. The most crucial event in Grosz's early life, however, was his service in the German infantry, during World War I, which resulted in his being temporarily institutionalized and enduringly embittered.

Returning to the Berlin art scene in 1918, Grosz became an active member of the irreverent Dada movement, and his post-war work reflected an increasingly political and anti-authoritarian message. In brutally caustic paintings and drawings, Grosz spared no one, as he vehemently attacked the military, the government, the upper class, and the common man. Themes such as murder, profiteering, prostitution, and general moral decline dominated his often grotesque imagery. His style at this time was influenced by the Italian Futurists whose work he had seen in Paris, and whose angular distortions of the modern world seemed well-suited to his own violent subject matter.

Through the publication of his drawings in a series of portfolios and books, Grosz began to attract an international audience in the 1920s. At the same time, the negative view of German society conveyed in these publications soon earned Grosz the animosity of his government. Arrested and tried repeatedly throughout the decade, Grosz finally moved to New York in 1933.[1] Four years later, his work was included in the notorious "Degenerate Art" exhibition staged by the Nazis, and in 1938, he was officially stripped of his German citizenship.

Physically removed from the volatile political and social conditions of his native country, Grosz initially drew with less cynicism and even began painting landscapes. His political activism revived with the start of World War II, however, and during the 1940s, Grosz painted nightmarish scenes of modern warfare. In 1958, in response to Germany's active solicitation of its many talented expatriots, Grosz returned to Berlin where he died the following year.

In retrospect, Grosz fully realized his early ambition to become a history painter. As a chronicler of one of the most violent periods in modern history, Grosz exchanged the grand style and romantic heroism of traditional history painting for caustic irony and shocking brutality and, thereby, succeeded in conveying the destruction and disillusionment of his time.

Eaten and to be Eaten, 1929
Watercolor on paper
20 x 27 in.
(l.r.: "Grosz 1929 Berlin")
Bequest of R. H. Norton 53.74

Eaten and to be Eaten is powerfully representative

of Grosz's work of the late 1920s. Painted in the midst of his protracted blasphemy trial, *Eaten and to be Eaten* presents a disturbing vision of impending doom, a warning to his countrymen of their imminent and horrifying fate.

As described by Grosz, German society in the 1920s appeared calm and joyous but was actually a "boiling caldron" of universal hate, dissension, and chaos, tentatively governed by the unstable Weimar Republic.[2] Signifying this situation in *Eaten and to be Eaten* through a series of vignettes, Grosz personifies the various character flaws which were blinding his countrymen to reality. Thus, the egotist, the glutton, the dreamer, and the drinkers completely ignore the man-eating menace in the upper right corner, pursuing, instead, the vanities and vices they exemplify.[3]

Intended as a nightmarish vision, *Eaten and to be Eaten* is permeated by a cloudy atmosphere which engulfs the figures, simultaneously separating and connecting them in an ambiguous, dreamlike space.[4] This hallucinatory quality is further enhanced by Grosz's style which, at this time, was strongly influenced by Surrealism. Although Grosz did not share the Surrealists' overriding interest in the subconscious, he found their dream-inspired imagery and irrational juxtapositions useful in conveying a world gone mad. Thus, the figures in *Eaten and to be Eaten* are variously cropped, overlapped and disfigured as they emerge from the disorienting swirl of clouds. Arranged in seemingly close proximity, the figures are, nevertheless, completely unaware of one another, adding to the scene's confusion. In all, it is a carefully constructed vision of a chaotic world.

Emphatically pessimistic, *Eaten and to be Eaten* was, nevertheless, prophetic. Like many of Grosz's images produced between the two World Wars, this painting reveals the acuity of Grosz's vision as he observed his society and predicted its tragic course. AMB

NOTES

[1] Grosz was first arrested in 1920 and tried for attacking the Reichswehr. In 1923, he was brought into court again, this time, for defaming public morals. In his trial of 1928, he was convicted of blasphemy and sacrilege, but this decision was finally reversed. For a succinct account of Grosz's trials, see John I. H. Baur, *George Grosz* (New York City, NY: The MacMillan Company, 1954), 21–22.

[2] George Grosz, *A Little Yes and a Big No* (New York City, NY: The Dial Press, 1946), 201–202.

[3] Grosz identified the figure in the upper left as "the 100% egoist," and described the figure in the lower right as being absorbed in his memory of the Rhineland. Letter to Ralph Norton, dated May 5, 1939. Norton Gallery of Art files. Gluttons and drinkers are recurring characters in Grosz's work.

[4] Ibid.

PROVENANCE

Norton Gallery, 1953.

EXHIBITION HISTORY

The Art Institute of Chicago, Chicago, IL, *George Grosz: A Survey of his Art from 1918–1938*, December 15, 1938–January 15, 1939, no. 4.

The Lowe Art Museum, University of Miami, Coral Gables, FL, *American Exhibition*, February 25–March 14, 1952.

Smithsonian Institution, Washington, D.C., *Master Watercolors and Drawings from the Norton Gallery of Art*, travelling exhibition, February 11, 1988–September 24, 1989, no. 20.

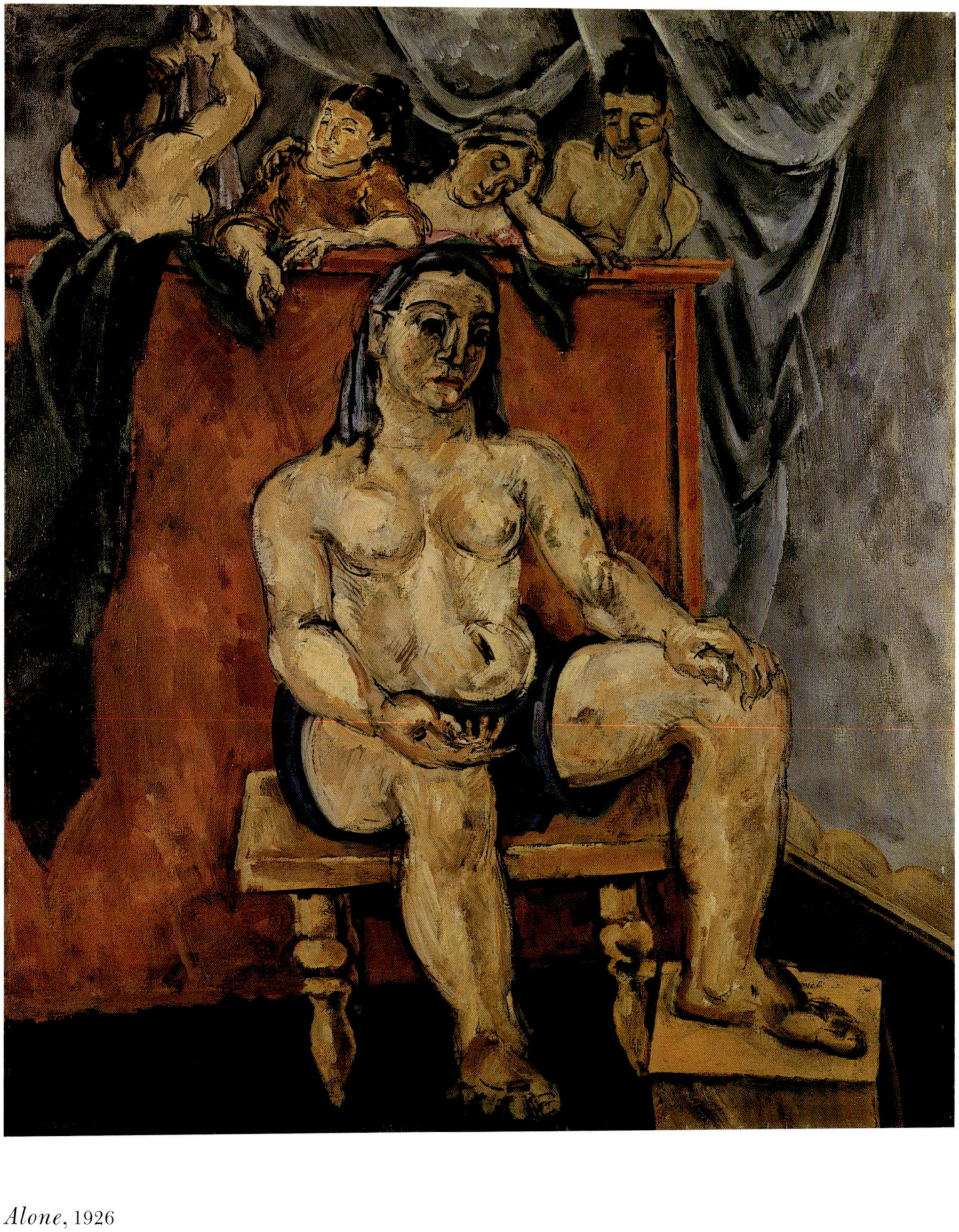

Alone, 1926
Oil on canvas
36 x 30 in.
Bequest of R. H. Norton

Max Weber

1881–1961

Among the most talented of America's early modernists, Max Weber played a crucial role in introducing European modernism to America. Painting with exceptional facility in Fauvist, Cubist and Futurist styles, writing intelligently on modern aesthetic theory, and organizing avant-garde exhibitions, Weber passionately promoted modernism, aiding its assimilation into American culture.

Born in Bialystok, Russia, Weber came to America with his family when he was ten years old. In 1898, he entered the Pratt Institute in Brooklyn, New York, where he studied with Arthur Wesley Dow, one of the most gifted and innovative art teachers of the time. Dow's expressive use of color and form and his appreciation of Oriental and European art history made an enduring impression on Weber.

After graduating from Pratt in 1900, Weber taught art in Virginia and Minnesota until he had saved enough money to go to Europe. Arriving in Paris in 1905, he studied at the Académie Julian, the Académie Colarossi, the Académie de la Grande Chaumiere, and finally, with Henri Matisse. Travelling through Europe and spending much of his time in museums, Weber acquired a broad, historical perspective of European, African, and Oriental art, which enhanced his understanding of even the most radical work of his contemporaries.[1] Stimulated by the fresh approaches to traditional issues that were being posited by Paul Cézanne, Pablo Picasso, Georges Braque, Henri Rousseau, and Henri Matisse, Weber became an ardent member of the modernist movement before returning to the United States in 1909.

In New York, Weber received encouragement from the influential art dealer Alfred Stieglitz. Working for a time in Stieglitz's gallery, *291*, Weber helped organize avant-garde exhibitions and wrote insightful articles for Stieglitz's progressive magazine *Camera Work*. In 1910, Stieglitz recognized Weber as a member of the American vanguard by including him in his landmark exhibition, *Younger American Painters*.[2]

Throughout this period, Weber restlessly explored a variety of styles. His earliest post-European work was strongly influenced by Matisse's bright, Fauvist palette and simplified forms. Within a year, however, his canvases revealed a greater interest in the formalism of Cézanne and the Cubists, and by 1913, he was painting views of New York City with the kaleidoscopic effects of Italian Futurism.

Beginning in the 1920s, Weber's work increasingly became less a recapitulation of various modern movements and more of a consistent, personal expression. His subject matter became more introspective, spiritual, and narrative, often dealing with aspects of his Russian-Judaic heritage.

Although Weber suffered the critical and public rejection of most American modernists prior to the Armory Show in 1913, he actually enjoyed critical, if not financial, success relatively early. His 1913 solo exhibition at the Newark Museum, for example, was the first ever given to an American avant-garde artist by a public museum.[3] From that time forward, his work attracted influential critical support and was widely exhibited, both here and abroad. In 1916, he published his *Essays on Art*, an insightful statement of early modernist aesthetics. By the 1950s, Weber was generally hailed as a leader of American modernism, and prior to his death in 1961, he was honored with major retrospective exhibitions by The Museum of Modern Art, The Whitney Museum of American Art, The Jewish Museum, and the Newark Museum. Although during his lifetime Weber was most highly praised for his late, expressionistic paintings, his current reputation rests largely on the cubist-inspired paintings of his youth.

Alone, 1926
Oil on canvas
36 x 30 in.
(l.l.: "Max Weber" ; verso: "1926")
Bequest of R. H. Norton 53.206

Weber's introspective and expressive work of the 1920s is powerfully represented by *Alone*. After briefly experimenting with abstract compositions in the 1910s, Weber returned to more traditional subject matter, creating forceful images of the complexity of the human condition.

Like many of Weber's paintings from this period, the precise narrative of *Alone* remains elusive. Its setting, the identity of its five figures, and their relationship to each other, are all ambiguous. Seated on a nondescript stool, with its left foot slightly elevated on a low pedestal, and wearing nothing except a cloth headdress and rather peculiar shorts, the central figure suggests a model posing in an artist's studio. This interpretation is reinforced by the background figures who, in their various stages of undress, fail to interact and appear to be additional models waiting their turns to pose.[4]

This potentially mundane subject is transcended, however, by Weber's sensitive use of gesture and posture to express the central figure's alienation, and the boredom of those behind. Extensive academic training had provided Weber with a thorough background in anatomy and drawing from life, and throughout his long career, he focused on the human body which he, like his teacher Matisse, viewed as the most expressive vehicle for subtle ideas.[5]

Stylistically, *Alone* illustrates Weber's continuing identification with European modernism. The massive, sculpturesque foreground figure, with its masklike face and purposefully distorted proportions, is closely related to Picasso's contemporary neoclassical nudes. By employing this style, both artists succeeded in elevating their figures above the particular and individual to express universal concepts and truths. This desire for universality may also explain the otherwise surprising, and uncharacteristic, androgyny of *Alone's* central figure. The contrast between this forceful figure and the more naturalistically portrayed, but comparatively ineffectual figures in the background, clearly illustrates the effectiveness of Weber's technique.

Compositionally, *Alone* relates to several other figural paintings by Weber, in which he arranges figures, such as the four in the background, in the form of a "W", a subtle form of signature.[6] Similarly, for the cover of his *Essays on Art*, Weber drew two seated figures facing each other and merging to form a "W". In 1939, Weber seems to have returned to *Alone* for inspiration in painting *The Balcony* (private collection). Using a similar setting and only slightly altering poses and composition, Weber, nevertheless, paints a very different image by radically changing his style.

Painted in the 1920s, *Alone* is a transitional work. Simultaneously exhibiting a continuing stylistic influence of European modernism, as well as the promise of the uniquely personal expression to come, *Alone*, nevertheless, stands on its own as a compelling and provocative image. AMB

NOTES

[1] Weber studied the ethnological collections, including African art at the Trocadero and Oriental art at the Musée Guimet. William Inness Homer, *Alfred Stieglitz and the American Avant-Garde* (Boston, MA: New York Graphic Society, 1977), 129.

[2] This exhibition additionally featured D. Putnam Brinley, Arthur B. Carles, Arthur Dove, Laurence Fellows, Marsden Hartley, John Marin, Alfred Maurer, and Edward Steichen.

[3] Percy North, *Max Weber: American Modern* (New York City, NY: The Jewish Museum, 1982), 20.

[4] In this context, it is perhaps significant that at this time Weber was teaching at the Art Students League in New York and would have had ready access to life-drawing classes. Although he was teaching still life, Weber drew from a model in the classroom. See Alfred Werner, *Max Weber* (New York City, NY: Harry N. Abrams, 1975), 62.

[5] North, 33.

[6] Ibid., 38–39.

PROVENANCE

A. P. Rosenberg & Co.; Ralph Norton, 1949, Norton Gallery, 1953.

EXHIBITION HISTORY

The Whitney Museum of American Art, New York City, NY, *Max Weber: Retrospective*, travelling exhibition, February 5–August 14, 1949, no. 31.

Wildenstein Gallery, New York City, NY, *Modern French and American Painting*, May 4–28, 1955.

Playhouse Gallery, Miami, FL, *Paintings and Sculpture from the Norton Collection*, January 12–24, 1959.

The Art Gallery, McCormick Place, Chicago, IL, *Inaugural Exhibition*, November 18–December 23, 1960, no. 25.

Museum of Fine Arts, St. Petersburg, FL, *Masters from the Norton Gallery*, April 16–May 21, 1978.

The Jewish Museum, New York City, NY, *Max Weber: American Modern*, travelling exhibition, October 5, 1982–November 5, 1983, no. 58.

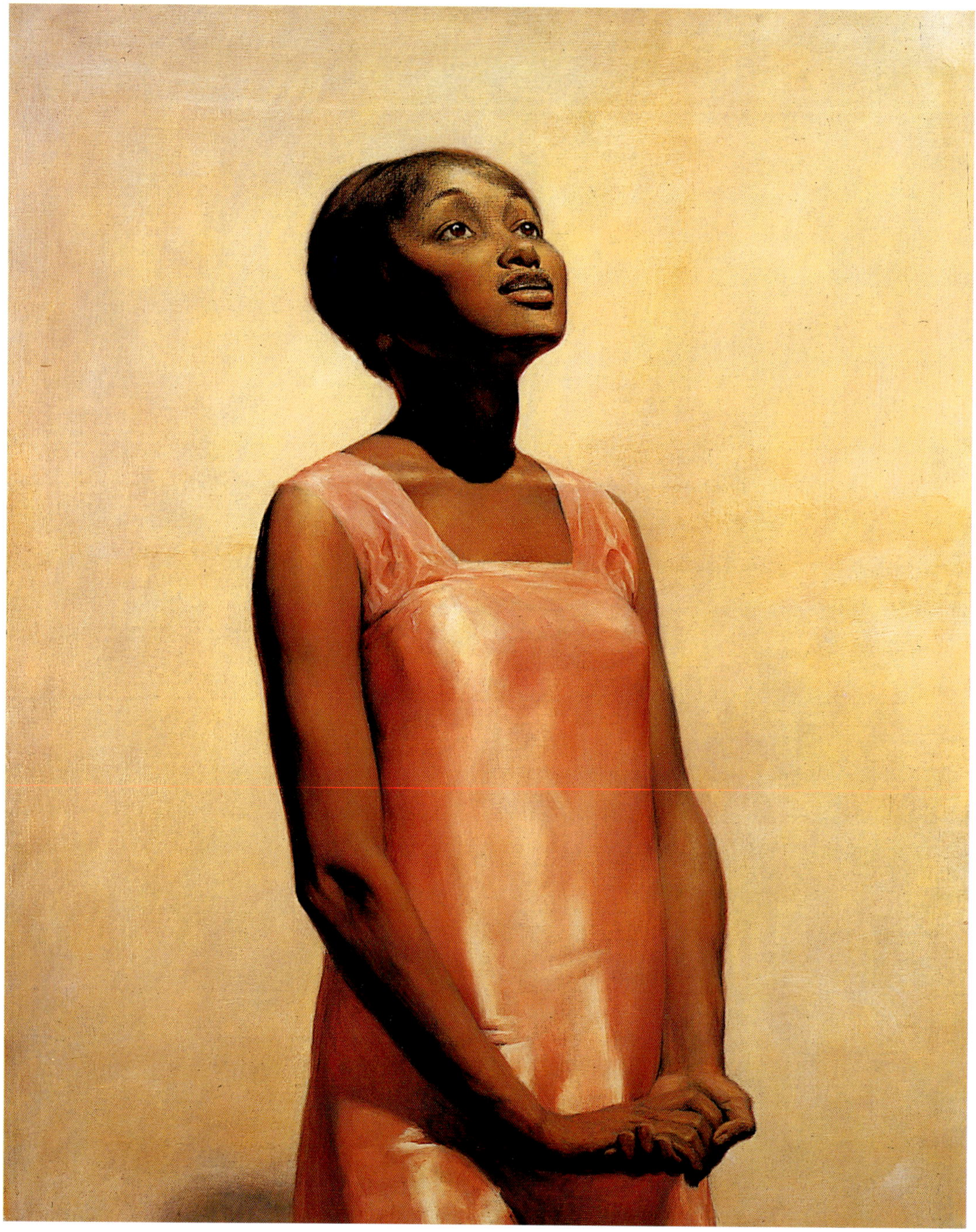

Ruby Green Singing, 1928
Oil on canvas
38 x 30 in.
Bequest of R. H. Norton

James Chapin

1887–1975

Born in West Orange, New Jersey, James Chapin received a traditional artistic education at several institutions, including Cooper Union and the Art Students League in New York, and the Royal Academy in Antwerp, Belgium. As a teenager and a young adult, Chapin produced his early artistic attempts in the styles of Paul Cézanne and the Post-Impressionists. The artist struggled through this initial stage in his career by making a living as a commercial illustrator, while longing to devote all of his time to painting.[1]

After moving to New Jersey in 1922, Chapin began to pursue a painting career, no longer working in European modes, but instead, in his own version of American Regionalist realism. Similar to the better-known Regionalist work of Thomas Hart Benton and Grant Wood, Chapin's American scenes present an expressionistic blend of figures and landscapes. The farmers and rural workers of New Jersey provided the inspiration for Chapin's depictions of American life.

Sharing in the popularity of Regionalist representations during the 1930s, Chapin's figural groupings and portraits of American workers became his most popular subjects. Chapin's Regionalist colleague Grant Wood admired his portraits of rural American workers because, "They were full of the pain and bleakness of a frugal existence on the land, yet possessed a subtle, melancholy beauty of their own."[2] In his early portraits, Chapin depicted the people of the rural areas around him in New Jersey, in an attempt to capture both their personalities and their way of life. In the 1930s, Chapin's subjects broadened to include urban workers, people in bars, boxers, baseball players, gangsters, and men and women of diverse backgrounds and races.

Chapin lived in the Northeast for much of his life, teaching, for a while, at the Pennsylvania Academy of the Fine Arts in Philadelphia and residing in New York City and in New Jersey for many years. In 1969, the artist moved to Canada in protest over the Vietnam War. Continuing to paint in a realist style, he remained there with his family until his death at the age of 88.[3]

Ruby Green Singing, 1928
Oil on canvas
38 x 30 in.
(l.r. and on verso: "James Chapin 28")
Bequest of R. H. Norton 53.29

When Chapin painted her portrait, Ruby Green sang as a contralto with Hall Johnson's Negro Chorus in Manhattan, a group devoted to singing spirituals. Green had graduated from the Juilliard School of Music, and she often performed for radio and television, as well as in concerts. The simple background of this painting may indicate that the popular singer posed for the artist in his studio, and her upward gaze suggests her own spirituality and that of her songs.[4]

Chapin often conveyed the dignity of his sitters through specific poses, as he once explained, "The symbol of the human gesture interests me a lot.... Not the gesture of hands or feet so much as the carriage of the human body and the human head." Chapin depicted the dignity of Ruby Green's presence in this portrait as a representation, not only of a particular individual, but also of the beauty and dignity of the African-American race. The artist claimed that in this portrait he aimed to portray "the beauty of Negro music and the Negro people." In his depictions of black women, Chapin often portrayed them, like Ruby Green, as noble individuals, full of pride, and as symbols for the beauty of their race.[5]

At the time of their production, Chapin's portraits, such as *Ruby Green Singing*, presented a new pictorial image of African-Americans, one that was individual and insightful, rather than stereotypical. The sympathy Chapin afforded his African-American subjects was not often found in the work of other white artists, and, in fact, such sensitivity toward black individuals, realized a definitive break with the traditional, stereotypical portrayals of them in secondary, often humorous, roles.[6]

Chapin completed this portrait the year before his first major exhibition in New York, in 1929. Since then, *Ruby Green Singing* has consistently succeeded in evoking an emotional response from a wide audience. Especially in the past few decades, Chapin's portrait has become an icon for the beauty of African-American spirituality and artistic expression. This symbolic function has been manifested primarily through the painting's inclusion in numerous textbooks and other publications. In the widespread reproduction of the painting, it has been associated not only with the spirituality of African-American music, but also with the great awakening of African-American culture in the 1920s, the Harlem Renaissance. LTJ

NOTES

[1] Christopher Hume, "James Chapin at Yaneff Gallery," *Artmagazine* 12 (February-March 1981): 48–49; Guy McElroy, *Facing History: The Black Image in American Art 1710–1940* (San Francisco, CA: Bedford Arts, 1990), 117.

[2] McElroy, 117.

[3] Hume, 48. Leonard E. Fisher, *Masterpieces of American Painting* (New York City, NY: Exeter Books, 1985), 132.

[4] McElroy, 117; *Music Educators' Journal* 53 (January 1967): 27.

[5] Alexander Eliot, *Three Hundred Years of American Painting* (New York City, NY: Time, Inc., 1957), 206; McElroy, 117.

[6] Alain Locke, *The Negro in Art* (New York City, NY: Hacker Art Books, 1979), 140, 204; McElroy, 117.

PROVENANCE

Frank K. M. Rehn, Inc., New York City, NY; Paul Sachs, Cambridge, MA; Frank K. M. Rehn, Inc., New York City, NY; Ralph Norton, 1930; Norton Gallery, 1953.

EXHIBITION HISTORY

Dallas Museum of Art, Dallas, TX, *Directions in Twentieth Century American Painting*, October 7–November 12, 1961, no. 37.

Museum of Fine Arts, St. Petersburg, FL, *Masters from the Norton Gallery*, April 16–May 21, 1978.

Corcoran Gallery of Art, Washington, D.C., *Facing History: The Black Image in American Art 1710–1940*, January 13–March 26, 1990, no. 117.

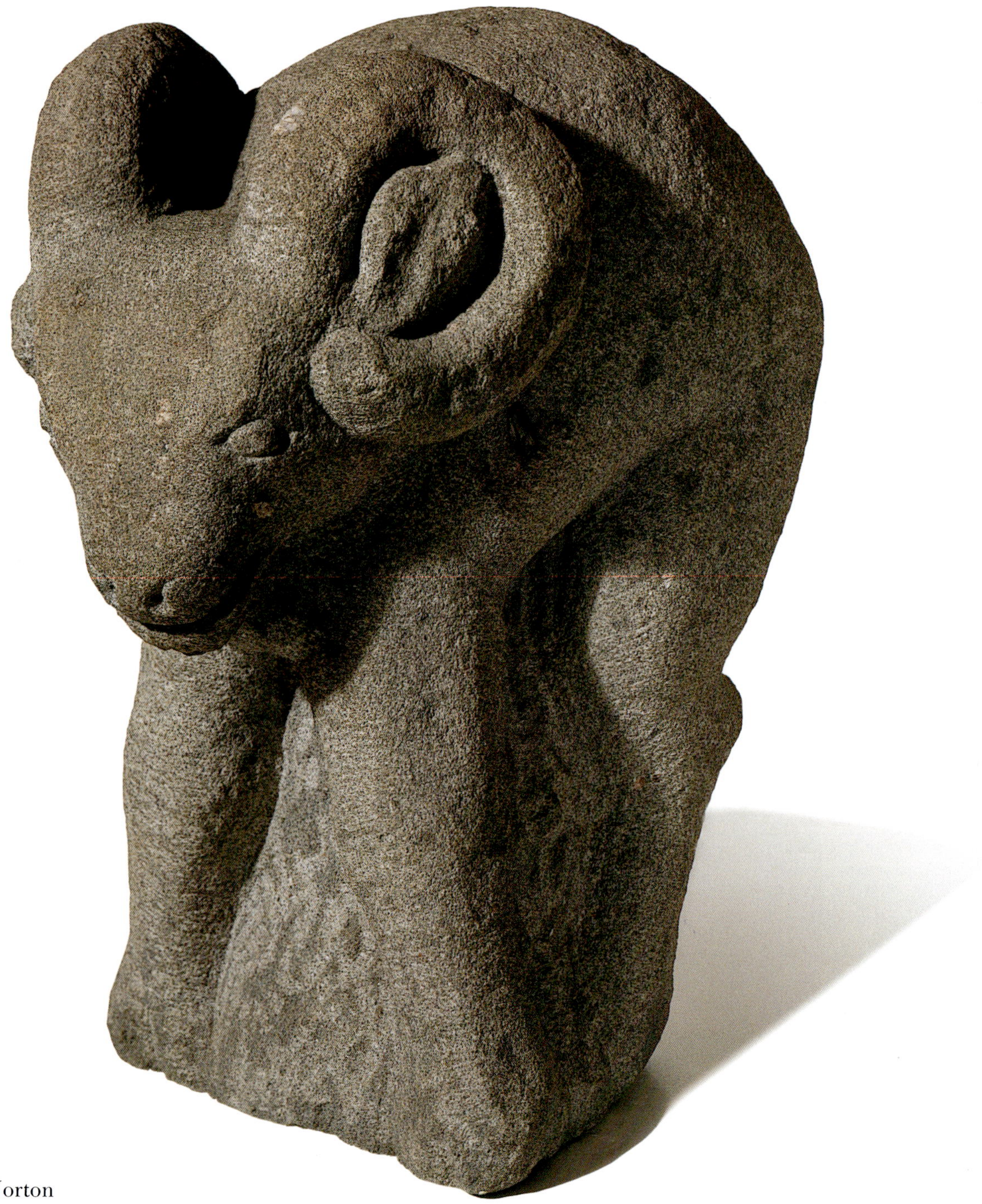

Ram, 1929
Fieldstone
18 x 12 x 9 in.
Bequest of R. H. Norton

John B. Flannagan

1895–1942

The sculptural work of John B. Flannagan is a modernist evocation of ancient, non-Western art. The naturalism of his simplified, animal carvings is complemented by an attendant pantheism, a quality quite distinct from the staid tradition of nineteenth-century American sculpture.

Born in Fargo, North Dakota, John Bernard Flannagan survived a difficult childhood. He suffered the loss of his father when he was six years old, and after years of financial struggle, his mother placed him and his brother in a Minnesota orphanage. Art was an early interest, and Flannagan entered the Minneapolis School of Art in 1913. He studied painting, and his pictures were exhibited in New York City in 1918. The same year, he joined the United States Merchant Marine, travelling to Europe and South America. He left the Merchant Marine after one year and moved to New York to pursue an artistic career in 1919.

Initially, Flannagan financially struggled in New York, but his fortunes improved in 1923, when he met Arthur B. Davies, a painter in Robert Henri's circle of anti-academy artists. Davies hired Flannagan to work on his farm in Congers, New York, providing him with a steady income. Davies' large art collection, which included pre-Columbian, antique, and Medieval sculpture, inspired the younger artist. Flannagan learned from Davies how to paint using wax, and with his encouragement, started to carve. Gradually, he made the transition from carved assemblage and wax painting, in which wax figures are mounted on board and painted, to sculpture.

In 1924, Flannagan exhibited paintings with Davies, Maurice and Charles Prendergast, William Glackens, Charles Sheeler, and Walt Kuhn at the Montross Gallery in New York. Three years later, the Weyhe Gallery of New York agreed to represent him, and the first of seven Flannagan exhibitions held at the gallery was successful. Fascinated by the history and culture of Ireland, his ancestral country, he travelled there for a year-long stay in 1931, a trip partly funded by the Weyhe Gallery. He spent 1932 and 1933 in Ireland as well, funded by a Guggenheim Fellowship. His intent, according to his application, was to study thirteenth-century sculpture and architecture and to assimilate its lessons in "an austere conception of art." [1] By the end of his visit, Flannagan had compiled a catalogue of Irish animal images and added Celtic carving methods to his sculptural abstraction.

During his lifetime, Flannagan's naturalistic animal studies were popular and were acquired by the Metropolitan Museum of Art, the Museum of Modern Art, and the Whitney Museum of Art. Still, the artist was unable to cope with his success or to overcome personal setbacks. He suffered from depression and alcoholism, a factor that would lead to the termination of his Weyhe Gallery contract. In 1935, he attempted suicide and spent seven months in a New York State hospital. Furthermore, after two serious automobile accidents in 1937 and 1939, and several brain operations, he endured chronic pain. Ordered by his doctors to give up the more strenuous practice of direct, stone carving, Flannagan learned to sculpt with hydraulic tools and adopted metal as his medium. He produced sculpture once again, and even exhibited his work. Nonetheless, Flannagan was despondent over his poor health and the curtailment of his preferred artistic method. He died, a suicide, in 1942.

Ram, 1929
Fieldstone
18 x 12 x 9 in.
(no inscription)
Bequest of R. H. Norton 53.64

Flannagan subscribed to a notion of "primitivism" in which a spiritual sensitivity was accorded to the artistic methods of ancient sculptors. He reasoned that their holistic approach involved a limited intervention with the chosen medium and a pantheistic belief in divinely guided forces of nature. *Ram*, a piece from his early stone period of 1926 to 1930, reflects his assimilation of the pantheist and primitivist aesthetic. Although his presentation of the ram is representational, the sculpture still retains an association with the rough, stone material. Flannagan believed that form was pre-existent in all stone and only awaited "the creative act of realization" to free it.[2] Appropriately, the ram's body emerges from rock, underscoring a unity of form and medium and their significance as forces of nature.

Flannagan consistently expressed his desire to produce a symbolic art, and his attraction to animal forms is directly related to this interest. In animals, he found both a fundamental dignity and a compositional design superior to that offered by the human figure. Accordingly, the form of *Ram* echoes with rhythmic contours and an insistently simplified line. The slight bow in the animal's spindly legs attaches a vulnerability to the figure that may, in fact, be a visual metaphor for youthful uncertainty and inexperience. The stone material, itself, is humble and ordinary—a reflection of Flannagan's aesthetic and of his dire financial straits in the late twenties when he collected his medium from the fields in rural New York State.

In subsequent periods of his career, Flannagan worked in more reductive styles and added allegory to the content of his sculpture. He inscribed animal images in a circular base to reinforce the physiological character of a dragon or a sleeping cat in his design, and to invoke the circle's symbolic associations with eternity and perfection. Flannagan's sculpture increasingly became monolithic, a development that has generated comparisons with the approach of Constantin Brancusi, the Rumanian-born modernist. The Flannagan sculptures of the early thirties share the tightly defined, uniform construction of the Brancusi form, which he had seen in Arthur B. Davies' collection. Yet, Flannagan did not refine his medium to the extent that Brancusi did. In the unfinished surface of sculptures, such as *Ram*, is the evidence of Flannagan's love for the organic and essential quality of fieldstone. Similarly, he exploited the color of bluestone in his sculpture *Jonah and the Whale*, 1937 (Minneapolis Institute of Arts) and the solidity of the granite-carved goat form in *Figure of Dignity*, 1932–33 (Metropolitan Museum of Art). These subjects served to communicate Flannagan's views on the cycles of life and the paradigmatic creations of nature. JF

NOTES

[1] John B. Flannagan, "Application to the John Simon Guggenheim Memorial Foundation for a Fellowship, November 1931," in Museum of Modern Art, *Five American Sculptors* (reprint, New York City, NY: Arno Press, 1969), 98–99.

[2] D.C. Miller, "The Image in the Rock," in *Five American Sculptors*, 7–8.

PROVENANCE

Artist; unknown private collection, Woodstock, NY, ca. 1930s–40s; Buchholz Gallery, New York City, NY, until 1951; Ralph Norton, 1951–53; Norton Gallery, 1953.

EXHIBITION HISTORY

The Art Gallery, McCormick Place, Chicago, IL, *Inaugural Exhibition*, November 18–December 23, 1960, no. 43.

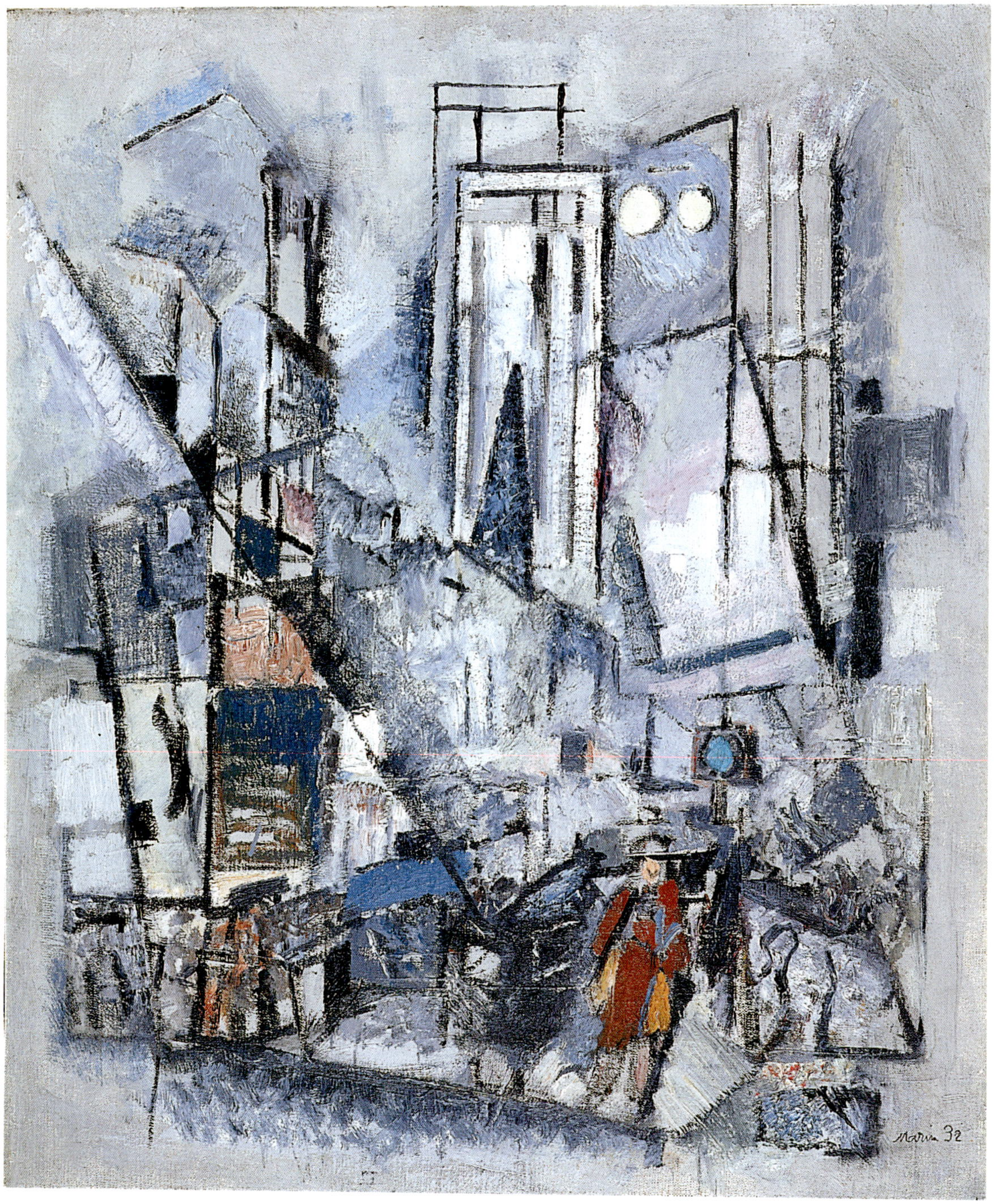

Looking Up Fifth Avenue from 30th Street, 1932
Oil on canvas
27 1/16 x 22 3/16 in.
Purchased through the R. H. Norton Fund

John Marin

1870–1953

John Marin, one of America's most talented modernists, abandoned a career as an architect at the age of twenty-nine in order to become an artist. He enrolled at the Pennsylvania Academy of the Fine Arts in 1899, where he studied under Thomas Anshutz and Hugh Breckenridge until 1901, then attended the Art Students League in New York City. In 1905, Marin travelled to Paris where he took courses at the Delecluse Academy and the Académie Julian. He remained in Europe for nearly five years, creating watercolor and oil landscapes in a style akin to James A.M. Whistler's tonalism. Marin came to know avant-garde Americans, like Arthur B. Carles, Max Weber, and Alfred Maurer, while abroad, and he exhibited at the radical Salon des Indépendents and the Salon d'Automne. Later, in 1913, Marin participated in the Armory Show held in New York City, an exhibit which revolutionized the American art world by introducing avant-garde artists, such as Pablo Picasso, Henri Matisse, and Marcel Duchamp.

Marin's primary goal as an artist was to record his personal, emotive responses to nature and to the urban environment. He achieved this end by working in an idiosyncratic form of Cubism, which was an approach to painting developed by Picasso and others in France. Noted for its planar, faceted look, Cubism had followers both in the United States and abroad.

Marin's patron Alfred Stieglitz, whom he met in 1909, aided Marin in developing his approach to painting. In fact, he encouraged all of the artists that he supported to develop an artistic philosophy. Like Marin, Georgia O'Keeffe, Arthur Dove, and Marsden Hartley—the other members of the Stieglitz circle—

each created individual visual means through which to convey their personal experiences of the world.

By 1912, Marin's mature style emerged in his paintings of New York City, which, together with portrayals of the Maine coast where Marin spent his summers, became his primary subject matter. Marin was particularly interested in depicting New York's buildings, for he was captivated by the interplay of architectural masses. Describing his fascination with the urban landscape Marin, wrote, "I see great forces at work; great movements; the large buildings and the small buildings; the warring of the great and the small; influences of one mass on another greater or smaller mass." [1] The buildings emotionally inspired Marin as well. "If these buildings move me," he wrote, "they too must have life.... It is this 'moving of Me' that I try to express, so that I may recall the spell I have been under and behold the expression of the different emotions that have been called into being." [2]

During the 1930s Marin began to use oils more regularly than he had in the past, and he introduced the human figure, especially the female nude. The oils focused more on brushwork than on subject matter until the 1940s and 1950s, when his work in both media became almost purely calligraphic and laced with weblike, black "ray" lines. This focus on brushwork paralleled the expressionism and the surface patterning of younger New York School painters, such as Jackson Pollock, but with one exception: Marin did not wish his paintings to give the impression that they continued beyond the limits of their frames, as did the Abstract Expressionists. "[A good painting will have] its boundaries as definite as the prow, the stern, the sides and bottom bound a boat.... My picture must not make one feel that it burst its boundaries.... That would be a delusion and I would have it that nothing must cut my picture off from its finalities." [3]

Looking Up Fifth Avenue from 30th Street, 1932
Oil on canvas
27 1/16 x 22 3/16 in.
(l.r.: "Marin 32")
Purchased through the R. H. Norton Fund 53.6

Looking Up Fifth Avenue from 30th Street typifies Marin's oeuvre in that it portrays a busy scene in New York City. Figures are visible in the foreground, the most prominent of which wears a brown coat and hat and hurries rapidly down the street. Other recognizable forms include skyscrapers, a steeple, and a traffic light.

Looking Up Fifth Avenue is a work created during the first period that Marin focused on oil painting. In addition to the years encompassing the late 1920s and early 1930s, Marin worked in oils a great deal from the mid-1940s until his death. Like the watercolors portraying the same scenes, the oils were executed relatively quickly in order to preserve the brief moment that inspired them.

In addition to the watercolor-like immediacy of the painting, Marin employs other means to create an overall sense of energy and spontaneity. His use of "ray" lines, for instance, add to the excitement through their dynamic diagonal placement. Scattered across the canvas, the black lines describe edges of buildings and other objects. The fragmented Cubist manner of representation also contributes to the feeling of excitement. Marin depicts objects—especially the buildings—from a variety of viewpoints, a tactic which has an exhilarating, almost dizzying, effect. The lack of a specific vanishing point or system of perspective creates energy. The eye moves rapidly around the composition in search of a focus, but unable to find one, resumes its disorienting quest.

Looking Up Fifth Avenue radiates energy. It beckons the viewer. One finds it easy to imagine hurrying through a crowd down one of New York City's most exciting thoroughfares. CMC

NOTES

[1] Ruth E. Fine, *John Marin* (New York City, NY: Abbeville Press in conjunction with the National Gallery of Art, 1990), 126.

[2] Ibid., 126.

[3] Ibid., 207.

PROVENANCE

Alfred Stieglitz, New York City, NY, c. 1948; John Marin Jr., NJ; Downtown Gallery, New York City, NY, 1956; Norton Gallery, 1956.

EXHIBITION HISTORY

Museum of Modern Art, New York City, NY, *John Marin: Watercolors, Oil Paintings, Etchings*, October 1936.

Biennale Internazionale d'Arte, Venice, Italy, 1950.

Art Galleries, University of California, Los Angeles, CA, *John Marin Memorial Exhibition*, February 1955.

Arts Council Gallery, London, England, *John Marin Paintings*, September 22–October 20, 1956.

High Museum of Art, Atlanta, GA, *Collectors' Firsts*, February 18–March 1, 1959.

The Art Gallery, McCormick Place, Chicago, IL, *Inaugural Exhibition*, November 18–December 23, 1960.

Florida Development Commission's Showcase, Rockefeller Center, New York City, NY, *Art in Florida*, July 1961.

The Corcoran Gallery of Art, Washington, D.C., *John Marin in Retrospect*, March 2–April 15, 1962.

American House, Berlin, Germany, *John Marin: Ölbilder und Aquarelle*, September 15–October 14, 1962.

University of Arizona Art Gallery, Tucson, AZ, *John Marin*, February 9–March 10, 1963.

Museum of Fine Arts, St. Petersburg, FL, *Masters from the Norton Gallery*, April 16–May 21, 1978.

Visual Arts Gallery, Florida International University, Miami, FL, *Treasures from the Norton Gallery of Art*, September 28– October 21, 1982, no. 16.

Pensacola Museum of Art, Pensacola, FL , *American and European Masterpieces of the Nineteenth and Twentieth Centuries*, September 22–November 16, 1984.

The Parrish Art Museum, Southampton, NY, *Marin in Oil*, July 18–September 20, 1987.

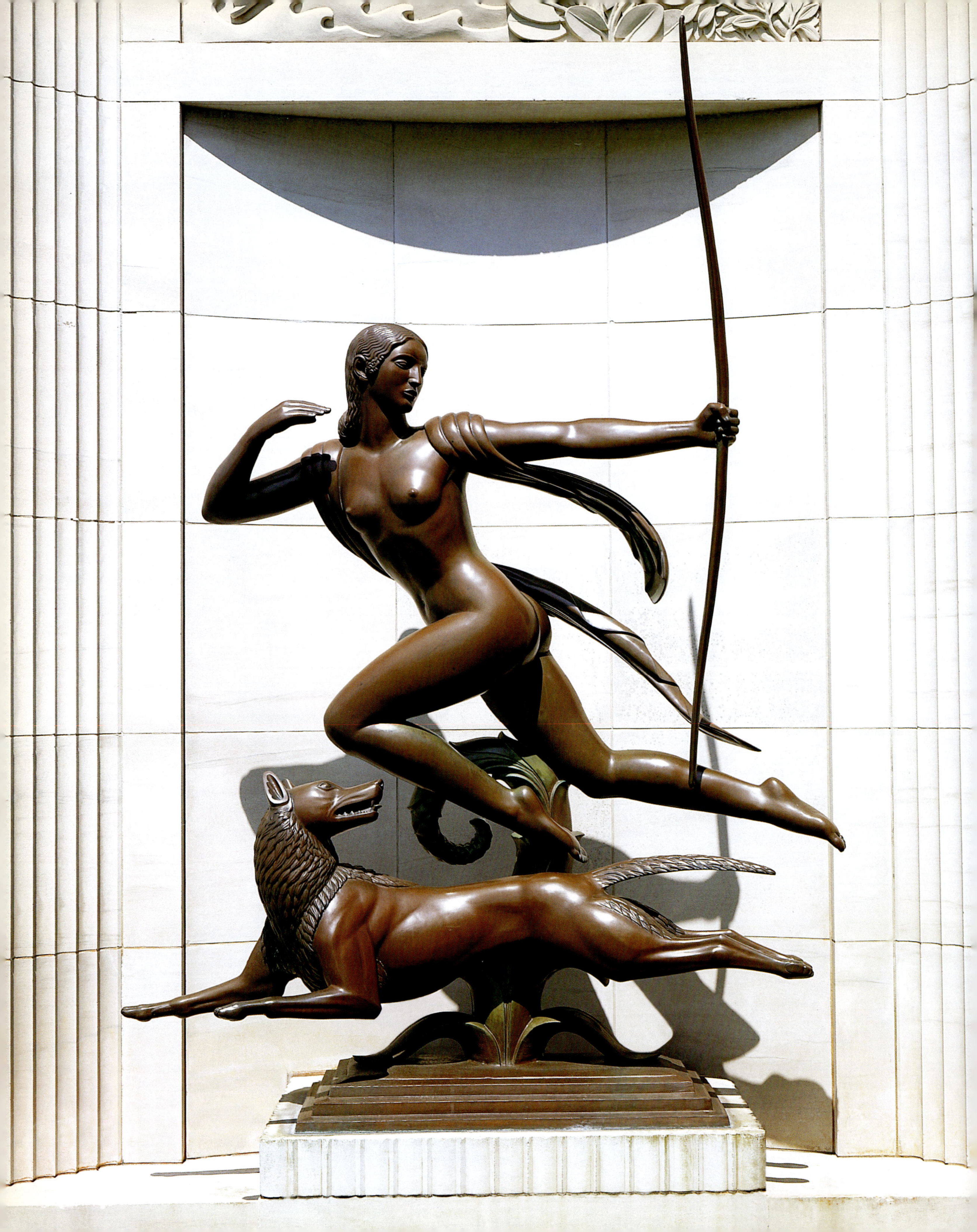

Paul Manship

1885–1966

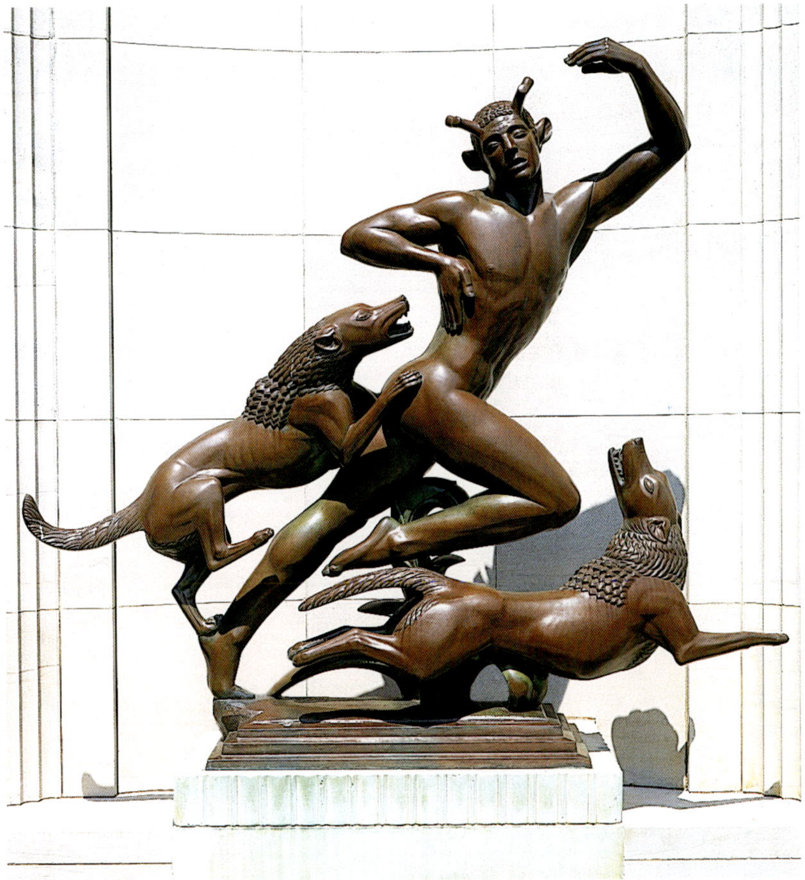

Diana and *Actaeon*, 1940
Nickel-bronze
11 x 82 x 23 3/4 in. *(Diana)*
85 x 95 x 23 3/4 in. *(Actaeon)*
Purchased through the Palm Beach Art League Construction Account

Paul Manship, 1885–1966

Maturing during the heat of early twentieth-century modernism, Paul Manship by-passed radical new approaches to the artistic enterprise and forged, instead, a unique style synthesizing moderate abstraction with traditional academicism. Originally from St. Paul, Minnesota, Manship studied painting at the St. Paul Institute of Art from 1892–1903, until a diagnosis of color blindness caused him to shift his focus to sculpture. In 1905, Manship briefly attended classes at the Art Students League in New York City, where he studied anatomy with the celebrated teacher of this subject, George Bridgman, and assisted the sculptor Solon Borglum. Manship also attended the Pennsylvania Academy of the Fine Arts for two years, where he chiefly worked with Charles Grafly. In 1909, the artist won a scholarship to attend the American Academy in Rome, a circumstance that generated a lifelong interest in ancient art. When Manship returned to the United States in 1912, his first show met with phenomenal success; all ninety-six bronzes sold. Due in part to the universal appeal of his work, the artist launched a career as a sculptor of public works.

Manship's mature style is marked by a formal vocabulary that draws heavily upon the art of ancient civilizations. While he was most inspired by archaic Greek forms, the influence of Egyptian, Minoan, and Assyrian art is evident, as well. His idiosyncratic use of ancient forms influenced a generation of followers at the American Academy in Rome, and it helped to formulate the conventions of Art Deco. This aesthetic, which predominantly affected the decorative arts, is characterized by a streamlined, geometricized classicism.

Manship's immense popularity was due primarily to a willingness to create works that existed comfortably within the settings of contemporary urban life—sites that included garden landscapes, city plazas, and especially twentieth century architecture. Unlike some modern sculpture, works such as New York City's Rockefeller Center's *Prometheus*, 1934, enhance rather than clash with the spaces they inhabit. Manship's affable personality facilitated his success, as well. He was the favored sculptor of many architects, city planners, and public works administrators.

To have achieved the status of Paul Manship's in one's own lifetime is a rare feat. It comes as a surprise, then, that the sculptor fell into obscurity during the decades following his death. In recent years, however, with the revival of interest in Art Deco, Manship's reputation has risen again.

Diana and *Actaeon*, 1940
Nickel-bronze
117 x 82 x 23 3/4 in. *(Diana)*, 85 x 95 x 23 3/4 in. *(Actaeon)*
(on each base: "Paul Manship")
Purchased through the Palm Beach Art League Construction Account 41.14.1 and 41.14.2

The Norton casts of *Diana* and *Actaeon* are the largest versions of several sculptures by Manship which portray this mythological story, and they constitute one of only a few complete pairs. The other works exist as single Dianas and Actaeons and were executed at various points, starting as early as 1911. In Greek mythology, the hunter Actaeon angers Diana, goddess of the hunt, by inadvertently glimpsing her at her bath. As retribution, she shoots him with an arrow that turns him into a stag. Failing to recognize his true identity, Actaeon's own hunting dogs chase and eventually devour him.

Manship realized the myth in two sculptural clusters. The Diana group portrays the goddess at the moment that she releases her arrow and a single hunting dog. The Actaeon group depicts the fleeing god, who is just beginning to sprout antlers, and two hunting dogs that tear viciously at his legs. The elements of both clusters are held together by plant-forms that serve the purpose of the single, supporting tree stump found in much Greek sculpture.

While the logical arrangement of the groups would place *Diana* on the left and *Actaeon* on the right, gallery founder Ralph Norton preferred to display the pieces in the opposite positions for aesthetic reasons. The groups occupy niches on the east facade of the gallery, and they are accompanied by a bas-relief which Manship executed, as well. A female personification of the abstract concept "interpretation" occupies the space above the niche in which the Diana group sits, and a personification of the concept "imagination," occupies the space above the Actaeon group. A third relief, "inspiration," is situated in the center of the façade over the gallery's entrance. Stylistically similar to *Diana* and *Actaeon*, the reliefs are independently powerful expressions. CMC

PROVENANCE

Norton Gallery, 1941.

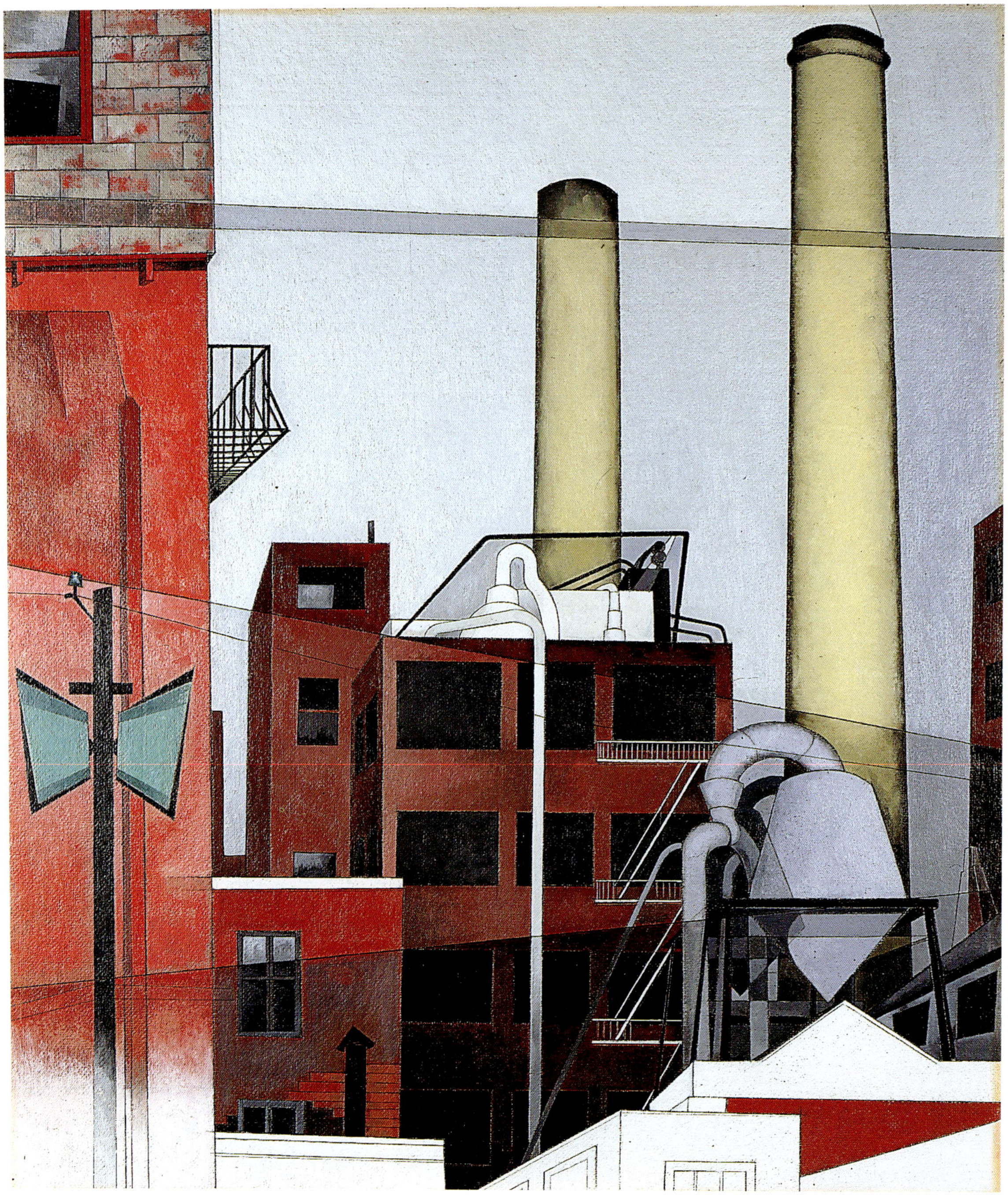

After All..., 1933
Oil on composition board
36 x 30 in.
Bequest of R. H. Norton

Charles Demuth

1883–1935

Charles Demuth has been called intriguing, enigmatic, complex, and paradoxical. At the same time that he was developing his own, highly acclaimed version of the Precisionist style of depicting contemporary, industrial America, he created a great number of exquisite, traditional still lifes. Although he was highly regarded in avant-garde artistic circles in New York and Paris, the artist spent much of his mature life living at home with his mother in his native town of Lancaster, Pennsylvania, which he fondly referred to as "the province."[1] Despite chronic poor health and an early death at age 52, he produced more than 900 paintings, and today he is considered one of America's leading modernists.

Born to a prosperous family in 1883, at the age of four, Demuth suffered a hip injury which left him permanently lame. His parents encouraged him to study art, and by 1896, he was drawing and painting with watercolors. He began his formal training in art at Philadelphia's Drexel Institute in 1904, and while a student there he met William Carlos Williams and began a lifelong friendship. In 1905, he entered the Pennsylvania Academy of the Fine Arts, where he studied with William Merritt Chase and Thomas Anshutz.

Demuth went to Paris, in 1904, for his twenty-first birthday, and the artistic climate so excited him there that he returned in 1907, and again for a prolonged stay from 1912–1914. Through the American artist Marsden Hartley, whom he first befriended in Paris, Demuth became a regular guest at the Saturday evening salon of Gertrude and Leo Stein, where he met Pablo Picasso, Henri Matisse and Marcel Duchamp, among others. While in Paris,

Demuth studied at the Académie Julian and the Académie Moderne, and although his painting remained conservative, he absorbed as much as he could from the Parisian avant-garde. Only when he returned to America, in the spring of 1914, did Demuth begin to adapt Cubist form to his own innovative style of modernist painting. He continued to visit Paris and maintained his ties to the Parisian artistic community, but as he wrote to Alfred Stieglitz, "I feel 'in' America—even though its insides are empty. Maybe, I can fill them." [2]

Demuth soon helped to fill the void which he perceived in American painting by playing a leading role in the development of Precisionism, a style of painting which was practiced by Demuth and a group of his contemporaries, including Georgia O'Keeffe, Charles Sheeler, and Preston Dickinson, during the 1920s and 1930s. These artists painted scenes of the American industrial landscape, employing both Analytic Cubism's restructuring of visible reality on the picture surface, and the Futurist use of Cubist form to capture the dynamism and energy of the modern machine. Unlike Futurism, however, Precisionism was not an ideological movement with a manifesto, but rather, a formal means used by a group of American artists to convey their generally positive, individual pictorial responses to modern urban America.

Demuth became severely ill and was forced to return from Paris in the spring of 1921. He was diagnosed as diabetic, and after a period of hospitalization returned to his family home in Lancaster. In spite of his poor health, Demuth continued to paint exquisite watercolor still lifes, as well as architectural views of Lancaster, in both tempera and oils. His illness increasingly drained his energy, although he was still able to produce an average of one painting per week. In 1923, Demuth began using the newly developed drug, insulin, to treat his diabetes, which slightly improved his health. He died at his mother's home in Lancaster, at the age of 52.

After All..., 1933
Oil on composition board
36 x 30 in.
(u.r.: "C. Demuth 1933")
Bequest of R. H. Norton 53.43

After All... is the last large oil painting completed by Demuth, and the last of a series of approximately 20 paintings of Lancaster architecture which he created between 1919 and 1933. This is one of several views the artist painted of the Armstrong Cork Company. Pale yellow smokestacks rising up from behind the brick building, in the center of the canvas, and the pentagonal mechanical apparatus, in the lower right, are balanced by the corner of a large, pinkish building which extends beyond the far left edge of the picture. Thin, diagonal lines, similar to Futurist "force lines" which convey movement and energy, cut across the image from left to right, dividing it into planes of varying tonal intensity and light. The dull gray of the background sky is echoed in the faceted shadows beneath the cyclone separator and in the trapezoidal lights, or loudspeakers, which project like the wings of a strange metallic butterfly from the top of a light pole in the lower left. The bold reds with which Demuth has painted certain architectural details contrast strikingly with the subdued tones of the rest of the industrial landscape.

After All... typifies the style known as Precisionism, in which clean, crisp outlines and smoothly painted surfaces were employed to delineate factories, skyscrapers, and other aspects of the modern American industrial landscape. The presence of implied social commentary in Demuth's Precisionist industrial paintings, such as *After All...* has been debated by scholars for over half a century. Some have suggested that the irony in many Demuth titles reveals his caustic attitude towards the industrialization of Lancaster and the modern world.[3] Others have countered that Demuth was a truly modern artist, whose paintings embraced the changes of modern industry as affirmations of faith in the machine.[4] The title of *After All...,* which was taken from the original title of an 1871 ode to American industry by Walt Whitman, "After All, Not to Create Only...," reinforces the argument that Demuth found many positive qualities to be celebrated in modern industrial subjects.[5] Although *After All...* does not glorify the modern factory overtly, the stylish, modern look of Cubism imposed on the dull machinery of the Armstrong Cork Company, especially the interplay of pipes and shadows in the lower right of the picture and the precision with which Demuth has rendered his forms, suggests that Demuth was not condemning American industrial progress. A passage written by Demuth titled, "Across a Greco is Written," which the artist published in *Creative Arts* in September 1929, provides insight into his artistic intentions.

"Paintings must be looked at and looked at and looked at.... They must be understood, and that's not the word either, through the eyes. No writing, no talking...will explain them. 'Look at that,' is all that can be said before a great painting, at least by those who really see it."[6]

An early commentator recognized in this statement an affirmation of the modernist credo, "Art for art's sake," as proof that Demuth did not regard art as a social function.[7] The contrast between the matter of fact presentation of the industrial subject in *After All...* and the delicate treatment of his exquisite, watercolor still lifes, simply confirms that Demuth was an extremely sensitive, delicate aesthete, capable of a myriad of different artistic responses to the people and things in his modern world. DM

NOTES

[1] Betsy Fahlman, *Pennsylvania Modern: Charles Demuth of Lancaster* (Philadelphia, PA: Philadelphia Museum of Art and the University of Pennsylvania Press, 1983), 13.

[2] Emily Farnham, *Charles Demuth: Behind a Laughing Mask* (Norman, OK: University of Oklahoma Press, 1971), 59.

[3] Alvord L. Eiseman, *Charles Demuth* (New York City, NY: Watson-Guptill Publications, 1982), 17.

[4] David Gebhard in *Charles Demuth: The Mechanical Encrusted on the Living* (Santa Barbara, CA: The Art Gallery of the University of California, Santa Barbara, CA, 1971), 10.

[5] Betsy Fahlman, "Charles Demuth's Paintings of Lancaster Architecture: New Discoveries and Observations," *Arts Magazine* 61 (March 1987): 27.

[6] William Murrell, *Charles Demuth* (New York City, NY: Whitney Museum of American Art, 1931), 7–8.

[7] Ibid.

PROVENANCE

Georgia O'Keeffe, ca. 1937–50; Downtown Gallery, New York City, NY, ca. 1950–52; Norton Gallery, 1953.

EXHIBITION HISTORY

Whitney Museum of American Art, New York City, NY, *Second Biennial Exhibition of Contemporary American Painting*, November 27, 1934–January 10, 1935, no. 1.

Whitney Museum of American Art, New York City, NY, *Demuth Memorial Exhibition*, December 15, 1937–January 16, 1938, no. 33.

Museum of Modern Art, New York City, NY, *Charles Demuth*, March 7–June 11, 1950, no. 156.

Fort Worth Art Center, Fort Worth, TX, *Inaugural Exhibition*, October 1–31, 1954, no. 24.

Moscow, U.S.S.R. (sponsored by the Whitney Museum of American Art), *American National Exhibition in Moscow*, July 25–September 5, 1959.

The Walker Art Center, Minneapolis, MN, *The Precisionist View in American Art*, November 13– December 25, 1960, p. 41.

Pennsylvania Historical & Museum Commission, *Charles Demuth of Lancaster*, September 24–November 6, 1966.

Indiana University Art Museum, Bloomington, IN, *The American Scene 1900–1970*, April 6–May 17, 1970, no. 70.

Museum of Fine Arts, St. Petersburg, FL, *The City and the Machine: Their Influence on Art between the Two World Wars*, October 6, 1973–November 4, 1973, no. 20.

Museum of Fine Arts, St. Petersburg, FL, *Masters from the Norton Gallery*, April 16–May 21, 1978.

Philadelphia Museum of Art, Philadelphia, PA, *Pennsylvania Modern: Charles Demuth of Lancaster*, July 16–September 11, 1983, no. 35.

Brooklyn Museum, Brooklyn, NY, *The Machine Age in America*, 1918–1941, October 17, 1986–February 16, 1987.

Whitney Museum of American Art, New York City, NY, *Charles Demuth*, October 14, 1987–January 17, 1988.

Arthur B. Davies

1862–1928

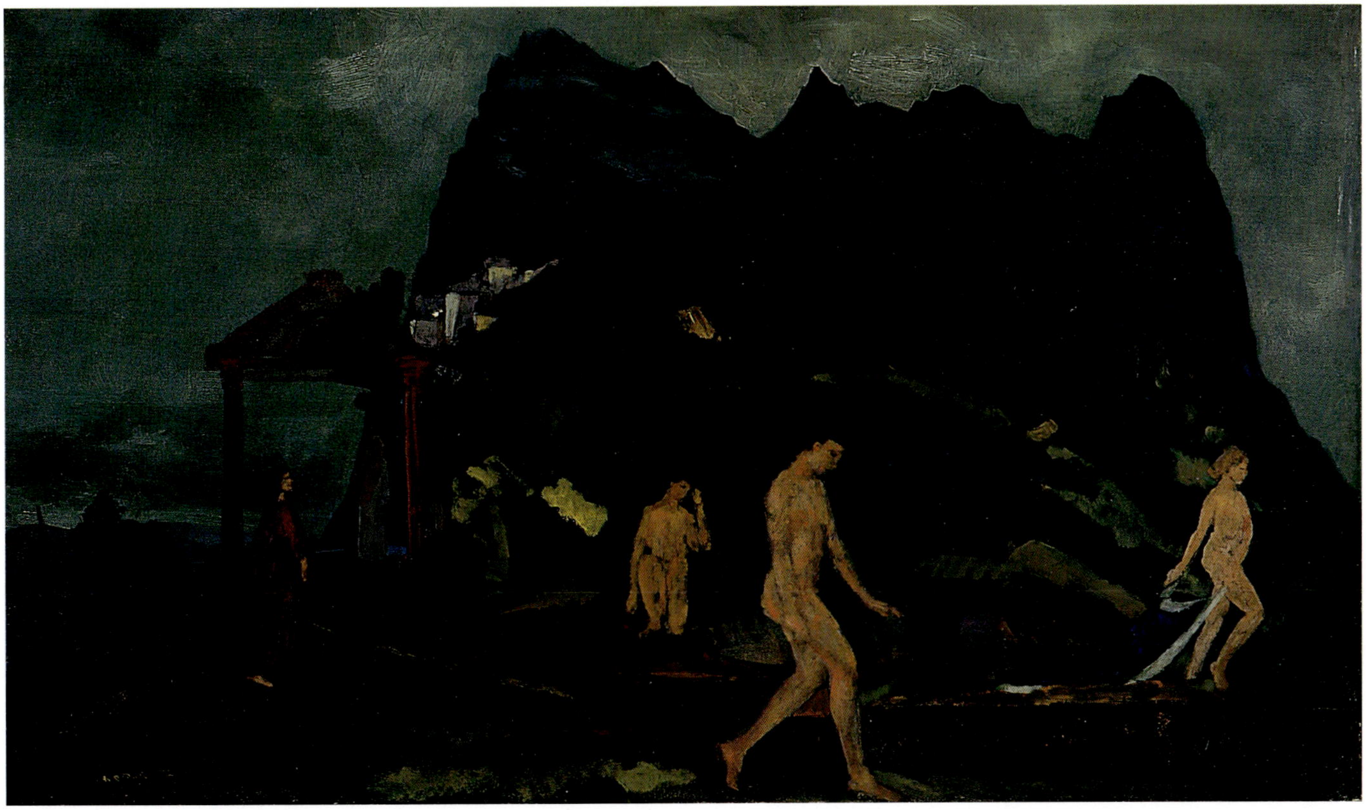

Umbrian Landscape, prior to 1913
Oil on paper on canvas
18 x 30 in.
Purchased through the R. H. Norton Fund

Arthur B. Davies, 1862–1928

Arthur B. Davies, born in Utica, New York, studied art with Dwight Williams and took courses at the Chicago Academy of Design in 1878. From 1880–1882, Davies worked in Mexico as an engineering draftsman, but he soon returned to Chicago to further his studies at the Academy. In 1886, Davies moved to New York City and enrolled at Gotham Art Students and the Art Students League. He went to Europe to study independently in 1893, where he absorbed a variety of romantic and decorative styles from the art of the Venetian painter Giorgione to Puvis de Chavannes and the Pre-Raphaelites.

Davies' characteristic style evolved after he returned from Europe. The type of painting for which he is best known portrays idealized female nudes in idyllic landscapes. The works exude an air of mystery and, occasionally, they include fantastic elements such as unicorns. Often, the paintings are allegorical or allude to myths, legends, or poems. Over the years, Davies' works became more horizontal and began to resemble friezes, testifying to his interest in Greek art, and he began to place his figures in elegant dance-like poses.

Though Davies' art was basically conservative, he, nevertheless, supported modernist trends. He exhibited with the anti-academic group The Eight in 1908, even though his work had little in common with their down-to-earth realism. In 1913, he organized the ground-breaking Armory Show, an exhibition which highlighted nontraditional American artists and introduced European avant-garde art to the United States. Influenced by the radical art included in the event, Davies began to work in a Cubist mode.

The artist experimented with a variety of media after 1918, when he revived an interest in lithography. Throughout this period, however, his subject matter remained the same. During the 1920s, Davies created aquatints and etchings, worked in chalk on paper, and designed tapestries and rugs.

Umbrian Landscape, prior to 1913
Oil on paper on canvas
18 x 30 in.
(l.l.: "A.B. Davies")
Purchased through the R. H. Norton Fund 92.26

Though Davies failed to date the majority of his paintings, we can be reasonably certain that he painted *Umbrian Landscape* prior to 1913. The work does not incorporate the Cubist forms that pervaded his work after the Armory Show. Furthermore, one may surmise that *Umbrian Landscape* is one of Davies' earliest pieces, because it lacks the compositional simplicity of his mature works.

Like numerous other works, the painting portrays idealized figures in an ethereal landscaped setting. Two clothed figures proceed down a path towards mountains in the distance, and three nude females engage in various activities. One wonders if a ritual has just been performed or will be performed in the near future. This inconclusiveness creates a narrative tension, which adds to a sense of mystery; the exact meaning of the painting, as is often the case with Davies' work, is not known. A similar mood is evident in works by Davies' contemporaries Kenyon Cox, Albert Pinkham Ryder, and Ralph Albert Blakelock, who like Davies, worked in primarily dark colors. Scholars of American art often categorize these artists' unusual paintings as "visionary," in order to distinguish them from more mainstream works done in "tonal" and Impressionist styles.

In addition to the fact that the painting refers to an ancient district—Umbria was located in north-central Italy—*Umbrian Landscape* reveals Davies' interest in ancient times through his use of classical architecture. Two columns supporting an entablature are represented on the painting's left side, beneath which the two clothed figures pass. These figures are shrouded in Greek-style robes. The frieze-like stances of the female nudes may be an additional allusion to antiquity. CMC

PROVENANCE

Kay Hillman, New York City, NY; Joseph H. Hirshhorn, New York City, NY; Norton Gallery, 1992.

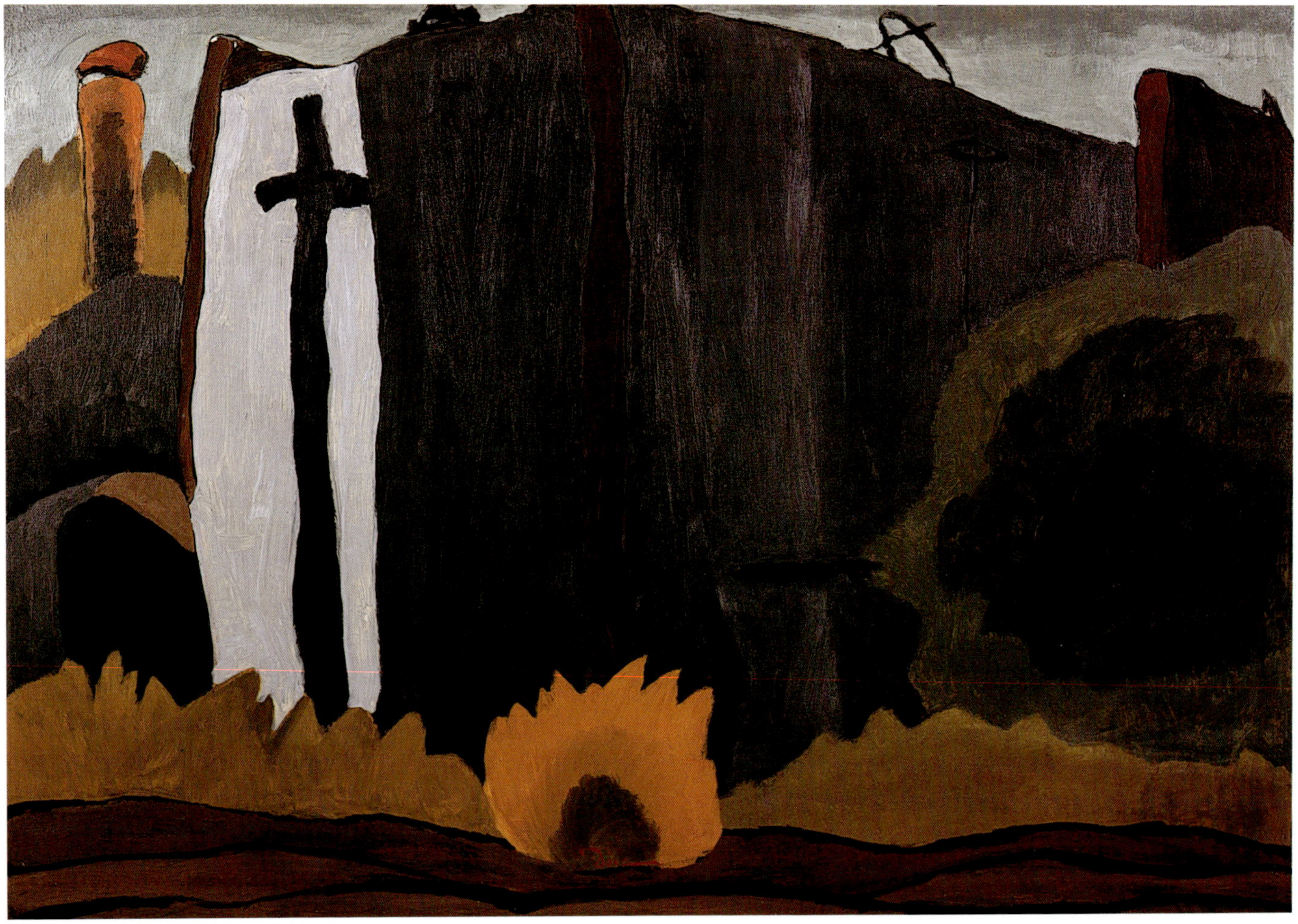

Power Plant II, 1938
Oil on canvas
25 x 35 in.
Purchased through the R. H. Norton Fund

Arthur Garfield Dove

1880–1946

At the beginning of the twentieth century, Arthur Dove was among the relatively small number of American painters experimenting with abstraction. Working in a variety of media and varying the degree of abstraction, Dove consistently maintained an interest in the essential expressiveness of art's formal elements of line, color, shape, texture, and pattern. For him, abstraction offered the means to this end.

Dove grew up in the Finger Lakes region of western New York State. Graduating from Cornell University in 1903, he moved to New York City with the intention of becoming a professional artist. His early success, however, came in the commercial realm of magazine illustration for *Collier's, The Illustrated Sporting News*, and other noted publications. In this period, he also drew with pastels and completed oil paintings. Two paintings from this time survive, *Portrait of Alfred Stieglitz*, ca. 1906 (Williams College Museum of Art) and *Stuyvesant Square*, 1907 (Hobart and William Smith Colleges), and they demonstrate Dove's interest in traditional genres and Impressionism.[1]

In 1908, Dove, apparently determined to further develop his talent, travelled to Paris to study art.[2] During his stay in France, he experimented with Fauvism, the bold and colorful style favored by André Derain and Henri Matisse. In France, Dove's work was included in the prestigious Salon d'Automne in 1908 and 1909. Yet, when exhibited at Alfred Stieglitz's 291 Gallery in New York City in 1910, it provoked hostility and confusion. American art critics were generally conservative viewers and were offended by modernist styles, from Fauvism and Cubism to abstraction and primitivism.

Upon his return to the United States, Dove began to work in a more abstract style. A series of small oil paintings executed shortly thereafter is the artist's distillation of landscapes and natural forms. The paintings merely suggest, rather than delineate, outdoor scenes. Dove's early works are abbreviations of form. The artistic elements, such as angular line, biomorphic shapes,and a palette limited to earthy and nonprimary colors, are very simply articulated. The paintings and drawings are Dove's subjective responses and emotive interpretations of what he had seen and experienced. This was no less true in the 1920s, when he produced mixed-media assemblages as well as paintings. At that time, Dove inventively used ordinary objects, such as denim, needlepoint, and hymnal pages, to make humorous portraits of his friends and to fashion visual idioms. The assemblages exemplified Dove's interest in the expressive possibilities of his materials, and they challenged notions of what could be considered art.[3]

Dove's work displays a range of abstraction, an indication of the artist's commitment to experiment in this mode. In the 1930s, his painting style was sometimes referential, as evidenced in the Norton's *Power Plant II*. He transforms a recognizable subject in this painting, distorting its form in order to present his interpretation of its energies and those of the natural surroundings. In *Willow Tree*, another 1938 painting in the Norton's collection, his approach is less representational. He abstracts the subject into an organic and biomorphic swirl, and, thus, locates a self-generative force within it. He continued to work in this manner in the 1940s, while integrating flat, geometric form into his abstraction.

Throughout his long career, Dove remained independent of movements and distant from artistic centers, working in Connecticut, the Finger Lakes region, and Long Island, New York. His art, nonetheless, was seen and admired by American audiences. It was frequently exhibited at Stieglitz's influential New York galleries, 291 and An American Place. In addition, the Washington art collector Duncan Phillips was a patron of the artist. Dove's work likely broadened the national taste and influenced the American public's appreciation of modernism. By the time of his death in 1946, the critical and historical perception of Dove had shifted from the practitioner of foreign styles, to the pioneering and original American artist.

Power Plant II, 1938
Oil on canvas
25 x 35 in.
(l.c.: "dove")
Purchased through the R. H. Norton Fund 57.23

Dove frequently took the American landscape as his subject, and in *Power Plant II*, he combines natural and industrial presences. The utility plant is girded by the colorfully rendered forms of nature. Grasses, earth, and trees appear brighter in hue than in reality, and their contours are dynamically jagged and rolling; a small shrub positioned in the foreground is virtually aflame with energy. The electrical power plant also swells with energy, exceeding our expectations of a real, architectural form. Straightforwardly expressed in title and visual imagery, the message of *Power Plant II* is pantheistic. The painting demands consideration of vital, coexistent presences.

The formal elements of *Power Plant II* advance the idea of a unified and continuous energy in the world. Color and shape are closely associated on a one-to-one basis—a characteristic typical of Dove's paintings from 1933–1938.[4] In *Power Plant II*, each shape, whether organic or geometric, is rendered in a unique hue. Spiky grasses are golden, and a tree radiates shades of green. In contrast, the utility plant is a dark, bluish gray which relates it to similarly colored rocks. The distinctions of shape give each form a separate identity, and yet, it is obvious that natural rock is the source material for the constructed building. The rock provides durability and solidity to an architectural form, and its natural energies animate the building in an anthropomorphic manner.

Dove's formalist strategies convey his holistic belief in the connectedness of all worldly things. The artist subscribed to the Futurist notion of dynamic forms, Henri Bergson's theory of an omnipresent flux in nature, and the theosophical belief in nature's unseen energies.[5] In *Power Plant II*, the stark pole notably engenders interpretations related to Dove's spiritual beliefs. As a telegraph pole, it may be a theosophical symbol for clairvoyance, an ability Dove believed he possessed.[6] Perhaps, another visual reading is that the pole represents a Christian cross juxtaposed against a symbol of the new religion of modernization and industrialization.

Power Plant II is an example of a referential turn in Dove's painting during the 1930s. Critics of that era noted the integration of recognizable subjects in his work. Some preferred the nonreferential abstraction which characterized his paintings and drawings of 1910–1920; others theorized that a more explicitly representational style made Dove's art more accessible to larger audiences. *Power Plant II* is more abstract than *Power Plant I* (private collection), a painting of the same year and the same theme. While *Power Plant I* is likely closer to the scene Dove actually saw, *Power Plant II* adds an emotional response to it. JF

NOTES

1 Barbara Haskell, *Arthur Dove* (Boston, MA: New York Graphic Society, 1974); Ann Lee Morgan, *Arthur Dove: Life and Work, with a Catalogue Raisonné* (London, England: Associated University Presses, 1984). William C. Agee mentions the Stieglitz portrait in a book review of Morgan's monograph, *Archives of American Art Journal* 24 (1984): 19. There is, however, uncertainty about the date of this painting, and its subject, which is not likely Stieglitz, and could be William Glackens, another New York painter.

2 Biographers have not been able to discover what specifically prompted Dove to give up illustration at this stage of his life. Wight and Haskell note that Dove had saved $4,000 for his trip and was additionally financed by his father. Haskell, *Arthur Dove*, 10; Frederick Wight, *Arthur Dove* (Berkeley, CA: University of California Press, 1958), 26.

3 Morgan, *Arthur Dove*, 49–52.

4 Ibid., 57.

5 Sherry Cohn, Arthur Dove: *Nature as Symbol* (Ann Arbor, MI: UMI Research Press, 1985), 63.

6 Ibid., 56–57. According to Cohn, theosophists and psychic researchers used the telegraph pole as an analogy for mental telepathy. In addition, Dove's son reported that his father believed that he, himself, had psychic powers.

PROVENANCE

Helen Torr Dove, the artist's wife, and William C. Dove, the artist's son, Huntington, NY, until 1957; The Palm Beach Art League, West Palm Beach, FL, 1957; Norton Gallery, 1957.

EXHIBITION HISTORY

An American Place, New York City, NY, *Arthur G. Dove: Exhibition of Recent Paintings, 1938*, March 29–May 10, 1938, no. 11.

Downtown Gallery, New York City, NY, *Special Exhibition of Paintings by Dove*, February 26–March 24, 1956, no. 17.

The Art Gallery, McCormick Place, Chicago, IL, *Inaugural Exhibition*, November 18–December 23, 1960, no. 7.

Museum of Fine Arts, St. Petersburg, FL, *Masters from the Norton Gallery*, April 16–May 21, 1978.

Pensacola Museum of Art, Pensacola, FL, *American and European Masterpieces of the Nineteenth and Twentieth Centuries*, September 22–November 16, 1984.

Andrew Wyeth

1917–

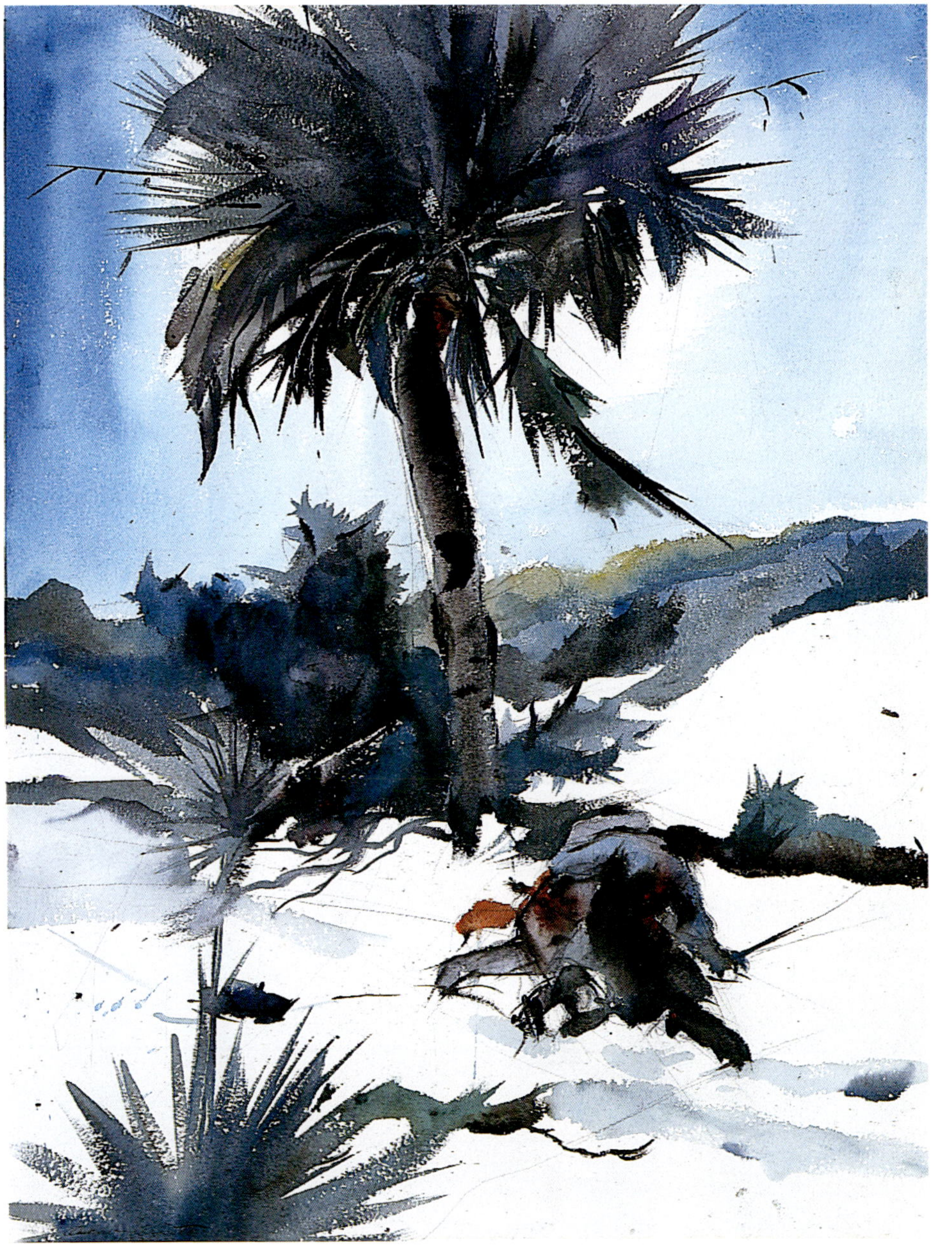

Pirate Country, 1937
Watercolor on paper
30 x 22 1/2 in.
Gift of Elizabeth C. Norton

Andrew Wyeth, 1917–

For much of this century, Andrew Wyeth has been the most popular painter in the United States. Wyeth is an accomplished draftsman, a skill he acquired under the tutelage of his father, the illustrator N.C. Wyeth (1882–1945). The elder Wyeth trained his son to carefully study his subjects, and then, to draw from memory and instill his images with an essential feeling of the subject matter. As a result, by the time he was a teenager, Andrew Wyeth was a sought-after illustrator whose work made the covers of *The Saturday Evening Post* and other publications. Wyeth, however, turned down a lucrative, full-time career in illustration in order to pursue fine art. His early watercolors, the Norton's *Pirate Country*, 1937, among them, evidence the freshness and rapidity of his draftsmanship and the narrative quality one finds in illustration. In a 1941 watercolor exhibition, Wyeth landscapes and portraits generated high praise and stylistic comparisons with the work of Winslow Homer and John Singer Sargent.

Wyeth learned a new approach during the mid-1940s and early 1950s, a shift that coincided with N. C. Wyeth's death in 1945 and Andrew Wyeth's ill health during 1950–1951. At that time, he assumed the drybrush technique in which the artist wipes most of the watercolor media from the brush with the fingers or a rag, reducing and controlling the amount of paint applied with each stroke. He frequently combined drybrush and traditional watercolor techniques, layering the distinct brushwork of the former over fluid washes of watercolor to build up forms. Since the 1940s, he has also painted in tempera, a media he favors because it allows him to gradually establish solid shapes and forms. Wyeth generally has worked with a muted palette, yet by varying his tonal values to emphasize the differentiation of forms, he convinces us of their verisimilitude. His style has remained virtually unchanged since the 1950s, although the artist has enlivened his compositions, during the last decade with dashes of bright, primary color.[1]

Wyeth scholars and his audiences often focus on the evoked drama and symbolism in his work, yet its modernist manifestations are just as important. Wyeth directs attention to formal details by abruptly cropping his scenes in the manner of American photographers Walker Evans and Edward Weston.[2] He also subtly distorts figures and objects to suggest compositional or textural unity among dissimilar things. Moreover, he tends to compress space in his paintings to make the landscape perfectly picturesque. Photographs of the landscapes which have inspired him reveal that Wyeth, like all artists, subjectively interprets what is before his eyes. However, unlike the most radical modernists, Wyeth does this without irony. His distortions do not disturb our expectations for the materiality of the rendered object and its presence in illusory three-dimensional space.

The subjects of Wyeth's paintings are his neighbors, and the geographical settings are around his birthplace of Chadds Ford, Pennsylvania, and his Maine summer home. His sitters include his Pennsylvania neighbors Karl Kuerner and Helga Testorf, and his Maine friends, the late Alvaro and Christina Olson. Painted in military uniforms and simple work clothes, the depicted subjects are visualizations of a positive, national heritage to many Americans.

Pirate Country, 1937
Watercolor on paper
30 x 22 1/2 in.
(l.l.: "Andrew Wyeth 1937")
Gift of Elizabeth C. Norton 47.41

In *Pirate Country*, Andrew Wyeth displays a master's facility with a difficult medium, and the narrative creativity of a seasoned illustrator. Inspired by Winslow Homer's Florida-theme watercolors of the late nineteenth century, the 1937 work is a product of Wyeth's youthful imagination: he visited Florida for the first time in 1939, two years after he drew this scene based on the state's historical past. Wyeth made the drawing after a visit to South Carolina, and its beaches may have served as the model for this picture's setting.[3] Like N. C. Wyeth's *Friar Tuck*, also in the Norton's collection, *Pirate Country* is a narrative-driven adventure. Andrew Wyeth's childhood drawings often were devoted to heroic tales of medieval chivalry and pirates, and as a young artist, he continued to exploit the story-telling potential of art.

Pirate Country is a balanced composition which retains a graphic immediacy. Wyeth manipulates tonal gradations and the expressive fluidity of the watercolor wash to give the drawing a convincing naturalism. He animates his images with economic brush strokes to reference representational form, such as the rounded contours of sand dunes. Furthermore, Wyeth's approach to line and color establishes a structural relatedness between the natural surroundings and the human actors in the picture. A dark palette of greens, blues, and browns gives similar volume to the palm's trunk and the tangled pirates, while the needle-like vibrancy of a pirate's sword resembles the spikiness of shoreline flora. Wyeth adds a crimson patch just to the left of the pirates, and also uses it to tinge the outline of pirate's crouched body. Against the supporting ground of white sand, this intensely red hue stands out and is an important testament to the bloodiness of the duel.

In contrast to *Pirate Country*, his mature work in tempera is less narrative, and instead, more somber and descriptive. Wyeth, in the mid-1940s, renounced what he termed "the visual cocktail," referring to the light-hearted subject matter and relative bright hues of his watercolors. His goal since then has been to imbue his pictures with the atmosphere of the particular location or the unique character of his sitter. Still, Wyeth does continue to paint in watercolor, explaining to an interviewer in 1973, "My wild side that's really me comes out in my watercolors."[4] JF

NOTES

1 Thomas Hoving, "Wyeth Since Helga," *Connoisseur* 220 (December 1990): 109.

2 Wanda M. Corn, *The Art of Andrew Wyeth* (Greenwich, CT: New York Graphics Society, 1973), 104, 106, 109.

3 N.C. Wyeth records a 1939 trip with his wife and son Andrew to Marjorie Kinnan Rawling's home in Florida. In Betsey James Wyeth, ed., *The Wyeths by N.C. Wyeth, 1901–1945* (Boston, MA: Gambit, 1971), 781; and Mary Landa, Wyeth Collection Curator, personal correspondence with author, 30 July 1944. In the past, *Pirate Country* has been incorrectly dated 1939.

[4] Corn, 55.

PROVENANCE

Carson, Pirie & Scott, Chicago, IL, 1937–40; Elizabeth C. Norton, West Palm Beach, FL, 1940; Norton Gallery, 1947.

EXHIBITION HISTORY

Whitney Museum of American Art, New York City, NY, *Contemporary American Sculpture, Watercolors, Drawings and Prints*, March 8–April 10, 1938, no. 205.

The Art Institute of Chicago, Chicago, IL, *Eighteenth International Exhibition of Watercolors, Pastels, Drawings and Monotypes*, March 23–May 14, 1939, no. 557.

University of Arizona Art Gallery, Tucson, AZ, *Andrew Wyeth: Watercolors, Temperas and Drawings*, March 16–April 14, 1963, no. 1.

Oklahoma Museum of Art at Red Ridge, Oklahoma City, OK [now Oklahoma City Art Museum, Oklahoma City, OK], *The Wonder of Andrew Wyeth: Temperas, Watercolors, Drybrush, Drawings (1939–1966)*, December 2–23, 1967, no. 23.

Wichita Art Museum, Wichita, KS, *Wyeth's World: An Exhibition of Watercolors, Temperas and Drawings by Andrew Wyeth*, September 15–November 15, 1967, no. 33.

The Society of the Four Arts, Palm Beach, FL, *Views of Florida by American Masters*, March 8–April 13, 1975, no. 45.

Greenville County Museum of Art, Greenville, SC, *Andrew Wyeth: In Southern Collections*, February 1–March 31, 1978, no. 25.

Museum of Art, Fort Lauderdale, FL, *Andrew Wyeth from Public and Private Collections*, January 12–February 28, 1983.

Pensacola Museum of Art, Pensacola, FL, *American and European Masterpieces of the Nineteenth and Twentieth Centuries*, September 22–November 16, 1984.

Canton Art Institute, Canton, OH, *Andrew Wyeth From Public and Private Collections*, September 15–November 3, 1985.

Smithsonian Institution, Washington, D.C., *Master Watercolors and Drawings from the Norton Gallery of Art*, travelling exhibition, February 11, 1988–September 24, 1989, no. 54.

Jacksonville Art Museum, Jacksonville, FL, *Andrew Wyeth: Southeastern Collections*, January 19–April 19, 1992, no. 3.

Reginald Marsh

1898–1954

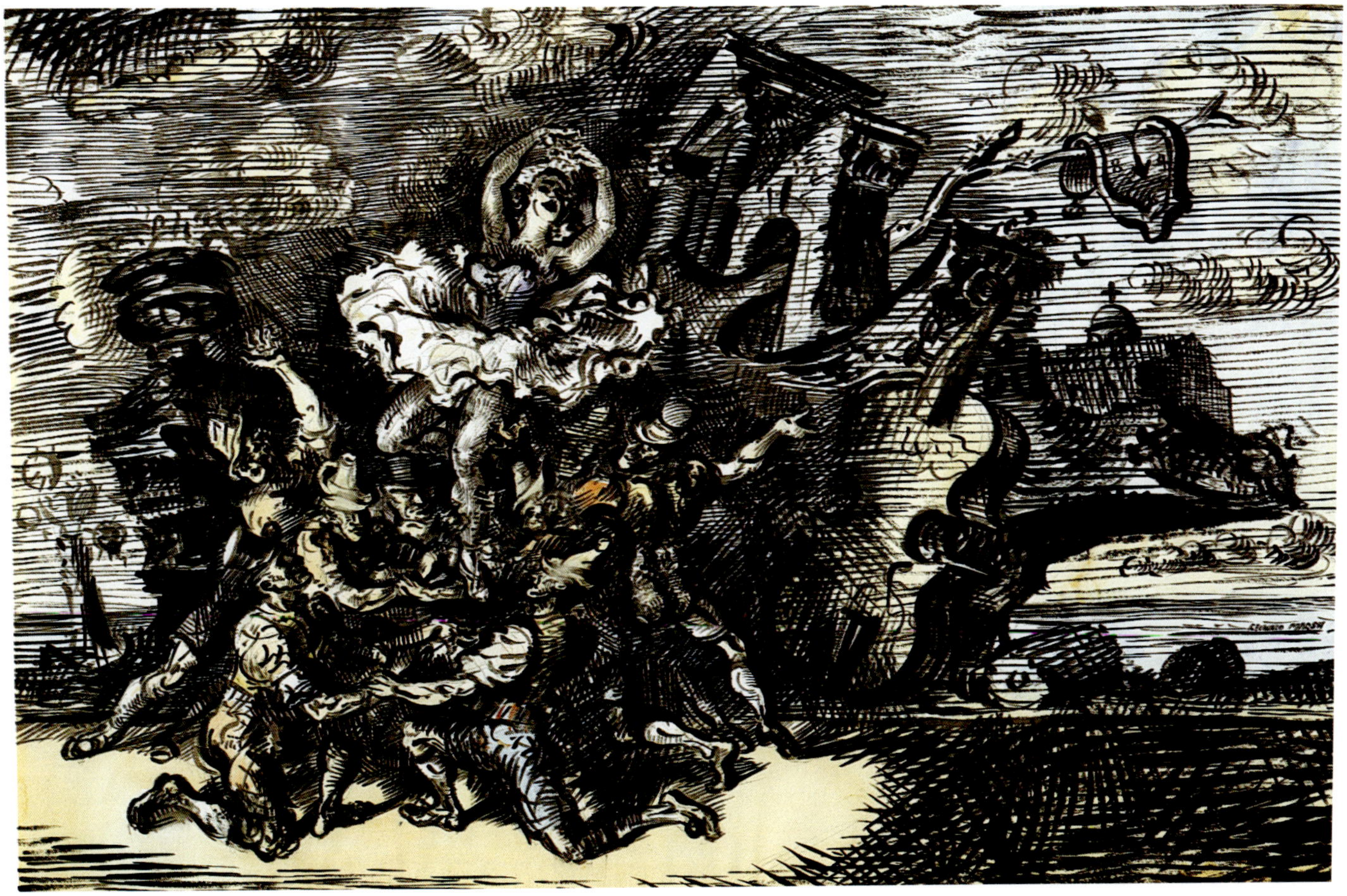

Italian Suite, 1940
Watercolor and black ink on paper
27 x 39 1/2 in.
Gift of Mr. and Mrs. Selig S. Burrows

Reginald Marsh, 1898–1954

The human quality of urban American culture during the Depression and post-Depression years has been preserved in the drawings and paintings of Reginald Marsh. With keen insight, the artist chronicles the activities, as well as the spiritual condition, of both the lower-and upper-class population of New York City.

Marsh was born in Paris in 1898, and his parents, who were both American artists, moved back to the United States in 1900 and settled in New Jersey, where Marsh spent his childhood. While attending Yale University from 1916–1920, he contributed illustrations to *The Yale Record* and became its art editor in 1920. After graduation, he settled in New York City as a free-lance newspaper and magazine illustrator. He became a staff artist for the New York *Daily News*, and then, from 1925–1931, for *The New Yorker*. Marsh also contributed to *Esquire*, *Fortune*, and *Life* throughout his career. The illustrative quality of his mature paintings is derived, in part, from his extensive magazine and newspaper experience during his early career.

In 1927, Marsh enrolled in classes at the Art Students League in New York. He studied briefly with the realist painter George Luks, and then, with Kenneth Hayes Miller. Miller encouraged Marsh to study the great art of past epochs, such as the Italian Renaissance and the Northern European Baroque, and to seek his subject matter in the spectacle of contemporary, urban life that surrounded him. Following his mentor's advice, Marsh sought out places such as Coney Island where he could observe "crowds of people in all directions, all positions, without clothing, moving—like the great compositions of Michelangelo and Rubens."[1] The theater also provided the artist with an opportunity to observe humanity on display. Marsh remarked that the theater was excellent training, because the artist had to sketch his subjects very quickly in order to capture them in action. Although most well known for his interpretations of vaudeville and burlesque shows, Marsh, also, frequented the Metropolitan Opera, which he reviewed and illustrated for various magazines during the 1920s.

Throughout his career as an artist and teacher, Marsh emphasized the importance of drawing, including the copying of old master works, as well as drawing from life. Marsh's work consistently revealed a preference for drawing over painting, the latter of which seemed to the artist "a laborious way to make a bad drawing. . . ."[2] After becoming frustrated with slow-drying oil paint, Marsh turned to the more fluid and spontaneous medium of watercolor, which he felt was more closely related to drawing. Between 1939 and 1940, Marsh created approximately 40 large watercolors, and during the 1940s, he began to use the inexpensive, flexible, and permanent medium of Chinese ink. During the last decade of his life, Marsh continued to pictorially explore the life and leisure activities of urban America, until his death in 1954.

Italian Suite, 1940
Watercolor and black ink on paper
27 x 39 1/2 in.
(l.r.: "Reginald Marsh")
Gift of Mr. and Mrs. Selig S. Burrows 91.4

Marsh painted several versions of *Italian Suite*, which suggests that the theme was especially important to the artist. The subject matter of the work is uncharacteristic for Marsh because it does not depict the everyday life of urban America. Rather, this drawing can be viewed as an allegorical response to the events of World War II. Although the United States did not enter the war in Europe until 1941, events in Europe during the preceding two years were troubling to many Americans, especially to an artist like Marsh, who looked to Europe as the origin of Western artistic tradition. In May 1939, Italy formed a political and military alliance with Nazi Germany, and by the end of June 1940, when France surrendered to Hitler's forces, most of Europe had been invaded by the Fascist alliance. Although Marsh did not depict explicitly war-related scenes, two of his water-colors, roughly contemporary with *Italian Suite*, con- tain references to the war in newspaper head-lines and movie marquees.

In the right foreground of the image, a tangle of muscular men in contemporary clothes form the base of a human pyramid that is topped by a robust, blonde ballerina wearing a ruffled tutu. Such an assembly of men supporting a beautiful starlet was a common element of the lavish dance numbers featured in Hollywood movies during the 1930s and 1940s. The title of the Norton's enigmatic drawing suggests ballet or classical music terminology. In addition, the domed church in the right background and the classical architec-tural ruins throughout the composition make a generalized reference to historical European cul-ture. Such an allusion by Marsh is probable, consid-ering that the artist travelled to Europe several times, during the 1920s and 1930s, to view the great art of the past, and placed much importance on the study of the Old Masters and their techniques.

The melted clock that appears draped over the limb of a dead tree in the right middle ground is nearly identical to the clock in Salvador Dali's well-known Surrealist painting *The Persistence of Memory*, 1931 (Museum of Modern Art, New York). Marsh would have certainly known of Dali's work by the time *Italian Suite* was conceived, because the Spanish painter's work became well known in the United States after he moved to Paris in 1929, and by 1940, Dali's art had been exhibited by leading galleries and museums in New York City. Marsh may have included the reference to Surrealism because the Western world, embroiled in World War II, had become a Surrealist nightmare.

In this drawing, Marsh portrays the ruins of traditional European culture embedded in the crumbling rock of civilization. As if unaware of the devastation behind her, the costumed balle-rina descends from the classical past into a tumul-tuous present that is dark and foreboding. The exaggerated movements of the strange mixture of men who form her human staircase contribute a feeling of anxious energy to the image. The balle-rina's movement creates a diagonal force down-ward to the left, which is countered by the upward right pull of the rocky outcropping to create a disquieting tension in the composition. Marsh's fluid, heavy brush strokes heighten the feeling of excited movement, and the dense webs of over-laid crosshatching intensify the ominous mood of this imaginary scene. Marsh has combined the expressive power of the brush with a sophisticated allegory to make a reference to the conditions of his world. DM

NOTES

[1] Reginald Marsh, "Let's Get Back to Painting," *Magazine of Art* 37 (December 1944): 296.

[2] Ibid., 292.

PROVENANCE

Norton Gallery, 1991.

EXHIBITION HISTORY

Newport Harbor Art Museum, Newport Beach, CA, *Reginald Marsh: Retrospective*, November 2– December 10, 1972.

Georgia O'Keeffe

1887–1986

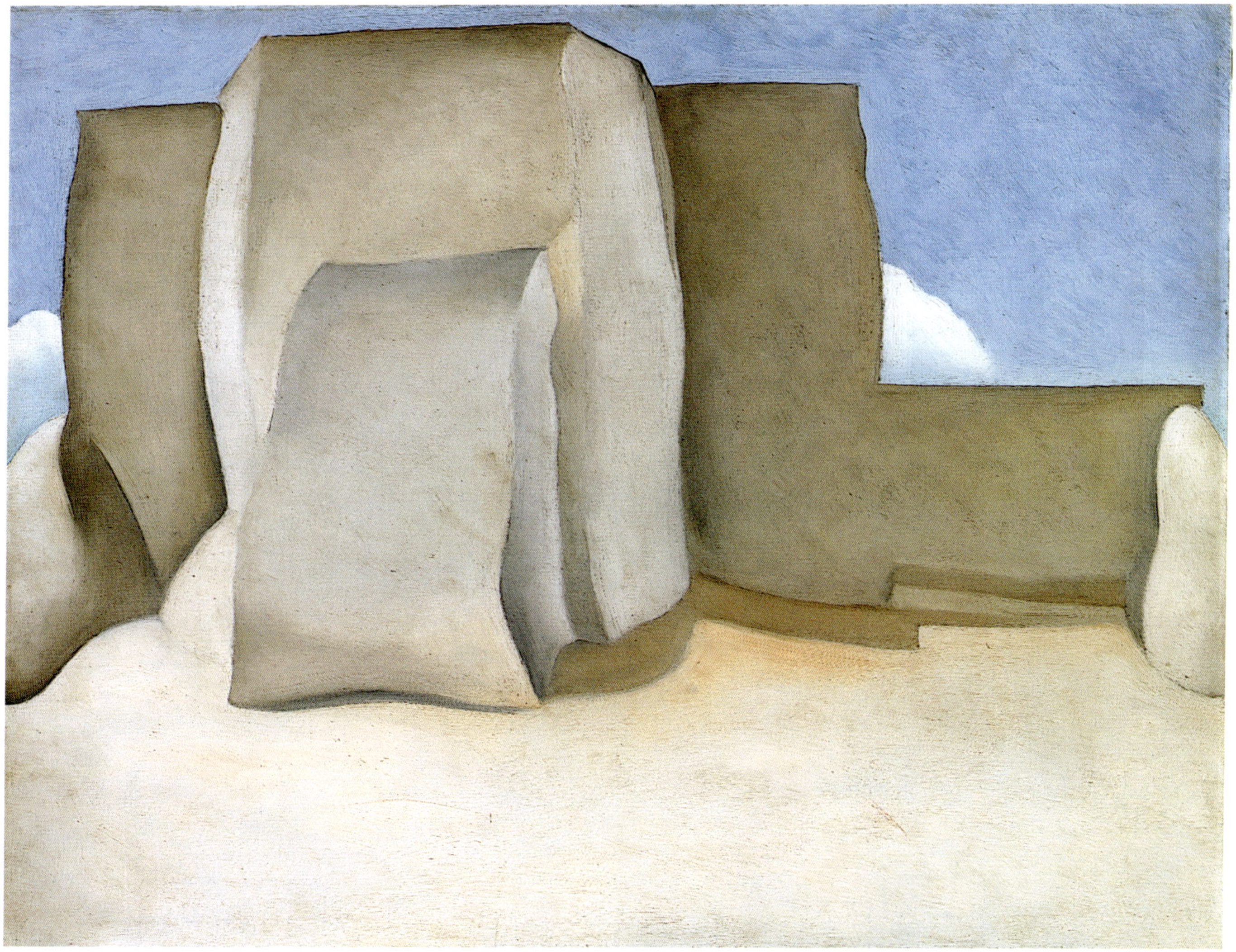

Ranchos Church No. 1, 1929
Oil on canvas
18 3/4 x 24 in.
Purchased through the R. H. Norton Fund

Georgia O'Keeffe, 1887–1986

Georgia O'Keeffe was one of the most independently creative artists of the twentieth century. As a primary member of the Stieglitz circle, she spent much of her career in the center of New York's modernist movement, yet retained, and continually renewed, her independent artistic vision.

O'Keeffe had extensive academic training, studying first at The Art Institute of Chicago and then at the Art Students League in New York where her instructors included William Merritt Chase and Kenyon Cox. The most important influence on her early work, however, was Arthur Wesley Dow with whom she studied at the Teacher's College of Columbia University in 1914 and 1916. Dow's emphasis on original design made a particularly strong and lasting impression on O'Keeffe. While studying in New York, O'Keeffe became interested in modernism and frequented Alfred Stieglitz's gallery where she saw avant-garde works by contemporary American and European artists.

In 1915, O'Keeffe accepted a teaching position in Columbia, South Carolina. There, removed from the distractions and influences of the New York art scene, she produced a highly personal series of abstract charcoals and watercolors which marked the beginning of her individual artistic development. Equally important, perhaps, was the role this series played in establishing O'Keeffe's relationship with Stieglitz. Presented with these drawings by a mutual friend, Stieglitz immediately hung them in his gallery and became an ardent and influential supporter of her work.

For the next few years, O'Keeffe held teaching positions, first in Virginia and then in Texas, and continued to experiment with form and color in abstract compositions. In 1918, at Stieglitz's invitation, she returned to New York and, with his financial support and encouragement, devoted herself to painting. They married in 1924. During this period, O'Keeffe began painting boldly enlarged and closely cropped images of single objects, particularly flowers, which paralleled stylistic developments in contemporary photography, most notably in the work of Stieglitz and his protégé Paul Strand.

Beginning in 1929, O'Keeffe spent part of each year in New Mexico and moved there, permanently, three years after Stieglitz's death in 1946. Towards the end of her life, living quietly in the desert, O'Keeffe became a symbol of the independent American artist. By the time of her death in 1986, O'Keeffe was internationally recognized as an early and influential leader of American modernism.

Ranchos Church No. 1, 1929
Oil on canvas
18 3/4 x 24 in.
(verso: "29")
Purchased through the R. H. Norton Fund 53.153

Painted during her first extended stay in New Mexico, *Ranchos Church No. 1* is O'Keeffe's celebratory response to the bright light and openness of the southwest desert. Thematically related to some of her earlier work, *Ranchos Church No. 1* is, nevertheless, executed with a new vitality and marks the beginning of her late, southwestern style.

O'Keeffe considered the mission church of Saint Francis of Assisi in Ranchos de Taos "one of the most beautiful buildings left in the United States by the Spaniards."[1] As with most of the approximately eight paintings O'Keeffe made of this subject between 1929 and 1930, *Ranchos Church No. 1* depicts the church from its imposing rear view. In this painting, O'Keeffe remains generally true to her model, making only subtle changes in order to enhance the overall sculptural quality of the building. Small details, such as cracks in the adobe and diminutive clerestory windows, have, for example, been eliminated. Moreover, by selecting a fairly low vantage point and filling most of the canvas with the image of the church, O'Keeffe enhances its size, lending monumentality to the comparatively small building. Similarly, her exaggeration of the natural curves of the adobe walls gives the church greater vibrancy.

O'Keeffe had been painting architectural subjects for several years prior to her trip to New Mexico, but the contrast between *Ranchos Church No. 1* and her roughly contemporary paintings of New York's architecture is striking. The sharp angularity and predominantly dark palette of her New York scenes, such as *City Night*, 1926, are replaced here with brightly colored, curvilinear forms. Moreover, whereas her New York buildings, generally shown from a sharply upturned angle, are disassociated from the land, the Ranchos Church organically merges with its site. This unification of church and land is even more apparent in subsequent paintings in the series, such as *Ranchos Church*, 1930 (Metropolitan Museum of Art), in which she eliminates the dark outlines with which she had delineated the building in the Norton's version.

In addition to reflecting O'Keeffe's enthusiastic response to a new venue, *Ranchos Church No. 1* suggests a lessening of Stieglitz's influence on her work. Working closely together in New York, at times exploring similar themes simultaneously, O'Keeffe and Stieglitz naturally shared certain impressions and directly influenced each other's work.[2] Thus, her New York scenes, contemporaneous with Stieglitz's photographic series on the city, share his emphasis on verticality and industrialization. In New Mexico, her vision was more her own, and the softer forms and brighter palette, especially the brilliant blue, of *Ranchos Church No. 1* become distinguishing characteristics of her southwestern paintings. AMB

NOTES

[1] Georgia O'Keeffe, *Georgia O'Keeffe* (New York City, NY: Viking Press, 1976), 62.

[2] For more information on O'Keeffe and Stieglitz and their reciprocal influence, see Alexandra Arrowsmith and Thomas West, eds., *Georgia O'Keeffe and Alfred Stieglitz, Two Lives: A Conversation in Paintings and Photographs* (New York City, NY: Harper Collins, 1992).

PROVENANCE

The Downtown Gallery; Norton Gallery, 1953.

EXHIBITION HISTORY

Mayo Hill Galleries, Delray Beach, FL, *Paintings by Georgia O'Keeffe*, March 16–April 11, 1953, p. 11.

Columbus Gallery of Fine Arts, Columbus, OH, *Art in the Homes of Columbus*, February 15–March 15, 1963.

Madison Art Center, Madison, WI, *Georgia O'Keeffe: Paintings*, February 25–April 12, 1984.

National Museum of American Art, Washington, D.C., *The Art of New Mexico, 1900–1945*, travelling exhibition, March 7, 1986–April 19, 1987.

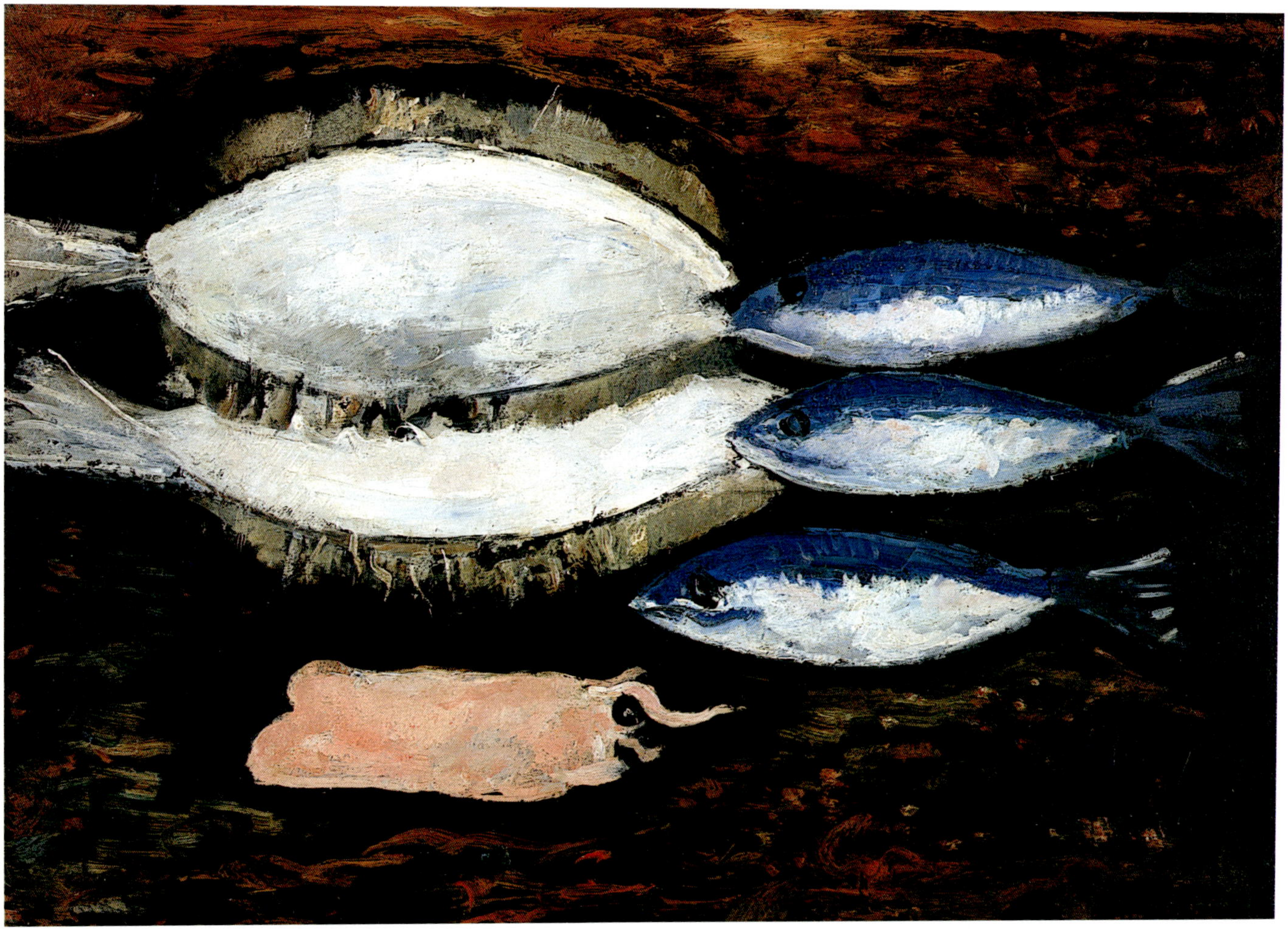

Flounders and Blue Fish, 1942
Oil on ragboard
16 3/4 x 22 3/8 in.
Bequest of R. H. Norton

Marsden Hartley

1877–1943

Born in Lewiston, Maine, where he spent a good deal of time out of doors, Marsden Hartley, at an early age, acquired a love for portraying nature. When he was thirteen, he executed for a professional naturalist, a group of detailed drawings which depicted flowers, moths, and butterflies. Hartley's interest in natural objects grew over the years until it became the primary subject matter of his canvases. Though other themes engaged his attention at times, he soon tired of them and always returned to portraying nature. This attention to nature, and the various modern styles he used to depict it, caused Hartley to stand out among early twentieth-century American artists.

Hartley moved from Maine to Cleveland, Ohio, in 1893, where he received his first art lessons under John Semon, and then attended the Cleveland School of Art (now the Cleveland Institute of Art) on a scholarship from 1898–1899. In 1899 Hartley moved to New York to attend the Chase School and studied under William Merritt Chase. He became dissatisfied with Chase's philosophy, however, and transferred to the National Academy of Design soon after. At the Academy, he worked with Edgar Ward, F. J. Dillman, and others.

Hartley did not begin to experiment with modernism until 1906. His first major venture into avant-garde representation was to paint landscapes in a "stitch" style similar to the Italian divisionist Giovanni Segantini. The works caught the attention of Alfred Stieglitz, who was the major promoter of American artists working in progressive styles at the time, and who became Hartley's greatest patron. Stieglitz exhibited the works, in 1909, at the Little Galleries of the Photo-Secession. Towards the end of the same year, Hartley created his well-known "Black Landscape" paintings, which were influenced by the dark, romantic canvases of the American protomodernist Albert Pinkham Ryder.

Hartley lead a nomad-like existence for most of his adult life, establishing himself in numerous cities throughout Europe and America. With each relocation—and corresponding change of environment—his art also changed, thus making it difficult to characterize his work stylistically. Key periods in Hartley's development include his first trip to Paris in 1912, where he experimented with Cubism and Fauvism, and the period from late 1912–1915, which he spent in contact with the Blaue Reiter ("Blue Rider") artists Wassily Kandinsky and Franz Marc. Works from the first German period are some of Hartley's most abstract. In typical Blaue Reiter fashion, many of the paintings contain mystical references to numbers and shapes. Several, however, such as the well-known *Portrait of a German Officer*, 1914–15 (The Metropolitan Museum of Art, New York), which makes reference to a young man with whom Hartley was then in love, make use of German military imagery.[1]

After leaving Germany, Hartley lived, intermittently, in Maine, New Mexico, France, Massachusetts, Mexico, Germany, Bermuda, and numerous other locations. He experimented with a variety of styles and degrees of abstraction, but references to his surroundings, and to natural objects such as seashells, fish, and birds, remained a constant. Hartley also explored other art media during these years, like lithography and painting on glass.

Some scholars believe that a "mature" style manifests itself late in Hartley's career. This style, which may be simply yet another aspect of the artist's ever-evolving mode of expression, is evident in the Dogtown Series created in Gloucester, Maine, in 1931. In these later works, a new somberness asserts itself, and the natural forms become more solid and frontal. Colors from this period are both darker and stronger, and forms are often outlined in heavy lines. Ryder's influence is, again, notably evident.

Flounders and Blue Fish, 1942
Oil on ragboard
16 3/4 x 22 3/8 in.
(l.r.: "MH")
Bequest of R. H. Norton 53.76

Hartley's *Flounders and Blue Fish* is typical in subject matter to many of his paintings, but stylistically, it is representative of his late work. Painted six months before his death, the work portrays an assortment of natural objects. The flounders, blue fish, and squid are native to Maine, and would have been familiar aspects of Hartley's everyday life. Like many of the painter's later works, each form is treated distinctly. The artist separates the individual sea creatures from the others by using black lines, and arranges all of the elements on a dark, flat, background. The fish seem to hover above this setting due to their luminous coloring, which contrasts greatly with the background.

One is immediately tempted to compare *Flounders and Blue Fish* to Ryder's *The Dead Bird*, c. 1890–1900 (The Phillips Collection, Washington, D.C.), which is similar both thematically and compositionally. But Hartley's work is not poignant in the manner that Ryder's work is, for his point was not to capture the pathos of the dead animals. Hartley often asserted that he was more interested in clarity of intellectual idea than in emotionalism in art. Thus, more so than Ryder's work, the piece is an experiment in formal and aesthetic concerns. CMC

NOTES

[1] See Jonathan Weinberg, *Speaking for Vice, Homosexuality in the Art of Charles Demuth, Marsden Hartley and the First American Avant-Garde* (New Haven, CT: Yale University Press, 1993), for a discussion of Hartley's homosexuality and its relationship to modernism.

PROVENANCE

A. P. Rosenberg and Co., 1951; Norton Gallery, 1953.

EXHIBITION HISTORY

Playhouse Gallery, Miami, FL, *Paintings and Sculpture from the Norton Gallery Collection*, January 12–24, 1959.

The Art Gallery, McCormick Place, Chicago, IL, *Inaugural Exhibition*, November 18–December 23, 1960.

Visual Arts Gallery, Florida International University, Miami, FL, *Treasures from the Norton Gallery of Art*, September 28–October 21, 1982, no. 6.

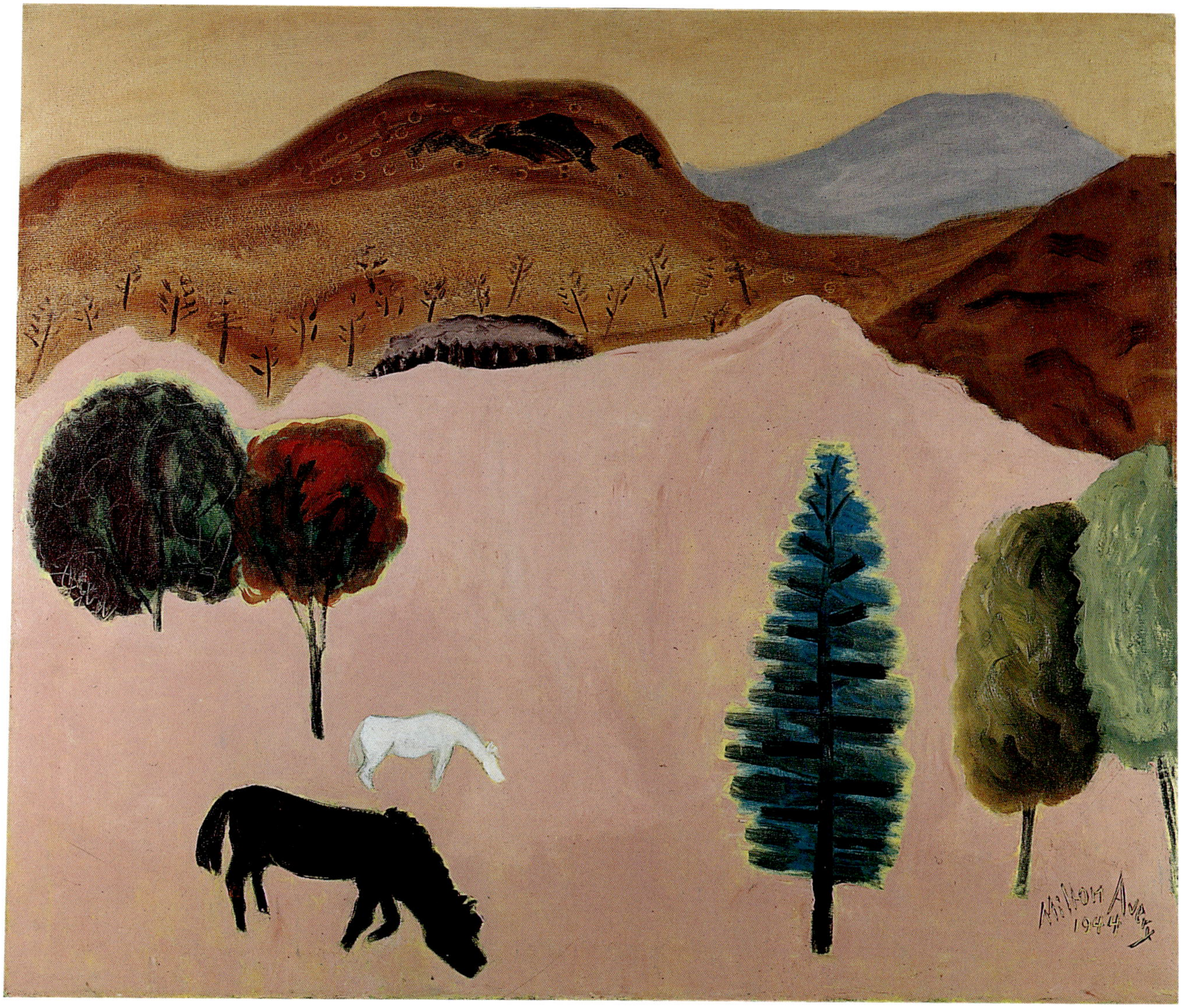

Landscape with Black and White Horses, 1944
Oil on canvas
27 x 36 in.
Purchased through the Palm Beach Art League
Construction Account

Milton Avery

1885–1965

Milton Avery's canvases are unique for their emphasis on the formal elements of color and shape and for their lyrical mood. These elements interested the artist more than realistically portraying objects or conveying philosophical, social, or political content. The latter issues concerned many of Avery's contemporaries, however, including Thomas Hart Benton, Grant Wood, Ben Shahn, and other painters of the American Scene.

Born in Sand Bank, New York, Avery moved with his family to Wilson Station, Connecticut, in 1898. Sometime between 1905–1911, he enrolled in a lettering class at the Connecticut League of Art Students to become a commercial artist, but he finished the term in the life-drawing class instead. Avery studied fine art at the League under Charles Noel Flagg until 1918, then transferred to the School of the Art Society of Hartford. He remained a student there until he was 34 years old, perhaps because he found it necessary to work while he attended school, in order to support the extended family with whom he lived.

Although Avery did not go to Europe until he was 67 years old, the influence of modern European art on his work is evident. He especially admired the Fauvism of Henri Matisse, whose broad areas of bright color and joyful subjects inspired Avery's own muted tonalities and whimsical scenes. Critics recognized Avery's connection to this artist, and honorably dubbed him the "American Matisse." [1]

To consider Avery only in terms of his relationship to European influences, however, is misleading. Because Avery trained in the United States and lived his entire life there, it is fitting to look, as well, to indigenous movements for his inspiration. Avery's rich pastel palette, for instance, draws, also, from American Impressionism that peaked at the turn of the century when Avery was coming into his own as an artist. The lyrical, at times naïve, quality of his paintings was no doubt fueled by exhibitions of folk art. During the 1930s, when critics and historians sought to establish an American aesthetic distinct from that of Europe, folk art gained new respect.

Avery's oeuvre is dominated by landscapes, seascapes, and the human figure, all treated as abstract shapes. The painter simplifies objects, or reduces them to their essences, rather than paints them realistically. Forms are flattened, and often appear parallel to the picture plane. Perspective is all but eliminated. Avery omits all detail, unless it is very important, and then, he uses it sparingly, and pointedly. What few details he does include often take the form of thin lines scratched into paint to reveal the canvas underneath.

Avery's influence is visible in the art of several younger artists. His work is especially evident in the oeuvres of Color Field painters Mark Rothko and Adolph Gottlieb, who were Avery's close, personal friends. Rothko appreciated Avery's use of broad areas of color, while Gottlieb benefitted from his lyrical approach to shape.

Landscape with Black and White Horses, 1944
Oil on canvas
27 x 36 in.
(l.r.: "Milton Avery 1944")
Purchased through the Palm Beach Art League Construction Account 46.11

Avery's love of color and shape is evident in *Landscape with Black and White Horses*, a painting created when the artist was almost sixty. Broad, flat areas of rich color describe a valley floor in the foreground and mountains and sky in the background. The vibrant pink of the field upon which two horses graze especially calls to mind Matisse.

Each object is treated as an abstract shape. The trees, horses, mountains, and field exist as flat areas of color with little or no modeling. A few details aid in describing the trees, but the horses and other elements in the composition consist of uniform hues. The two horses, in fact, one black and one white, are the most abstract components rendered. With their simplified, geometric forms, they, again, call to mind Matisse, in that they resemble this artist's decorative paper cut-outs.

The entire scene is calm and inspires feelings of well-being. The horses graze quietly in the field, and the trees stand motionless next to them. There is no suggestion of movement, not even the hint of a breeze. *Landscape with Black and White*

Horses portrays a land that is eternally placid. One critic, paraphrasing Avery's philosophy on art, wrote in 1952, "Objects in nature, whether static or in motion, are seized [by Avery] at a fleeting moment, as in a snapshot, and translated into abstract color and form."[2] CMC

NOTES

[1] Robert Hobbs, *Milton Avery* (New York City, NY: Hudson Hills Press, 1990), 225.

[2] Ibid., 173.

PROVENANCE

Purchased from Paul Rosenberg and Company, New York City, NY, through the Art Institute of Chicago, 1946.

EXHIBITION HISTORY

Playhouse Gallery, Miami, FL, *Paintings and Sculpture from the Norton Gallery Collection*, January 12–24, 1959.

The Art Gallery, McCormick Place, Chicago, IL, *Inaugural Exhibition*, November 18–December 23, 1960.

Visual Arts Gallery, Florida International University, Miami, FL, *Treasures from the Norton Gallery of Art*, September 28–October 21, 1982, no. 1.

Albany Museum of Art, Albany, GA, *Pioneers of Modernism*, September 1, 1993–January 15, 1994.

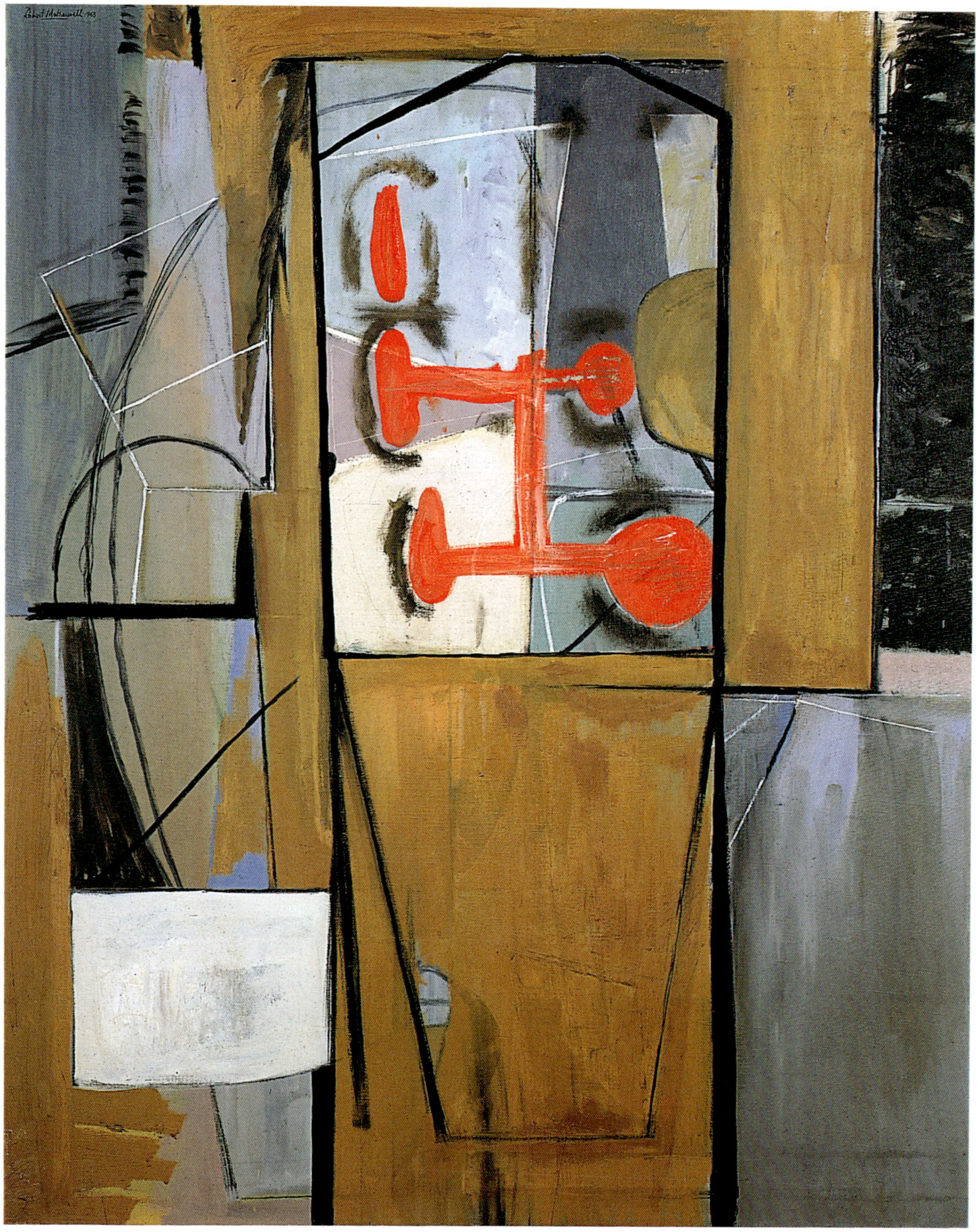

Personage, 1943
Oil on canvas
48 x 30 in.
Purchased through the Palm Beach Art
League Construction Account

Robert Motherwell

1915–

A leading innovator in abstract painting for almost half a century, Robert Motherwell is one of the artists who originated Abstract Expressionism. Born in Aberdeen, Washington, Motherwell grew up in Utah and California. He studied briefly at the School of Fine Arts in San Francisco before entering Stanford University, where he received a B.A. degree in philosophy in 1937. Intending to study philosophy, Motherwell entered a graduate program at Harvard University. In 1938, he moved to France to finish writing a book on the French Romantic painter Delacroix, and when he returned the following year, he entered Columbia University to study art history with Meyer Shapiro. Through Shapiro, he met several European Surrealists who were in exile in New York, including André Breton, Max Ernst, Yves Tanguy, and the Chilean painter Roberto Matta Echaurren. He and Matta travelled to Mexico together in 1941, where Motherwell experimented with the Surrealist technique of automatic drawing and painted his first major paintings. Motherwell was impressed with Mexican folk art which featured intentionally crude renderings of skeletons, coffins, and other images of death.[1] In 1942, he settled in New York and completely abandoned his university studies to concentrate on painting.

Motherwell was making collages in 1943, when he and Jackson Pollock were invited to participate in an international collage exhibition at Peggy Guggenheim's gallery, Art of This Century. Unlike slow-drying oil paint, collage allowed the artist to add new shapes to his work immediately, and to experiment freely with their configuration. Motherwell translated his emotional and formal discoveries with collage into his oil paintings of the next several years, resulting in a fresh spontaneity and innovative freedom that he had not achieved earlier.

Motherwell had his first, critically successful one-artist show at the Art of This Century gallery in 1944. The same year, he moved to East Hampton, New York, where Pollock and Lee Krasner had been living, and where he met Mark Rothko in 1946. In 1948, he painted the first of his series of monumental, abstract *Elegies*, featuring large, ovoid areas of thick, dark paint which resemble the torn shapes of his collages, squeezed between vertical rectangles that seem to hold the ovoid shapes tightly in place. These paintings, for which the artist is best known, were inspired by his profound reaction to the well-publicized brutality of the Spanish Civil War.[2]

During the 1950s, Motherwell's experiments with color were restricted largely to his collages, but in the 1960s, he began to work on his *Open* series of paintings, in which he explored the use of sensuous color and brush stroke on a large scale. Like the paintings of his earlier years, these large, color abstractions embody the artist's feelings about the world, sensations which can not be put into words. In the last two decades, the artist has continued to produce works in oil, collages, and prints, and he has been recognized internationally for his significant contribution to modern painting.

Personage, 1943
Oil on canvas
48 x 30 in.
(u.l.: "Robert Motherwell 1943")
Purchased through the Palm Beach Art League
Construction Account 46.10

Painted shortly after Motherwell made his first collage, *Personage* represents an important stage in the artist's formative years. Originally untitled, the artist called the painting *Dead Personage*, in 1944, and later, shortened the name to *Personage*. In a letter of 1946, the artist related the painting to the theme of "dead (and assassinated) political leaders," a theme which had fascinated him for several years.[3] The morbid subject, abstract shapes, and brooding earth tones of the painting reflect his concurrent discoveries in collage, the influence of Surrealism, and the artist's understanding of painting as a way to express his personal reactions to life's experiences.

Personage was painted in layers, similar to the layering process in the construction of collage. First, Motherwell applied coats of thin, gray and red paint in biomorphic shapes, some of which are still visible in the upper left of the canvas. Next, thicker rectangular areas of opaque ochre pigment were applied in the center of the canvas, leaving a window in the top center through which curved and angled lines are visible. The random, spontaneous quality of the white and black lines which activate Motherwell's painted surface, particularly in the top center and left of the composition, recalls Surrealist automatic drawing. Robert Saltonstall Mattison, a leading scholar of Motherwell's work, has noted that the loosening of structure in this composition, as compared with Motherwell's earlier oil paintings, is "due to the increased freedom in mixing shaped areas of color and drawing with paint" that the artist experienced working with collage.[4]

The rectangular shape in the center has been identified, by the artist, as a coffin, and the red shapes which appear through the opening in its top suggest the bloody skeleton of the deceased. The predominant tones of gray and ochre convey a mood of sadness. Motherwell described the image as "somber, mournful, subdued, with an undertone of violence, but deliberately generalized...."[5] Mattison has related Motherwell's concern with images of violence and death during this period to his depressed state of mind resulting from the cataclysmic events of World War II, a stressful marriage, and his father's death in 1943. In a statement issued eight years after *Personage* was painted, Motherwell eloquently summarized his use of art to express a fundamental response to modern life.

"The need [which abstract art fulfills] is for felt experience—intense, immediate, direct, subtle, unified, warm, vivid, rhythmic. Everything that might dilute the experience is stripped away."[6]

Personage does not depict a specific assassination victim, or an identifiable episode of violence, rather, in monumental, painterly terms, it expresses the impact of such occurrences on the sensibility of the artist. DM

NOTES

[1] Robert Saltonstall Mattison, *Robert Motherwell: The Formative Years* (Ann Arbor, MI: University of Michigan Press, 1987), 93–95.

[2] For a thorough discussion of the meanings associated with Motherwell's *Elegy* series and their relationship to the Spanish Civil War, see Mattison, 200–207.

[3] Robert Motherwell, letter to a Mr. McKim of East Hampton, New York, dated 22 February 1946, Registrar's files, Norton Gallery and School of Art, West Palm Beach, FL.

[4] Mattison, 97.

[5] Motherwell, letter to Mr. McKim.

[6] Robert Motherwell, "What Abstract Art Means to Me," *The Museum of Modern Art/Bulletin* 18 (Spring 1951): 12.

PROVENANCE

Kootz Gallery, New York City, NY, until 1946; Norton Gallery, 1946.

EXHIBITION HISTORY

Society of the Four Arts, Palm Beach, FL, *Abstract Expressionist Paintings*, January 18–February 10, 1946, no. 27.

Playhouse Gallery, Miami, FL, *Paintings and Sculpture from the Norton Collection*, January 12–24, 1959.

The Art Gallery, McCormick Place, Chicago, IL, *Inaugural Exhibition*, November 18–December 23, 1960, no. 20.

Herbert F. Johnson Museum of Art, Cornell University, Ithaca, NY, *Abstract Expressionism: The Formative Years*, March 30–May 14, 1978, no. 95.

Visual Arts Gallery, Florida International University, Miami, FL, *Treasures from the Norton Gallery of Art*, September 28–October 21, 1982, no. 18.

Albright-Knox Museum, Buffalo, NY, *Robert Motherwell*, October 1, 1983–January 31, 1985, no. 6.

Solomon R. Guggenheim Museum, New York City, NY, *Peggy Guggenheim's Other Legacy*, March 6–May 3, 1987, p. 30.

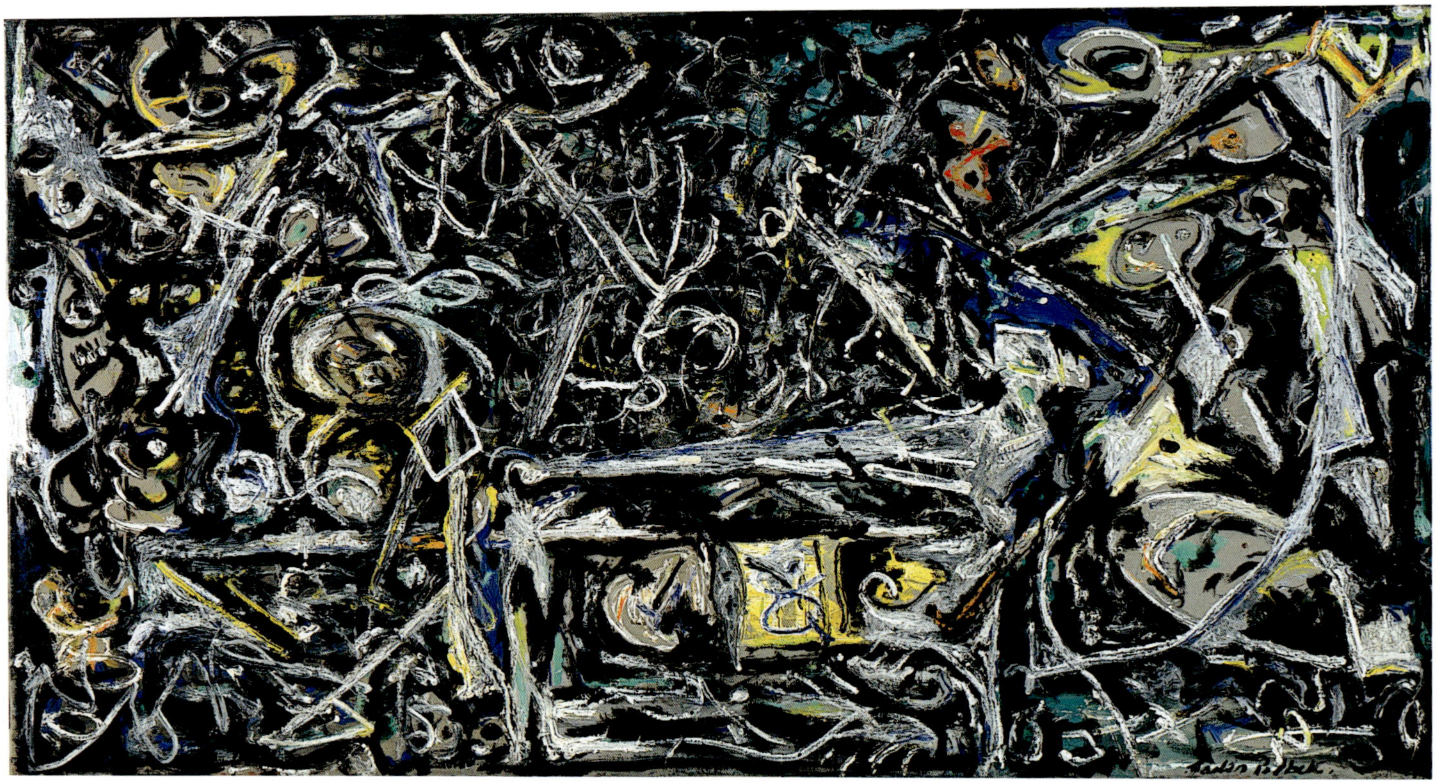

Night Mist, 1945
Oil on canvas
36 x 74 in.
Purchased through the R. H. Norton Fund

Jackson Pollock

1912–1956

Jackson Pollock was a leader of the New York School, a group of American artists whose bold, new abstraction drew worldwide critical attention away from Paris during the years following World War II. Working in nontraditional art materials, such as latex house paint, Pollock also dared to eliminate the traditional support and vertical orientation of his paintings by laying his unstretched and unprimed canvas on the floor to work. The act of painting became a vigorously physical process, and led the critic Harold Rosenberg to remark, "At a certain moment, the canvas began to appear to one American painter after another, as an arena in which to act.... What was to go on the canvas was not a picture, but an event." [1] Pollock and his companions, who developed this intuitive, gestural approach to painting, have been called Action Painters, and the intensely compelling images which resulted became known as Abstract Expressionism.

Paul Jackson Pollock was born in Cody, Wyoming. At a very young age he moved with his family to Arizona, and then to southern California, where he spent most of his youth. Pollock's later preference for extremely large-scale paintings that seem to engulf the viewer has been attributed, in part, to the awe he experienced as a child before the vast expanse of the desert Southwest. He attended Manual Arts High School in Los Angeles, where a teacher first introduced him to theosophy and the teachings of Krishnamurti, a late-nineteenth-century Hindu prophet and teacher. Mystical and occult figures which have been identified in Pollock's paintings of the 1940s suggest that the artist maintained his interest in Eastern mysticism and occultism throughout his early career.[2] In 1930, he followed his brother Charles, also an artist, to New York and enrolled in classes taught by Thomas Hart Benton at the Art Students League. Pollock's student drawings and paintings from the early 1930s resemble the baroque expressiveness of his teacher's figural style, and Benton's insistence on discovering American subject matter, undoubtedly, encouraged Pollock to spend several summers travelling across the country. It was on these trips that Pollock became intrigued by the ritual process of Native American sand painting, which was one inspiration for the "action paintings" of his mature career.

Before enrolling in Benton's classes, Pollock had been impressed by the work of the Mexican muralists Diego Riviera and José Clemente Orozco. In New York, Pollock watched Riviera paint murals for the New Workers' School, and then, began working in the experimental workshop of David Alfaro Siquieros, another Mexican artist who was investigating the use of nontraditional paints and the use of "controlled accidents" in mural painting. In 1935, Pollock began working for the Federal Art Project of the Works Progress Administration, where he gained further exposure to large-scale mural painting. During these formative years, Pollock also frequented the museums and galleries of New York, where he was influenced by Picasso's Analytic Cubism, and the Surrealism of André Masson and Joan Miró.

In 1943, Pollock met Peggy Guggenheim, who had just opened her gallery, Art of This Century. Two years later, she granted Pollock his first one-man show, which afforded him major critical exposure. Through Guggenheim, Pollock also became familiar with several of the European Surrealists who had fled the Nazis. He was greatly interested in the Surrealists' use of psychic auto-matism, a process by which rational control is suspended to allow the unimpeded flow of images from the unconscious mind onto the paper or canvas. Pollock had used the same technique with his Jungian therapist during treatment for alcoholism and depression, during the mid-1930s.

Both Pollock's reputation and the size of his canvases grew during the late 1940s. By 1950, he was, literally, dripping and throwing house paint from overloaded brushes onto enormous spans of unprimed canvas spread on his studio floor. The compelling physicality of the dense webs of flowing pigment which result from this process created monumental paintings unknown in previous art and catapulted Pollock into international stardom. His career was tragically cut short at the age of 44, when he was killed in an automobile accident.

Night Mist, 1945
Oil on canvas
36 x 74 in.
(l.r.: "Jackson Pollock")
Purchased through the R. H. Norton Fund 71.14

Night Mist has been called "transitional" with regard to style and method, because it was painted during that critical juncture when Pollock was moving away from his earlier mode of Cubist-based, symbolic figuration, towards complete abstraction and unrestrained expressionism. In this painting, vestiges of human figures, birds, biomorphic creatures and symbolic forms can be discerned struggling against the angular strokes of dark, heavy paint, which interlace to form the remnants of a geometric, Cubist structure. The slashing marks of dark paint and the energized lines of lighter pigment in *Night Mist* convey the force of the artist's gestures during the act of painting.

Certain scholars have attempted to reveal an iconography of Jungian symbols and other archetypal images in Pollock's transitional paintings of the early 1940s. One scholar has identified the white, diamond-shaped lozenge in the left center of *Night Mist* image as female genitalia, located at the apex of an inverted "V" which would represent a figure's legs.[3] The torso of the figure continues upward from the diamond, with a figure eight turned on its side to indicate breasts, and a long neck, topped by a saucer-shaped head. In the middle of the far right of the canvas, two reddish-gray ovals outlined in black, with details in black and white, can be identified as the heads and facial features of additional figures. The ovals are connected to narrow shapes which resemble torsos extending downward, and a curved line extends below the face on the far right, suggesting shoulders and arms.

Figures such as these in Pollock's paintings can be related to the archetypal images frequently found in Native American art, which Pollock is known to have admired. They may also refer to the mythic images which figure prominently in the psychological writings of Carl Jung. Pollock had undergone several years of therapy with a Jungian psychoanalyst before *Night Mist* was painted, and the artist was well-versed in Jung's theories, although he had probably not read Jung's texts himself. In his recent study of meaning in Pollock's paintings, the scholar Claude Cernuschi has convincingly argued that while it is unlikely that Pollock consciously included Jungian symbols in his paintings, the images which surfaced, unconsciously, while he was exploring the use of psychic automatism, would have been in keeping with the artist's personal interest in mythic themes and symbols.[4] Similar symbolic forms were also common in Native American painting, which the artist esteemed, and in the work of Picasso and Miró, the two artists whom Pollock admired the most.

The vigorous brushwork and the dense web of calligraphic lines in *Night Mist* create the illusion of depth, while at the same time emphasizing the materiality of the flat surface and the gesture of the artist during the process of painting. Although it is a work in oil, created in the traditional mode of easel painting, *Night Mist* looks forward to the most famous period of Pollock's career, in which the artist flung latex house paint over unstretched canvas on the studio floor to create a new pictorial space that is energized by the physical act of its creation. When Pollock painted *Night Mist*, he was on the verge of a breakthrough which forever changed the course of twentieth-century art. DM

NOTES

1 Harold Rosenberg, "The American Action Painters" (1952), reprinted in Herschel B. Chipp, *Theories of Modern Art* (Berkeley, CA: University of California Press, 1968), 569.

2 Jonathan Welch, "Jackson Pollock's 'The White Angel' and the Origins of Alchemy," *Arts Magazine* 53 (March 1979): 138–41. Welch has identified a female figure in *Night Mist* which is similar to a female angel in *White Angel*, painted by Pollock in 1946, which Welch associates with the practice of alchemy.

3 Ibid., 139.

[4] Claude Cernuschi, *Jackson Pollock: Meaning and Significance* (New York City, NY: Harper Collins, 1992), 62–76.

PROVENANCE

Marlborough-Gerson Gallery, New York City, NY; Harry W. Anderson, Atherton, CA; Harold Diamond Gallery, New York City, NY; S. I. Newhouse Jr.; Bodley Gallery, New York City, NY; Norton Gallery, 1971.

EXHIBITION HISTORY

Art of this Century Gallery, New York City, NY, *Jackson Pollock*, March 19–April 14, 1945, no. 9.

Marlborough Gallery, London, England, *Jackson Pollock*, June 1961, no. 43.

Kunstverein für die Rheinlande und Westfalen, Kunsthalle, Düsseldorf, Germany, *Jackson Pollock*, September 5–October 8, 1961, no. 69.

Marlborough-Gerson Gallery, New York City, NY, *Jackson Pollock*, January–February, 1964, no. 71.

Marlborough Gallery, New York City, NY, *Jackson Pollock, Black and White*, March 1969.

Herbert F. Johnson Museum of Art, Cornell University, Ithaca, NY, *Abstract Expressionism: The Formative Years*, March 30–May 14, 1978, no. 2.

Musée National de l'Art Moderne, Paris, France, *Jackson Pollock*, January 21–April 19, 1982.

Center for Fine Arts, Miami, FL, *In Quest of Excellence: Civic Pride, Patronage, Connoisseurship*, January 14–April 22, 1984, no. 188.

Los Angeles County Museum of Art, Los Angeles, CA, *The Spiritual in Art, Abstract Painting 1890–1985*, November 23, 1986–March 8, 1987, no. 21.

Museum of Contemporary Art, Los Angeles, CA, *Individuals: A Selected History*

Edward Hopper

1882–1967

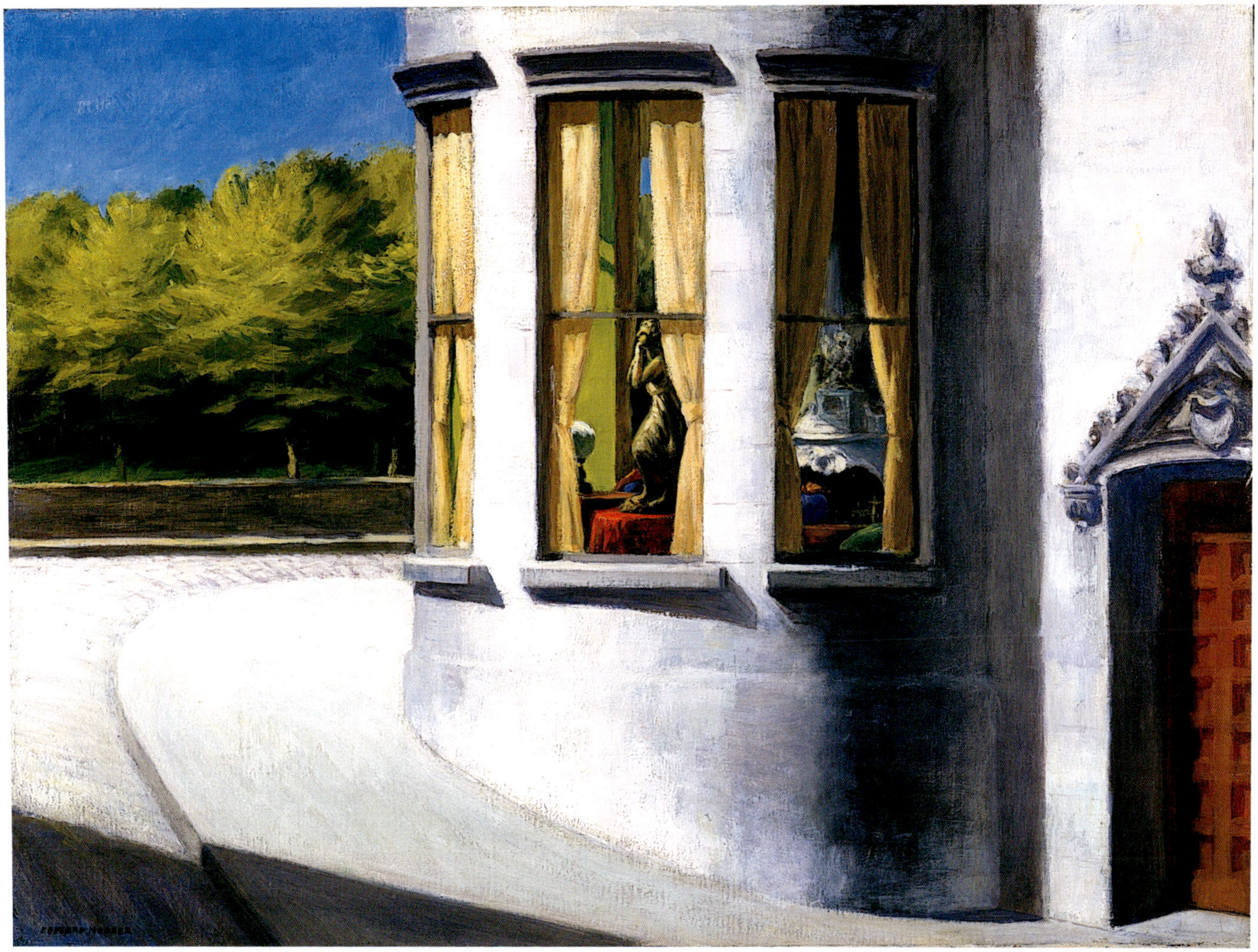

August in the City, 1945
Oil on canvas
23 x 30 in.
Bequest of R. H. Norton

Edward Hopper, 1882–1967

Edward Hopper, the foremost American Scene painter, studied art under Robert Henri at the New York School of Art from 1900–1906. Henri and his circle zestfully painted all facets of life in New York City, including its less genteel or seamier sides, in bold, slashing brushwork. This approach differed from the refined subject matter and tamer manner of representation preferred by the National Academy of Design. While Hopper's mature works are far more reserved in tone than Henri's, they, nevertheless, reveal his teacher's interest in portraying the scenes of contemporary city life. Hopper and other artists, such as Grant Wood, Ben Shahn, and Andrew Wyeth, who depicted life in the United States, came to be known as American Scene Painters.

Hopper travelled overseas several times and visited a number of European capitals during the years 1906–1910, but he was unaffected by avant-garde styles such as Cubism and Fauvism. Despite this fact, he sold his first picture at the 1913 Armory Show in New York City, the exhibition which largely showcased non-academic American artists and brought radical European styles to the United States. His early success was short-lived, however, and Hopper turned to commercial and graphic art to earn a living. A series of etchings created during the years 1915–1923 helped him to clarify his artistic focus, and by 1923, he had taken-up oils again, and his hallmark realistic approach to painting had developed.

Hopper's oeuvre is noted for its remarkable consistency of style and subject matter. A typical painting by the artist portrays one of several recurrent themes in a naturalistic manner. Hopper's primary subjects include cityscapes devoid of human inhabitants, single figures or groupings of people in urban or countryside interiors viewed from the outside, and people outdoors, but in relation to architectural settings. What is striking about his scenes is that his figures all give the appearance of being lost in thought, and even appear dazed or oblivious to their surroundings. Whether or not Hopper intended it, critics often read this quality as commenting on issues like the cynicism of modern society and the increasing lack of communication between people.[1]

Hopper's use of formal elements aided him in creating this introspective mood. Colors, for instance, are luminous, yet they are also cold; weak morning or evening light illuminates many of his scenes, giving them an eerie, stage-set quality. Figures depicted indoors are often boxed-in by compositional elements, creating cramped, claustrophobic atmospheres.

Today, Hopper's work is extremely well known, and the impact of his paintings on American culture has been tremendous. Paintings, such as *Nighthawks*, 1942, which portrays several figures in a lonely cafe, adorn countless book jackets and are often used in advertising and for other purposes. Numerous contemporary artists and illustrators working in a Hopperesque manner continue his legacy of conveying the psychologically remote.

August in the City, 1945
Oil on canvas
23 x 30 in.
(l.l.: "EDWARD HOPPER")
Bequest of R. H. Norton 53.84

Many of Hopper's paintings, like *Eleven A.M.*, 1926 (Hirshhorn Museum and Sculpture Garden, Washington, D.C.), and *Morning Sun*, 1952

(Columbus Museum of Art, Ohio), portray women bathed in sunlight peering out of windows.[2] In *August in the City*, however, Hopper replaces the woman with a statue. With the human element present only in symbolic terms, the sense of desolation is more profound than in many of Hopper's other works. This mood is further compounded by the room's Victorian decor, which hints of days past and things forgotten.

Also, like many of Hopper's other paintings, the sculpture is contained within an architectural setting—here, a Manhattan apartment building adjacent to Riverside Park—and the viewpoint is from the outside looking in. Corners of buildings and interesting architectural forms, such as rooms that jut out, dormer windows, and mansard roofs, especially fascinated Hopper. In *August in the City*, the room makes up the first floor of a corner turret. In an identical format to *Nighthawks*, the sidewalk curves around the structure and emphasizes its roundness. By depicting the room's curtains slightly open, Hopper invites the viewer to peer into the space and to experience the heat and stillness of a deserted, urban residence in August.

Color, shape, and light are important formal components of *August in the City*. The painting incorporates broad flat areas of simple colors, such as red, blue, green, and yellow. The sky, for instance, is an even shade of blue, while the trees are green, the curtains yellow, and the doorway dark red. Shapes are generalized or abstracted to a degree, and they are sometimes repeated. A row of similarly round trees lines the rectangular shape that makes up the road, for example, while the curtains consist of six identical bow-shapes positioned parallel to each other. The light has a chiaroscuro effect. Hopper paints sunlight that enters the scene from an angle and dramatically illuminates the building, like a spotlight. Objects are either fully visible or in deep shadow. CMC

NOTES

[1] Hopper had mixed feelings about critics who found meaning beyond the literal in his works. J. Daniel Selig, "The Reality of Realism: Hopper's 'Sunlight on Brownstones,'" *Wichita Art Museum Bulletin* (Winter 1973).

[2] For an interpretation of the meaning of sunlight in Hopper's paintings, see Ian Jeffrey et al., *Edward Hopper* (London, England: Hayward Gallery, 1981), 11–15.

PROVENANCE

Frank K. M. Rehn, Inc., New York, 1947; Norton Gallery, 1953.

EXHIBITION HISTORY

Whitney Museum of American Art, New York City, NY, *Edward Hopper: Retrospective Exhibition*, February 11–March 26, 1950.

The Art Institute of Chicago, Chicago, IL, *Sixtieth Annual Exhibition: Painting and Sculpture*, October 25–December 16, 1951.

Lowe Art Gallery, University of Miami, Coral Gables, FL, *American Exhibition*, February 25–March 14, 1952.

Worcester Art Museum, Worcester, MA, *Five Painters of America*, February 17–April 3, 1955.

The Art Gallery, McCormick Place, Chicago, IL, *Inaugural Exhibition*, November 18–December 23, 1960.

Columbus Gallery of Fine Arts, Columbus, OH, *Art in the Homes of Columbus*, February 15–March 17, 1963.

University of Arizona Art Gallery, Tucson, AZ, *Edward Hopper*, April 20–May 19, 1963.

Whitney Museum of American Art, New York City, NY, *Edward Hopper*, September 29–November 29, 1964.

New Jersey State Museum, Trenton, NJ, *Focus on Light*, May 20–September 10, 1967.

Lowe Art Gallery, University of Miami, Coral Gables, FL, *Magic and Super Realism*, December 16, 1967– February 6, 1968.

Hayward Gallery, London, England, *Edward Hopper 1882–1967*, February 11–March 29, 1981, no. 100.

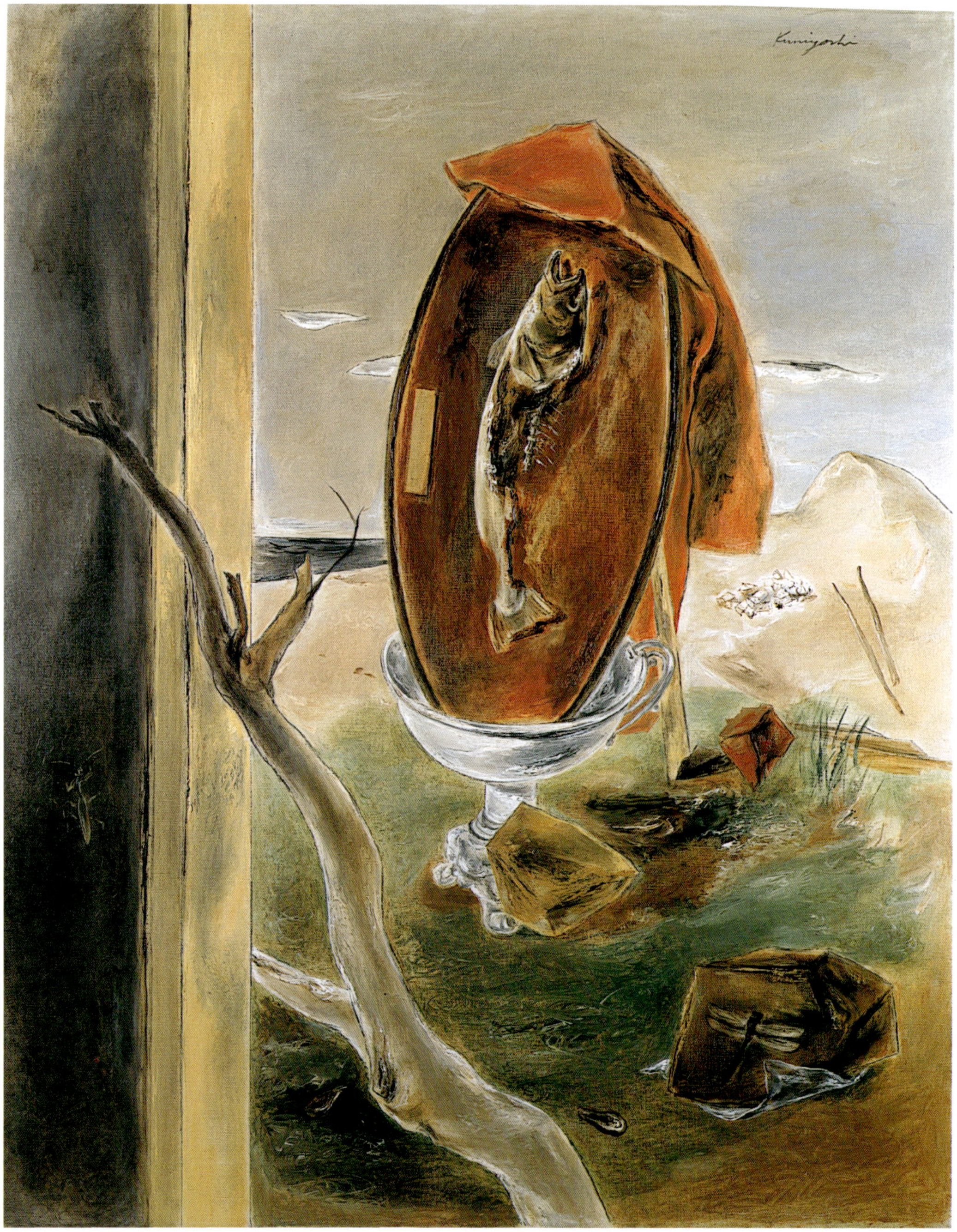

Rotting on the Shore, 1945
Oil on canvas
46 1/8 x 36 1/8 in.
Bequest of R. H. Norton

Yasuo Kuniyoshi

1893–1953

A leading master of American still life painting, Japanese-American artist Yasuo Kuniyoshi possessed the rare ability to convey the spiritual condition of American life through the careful arrangement of inanimate objects. Born in Japan, Kuniyoshi came to the United States in 1906 and settled in California. Four years later, he moved to New York, where he enrolled in classes taught by Kenneth Hayes Miller at the Art Students League. When he left the Art Students League in 1920, Kuniyoshi was producing symbolic, fantastic landscapes in which the drawing was freely distorted for plastic or decorative effect, and the background rose almost vertically to parallel the picture plane. These characteristics were derived from the art of his native Japan, but were also central to modernist styles which were being advanced in New York and Paris. In the late 1920s, he made two extended visits to Paris, where he recalled being "impressed with my French contemporaries, especially for their keen understanding of their medium."[1] Interestingly, he was not greatly influenced by Cubist or Expressionist abstraction during these trips, but rather, by a general emphasis, which he observed, on painting directly from the object.

For years, Kuniyoshi had drawn his images from his imagination or memories. Upon his return from Paris in 1928, he began to paint directly from models in a realistic style which reflected the artist's fascination with the physical properties of objects. Far from copying the mere appearance of nature, however, Kuniyoshi was sensitive to the inner significance of things, a trait which he believed stemmed from his cultural background. "...the Oriental artists... have always remembered that art is not a metaphor—

not imitation of nature, but the creation of an equivalent of nature in plastic terms."[2]

In the early 1920s, Kuniyoshi bought an inexpensive camera and began to support himself photographing works of art for reproduction. He soon became well known in New York art circles that included some of the most prestigious galleries and private collectors among his clients. As he worked with his camera, Kuniyoshi discovered that the sudden cropping of images and the tilted perspective which could be achieved through the camera lens were well suited to his personal aesthetic inclinations. He began to explore the use of the camera to do more than document other people's art; for Kuniyoshi, photography became a medium for his own creative expression.

The U.S. involvement in the Pacific during World War II profoundly affected Kuniyoshi. A few days after the Japanese attacked Pearl Harbor on December 7, 1941, the artist was forced to surrender his camera and binoculars to the New York City Police Department. Although he considered himself an American, the National Origins Act of 1924 had prevented him from becoming a United States citizen, and now in 1941, he was considered an enemy alien in his own country. Despite his public denouncements of Japanese aggression, Kuniyoshi was interned in his New York studio, and the Justice Department impounded his financial assets.[3] He responded by returning to his earlier mode of symbolic naturalism with underlying themes of desolation, decay, and the transitory nature of life, and he continued in this direction until his death. In spite of the racial discrimination which he experienced, Kuniyoshi explained that his art was a product of the American environment, which "temper[s] and shape[s] the American, no matter where the individual first came from."[4]

Rotting on the Shore, 1945
Oil on canvas
46 1/8 x 36 1/8 in.
(u.r.: "Kuniyoshi")
Bequest of R. H. Norton 53.100

Two years after he completed *Rotting on the Shore*, Kuniyoshi wrote, "I would say that the war for the past few years has been the backdrop for a great number of my works. Not necessarily the battlefield, but war's implications: destruction, lifelessness, hovering between life, death, loneliness."[5] Although the Norton painting represents a return to the symbolic mode of Kuniyoshi's youthful work, the colors, textures, and thematic content of the still life reflect a new sense of gravity for the mature artist.

By 1940, Kuniyoshi's sheer joy in painting became overshadowed by the profound impact of world events. His palette darkened, and the subject matter of his still life arrangements began to reflect new concerns. The artist explained his introduction of broken, decaying objects in unusual configurations into his painting: "If a man feels deeply about the war, or any sorrow or gladness,...you can use symbols to say clearly how the sorrow or gladness is felt deeply in your heart, although the physical expression of it is just still life...."[6]

Rotting on the Shore embodies Kuniyoshi's visual expression of the sorrow and sadness he experienced as a Japanese-American during World War II. A mounted fish is featured in the center of the canvas, resting in a silver goblet. Rather than the carefully preserved prize catch that one would expect, however, Kuniyoshi presents a decomposing salmon. The crumpled debris which surrounds the base of the goblet underscores the theme of destruction and decay, and the blood-red shroud which falls over the top of the oval trophy can be compared to a stained burial shroud. The barren tree which rises from the bottom center of the canvas recalls the spiky trees and shrubs of Kuniyoshi's earlier paintings and symbolizes the ephemerality of life and the passage of time. The fish and the tree were once living things that Kuniyoshi would have delighted in painting. In 1945, he presents them in the tradition of memento mori still lifes, as morbid reminders of the mortality of all living things.

In *Rotting on the Shore*, Kuniyoshi has cleverly altered the arrangement of interior and exterior space in traditional still life painting by positioning his objects within a bleak landscape, outside what appears to be a doorway or window. The landscape is pictured from a bird's-eye perspective that tilts it forward towards the surface of the canvas and enhances the fantastic quality of the scene. The artist has stacked the objects in an unstable configuration, but his skillful balance of rich reds and deep earth tones throughout the composition seems to visually hold the still life in place. As in the still lifes of Cézanne, outlines define Kuniyoshi's forms, which are adeptly modelled to show their three-dimensionality, and a patch of bare canvas at the top left of the picture emphasizes its nature as a two-dimensional representation of reality. Kuniyoshi has masterfully created an eloquent record of his personal response to his contemporary world. DM

NOTES

[1] Lloyd Goodrich, *Kuniyoshi* (Tokyo, Japan: National Museum of Modern Art, 1954), n.p.

[2] Kuniyoshi, in a lecture delivered at the American Abstract Artists Eighteenth Annual Exhibition, New York, quoted by Douglas Dreishpoon in "Yasuo Kuniyoshi and Photography: Balancing Painterly Vision," *Arts Magazine* 58 (January 1984): 114–115.

[3] Frank Riehlman and Tom Wolf, "Yasuo Kuniyoshi, Painter/Photographer," in *Yasuo Kuniyoshi: Artist as Photographer* (Annandale-on-Hudson, NY: Edith C. Blum Institute in cooperation with the Norton Gallery and School of Art, 1983), 7.

[4] Ibid., 16.

[5] Goodrich, *Kuniyoshi*, n.p.

[6] Ibid., 33.

PROVENANCE

Downtown Gallery, New York City, NY, until 1950; Norton Gallery, 1950.

EXHIBITION HISTORY

Carnegie Institute, Pittsburgh, PA, *Painting in the United States*, October 9–December 7, 1947.

University of Illinois, Urbana, IL, *Exhibition of Contemporary American Painting*, February–April, 1949, no. 63.

School of Fine Arts, State University of Iowa, Iowa City, IA, *Paintings by American Masters*, June 17–July 31, 1953, no. 18.

The Art Gallery, McCormick Place, Chicago, IL, *Inaugural Exhibition*, November 18–December 23, 1960, no. 14.

University Gallery, University of Florida, Gainesville, FL, *Yasuo Kuniyoshi*, February 7–March 30, 1969, no. 30.

Norton Gallery and School of Art, West Palm Beach, FL, *Yasuo Kuniyoshi: Artist as Photographer*, October 29–December 4, 1983, no. 38.

National Museum of Modern Art, Tokyo, Japan, *Yasuo Kuniyoshi: Retrospective*, February 20–April 1, 1990.

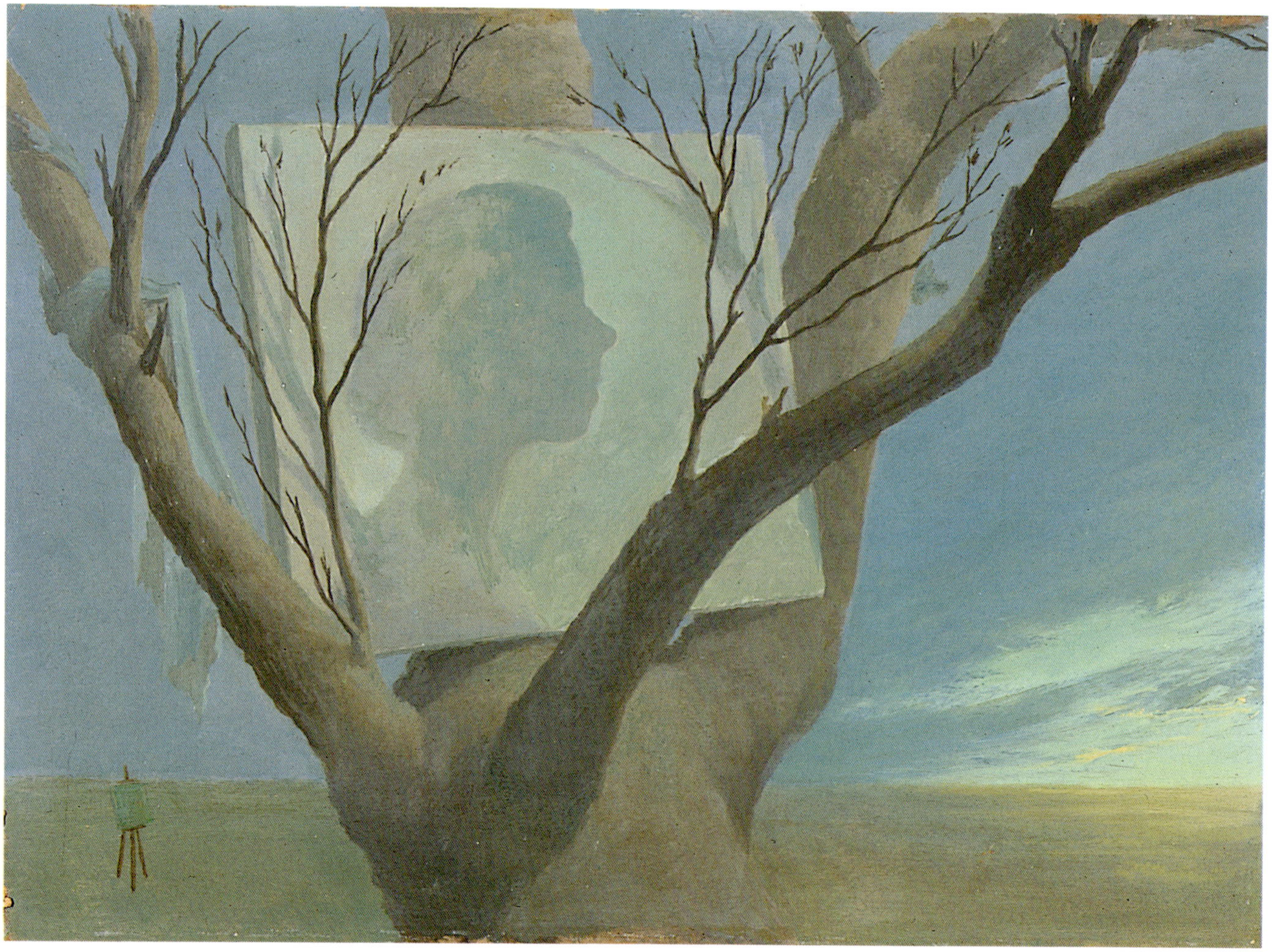

Self-Portrait in a Tree, 1950
Oil on board
11 7/8 x 16 in.
Purchased through the Rose L. Kraft Fund

Helen Lundeberg

1908–

Helen Lundeberg was a founder of Post-Surrealism, one of the first modernist movements in American art to originate on the West Coast. With her husband, Lorser Feitelson, she pioneered a new type of painting in which the subjective content of Surrealism is coupled with a classical interest in pictorial structure and form. Always a serious student who enjoyed analytical subjects, such as algebra and geometry, and who read extensively, Lundeberg began to study art in 1930 at the Stickney Memorial School of Art in Pasadena. There, she met Feitelson, who was her teacher and a formidable influence on her art.

At the Stickney School, Feitelson stressed analysis of the structural principles of Renaissance master paintings, as well as the work of leading modern artists. Lundeberg shared Feitelson's desire for an intellectual approach to painting. In the early 1930s, the two artists co-founded Post-Surrealism, originally called New Classicism or Subjective Classicism, a movement that called for an integrity of subject matter and pictorial structure.[1] Unlike Surrealism, in which images from the unconscious mind are typically juxtaposed in illogical arrangements, Post-Surrealism's combinations of elements were designed to unite form and content using both structural and psychic associations. Instead of undermining the viewer's rational sense of reality, the Post-Surrealists sought to create a new gestalt which would involve the viewer in rational, metaphysical speculation.[2] In 1934, Lundeberg published the theoretical manifesto of Post-Surrealism, *New Classicism*, and exhibited as a Post-Surrealist at the Fine Arts Gallery of San Diego and in the first group show of Post-Surrealism at the Centaur Gallery in Hollywood.

Lundeberg had exhibited her first figure painting at the Fine Arts Gallery of San Diego in 1931. In 1933, she began to paint easel paintings for the Public Works of Art Project (PWAP) under the Federal Works Progress Administration (WPA), and in 1936, Lundeberg and Feitelson were included in the landmark exhibition *Fantastic Art, Dada and Surrealism*, at the Museum of Modern Art in New York. Lundeberg continued to paint and exhibit Post-Surrealist paintings until the early 1950s, when she began to explore isolated architectural spaces using increasingly flattened, geometric areas and elongated shadows in her painting. By 1958, a joint exhibition with Feitelson at Scripps College in Claremont, California, revealed how much her style had diverged from that of her mentor, and in 1959, she began a new series of paintings in which flat geometric areas suggested empty architectural vistas, landscapes, or interiors, using a limited palette of subdued hues. Since Feitelson's death in 1978, Lundeberg has continued to produce subtly abstract paintings which explore variations of hue or tone while emphasizing classical pictorial structure.

Self-Portrait in a Tree, 1950
Oil on board
11 7/8 x 16 in.
(verso top half: "Helen Lundeberg "Self Portrait" 1950")
Purchased through the Rose L. Kraft Fund 94.1

Self-Portrait in a Tree is one of several paintings in which Lundeberg's own portrait is combined with unexpected objects to create a Post-Surrealist image. In the picture, a muted blue-gray silhouette of the artist appears on an unframed rectangular canvas, resting in the fork of a barren tree. When confronted with an image such as this, which is instantly recognizable and at the same time ambiguous and incomprehensible, the viewer wants to read the elements of the picture to discern its meaning. For Lundeberg, however, the formal aspects of the image convey as much meaning as the association of particular elements. The straight edges of the depicted canvas bearing her portrait contrast with the irregular, organic branches of the tree which surround it. Her "portrait," in the form of a muted silhouette, remains somewhat ambiguous, whereas the tree is rendered with the utmost clarity. As in *Double Portrait of the Artist in Time*, 1935 (Collection of the artist), or *Selma*, 1957 (Collection of the artist), the reality of her painted representation is contrasted with the reality of the natural world. Lundeberg described these Post-Surrealist paintings, such as *Self-Portrait in a Tree*, as "'idea entities,' through arrangements of depicted forms... contemplation of the sequence of meanings or associations attached to these forms created the pictorial aesthetic."[3] The unsettling effect of the questions raised by *Self-Portrait in a Tree* is enhanced by the use of eerie blue-greens and grays, despite the calming effect of overall tonal harmony throughout the composition.

Self-Portrait in a Tree was painted the same year that Lundeberg painted *A Quiet Place*, the first painting in which the artist decisively broke from Post-Surrealism and moved towards increasing abstraction and simplification. The Norton painting, therefore, is one of the last specifically Post-Surrealist paintings that the artist created. As in a Surrealist painting, the unusual combination of elements in Lundeberg's work leads to new associations which alter traditional meanings. Unlike the Surrealists, however, Lundeberg has not employed automatism to release images directly from her unconscious. Rather, the artist has carefully designed the arrangement of elements to create pictorial unity. *Self-Portrait in a Tree* is evocative and poetic, yet the riddle of its private world remains unexplained. DM

NOTES

[1] Henry T. Hopkins, in *Lorser Feitelson and Helen Lundeberg: A Retrospective Exhibition* (San Francisco, CA: Museum of Modern Art, 1980), 13.

[2] Diane Degasis Moran, "Helen Lundeberg," in *Lorser Feitelson and Helen Lundeberg: A Retrospective Exhibition* (San Francisco, CA: Museum of Modern Art, 1980), 24.

[3] Ibid., 25.

PROVENANCE

Artist; Tobey Moss Gallery, Los Angeles, CA, until 1994; Norton Gallery, 1994.

EXHIBITION HISTORY

La Jolla Museum of Art, La Jolla, CA, *Helen Lundeberg Retrospective*, December 1971–February 1972.

Sesnon Art Gallery, University of California at Santa Cruz, Santa Cruz, CA, *Helen Lundeberg/A Retrospective View*, November–December 1988.

Palos Verdes Art Center, Palos Verdes, CA, *Two Views, 1970–1987: Helen Lundeberg & Martha Alf*, November 1987–January 1988.

Muckenthaler Art Center, Fullerton, CA, *Helen Lundeberg*, April–July 1990.

Tobey C. Moss Gallery, Los Angeles, CA, *California Modernists*, November–December 1990.

Los Angeles Art Association, Los Angeles, CA, *Lundeberg and Feitelson: Together Again*, February–March 1993.

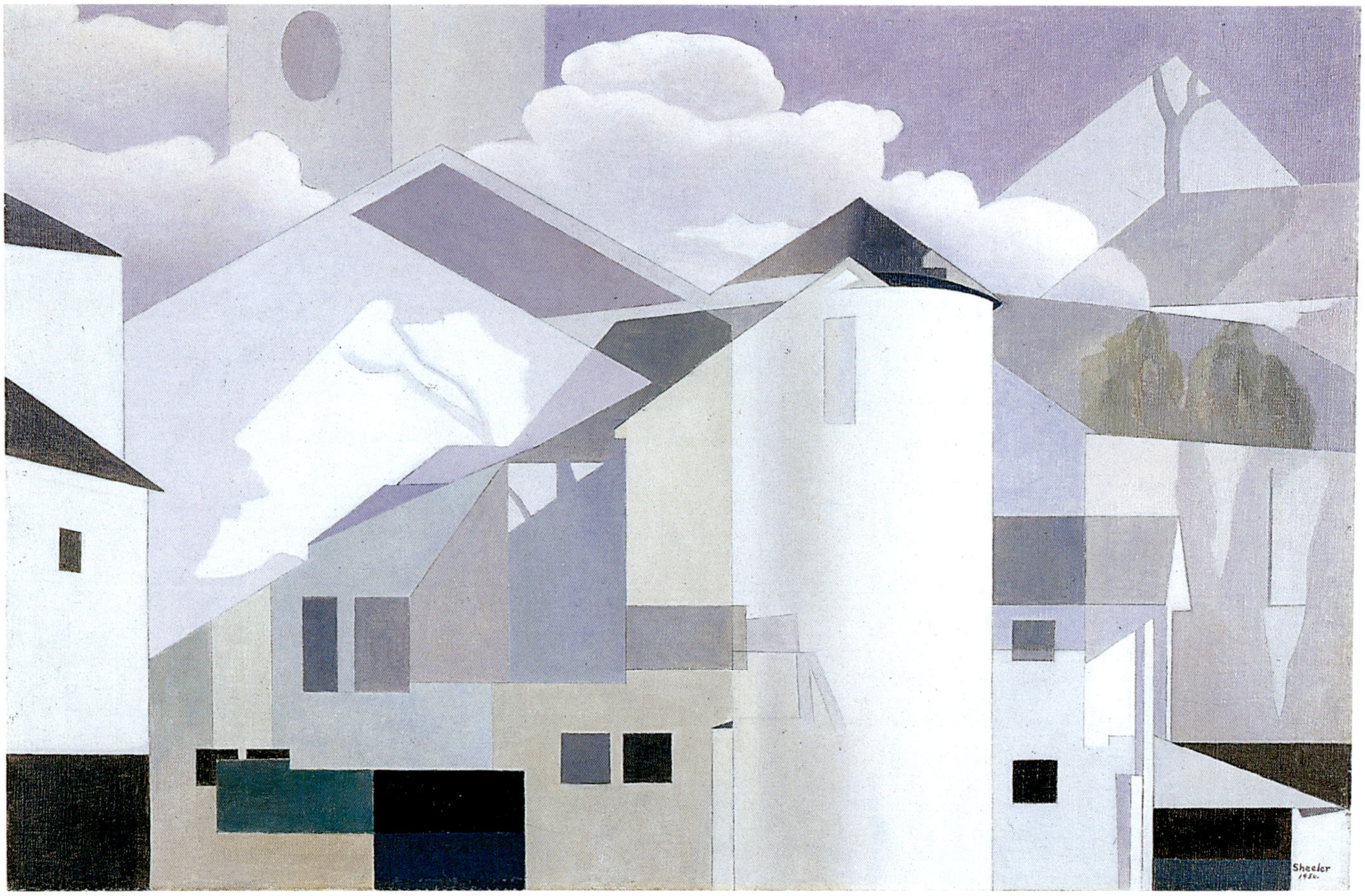

Shadow and Substance, 1950
Oil on canvas
20 x 30 in.
Bequest of R. H. Norton

Charles Sheeler

1883–1965

Charles Sheeler was among the first American artists to embrace European modernism. Best known today for his crisp, semi-abstract paintings of American industry and vernacular architecture, Sheeler was also an innovative photographer who helped established that medium as a fine art.

Born in Philadelphia, Sheeler received his training there as well, studying applied design at the School of Industrial Art, and painting at the Pennsylvania Academy of the Fine Arts, where his primary instructor was William Merritt Chase. Strongly influenced by Chase's flamboyant impressionist style, Sheeler's early work was characterized by a heavy, textural application of paint and a brilliant palette. In 1908, just two years after leaving the Academy, Sheeler had his first solo exhibition in Philadelphia and began exhibiting in New York.

Despite these encouragements, Sheeler found it difficult to support himself by painting, and in 1912, became an architectural photographer. What began as a necessity became an avocation, and within two years, Sheeler was exploring photography's artistic possibilities, as well as using his photographs as models for paintings.

In 1913, Sheeler exhibited six paintings in the landmark Armory Show exhibition in New York City. From that time forward, he became increasingly involved in the New York art scene. Visiting Alfred Stieglitz's progressive gallery, participating in the modernist gatherings at the home of Walter Arensberg, and working as an assistant in the Modern Gallery, Sheeler became well acquainted with the avant-garde movements and theories which were revolutionizing turn-of-the-century art.

Partially as a result of these experiences, Sheeler's painting took a new direction in the mid-1910s. Rejecting his earlier impressionistic style, Sheeler became interested in the work of modern European masters, such as Cézanne, and the Cubist painters Braque and Picasso. From these, he acquired a new appreciation of form, and he began to paint more sharply defined, linear compositions. This style, while influenced by Cubism, was closely related to Sheeler's photography and can also be traced to his early training in mechanical drawing.

Labeled "Precisionism" by contemporary critics, Sheeler's mature style was, in fact, architectonic in its clarity. Using a subdued palette and almost invisible brush strokes, Sheeler created deceptively simple images of both the modern industrial world and the rural vernacular past. Barns, factories, machinery, and Shaker interiors, for instance, were all painted in an abstract, yet entirely legible, style. With the eye of a photographer, Sheeler carefully selected his vantage point and cropped his images to maximize their power. Yet, while many of his paintings appear photorealistic, they vary considerably from his photographs of the same subjects, revealing his manipulation of light, shadow and composition to achieve desired effects.

In a career that spanned a half century, Sheeler's work never stagnated. Until his incapacitating stroke of 1959, Sheeler continued to develop new techniques, both in photography and painting, and to explore new avenues of artistic expression.

Shadow and Substance, 1950
Oil on canvas
20 x 30 in.
(l.r.: "Sheeler 1950")
Bequest of R. H. Norton 53.175

Sheeler first became interested in vernacular architecture through the barns of Bucks County, Pennsylvania, where he rented a weekend cottage during the 1910s. The proportionate relationships, contrasting textures, and underlying order of these functional structures made them ideal subjects for Sheeler's early studies in abstraction. Returning to the subject in 1950, Sheeler produced *Shadow and Substance*, a remarkably fresh interpretation of a familiar theme.

Although related to Sheeler's earlier experiments with Cubism, *Shadow and Substance* goes beyond the dissection of form and, as its title suggests, explores the nature of substance. In the late 1940s, Sheeler began experimenting with overlaying photographic negatives to create double exposures and, in *Shadow and Substance*, he translated this effect into paint.[1] By juxtaposing and overlapping transparent and solid shapes, Sheeler set up a contrast between tangible and intangible form, which he then enhanced by reversing their natural order. Thus, Sheeler's solidly painted clouds and shadows appear more substantial than his clearly outlined, but thinly painted buildings.

While strikingly innovative, *Shadow and Substance* nevertheless retains several elements which had distinguished Sheeler's earlier barn compositions. For example, by emphasizing the geometric rationality of the barns' design, Sheeler has rendered his ostensibly humble subject with classical dignity. Also, in common with earlier barn studies, *Shadow and Substance* contrasts realism and abstraction. Certain architectural elements, such as the nearly centered silo and profiled gables, are solidly painted and immediately recognizable, thereby anchoring the composition. By juxtaposing these relatively naturalistic elements with much flatter, abstracted shapes, Sheeler creates a lively tension between surface pattern and illusionary depth which is reminiscent of his earlier work.

In keeping with Sheeler's abstract objectives, the barns depicted in *Shadow and Substance* cannot be positively identified. Sheeler's early appreciation of Bucks County barns was later extended to those in New England and, by the time he painted *Shadow and Substance*, he was combining and superimposing elements from a variety of structures, eliminating individual details and textures to emphasize fundamental form. Ultimately, *Shadow and Substance* is most intriguing for the glimpse it provides of Sheeler's diligently refined, mature vision. AMB

NOTES

[1] This technique is thoroughly explained in Carol Troyen and Erica E. Hirshler, *Charles Sheeler: Paintings and Drawings* (Boston, MA: Little, Brown and Co., 1987), 42.

PROVENANCE

The Downtown Gallery; Norton Gallery, 1950.

EXHIBITION HISTORY

Whitney Museum of American Art, New York City, NY, *Contemporary American Painting*, November 10–December 31, 1950, no. 122.

Worcester Art Museum, Worcester, MA, *Painters Choice*, November 6–December 14, 1952, p. 3.

The Art Gallery, McCormick Place, Chicago, IL, *Inaugural Exhibition*, November 12–December 23, 1960, no. 21.

Allentown Art Museum, Allentown, PA, *Charles Sheeler Retrospective*, November 17–December 31, 1961, no. 40.

Atlanta Art Association Galleries, Atlanta, GA, *Landscape into Art*, February 6–25, 1962, no. 77.

Museum of Fine Arts, St. Petersburg, FL, *Masters from the Norton Gallery*, April 16–May 21, 1978.

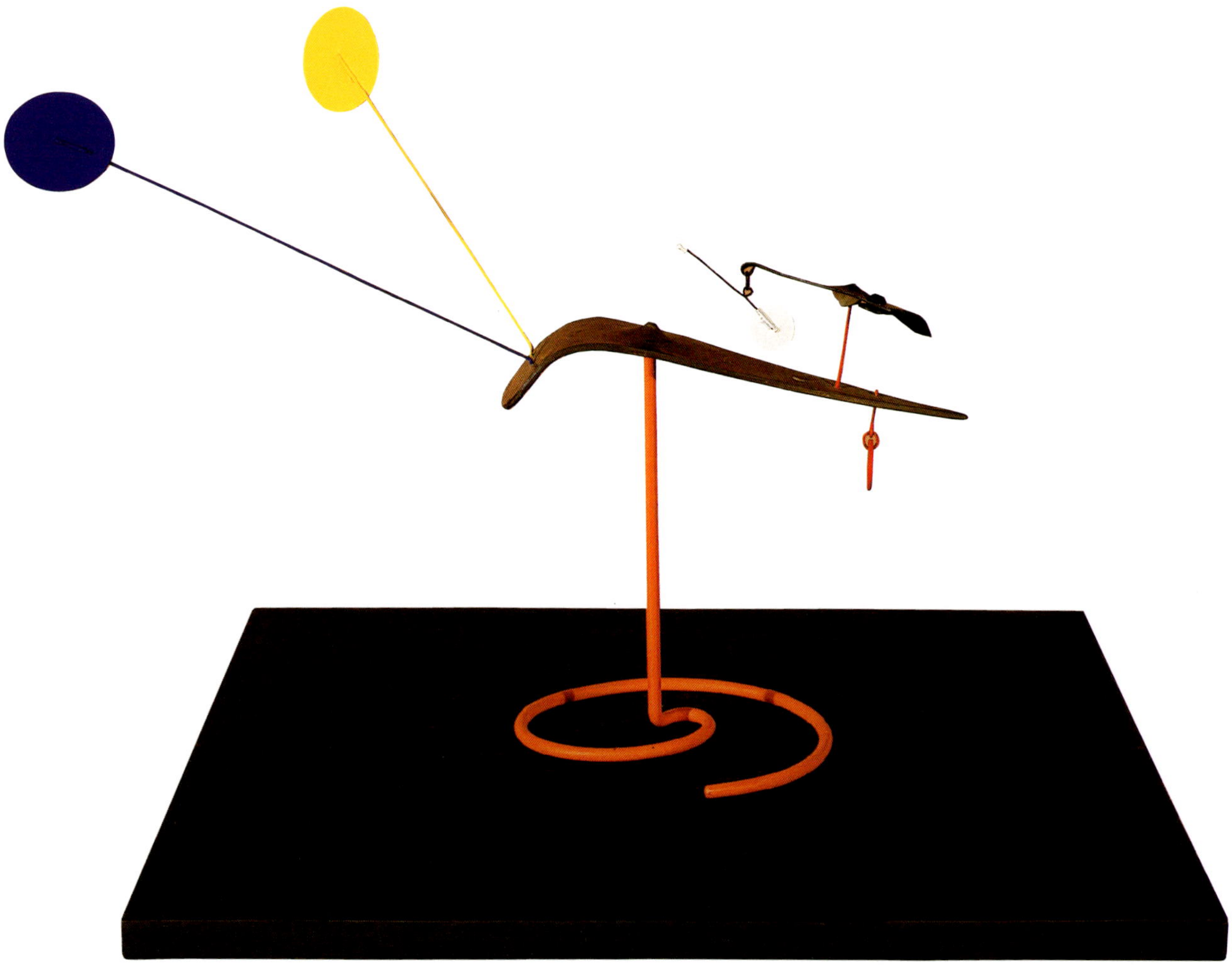

Brass Beak with Yellow and Blue Eyes, 1950
Painted metal
8 in.
Bequest of R. H. Norton

Alexander Calder

1898–1976

With a rare combination of whimsical creativity and technical sophistication, Alexander Calder substantially changed the concept of public sculpture in America. At a time when waning commissions for monumental sculpture were largely dominated by bronze, allegorical figures and heroes on horseback, Calder introduced his colorful creatures and kinetic abstractions, inspiring a resurgence in the patronage of public sculpture.

Although born into a family of painters and sculptors, Calder did not decide to become an artist until he was twenty-five.[1] Preparing instead for a career as a mechanical engineer, he entered Stevens Institute of Technology in Hoboken, New Jersey, receiving his degree in 1919. Calder's engineering career proved to be brief, but it provided him with a technical expertise that aided his later sculptural achievements.

Deciding to become a painter, Calder began attending courses at the Art Students League in 1923. Two years later, on assignment as a freelance illustrator, Calder went to the Ringling Brothers and Barnum and Bailey Circus and became inspired. Within a year, he was translating his outline drawings into a miniature circus in wire. Presenting his *Circus* in performances during the 1940s, Calder met many of the European modernists who would influence his subsequent artistic development, most notably Joan Miró and Piet Mondrian.

Calder met the Spanish surrealist Miró in 1928 and became interested in abstraction through Miro's biomorphic imagery. Visiting Mondrian's studio two years later, Calder had the sudden notion that Mondrian's more geometric abstractions might oscillate with great effect, an inspiration that eventually led to the mobiles which made Calder famous.[2]

Calder began exhibiting stationary, abstract sculptures, known as "stabiles," in 1931. The following year, he introduced his first kinetic sculptures. Comparatively simple, these first "mobiles" were hand-cranked or motorized machines and were soon succeeded by more graceful, wind-activated versions.

Calder's sculptural innovations owed a great deal to his early training. With an engineer's understanding of modern materials, tensile strength, and the physics of balance, Calder liberated sculpture from its traditional base and set it in motion. With the eye of a painter, he applied vivid color to his creations, animating them even further.

By 1950, Calder enjoyed an international reputation and, for the rest of his career, was inundated with commissions for monumental public sculpture. Nevertheless, he remained remarkably prolific in other areas, including illustrating and writing books, producing theatrical sets, and designing tapestries and lithographs.[3]

Today, Calder is generally recognized as a highly versatile artist and a founder of modern sculpture. With a rare combination of talents, Calder explored new avenues in three-dimensional expression and inspired a new generation of kinetic and abstract sculptors.

Brass Beak with Yellow and Blue Eyes, 1950
Painted metal
8 in.
(on beak: "CA")
Bequest of R. H. Norton 53.21

Brass Beak with Yellow and Blue Eyes is a delightful example of Calder's particular, witty approach to sculpture. Its abstracted animal form, delicate counterbalance, and skillful use of brilliant color all typify the singular appeal of Calder's mature style.

From cockroaches and spiders to elephants and lions, Calder enjoyed fashioning creatures in virtually every medium and scale. Birds were a favorite subject and although a few of these, such as his *Flamingo* in the Federal Center Plaza of Chicago, are monumental stabiles, most are moderately scaled mobiles that more nearly reflect the size and animation of their subjects.

In *Brass Beak with Yellow and Blue Eyes*, Calder has abstracted those features named in the title and used them in a playful balance to represent a bird. Set on an improbably thin, linear base, the triangular beak is delicately balanced by visually dissimilar, but nevertheless equal, counterweights. Moreover, Calder positioned the blue and yellow eye discs so that the slightest breeze will set the beak in motion, revolving and bobbing upon its base.

Color contributes immensely to the artful balance of this work. Using the primary colors along with black and white, Calder alternately increases and reduces the visual weight of his forms, while enhancing and reducing perceived distances between them.

In 1967, Calder returned to *Brass Beak with Yellow and Blue Eyes* to recreate a part which had been lost years before. Upon replacing the black and white balance which sits on top of the beak and repainting the sculpture, Calder signed its beak, suggesting his continued satisfaction with the bird he had created seventeen years earlier. AMB

NOTES

[1] Calder's father, Alexander Sterling Calder, and grandfather, Alexander Milne Calder, were both accomplished, academic sculptors. His mother, Nanette Lederer, was a painter.

[2] Patterson Sims, *Alexander Calder* (New York City, NY: Whitney Museum of American Art, 1981), 3–4.

[3] The Norton Gallery owns two additional works by Calder from this period: *Balloons*, 1973, lithograph; and *Spirales*, n.d., Aubusson tapestry.

PROVENANCE

Curt Valentin Gallery, Inc., New York City, NY, 1950; Ralph Norton, 1951; Norton Gallery, 1953.

EXHIBITION HISTORY

The American Federation of Arts, *Tradition and Experiment in Modern Sculpture*, travelling exhibition, 1951–1952, no. 2.

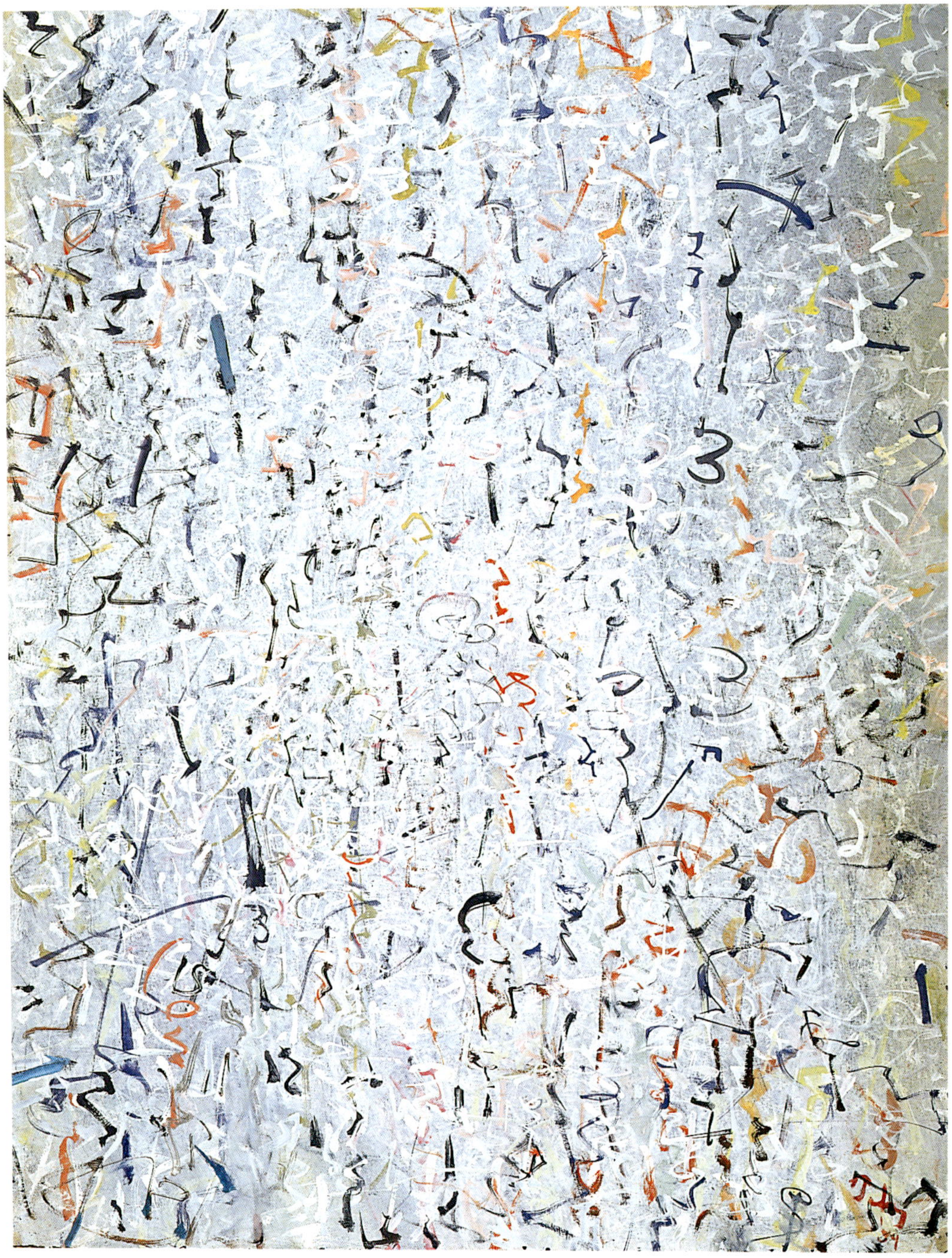

The Avenue, 1954
Tempera on paperboard
39 x 29 3/4 in.
Purchased through the R. H. Norton Fund

Mark Tobey

1890–1976

Mark Tobey's paintings are marked by "white writing," a manner of drawing light or white lines against a darker background. The realization of this abstract style came late in his career, after years of experimenting with representation. He spent his boyhood in the Midwest, and as a teenager, he studied at The Art Institute of Chicago. Although Tobey visited the Armory Show when it travelled to Chicago from New York in 1913, he was initially unimpressed by European avant-garde art. In those early years of his career, he did charcoal portraits, and the human image was a major motif in Tobey's art until the mid-1940s. His treatment of the figure swung from naturalistic to abstracted, and frequently, the human form was woven into a fragmented, Cubist framework.

In the years after the first World War, Tobey pursued an interest in a new visual language. His aesthetic was informed by the Bahá'í Faith to which he had converted in 1918. The creed of Bahá'í , a Persian religion founded in the nineteenth century, is based upon ideals of world unity and the relatedness of living beings. Applying Bahá'í to his visual art, Tobey argued against the hierarchies between form and ground, and the object and space. He envisioned a unified, dynamic expression, organized around the pleasing qualities of space, line, and color.[1] Tobey's holistic thinking was additionally influenced by calligraphy. In 1923, he moved to Seattle, where he taught at a progressive art school and studied Chinese calligraphy with artist Teng Kuei. Tobey adapted calligraphy's linearity to his art and adopted the spiritual and metaphysical discipline required of the calligrapher.

While Tobey is sometimes placed in the limiting, regionalist role of Seattle artist, he regularly visited and lived in numerous locales, among them Paris, Barcelona, Istanbul, Beirut, Hong Kong, and New York. His journeys were sometimes work related, as was the case when he intermittently taught in England between 1931 and 1938. Other trips were devoted to Bahá'í pilgrimages, tours of major art collections, and stays at Buddhist monasteries. For years, Tobey supported himself by teaching art, and this occupation afforded him a flexible schedule and the financial means to travel.

Tobey's "white writing" paintings date from 1935, and his first, *Broadway Norm* (Collection of Carol Ely Harper, Seattle), was painted while he was in England. White writing followed his investigations of Precisionism, Surrealism, organic abstraction, and calligraphy. Tobey hoped to break apart conventional form and open up the pictorial space. In his figurative pictures, white writing loosely depicts the "bright lights" aspect of urban life, while in nonreferential works, it is a linear network which appears to illuminate the composition. Through the 1930s and 1940s, he continued to paint representational and Cubist-influenced pictures, even as he assumed an increasingly abstract style.

Tobey gradually rose to prominence on the national art scene. In the 1930s and early 1940s, his work was seen at the Museum of Modern Art, The Art Institute of Chicago, and the Metropolitan Museum of Art. After a one-man exhibition at New York's Marion Willard Gallery in 1944, Tobey gained additional notoriety. Critics deemed him the successor to Paul Klee, the Swiss abstractionist whose ideographic style was known and admired by Tobey. Furthermore, Tobey benefited from growing acceptance in the United States of abstract art, and in particular, Abstract Expressionism. His international reputation spread rapidly. After the success of his one-man exhibition in Paris in 1955, Tobey—rather than his now well-known contemporary Jackson Pollock—became the most celebrated American artist in European circles. Representing the United States at the Venice Biennial twice during the 1950s, he won the competition's first prize in 1958. In 1960, the same year he declined to accept membership in the American Academy of Arts and Sciences, Tobey moved to Basel, Switzerland, where he lived until his death in 1976.[2]

The Avenue, 1954
Tempera on paperboard
39 x 29 3/4 in.
(l.r.: "Tobey '54")
Purchased through the R. H. Norton Fund 59.16

In *The Avenue*, Tobey's disciplined use of color is articulated in an array of contrasting brush lines. The full inventory of Tobey's "brush signs," as the art historian William C. Seitz termed them, is here—from the Art Nouveau arcs and zigzag flourishes, to the vibrating bolts and codified dashes and dots. Line charges the entire composition and, hence, supports Tobey's assertion that space is "a kind of living thing... all loaded with life."[3] The varied and layered brush strokes seem impetuously applied, and yet the convincing establishment of depth in the painting demonstrates the artist's ability to creatively evoke space and grounds.

The Avenue is a rejection of centralized images and illusory three-dimensionality. Tobey painted flatly and densely to convey a state of flux. Moreover, he believed that painting was a performance, and it is easy to link his application of the media in terms of musical and dance metaphors, considering his love of, and appreciation for, those arts. Arranged across the mauve canvas background, the lines of primary color and gray and white tones seem to perform. Like calligraphic characters, they dance to an infectious, improvisational rhythm.[4] *The Avenue* is smaller and less bombastic than Abstract Expressionist examples from the same period, notably, the signature drip paintings of Jackson Pollock and the heavily worked figuration of Willem de Kooning. Yet the Norton's painting, too, belongs to the decade of action painting. Tobey shared with these virtuosos of the large canvas, a concern with implied motion and process. Gesture, in a realized form on the canvas and in the artist's practice, is central to an appreciation of Tobey's art. He painted physically, dancing before the easel, and lightly wielding his brush so that it moved sprightly across the canvas surface.[5] Tobey's active approach was similar to Pollock's, and the artists may have influenced each other.

Tobey painted in an abstract manner, and yet he maintained that his works, unlike pure abstraction, were connected to life and its experiences. Typically, his titles are referential and locate his source of inspiration. One interpretation of *The Avenue* holds that the painting's palette evokes city smog, fog, and lights, and that its multi-directional lines suggest urban crowds and their movements. Swirls and strokes may resemble fragmented, architectural elements, signs, and other aspects of visual cacophony in the modern city. While Tobey's brush strokes may be linked to urban iconography, they are abstract enough to suggest the artist's deep reflection upon the subject, and subsequently, his nonfigurative rendering of modern urban life.

Painted in New York City during a time of intense productivity for the artist, *The Avenue* is distinct from other cityscapes. It is significantly larger than his preceding works and may have been a response to his dealer's request that he paint larger pictures to satisfy an audience clamoring for expansive Abstract Expressionist-type canvases. However, as the art historian Eliza Rathbone has observed, Tobey did not directly convert to this influential avant-garde style. Instead, he followed his career-long tendency to experiment and improvise, especially according to meditative approaches traditionally practiced by Asian artists.[6] For a brief period in 1957, Tobey worked in the broad brush and black ink style of Japanese *sumi*. While some of these compositions are large, others are not, and the variation in their scale and the presentation of the medium (from a flung looseness to a dense painterliness) indicate that the artist sought to plumb the range of expressive possibility.

In subsequent decades, Tobey broadened his palette to include diverse chromatic harmonies and more intense, background hues. Collaged elements also appeared in his later work, giving it a vitality and decorative energy. JF

NOTES

[1] Fred Hoffman, "Mark Tobey's Paintings of New York," *Artforum* 17 (April 1979): 26; Katherine Kuh, "Mark Tobey," in *The Artist's Voice* (New York City, NY: Harper and Row, 1962): 236, 240.

[2] Major biographers have not explained Tobey's refusal of the honor.

[3] William C. Seitz, *Mark Tobey* (New York City, NY: Museum of Modern Art, 1962), 22–23.

[4] Eliza C. Rathbone, "The Role of Music in the Development of Mark Tobey's Abstract Style," *Arts* 58 (December 1983): 99.

[5] Ibid.

[6] Eliza C. Rathbone, *Mark Tobey: City Paintings* (Washington, D.C.: National Gallery of Art, 1984), 99.

PROVENANCE

Artist, 1954–59; Norton Gallery, 1959.

EXHIBITION HISTORY

Museo d'Arte Moderna, Venice, Italy, XXIX Biennale d'Arte, *U.S. Representation: Lipton, Rothko, Smith, Tobey*, June 14–October 19, 1958, no. 57.

Museum of Modern Art, New York City, NY, *Mark Tobey*, September 17– November 4, 1962.

Whitney Museum of American Art, New York City, NY, *Between the Fairs: 25 Years of American Art, 1939 to 1964*, June 24–September 23, 1964, no. 129.

National Gallery of Art, Washington, D.C., *The White House Festival of the Arts*, June 15–July 11, 1965.

Museum of Fine Arts, St. Petersburg, FL, *Modern Masters from the Norton Gallery*, April 16–May 21, 1978.

National Gallery of Art, Washington, D.C., *Mark Tobey: City Paintings*, March 18–June 17, 1984, no. 40.

José de Creeft

1884–1982

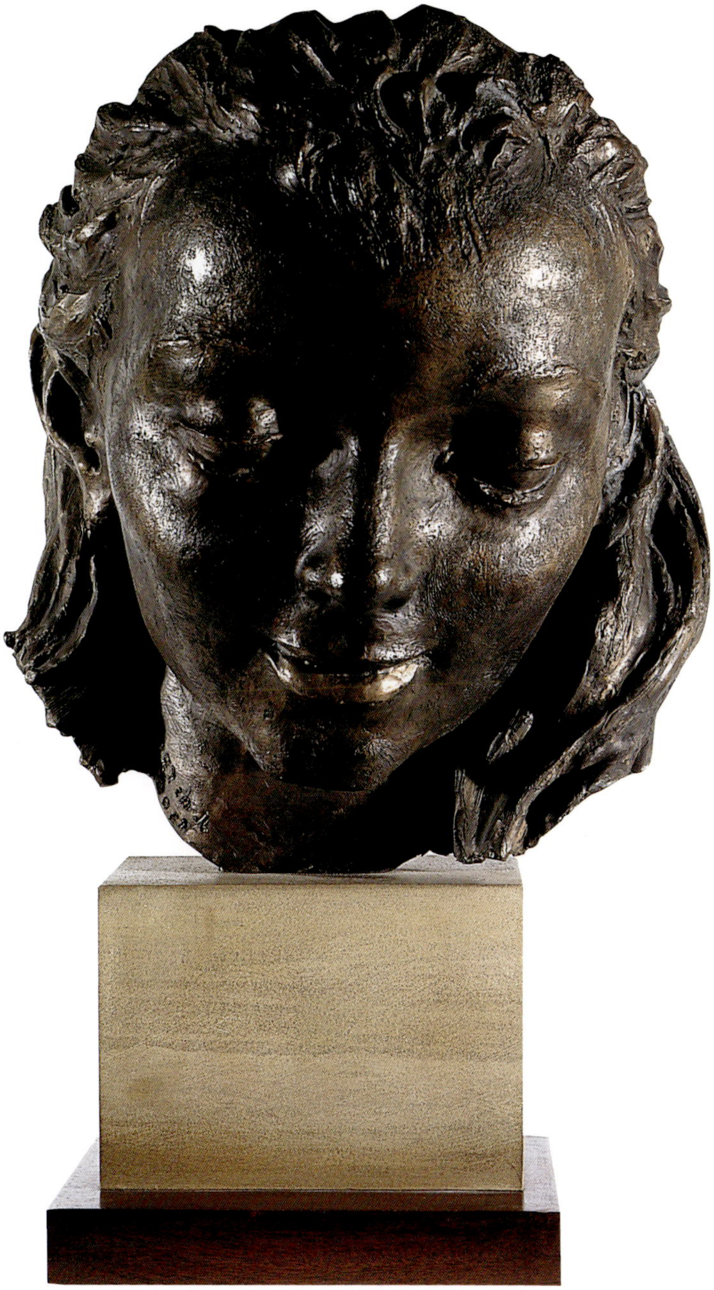

Alice (Head of Alice in Wonderland), ca. 1960
Bronze
21 x 14 in.
Gift of George T. Delacorte

José de Creeft, 1884–1982

José de Creeft's formal education in Europe provided him with the skills of modelling and casting which allowed him later to pursue his own artistic techniques. In his native Spain, de Creeft served as an apprentice under the government's official sculptor Augustín Querol, and in Paris, he enrolled at the Académie Julian, an internationally renowned center of conservative artistic training. According to the Académie's program at the turn of the century, de Creeft learned to create small clay or plaster models, which trained craftsmen then translated into full-size works using precise measuring devices. De Creeft succeeded with this method, but he soon left the Académie to study the carving skills of the craftsmen who actually executed the works in stone or cast metal. Joining the commercial sculpture firm Maison Greber, de Creeft learned the techniques of carving and sculpting that would inspire him to carve directly onto his own chosen medium.

By carving his images by hand in wood or stone without the use of models, de Creeft became part of a leading avant-garde sculptural movement in the United States, "direct carving." Many U.S. sculptors, including John Flannagan, Robert Laurent, and William Zorach, had begun to revive the method when de Creeft arrived in this country in 1929. De Creeft described the importance of each unique medium for the final sculptural outcome: "Materials have qualities which will speak to you if you, listen."[1] De Creeft's carvings illustrate his constant interaction with the particularities of each individual piece of wood or stone. This is often manifest through the elegant patterns created by de Creeft's sculptural forms and the natural grain of his chosen medium.

Always a versatile artist, de Creeft was not limited to direct carving methods in wood and stone, and throughout his career, he continued to work in a variety of techniques and with a range of different materials. He did not reject the use of clay and plaster models altogether, and continued to use them for his cast-metal pieces. While his directly carved sculptures tend to be more abstract, de Creeft's cast pieces are often more traditional portraits or figural subjects.

De Creeft also ventured into the Cubist constructionism popular with his colleagues in Spain, and he created several witty sculptural constructions of found, man-made objects. Above all, however, de Creeft continued to uphold his artistic ideals by having direct contact with each individual sculpture and its materials throughout the entire creative process.

After numerous awards, commissions, exhibitions, and a distinguished teaching career, de Creeft died in New York City in 1982, the year before a major retrospective of his work at the National Museum of American Art.

Alice (Head of Alice in Wonderland), ca.1960
Bronze
21 x 14 in.
(l.r.: "J. de Creeft/1 of 8")
Gift of George T. Delacorte 83.17

Alice is a bronze cast made from a larger sculptural group, *Alice in Wonderland*, commissioned for New York City's Central Park by George Delacorte as a memorial to his wife Margarita. This bronze sculpture may have been cast shortly after the sculptural group, perhaps as a personal commission from Mr. Delacorte. This work appears to be identical to the head of Alice in the Central Park sculptural group, but it seems to have been conceived of by de Creeft as an aesthetic whole.

Alice recalls many of de Creeft's female portraits. The female figure is central to de Creeft's oeuvre, not only in realistic portraits, but also in figural abstractions. For a young girl, *Alice* has a certain sophistication, but she displays much more naïveté and simplicity than in de Creeft's depictions of older females. De Creeft's portrayal of Alice as a smiling, innocent child, however, may have been the result of a conscious attempt to make her more youthful. His previous plaster cast had been criticized by the Park Commission for its too mature depiction of Alice, and de Creeft was requested to change her expression for the final sculpture group.[2]

De Creeft's first exhibition consisted of children's portraits, and he continued to do portrait heads of famous and fictional persons throughout his career, many cast in bronze. Although bronze casting was not de Creeft's most innovative sculptural work, he continued to use the medium, especially for portraits. Besides a certain permanence of the metal itself, de Creeft may have found the more traditional techniques of modelling and bronze casting appropriate for portraiture. The use of plaster models for commissioned sculptures may also have allowed for preliminary changes that otherwise would have been impossible.

Like de Creeft's other bronze portraits, *Alice* betrays the artist's admiration for the powerful sculpture of Auguste Rodin, whom de Creeft met in Paris in 1905. Although de Creeft's works often do not appear as "unfinished" as Rodin's, his sympathy with the famous sculptor surfaces in many of de Creeft's bronze sculptures. *Alice*, with the rough edges around her hair, creates an aesthetic similar to the energetic forms of Rodin's sculptures, and the textural variations on Alice's skin and eyelids also recall the work of the French sculptor.

De Creeft created the *Alice in Wonderland* sculptural group as an addition to the pool area for children near the Conservatory in Central Park. Constructed according to the design of Fernando Texidor, de Creeft's commission from the Delacorte Foundation was completed within four years, and the dedication of the finished work took place on May 7, 1959. Other public sculpture projects occupied de Creeft during this time, and like the *Alice* group, these allowed the artist to work with larger, more complex arrangements, intended for a specific audience.[3] With the *Alice* group, de Creeft had his own seven-year-old daughter in mind. "While the style and material is not my usual, I like the subject and accepted the commission at the urging of my daughter, Donna. I built in areas as steps for climbing, made all surfaces and edges smooth so kids won't get hurt or tear clothing...."[4] LTJ

NOTES

[1] Jules Campos, *The Sculpture of José de Creeft* (New York City, NY: Da Capo Press, 1972), 14. The primary source for dates and biographical information is Adelyn Breeskin, *José de Creeft: Sculpture and Drawings* (Washington, D.C.: National Museum of American Art, 1983).

[2] José de Creeft, "Correspondence and material on 'Alice in Wonderland' sculpture in Central Park, New York," de Creeft Papers, Archives of American Art, microfilm roll D150.

[3] These commissions included: the Ellen Phillips Samuel memorial in Fairmount Park, Philadelphia (1949); a mosaic mural for the nurses' residence at the Bronx Municipal Hospital Center (1962); and a relief for the Public Health Laboratory at Bellevue Hospital in New York City, NY (1966). Breeskin, 25, 37.

[4] Frederick Fried, *New York Civic Sculpture: A Pictorial Guide* (New York City, NY: Dover Publications, 1976), 110. Breeskin, 36.

PROVENANCE

George T. Delacorte; Norton Gallery, 1983.

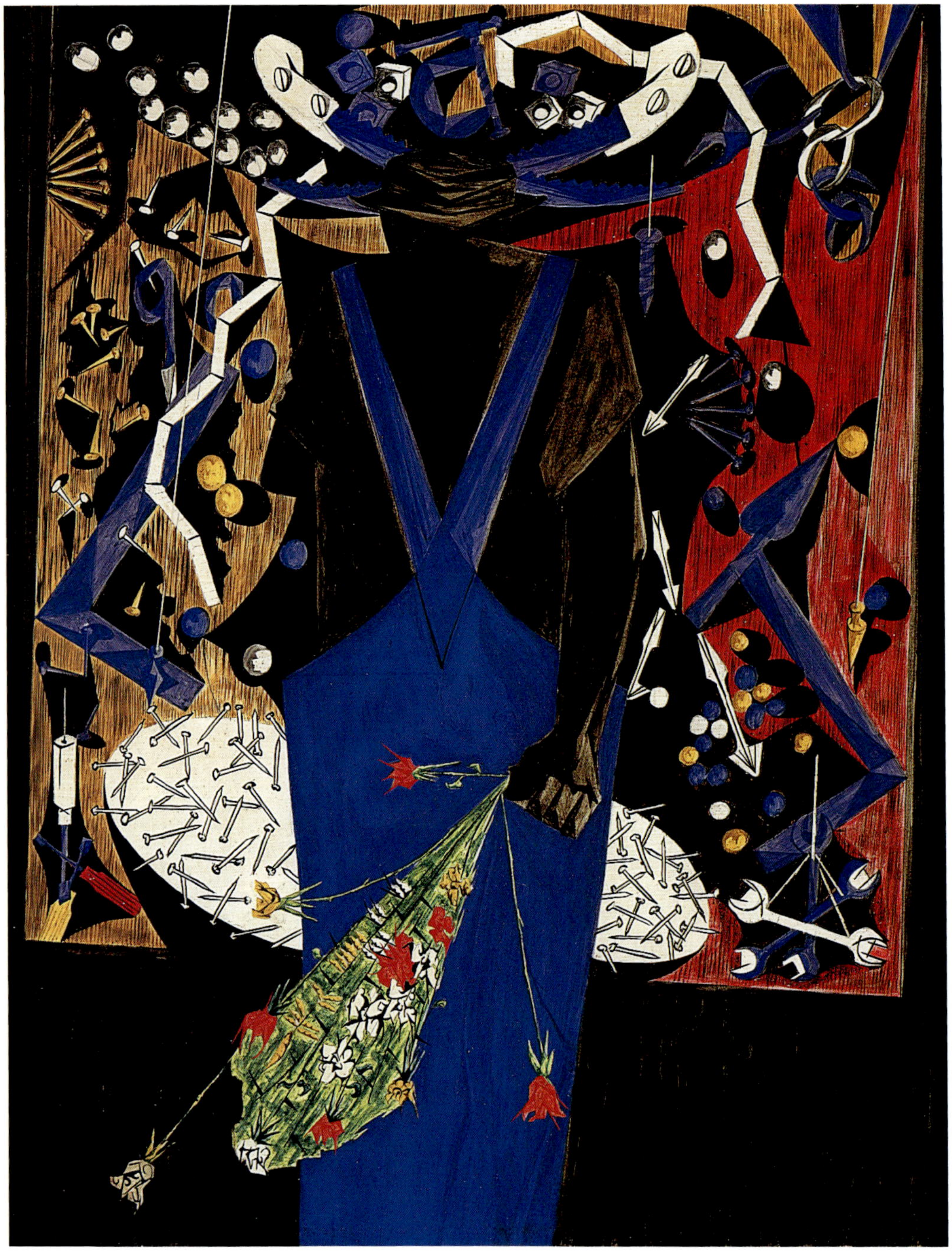

Man with Flowers, 1954
Tempera on gessoed masonite
15 3/4 x 11 3/4 in.
Purchased through the R. H. Norton Fund

Jacob Lawrence

1917–

A prolific artist, Jacob Lawrence established a signature style of figural expression early in his career. He continues to employ an economic language of line and color to translate historical subjects, as well as ordinary and everyday images, into powerful dramas.

Born in Atlantic City, New Jersey, Lawrence was a child of "The Great Migration," the exodus of black southerners which began during World War I and continued through mid-century. His parents separated in 1924, and Lawrence's mother moved her three children to New York City where the artist began his training in 1930. At the Utopia Children's House, a Children's Aid Society program in Harlem offering an after-school arts and crafts curriculum, Lawrence studied with Charles Alston, an African-American painter. He also worked with the African-American sculptor Henry Bannarn at the Harlem Art Workshop from 1932–1934. Lawrence continued to study with these two artists when the workshop, at first housed in a public library, moved to Alston's and Bannarn's studio at 306 West 141st Street. Called "306" for short, this studio was the Harlem headquarters for a Work Projects Administration (WPA) art program, and it attracted the African-American literati, among them the writers Countee Cullen and Langston Hughes, and the art historian Alain Locke.[1] "306" was Lawrence's haunt, an environment in which he received encouragement to develop his talent. His colorful tempera works on paper from this period bear evidence of the artist's precocious design sensibility and interest in painting the Harlem scene.

In 1936, Lawrence journeyed outside the Harlem community to the American Artists School in downtown Manhattan, where he studied with the painters Anton Refregier and Philip Reisman. Social realists, Reisman and Refregier likely fueled the young artist's desire to make African-American experiences and history the subject of his art. Lawrence began his practice of history painting in 1938 with *Toussaint L'Ouverture* (The Amistad Research Center's Aaron Douglas Collection, New Orleans), a forty-one panel series on the life of the eighteenth-century Haitian revolutionary. Subsequent biographical series on the African-American abolitionists Frederick Douglass, 1939, and Harriet Tubman, 1940, (both in Hampton University Museum, Hampton, Virginia) were exhibited in New York, Baltimore, and Washington, D.C., garnering increased public notice for the young artist. While he worked as an easel painter for the WPA art projects from 1938–1939, Lawrence was also recognized as a narrative painter who frequently expanded his ideas beyond a single frame.

The success of Lawrence's 1940–1941 series *The Migration of the Negro* (The Phillips Collection, Washington, D.C. and the Museum of Modern Art, New York), accelerated his professional career. Like the preceding series, *The Migration* is a multipanel series of bold, flatly painted images accompanied by prosaic captions. However, this series is distinctive for its collective subject—the anonymous Black masses—and its successful communication of the unrelenting tide of human movement. In the 1940s, *The Migration* was exhibited widely, opening at Edith Halpert's Downtown Gallery in New York and travelling to The Phillips Collection in Washington, D.C. and other major art venues.

Throughout the 1940s and 1950s, when Abstract Expressionism burgeoned and became the dominant style, Lawrence maintained his preference for figural expression. Drafted into the Coast Guard in 1943, he painted energetic scenes of ship life for the 1947 *War* series (The Whitney Museum of American Art). The *Hospital* series, 1950 (various collections), is based on his nine-month stay in a psychiatric hospital for treatment for depression. Lawrence also experimented with a more decorative and compositionally complex style during this period. His representations were more delicately drawn, and his palette expanded to include sparkling hues.

During the 1960s, Lawrence travelled to Nigeria, making the West African crossroads and marketplaces the subjects of his paintings. The civil rights struggle in the United States was another theme in his repertoire. Although his art is frequently categorized under the rubric of protest art, Lawrence has rejected that term. "I never use the term 'protest' in connection with my paintings. They just deal with the social scene.... They're how I feel about things." [2]

For much of his career, Lawrence has combined his artistic pursuit with a teaching career, holding posts at Black Mountain College, Pratt Institute, Brandeis University, the New School for Social Research, and the University of Washington at Seattle. Recognized by his peers as a modern master, Lawrence was named to the National Institute of Arts and Letters in 1965 and to the American Academy of Arts and Letters in 1983. His late career has been distinguished by his publication of print portfolios, children's literature, and mural commissions throughout the United States.

Man with Flowers, 1954
Tempera on gessoed masonite
15 3/4 x 11 3/4 in.
(l.l.: "Jacob Lawrence 54")
Purchased through the R. H. Norton Fund 95.21

In 1968 Jacob Lawrence began to explore the theme of "Builders"—images of working carpenters surrounded by their tools and building materials. Lawrence's fascination with tools stems from his childhood in Harlem. Recalling his interaction with cabinetmakers in that community, Lawrence has said that he found their tools "aesthetically beautiful, like sculpture." [3] Like the thematically related *Cabinetmakers*, 1946, and *Cabinetmaker*, 1957, (both in the Hirshhorn Museum and Sculpture Garden, Washington, D.C.), *Man with Flowers* is a significant and prescient articulation of Lawrence's "Carpenter Cubism." [4]

The Norton's painting is a frame within a frame as the viewer observes a man standing before a galaxy of tools and building materials. The figure, rendered as a simple form of planar color areas, strikes a pose that resembles our own as we size up the art object. But the exaggerated scale of Lawrence's human subject borders on the massive: this form is monolithic. Like a nervous suitor, the man holds the bouquet behind his back, and his mallet-like fist threatens to crush the fragile rose stems. Although his grasp is awkward, this ordinary and anonymous person enjoys beauty through the flowers that he holds and the ornamental materials upon which he gazes.

Man with Flowers presents an opportunity to expand and examine common notions of beauty. In most of Lawrence's "Builders" paintings, meaning is derived from the symmetry and refinement of tools wielded by able craftsmen. The Norton's painting, in contrast, is not a workshop scene. Its able-bodied hero is contemplative, and, perhaps, pondering the essential nature of things in his world. Closest to the picture plane are the complementary-colored flowers, their delicacy communicated through Lawrence's rendering of filament-thin stems. In contrast, the bouquet is bounded by a strict, mechanical outline that is diametrically opposed to the free-floating tools and building materials. The inventory of objects includes nuts, screws, nails, measuring tape, and chain links, and it is testament to Lawrence's appreciation for the simple and practical structure of craft instruments. These implements are expressly transformed into objects d'art: criss-crossed wrenches, saws, and wood chisels are arranged like mobiles; trompe l'oeil nails are spread into an elegant fan pattern; and weighted balls are colored and shaded to contribute to the painting's color scheme. These items of craft are integral to the picture: their heft, mass, and sharpened points create elliptical voids, wedges, and graceful arcs in the grainy mid-ground picture plane. All the depicted tools are hand-held ones that require the manual effort and the imaginative input of the human agent.

The moment of meditation depicted in *Man with Flowers* lends itself to metaphoric interpretation. As emblems of beauty, the plumb and flower stems are aesthetic equivalents, each constructed with a graceful, linear element. Lawrence effectively establishes the parallel between the natural and man-made worlds, with the figure mediating between these realms and confronting beauty in its distinct manifestations. Nonetheless, Lawrence' s intention in *Man with Flowers* and in the "Builders" works that would follow it, is to place human activity at the center of his art. For Lawrence, the human body is yet another beautiful and functional tool, and in his images of working people, he communicates his belief in human kind's constructive potential. JF

NOTES

[1] Ellen Harkins Wheat, *Jacob Lawrence: American Painter* (Seattle, WA: University of Washington Press, 1986), 30.

[2] Ibid., 114.

[3] Ibid., 143.

[4] Robert Pincus-Warren, "Jacob Lawrence: Carpenter Cubism," *Artforum* 13 (September 1974): 67. Pincus-Warren used this term to describe Lawrence's pragmatic and figural translation of Cubism.

PROVENANCE

Artist, 1954; Leonard and Ruth Bocour, 1954; Midtown Payson Galleries, New York City, NY, 1994; Norton Gallery, 1995.

EXHIBITION HISTORY

American Federation of Arts, New York City, NY, *Jacob Lawrence* (retrospective exhibition), 1960.

Whitney Museum of American Art, New York City, NY, *Jacob Lawrence*, May 16–July 7, 1974.

Midtown Payson Galleries, New York City, NY, *Jacob Lawrence: An Overview, Paintings, 1935–1994*, January 12–February 25, 1994.

Sam Francis

1923–1994

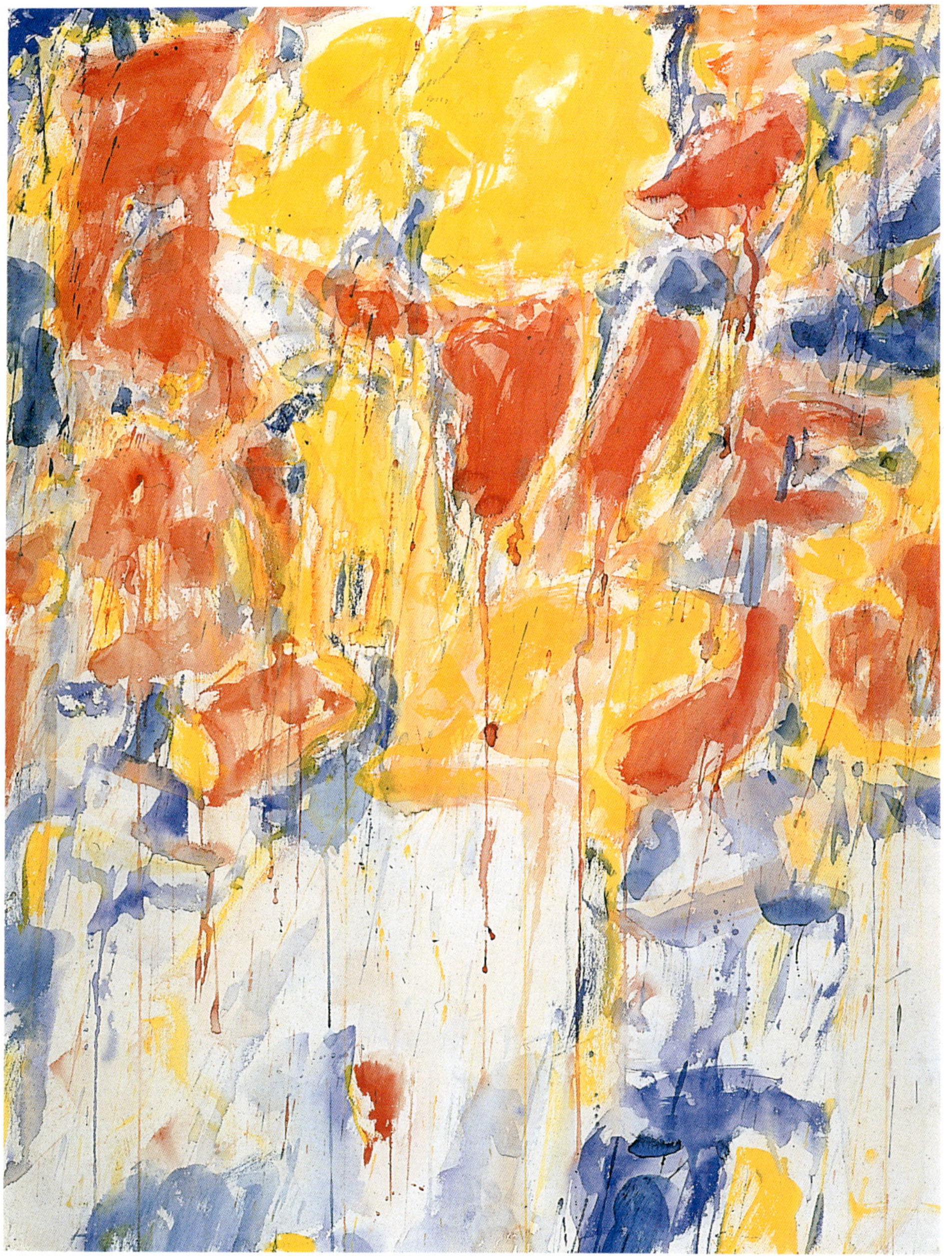

Untitled, 1956
Watercolor on paper
30 3/4 x 22 3/4 in.
Gift of Michael and Elizabeth Rea

Sam Francis, 1923–1994

Sam Francis is one of the rare masters of twentieth-century painting whose art transcends national boundaries and regional categorization. Born in San Mateo, California, his early interests included literature and Eastern philosophy. In 1941, Francis entered the University of California at Berkeley to study botany, later changing his major to psychology and medicine. Francis left college, after two years, to serve in the Army Air Corps during World War II, but an accident in a training plane left him confined to bed for several years with a severe spinal injury. While recuperating in 1944, Francis made his first paintings from his hospital bed. The artist recalled, "Painting became a way back to life for me.... I painted to stay alive." [1]

After his three-year hospital stay, Francis moved to Carmel, California, where he joined a small colony of artists and writers. His early paintings include Cubist portraits and fantastic landscapes inspired by Giorgio de Chirico, Joan Miró, and Paul Klee. Determined to be a painter, he returned to the University of California at Berkeley to study art and art history, earning his Bachelor of Arts degree in 1949 and his Master of Arts degree in the following year.

The legacy of Hans Hofmann, who had taught art at Berkeley during the 1930s, influenced Francis to work towards greater abstraction in his painting. However, the work of Clyfford Still and Mark Rothko, both of whom had taught at the California School of Fine Arts in San Francisco during the late 1940s, had the most profound influence on the young artist. Francis was especially drawn to Rothko's floating, biomorphic shapes and to the saturated hues applied in thin layers of translucent oil washes which seemed to breath pure light. Unlike Rothko, Francis was not concerned with mythic content, but with his painting materials as a vehicle for the expression of his immediate experiences of nature in a personal, abstract idiom.

In 1950, Francis moved to Paris and spent the next eight years painting, exhibiting, and travelling throughout Europe and Asia. His paintings evolved from large, nearly monochromatic canvases, across which pale, cellular shapes drifted through an atmospheric haze resembling the Paris sky, into images in which bold primary colors saturate large, organic shapes, vying for position within the picture plane. The vibrant, light-filled colors of his paintings during the mid-1950s can be compared to the brilliant colors of the sun-bathed landscape in the south of France where Francis travelled during this time, and to the light-filled atmosphere on the coast of his native California.

Already well known in Europe, in 1956 Francis's work was introduced to the American public in the *Twelve Americans* exhibition at the Museum of Modern Art in New York. In 1959, the artist moved to New York, and three years later, he settled in Santa Monica, California, where he lived until his death in 1994.

Untitled, 1956
Watercolor on paper
30 3/4 x 22 3/4 in.
(no inscription)
Gift of Michael and Elizabeth Rea 91.43

Many of Sam Francis's admirers view the period of this watercolor as the finest period of the artist's work. By the mid-1950s, the artist had restricted his palette to the three primary colors and had focused his work on the dual concerns of space and color. As in many of his oils and watercolors, the intense areas of vibrant, saturated colors in this painting are confined within large, amorphous, cellular shapes which seem to push together in the top of the image, exposing the white of the paper below. The vivid reds and yellows seem to pulsate as they bulge against the contours of their shapes, which are bounded by flowing washes of blue. These crowded color cells contrast sharply with the large areas of stark white paper which are visible below, in the lower half of the image, and in small patches throughout the composition. The white ceases to function as mere background or support, as the saturated areas of color appear to push against the empty void to establish a dynamic tension. The drips of paint which trickle down towards the bottom of the paper intensify the downward propulsion of the large color cells. The thinness of the paint in certain spots, however, combined with the patches of white paper that peek through even the most densely painted color areas, emphasize that the masses of color which jostle for space above the energized void are only thin layers of pigment applied to the flat surface of the paper.

For the artist, beauty in his painting results from the union of opposites. "One image contains all imaginable pairs of opposites, therefore, all things are called by one name."[2] Though not interested in conveying epic themes or allusions to mystical truths, Francis communicates on a fundamental level, establishing a dialectic in his paintings between the presence of color and the absence of the void. His painting explores the energy which can be created with liquid paint and paper alone. In his insistence on exploring the possibilities of color and space—two basic elements of art—Francis has been compared to Piet Mondrian, Yves Klein, and Barnett Newman, three of the most highly regarded masters of twentieth-century art.[3] DM

NOTES

[1] Diane W. Upright, "Sam Francis in the 1950s," in *Sam Francis: The Fifties* (Washington, D.C.: The Phillips Collection, 1980), 7.

[2] Pontus Hulten, *Sam Francis* (Bonn, Germany: Kunst- und Austellungshalle der Bundesrepublik Deutschland, 1993), 54.

[3] Ibid., 23, 25; see also Robert Elkon, "Introduction," in *Sam Francis: The Fifties*, (Washington, D.C.: The Phillips Collection, 1980), 5.

PROVENANCE

Robert Elkon Gallery, New York City, NY; Mr. and Mrs. Michael Rea, Washington, CT; Norton Gallery, 1991.

EXHIBITION HISTORY

The Phillips Collection, Washington, D.C., *Sam Francis: The Fifties*, March 1–April 13, 1980, no. 19.

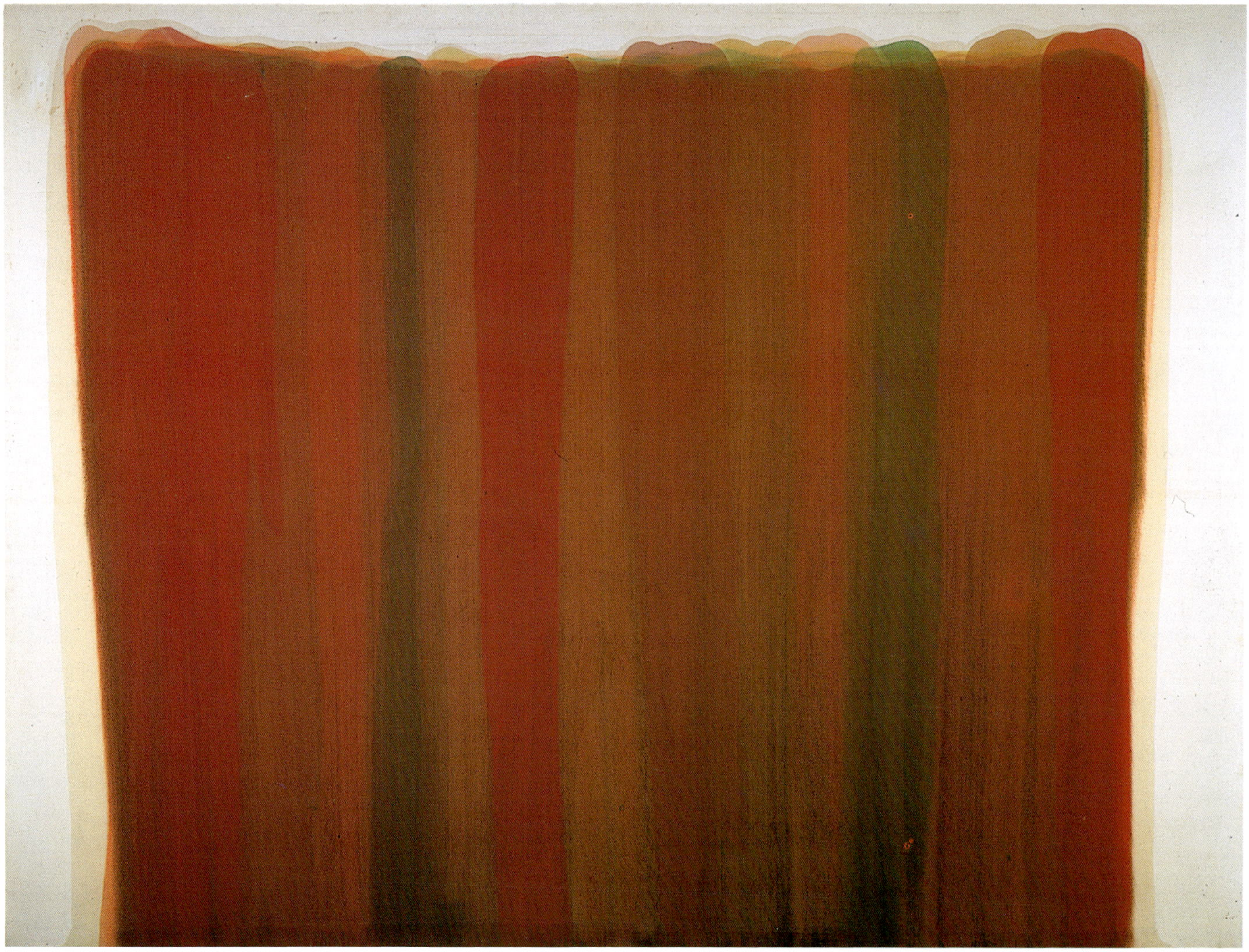

Autumnal, 1959
Acrylic on canvas
73 3/4 x 104 in.
Gift of Mrs. Dorothy H. Rautbord

Morris Louis

MORRIS LOUIS BERNSTEIN, 1912–1962

Among the more important additions to the modernist canon are the color-stained paintings made by Morris Louis during the last eight years of his life. His belief in the communicative quality of color reflected a formalist concern shared by the Abstract Expressionists, and yet, Louis' explorations also refute the personalized expression of that style. Influenced by the dictum of the critic Clement Greenberg, Louis strove to make "painting about its own means."[1]

Louis' commitment to color abstraction was made late in his career. Born in Baltimore, he studied at the Maryland Institute of Fine Arts from 1927–1932. During the Depression, he worked on federal art projects, first in Baltimore, and then in New York City. Louis' earliest surviving paintings—expressionist landscapes and neoclassical portraits—demonstrate his admiration for Max Beckmann, but increasingly, he assimilated Cubism and Surrealist automatism. By the 1940s, Louis had moved permanently to the Washington, D.C., area and was participating in local art competitions and exhibitions.

Louis' color purism began in 1954 and manifested itself in three innovative series: "Veils," "Unfurleds," and "Stripes." In April of the previous year, Louis and Kenneth Noland, a fellow Washington artist, visited New York City to meet artists and critics and to survey the contemporary art scene. Louis' veils are particularly indebted to one painting he saw in New York: Helen Frankenthaler's 1952 masterpiece *Mountains and Sea* (Collection of Helen Frankenthaler). Her method of staining canvas soon became Louis's preferred method as well. In two periods of veil production, 1954 and 1958–1959, he poured acrylic paint on expanses of unstretched, unsized canvas, creating layered, atmospheric compositions that take on the texture of the canvas itself. His next major paintings, the "Unfurleds" of 1960–1961, are characteristically defined by ribbons of paint poured across the lower corners of the picture. In the "Stripes" of 1961–1962, the tension and drama of chromatic relationships are generated from the juxtaposition of the color bands and their vibration against the white ground.

Louis' career was launched with the support of the New York art critic Clement Greenberg, whom he met in the mid-1950s and with whom he corresponded regularly. Greenberg periodically visited Louis in Washington to critique his paintings and to encourage the artist to work in a manner that would distinguish his art. Louis respected the critic's opinions, and at one point, destroyed more than 300 of his paintings that he and Greenberg believed were inferior. Despite the rashness of this act, Louis still managed to produce paintings in significant numbers, and Greenberg brought his work to the attention of the art world. A 1959 exhibition organized by Greenberg for French & Company earned the artist critical acclaim. The following year, Louis had four, one-man shows and was heralded in art journals. Seen in European as well as American art venues, his work was placed on the cutting edge of modernist art.

In the summer of 1962, Louis was stricken with lung cancer which rendered him unable to paint. He died at home in September 1962. Louis' artistic stature continued to grow in the years following his death because his work demonstrated that abstraction without symbols could successfully express beauty and offer meaning. He has come to be regarded as a transitional figure between two generations of painters: the Abstract Expressionists and the practitioners of Minimalism and color field abstraction.

Autumnal, 1959
Acrylic on canvas
78 3/4 x 104 in.
(no inscription)
Gift of Mrs. Dorothy H. Rautbord 91.1

Autumnal is a typical "veil" painting that well represents Louis's chromatic aesthetic. It is a strong, physical image of poured, mingled color, and simultaneously, a romantic and ethereal statement. The related red and orange hues appear woven into the canvas, giving the effect of merged pictorial grounds. The billowing movement in this painting is similarly connected to Louis' method of production. Thinned to enable even pouring, the acrylic paint flows in accordance with the laws of gravity and glows with a mysterious luminosity.[2] In this picture without figures or subjects, Louis' skillful and sensitive manipulation of the formal element brings forth the emotive content of color.

In 1958 and 1959, Louis painted 126 different veil pictures, a measure of his perfectionism and ingenuity. Guided by a learned color sensibility, and like Jackson Pollock, in search of the fortuitous accident, Louis regularly varied the color combinations, experimented with pigment quality and the amounts applied, and adjusted the position and tautness of the canvas surface. Furthermore, unlike other abstractionists who examined the real object and then tried to paint its essences, Louis received his inspiration during the making process.[3] He did not begin with a subject in mind, and he rarely titled his paintings. That task often fell to his wife and friends, such as Clement Greenberg and William Rubin, the curator at the Museum of Modern Art in New York. The material results of his painting were Louis' focus, and fittingly, the veils and his other painting series provoke subjective responses and interpretations.

Autumnal was created at a significant juncture of Morris Louis' career, and it anticipates a transition to other themes of color abstraction. The painting was one of the last of the veil type, and after a year-long period of experimenting with a wider palette and more distinctly defined contours, Louis developed the "Unfurleds" in 1960. This series, characteristically, has the gestural expressiveness of all the veils and the variegated, chromatic power of later examples, such as *Autumnal*. The "Unfurled" and subsequent "Stripe" series are veritable showcases of color, in which the large sections of unpainted canvas actively participate in the composition.

Louis' paintings are cornerstones of the Washington (D.C.) Color School, a canonical label applied to a diverse group of area painters—among them Kenneth Noland, Gene Davis, Thomas Downing, Paul Reed, and Howard Mehring—whose works were first exhibited together in 1965. While Louis did not live to see this exhibition, his works clearly belong among these artists who shared a deep interest in the autonomous power of brilliant, synthetic color.[4] JF

NOTES

[1] Arthur Danto, "Morris Louis," in *Encounters and Reflections: Art in the Historical Present* (New York City, NY: Farrar, Straus, Giroux, 1990), 47. For Greenberg's clearest articulation of modernist art, see "Modernist Painting," in *Clement Greenberg: The Collected Essays and Criticism*, vol. 4, ed. John O'Brian (Chicago, IL: University of Chicago Press, 1989), 85–93.

[2] Diane Upright, *Morris Louis: The Complete Paintings* (New York City, NY: Harry N. Abrams, 1985), 52. The resin stabilizer in magna acrylic paint causes this effect.

[3] John Elderfield, "Morris Louis and Twentieth-Century Painting," *Art International* 21 (May-June 1974): 28.

[4] Stephen S. Prokopoff, *Two Generations of Color Painting* (Philadelphia, PA: Institute of Contemporary Art and the University of Pennsylvania, 1970); LeGrace G. Benson, "The Washington Scene: Some Preliminary Notes on the Evolution of Art in Washington D.C.," *Art International* 13 (1969): 23.

PROVENANCE

Park International, New York City, NY; Dorothy H. Rautbord, Palm Beach, FL, until 1991; Norton Gallery, 1991.

EXHIBITION HISTORY

Galleria dell'Ariete, Milan, Italy, *Morris Louis*, November 23–December 20, 1960, no. 1.

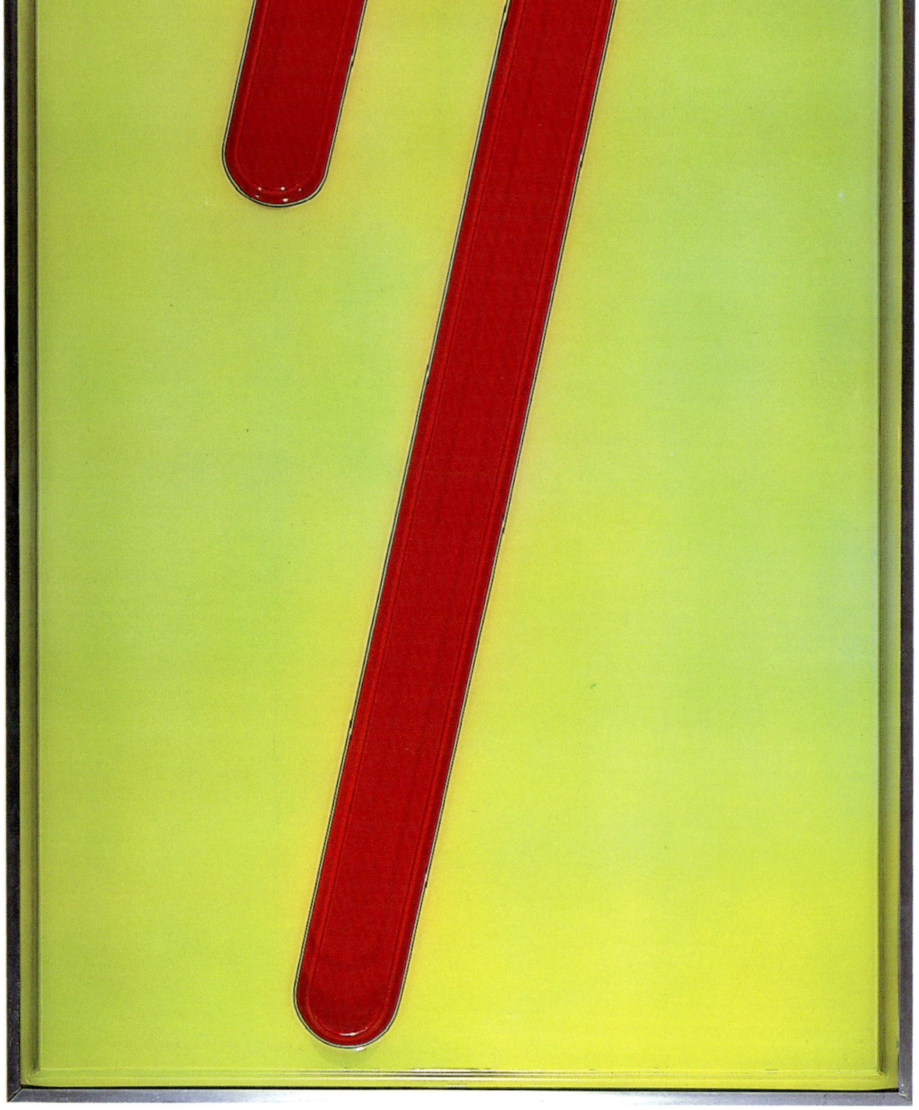

Craig Kauffman

(ROBERT) CRAIG KAUFFMAN, 1932–

An originator of the "L.A. look" of the 1960s, Craig Kauffman is well known for his brightly painted, plastic abstractions which countered the gesturalism of Abstract Expressionism and paralleled the developments of Pop Art and Minimalism. From an early age, Kauffman showed an interest in art, taking-up oil painting when he was eight years old. In high school, the Los Angeles native designed plaques and emblems for student organizations and won a statewide architectural competition. In 1950, he enrolled in the architecture school at the University of Southern California. Influenced by the works of Henri Matisse and local exhibitions of Abstract Expressionism, Kauffman decided to study painting. In 1952, he transferred to the art department at the University of California at Los Angeles, where he received his Bachelor of Arts degree in 1955 and his Master of Arts degree in 1956.

Kauffman participated in the first group show at the Ferus Gallery of Los Angeles in 1957, and in the following year, he was honored with a one-man exhibition there. His paintings of the period are related to Abstract Expressionism, and yet they are uniquely purist and distinguished for their open areas of unpainted canvas. Personal and sexual symbolism also is an integral aspect of these early, colorfully expressive paintings.

Kauffman's major contribution to contemporary art is the Plexiglas "painting." In 1964, he began to make low-relief molds that were inspired by plastic objects and signs manufactured for commercial use. He employed forms related to the organic shapes of his earlier work and experimented with intense color combinations and the effects of atmospheric light upon slick surfaces.

Chartreuse-Red, 1959
Acrylic lacquer on
vacuum-formed Plexiglas
90 x 46 1/2 in.
Gift of Eleanor and Herman Levine

His wall-reliefs of the late 1960s are central to his cool formalism, or "finish fetish," a term applied to slick and sensual art made of high-technology materials.

In 1970, Kauffman, who had taught at University of California campuses in Berkeley and Irvine during the previous decade, accepted a year-long teaching position at the School of Visual Arts in New York. He returned to painting in the 1970s because of his rekindled interest in drawing and his desire to produce two-dimensional art that was less abstract.[1] The resulting pictures, done on silk and muslin supports, are still spare, yet they assert a painterly, expressionistic quality. Kauffman purposefully drew attention to the structure of a stretched and framed canvas by integrating into these works Plexiglas separations and exposed wood supports. The works strike the viewer almost as pictures viewed from the back and also recall stained-glass windows and the mature compositions of Piet Mondrian. Kauffman's works make reference to the physical character of the conventional picture, and they question the relationships struck among illusion-giving visual elements, such as line and color.

An artist with an international reputation who frequently exhibited his work in Europe, as well as in the United States, Kauffman maintained studios in southern California and New York during the 1980s. Currently, he divides his time between Los Angeles and Manila. In his recent paintings, he has reintegrated the abstract biomorphism characteristic of his early style and continues to use plastic components.

Chartreuse-Red, 1959
Acrylic lacquer on
vacuum-formed Plexiglas
90 x 46 1/2 in.
(no inscription)
Gift of Eleanor and Herman Levine 93.13

Kauffman's persistent interest in light and color is manifest in his wall-relief works of the 1960s. He often worked in series, reusing each plastic mold several times and varying the chromatic personality of a given form with different combinations of high-key acrylic paint. Although some of these works are unnamed, others, such as the Norton's *Chartreuse-Red*, have titles that underscore the autonomous power of color. Yet, the subject matter of this work is not solely the straightforward confrontation of monochromes. Color, more accurately, is a determinist agent in *Chartreuse-Red* that mediates issues of compositional structure, surface, and pictorial image.

Kauffman's use of a translucent and sculptural Plexiglas complicates our reception of *Chartreuse-Red*. The synthetic material endows the work with a complex reflectivity, tempering the energy of the red, genital-like form which enters the viewer's space and also pulls the glance downward. Seeing *Chartreuse-Red* is a heightened, psychological experience that is related to our natural enthrallment with shiny cars and bright neon lights. It is an alluring work that effectively reminds us of southern California and its associations: a sunny climate, plastic and aerospace manufacturing, and a glamorous film and television industry.

A paradigmatic work of the Los Angeles "finish fetish" type, *Chartreuse-Red* illustrates why Kauffman was considered a leader and an innovator among his California peers. According to Billy Al Bengston, a celebrated artist of the L.A. circle, "Kauffman was the first southern California artist ever to paint an original painting,"[2] a comment that underscored the pre-1950s reputation of the region's artists as imitators, rather than innovators. The critic and artist Peter Plagens has linked Kauffman's earliest work to the confidence of these artists during the 1960s; a boldness that encouraged them to develop styles independent of ideas imported from Paris, New York, and San Francisco.[3] While Kauffman has downplayed the notion of ideological unity among southern California artists during that time, he has suggested that the synthetic makeup of their work was indeed a rejection of art world conservatism and conformity. Appropriately, the "L.A. look," once dismissed as hedonistic, has been reassessed over the last decade. Kauffman's wall-reliefs in particular are increasingly recognized as influential statements of optimism and modernity.[4] JF

NOTES

[1] Josef Woodard, "Craig Kauffman: Fabricator and Sculptor," *Artweek* 22 (April 4, 1991): 21.

[2] Billy Al Bengston, "Late Fifties at the Ferus: A Participant Refuses to Take the Show Lying Down," *Artforum* 7 (January 1969): 35.

[3] Peter Plagens, *The Sunshine Muse: Contemporary Art on the West Coast* (New York City, NY: Praeger, 1974), 105.

[4] Dan Cameron, "High-Tech Redux: L.A. Art of the Sixties Is Being Re-Assessed in Terms of the Art of the Late Eighties," *Flash Art* 141 (Summer 1988): 102–103; Greg Schneider, "Only Skin Deep: *Finish Fetish: L.A.'s Cool School* at USC Fisher Gallery," *Artweek* 22 (April 4, 1991): 1.

PROVENANCE

Philip Johnson Collection, New Canaan, CT, 1965–76; Eleanor and Herman Levine,Palm Beach, FL, 1976–93; Norton Gallery, 1993.

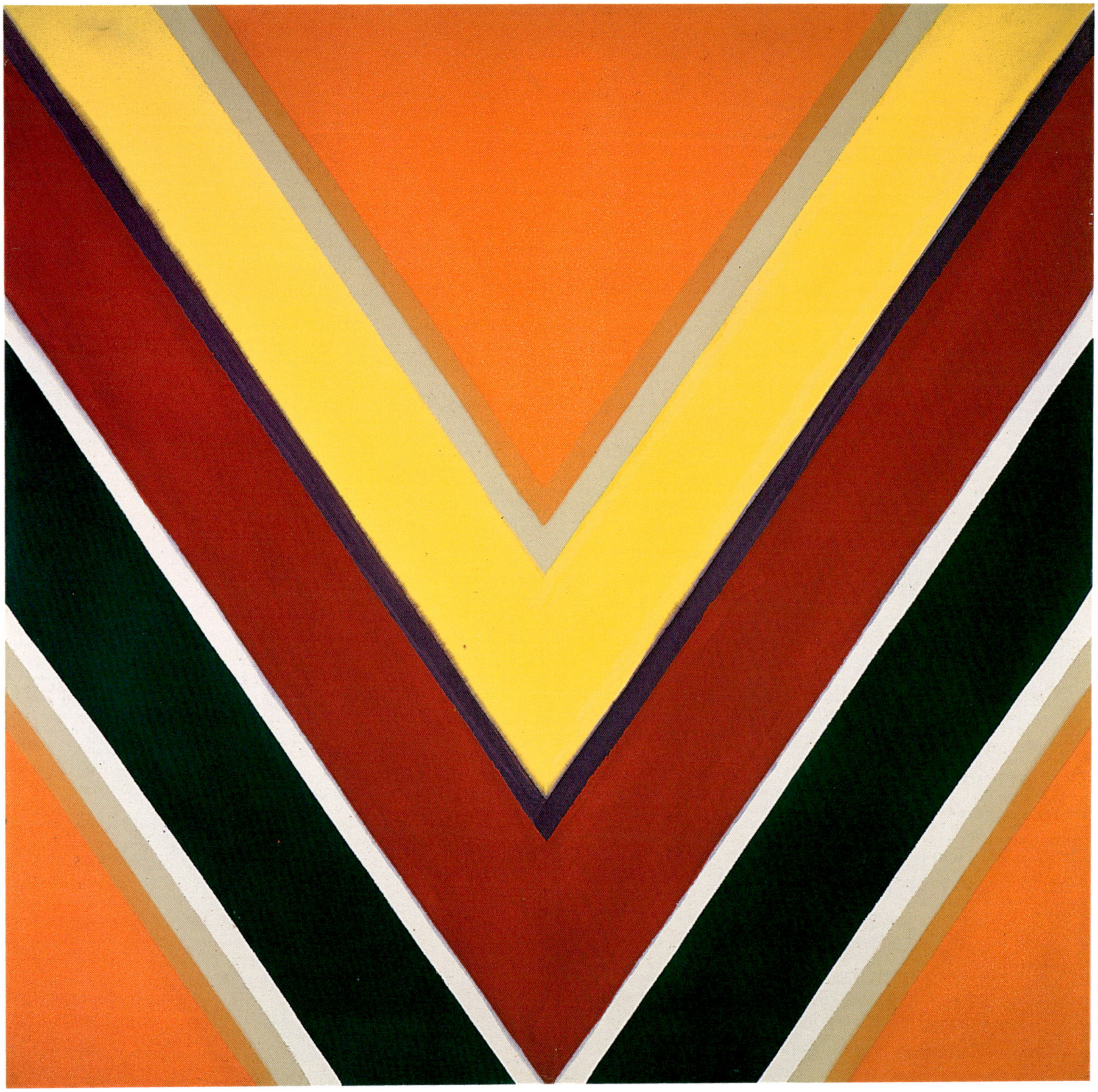

Thrust, 1963
Acrylic on canvas
45 x 45 in.
Gift of Mrs. Dorothy H. Rautbord

Kenneth Noland

1924–

Kenneth Noland's geometric abstraction effectively marked the advent of minimalist art and the passing of Abstract Expressionism. In the manner of the latter style, he consistently painted on large canvases, but his chosen forms were circles, chevrons, stripes, and other geometric shapes. Flat, colorful, and stated with utter clarity, Noland's icons contrast with the more personal and paint-erly touch of Abstract Expressionism.

From the start of his career, Noland was grounded in modernist abstraction. An Air Force veteran of World War II, he studied art in the United States and France under the GI Bill in the late 1940s. For two years, he attended Black Mountain College, an avant-garde arts center in his home state of North Carolina, and his mentor there was the painter Ilya Bolotowsky. During his student years, Noland came to admire Piet Mondrian's nonobjective designs, Bolotowsky's related manner of geometric abstraction, and Paul Klee's colorism.

Settling in Washington, D.C., in 1949, Noland taught art in workshops, at local art schools, and at Catholic University. Within this artistic community of Washington, Noland was a conduit of information. He occasionally visited the painter-sculptor David Smith and the critic Clement Greenberg in New York and mingled with their group. Noland brought back the ideas he had heard circulating, sharing the avant-garde concepts and his understanding of them with the Washington painters Morris Louis, Anne Truitt, Tom Downing, and Howard Mehring. During this experimental period of his career, Noland, himself, assumed the styles of Jackson Pollock, Willem de Kooning, Mark Rothko, and Clyfford Still.

He and Louis, after seeing Helen Frankenthaler's painting *Mountains and Sea* (collection of Helen Frankenthaler) in 1953, adopted her method of staining color into the canvas. Noland switched from oil paints to acrylic and plastic-based ones and subsequently, he developed a method of rapid, assured painting because this new medium made alterations or reworking difficult.

In the late 1950s, Noland began to paint his seminal "circle" series. Unlike the allover compositions of the Abstract Expressionists, these paintings have a discernible, central image. Consisting of crisp and loose circles and rings in a concentric organization, the brilliantly colored forms dominate the unpainted portions of his large canvases.

Noland moved to New York in 1962, but soon left for the quieter setting of Vermont in 1963. He settled near his friend David Smith and close to the academic and cultural environment of Bennington College. In subsequent years, the English sculptor Anthony Caro and the painter Jules Olitski joined the Bennington faculty, and Noland enjoyed the fraternal quality of the rural artistic circle.

During the purist revival of the 1960s, Noland was a major figure. His work influenced a proliferation of nonreferential art objects which exceeded the conventions of sculpture and painting. Noland's abstraction informed art criticism and theory as well. Without representational images to interpret, art historians and critics expanded the discourse, increasingly employing philosophical and psychological theory to address the new, austere art.

Interestingly, Noland, himself, has attached little extra-artistic meaning to his work. "Artists," he has stated, "have always sought formal economy and an essential expressivity."[1] Still living in Vermont, he continues to work in abstract modes. In a recent interview, Noland confidently predicted that abstraction would retain its validity, despite the current dominance of multimedia and socially conscious art. "It's a fertile field that we have barely explored, and young artists will return to it."[2]

Thrust, 1963
Acrylic on canvas
45 x 45 in.
(no inscription)
Gift of Mrs. Dorothy H. Rautbord 91.2

Thrust asserts a structural force typical of Noland's color geometric designs. Equal importance is given to color, line, pattern, and shape, and as a result, the interlocking chevrons comprise an almost irreducible and complex visual element. This iconic form forces the eye to follow the interaction of warm and cool colors and of varying tones on the evenly painted surface. Concurrently, its vertices insistently pull the entire composition and the viewer's glance downward, while its diagonals race to the canvas edges. Expressive dynamism is the content and subject matter of *Thrust*. Rather than describe or detail, the work resonates with its physical presence.

The chevron paintings may have been influenced by the strong diagonals in Morris Louis's "Unfurled" paintings, in which roughly parallel ribbons of paint emanate from the lower corners, creating a central area of unpainted canvas. However, the methods of Noland and Louis significantly differed. Noland preceded Louis in the use of unsized canvas, which the former employed to experiment with the pigment's finish and consistency at the picture's center. Moreover, although Louis eschewed the paintbrush in his late career,

Noland did not immediately do so. Precisely diagrammed and measured in pencil first, most of the chevrons were then painted freehand or with rollers. From a distance, *Thrust* looks sharply defined, yet upon closer scrutiny, its edges reveal themselves to be related to Noland's first concentric circle paintings and to possess some of their painterliness.[3]

Thrust was painted in 1963, the year Noland began to gain recognition. After the circles, he painted series of chevrons, diamonds, stripes, and linear grids to serve his formalist purposes in the late 1960s and throughout the 1970s. His reputation was made upon the abstract exploration of numerous geometric structures, color combinations, and pictorial orientations. Noland also began to make sculpture in the 1960s, inspired by the work of Smith and Caro. The structures are stainless steel assemblages of intersecting planes, and like his gridlike paintings of the same period, called "plaids," they recall the look of Mondrian. In 1985, he completed an architectural mural, evocative of the plaids, for the Wiesner Building at the Massachusetts Institute of Technology. Noland's more recent work, which consists of painted canvas slices that are mounted on wood supports and bordered by Plexiglas, continues this spatial investigation. JF

NOTES

[1] Diane Waldman, "Color, Format and Abstract Art: An Interview with Kenneth Noland," *Art in America* 65 (May-June 1977): 100.

[2] Michael Kimmelman, "Three Art Stars of the 60's Rise and Shine Again," *The New York Times*, 5 May 1994, B5.

[3] Barbara Rose, *American Art Since 1900* (New York City, NY: Praeger, 1975), 195.

PROVENANCE

Dorothy H. Rautbord, Palm Beach, FL; Norton Gallery, 1991.

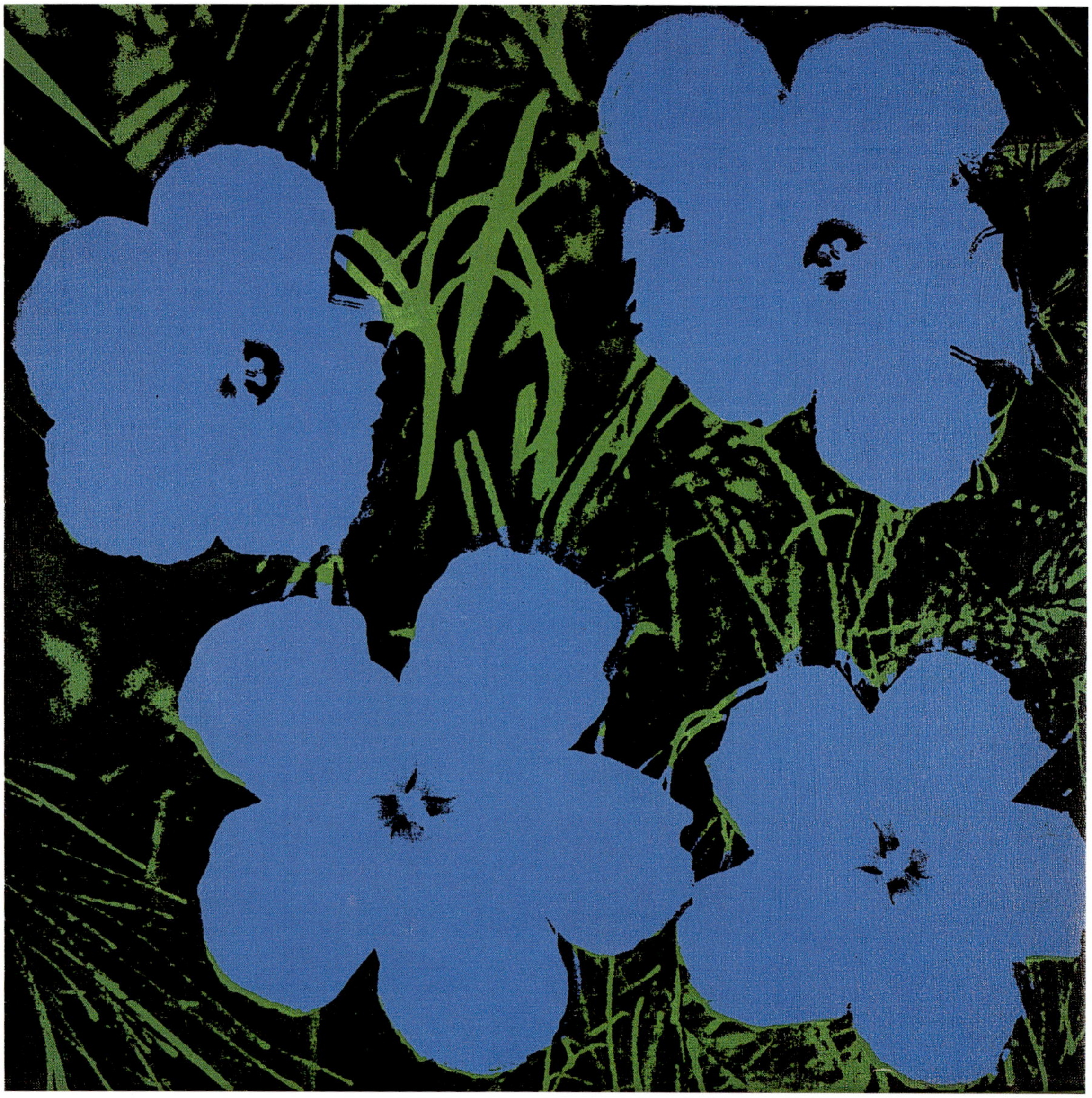

Flowers, 1964
Acrylic silkscreen on canvas
24 x 24 in.
Acquired through deaccession

Andy Warhol

ANDREW WARHOLA, 1928–1987

Among the most famous artists of the twentieth century, Andy Warhol broadly influenced visual culture with his silkscreen portraits of celebrities and depictions of news events and icons of modern society. Rather than bemoan the unending cycle of mass production and conspicuous consumption, Warhol made serial images that ironically acknowledged the banal, the gruesome, and the machine-made.

Warhol was born in McKeesport, Pennsylvania, and the year 1928 is widely accepted as the date of his birth. Another source states that Warhol was born in Forest City, a small town northeast of Scranton, Pennsylvania, in 1925.[1] After graduating from Carnegie Institute of Technology in 1949 with a degree in pictorial design, Warhol moved permanently to New York City and began a successful career as an illustrator. He designed graphics for major Manhattan departments stores and national fashion magazines until the late 1950s, when he embarked upon a career in fine art.

Warhol drew his motifs from the commercial and popular cultural realm which he knew so well. Starting in 1960, he did a series of paintings based on comic strip panels, Coca-Cola bottles, Del Monte peach cans, and pages from tabloid newspapers. Although these representational pictures bore the drip marks of Abstract Expressionism, they embodied a marked alternative to this dominant style of the 1950s. Warhol, like Jasper Johns, Roy Lichtenstein, and Robert Rauschenberg, was attracted to the crisp quality of these everyday images and sought to incorporate this effect in his style. Exhibited at the Ferus Gallery of Los Angeles in 1962, the early Warhol paintings helped to set the standard of advertising copy slickness in Pop art.

Warhol modified the commercial look of his art after 1962, increasingly employing the silkscreen process. Furthermore, he added the genre of portraiture to his repertoire. *Marilyn Diptych*, 1962 (Tate Gallery), the first of many celebrity studies, epitomizes the hard-edged approach employed by Pop and Minimalist artists of the 1960s. A combination of oil and acrylic painting and enamel silkscreen, the picture consists of fifty, photographically reproduced head shots of the actress Marilyn Monroe. One-half of the work presents her likeness in garish colors, while the remaining images are black and white, and partly smeared, as a result of mechanical error. Mass-produced in the artist's New York studio "The Factory," the photographic silkscreens of movie stars and wealthy art collectors commented on the fleeting nature of fame and fortune. In the manner of Warhol's sculpture of consumer items, such as Campbell soup cans and Brillo soap pads, the portraits effectively transformed the banal and the commonplace into an art which appeared impersonal and anonymously made.

Warhol, himself, became the focus of international attention in the mid-1960s. Mainstream culture absorbed his ironic use of popular images and the mechanical process of silkscreening. His interests also extended to other creative arenas. He promoted avant-garde rock-n-roll bands, most notably the Velvet Underground, and he made off beat, improvisational movies that earned critical acclaim and spawned admiring imitations. In 1968, following a life-threatening incident in which an actress who had worked in his films shot him, Warhol undertook several publishing ventures. While recuperating, he founded *Interview* magazine, a cornerstone of celebrity journalism, and wrote and edited books on Pop art and his role in the movement.

In the 1970s, Warhol embraced computers and advanced media technology that allowed him to electronically plan and design his work. This allowed his production pace to accelerate to an even greater extent. For the last decade of his life, however, Warhol returned to painting and created mixed-media paintings on metal-painted canvases. He suffered a fatal heart attack following gall bladder surgery in 1987.

Flowers, 1964
Acrylic silkscreen on canvas
24 x 24 in.
(verso l.r.: "Andy Warhol 64")
Acquired through deaccession 86.33

A subject seemingly more appropriate for wallpaper design than for the fine art of the late twentieth century, flowers interested Andy Warhol for their very ordinariness. In the 1950s, Warhol incorporated floral motifs into his commercial illustrations and made line drawings of this subject as well. The Norton's picture was inspired by a photograph he saw in *Modern Photography* in 1964. Warhol altered the photographic representation of seven hibiscus flowers by reducing their number to four and shifting the position of the blossoms in the pictorial space. Over a two-month period, the artist and his associates at The Factory produced more than nine hundred, painted versions of *Flowers* with variations in scale and color.[2]

Flowers illustrates how Warhol adapted and

translated a traditional still life genre into a Pop Art style. He radically distorted his subject, flattening and simplifying it into a recognizable visual sign for flora in nature, boxed into a square and restrictive frame. The hovering flowers and the background of grassy blades are bereft of naturalistic character, and their essence is restated in the language of mechanization. Warhol left some edges uneven and unfinished to underscore the process of his silkscreen method. Formally imperfect and imbued with a boisterous chromatic personality, *Flowers* is a marked contrast to the decorative predictability of wallpaper and yet the picture demonstrates the close relationship of commercial and fine arts.[3]

Warhol produced *Flowers* and some related silkscreens of single or double flower subjects in 1964. A second and third burst of activity around this theme occurred in the 1970s. Taking advantage of the lucrative climate for graphic works, Warhol reintroduced the 1964 flower motif in a portfolio of screenprints in 1970. Four years later, he returned to a more conventional style of presenting floral displays. He made black and white, and colored screenprints of camellias, carnations, and broad-leafed plants arranged in vases and posed firmly on tables or some form of support. Unlike the 1964 flowers, which were inspired by a single photographic image, the 1974 versions were based on illustrations culled from a wallpaper catalogue and books on floral design. Inspired by these sources, the artist made representational, freehand drawings that were made into photographic silkscreens. JF

NOTES

[1] Elizabeth Hoffman, *Explorations: The Visual Arts Since 1945* (New York City, NY: Harper Collins, 1991), 109.

[2] Frayda Feldman and Jörg Schellman, ed., *Andy Warhol Prints* (New York City, NY: Ronald Feldman Fine Arts, 1989), 14–15, 134–35; David Bourdon, "Andy Warhol: Flowers," *Arts Magazine* 50 (November 1975): 86; David Bourdon, *Warhol* (New York City, NY: Harry N. Abrams, 1989), 192–93.

[3] Bourdon, *Warhol*, 190–91; Feldman and Schellman, 17.

PROVENANCE

Norton Gallery, 1986.

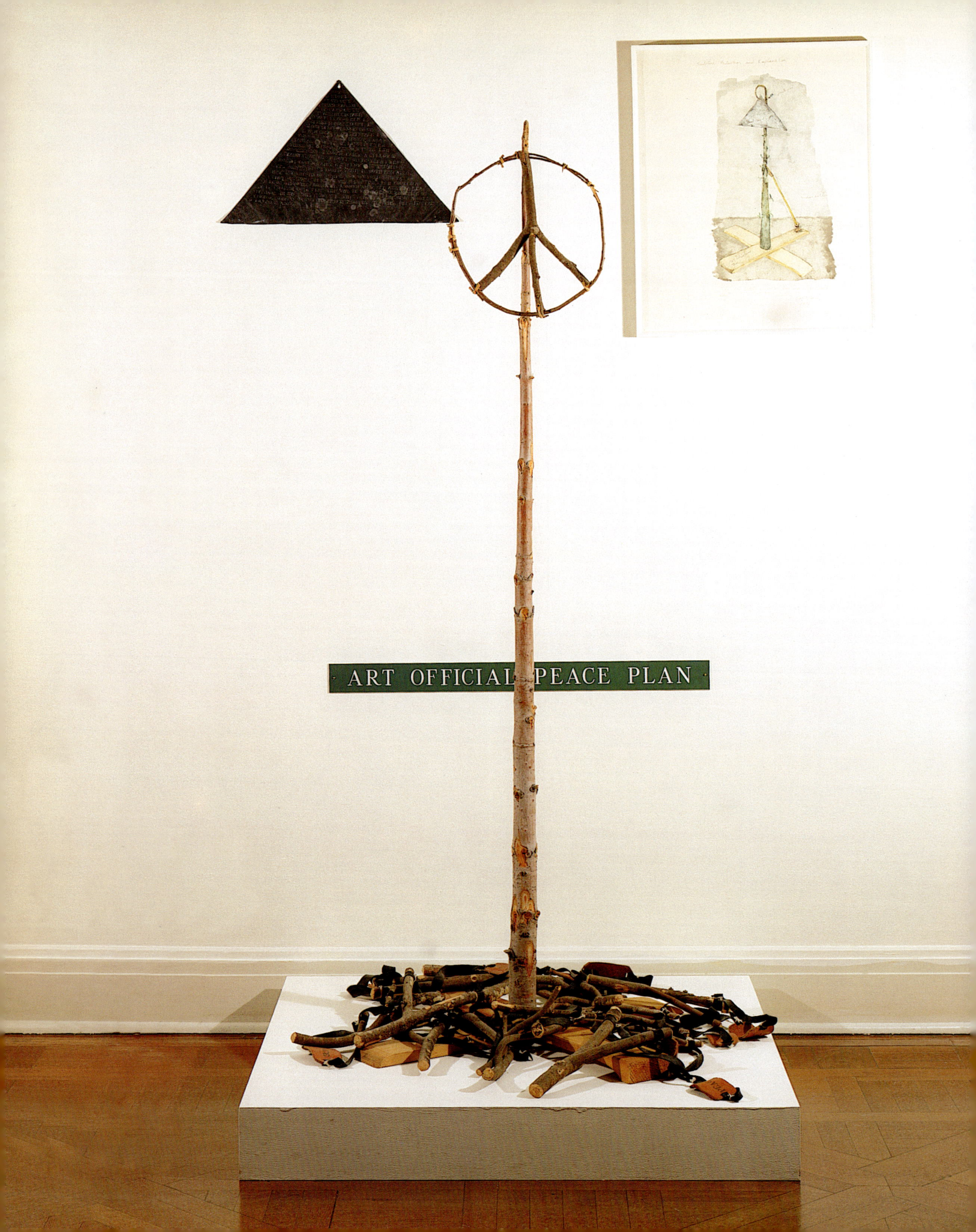
ART OFFICIAL PEACE PLAN

William T. Wiley

1937–

A leader of the California Funk Art movement of the late 1960s, in which artists parodied mainstream styles of modern art using humble materials and ordinary, vulgar subject matter, William T. Wiley is known both for his witty, irreverent social commentary and his consummate skill as a draftsman and watercolorist. Born in Bedford, Indiana, he moved frequently with his family before settling in the small town of Richland, Washington. Encouraged by an exceptional high school art teacher to pursue vanguard styles of abstract painting, Wiley earned a scholarship to study at the California School of Fine Arts (now the San Francisco Art Institute) in 1956. A decade earlier, Clyfford Still and Mark Rothko had introduced their rich, evocative styles of Abstract Expressionism to the San Francisco Bay area during their tenure as instructors at the Art Institute. The painterly expressionism of Still and Rothko was transformed into a lyrical, figurative abstraction by the artists who remained on the faculty, such as Wiley's teacher Frank Lobdell.

As a student of Lobdell, Wiley produced vigorous abstract expressionist paintings with stark contrasts of color and value, sometimes including figuration with allusions to cultural commentary. He also discovered the work of artists such as Rembrandt, Georges Seurat, and Marcel Duchamp, who became lifelong inspirations. While still a student, Wiley's prodigious talent was recognized by the San Francisco Museum of Modern Art, where he was given a one-person show in 1960.

Wiley taught at the University of California, Davis, from 1962–1973, where he was instrumental in the development of

Art Official Peace Plan, 1970
Wood, slingshots, sign,
lead plaque, watercolor
69 x 50 x 27 in.
Purchased through the
R. H. Norton Fund

Funk Art. Like his fellow faculty member Robert Arneson, Wiley produced satirical paintings and sculptures with metaphorical content directed at society. During this period, Wiley's art often possessed an introspective, self-referential quality. He began to seriously question his reasons for making art in 1967, and after a several month hiatus, he started to incorporate watercolors into his mixed-media assemblages. The artist explained, "And at that point, I connected with watercolor. I liked the idea that I could fit as much as I could possibly get out of art, right here in my lap." [1]

Wiley's art, since that time, has often included assemblages or "constructions" comprised of found-object sculpture, accompanied by exquisite, realistic watercolors and expressively brushed, abstract paintings on canvas. The artist characteristically scribbles words and phrases on surfaces throughout his constructions. The whimsical quality of his punning graffiti belies the social or metaphysical questions that lurk beneath his surfaces. Emblematic forms, such as the triangle, reappear throughout Wiley's work as personal symbols with a multitude of meanings. As in Surrealist art, odd juxtapositions of familiar objects, words, and imagery in Wiley's constructions produce countless new possibilities of meaning which are different for every viewer.

The artist's use of ordinary materials and recognizable imagery assures the accessibility of his art to a general audience, however, his rich layering of personal symbols and esoteric content creates a depth of meaning which cannot be plumbed without careful contemplation. It is Wiley's intention that the precise interpretation eludes the viewer. "...I think art is such a wonderful concept in that that's one of its main functions—to remain undefined." [2] Wiley's complex and enigmatic art has been described as reflective, both of himself, and as a mirror of contemporary society.

Art Official Peace Plan, 1970
Wood, slingshots, sign, lead plaque, watercolor
69 x 50 x 27 in.
(l.r.: "Wm T. Wiley / 1976")
Purchased through the R. H. Norton Fund 94.14

Produced in response to the Vietnam War, the collection of items which comprises *Art Official Peace Plan* connotes a multitude of meanings that range from playfully ironic to critically subversive. The central focus of Wiley's installation is a five-foot-nine-inch-tall wooden pole, with a peace symbol made of vines, twine, and rawhide suspended from its curved top. Scattered over the X-shaped base of the pole are several wooden slingshots whose Y-shapes resemble the central lines of the peace symbol above. The triangle of the slingshots and peace sign is echoed in the heavy piece of sheet-lead mounted on the wall behind the sculpture, which reappears in the watercolor image that is also displayed on the wall as a part of the piece. In the watercolor, the triangular form takes the place of the peace sign, and the wooden pole is depicted as a sapling tree with delicate leaves sprouting from its trunk. Below the sheet-lead and watercolor is a narrow, rectangular plaque, or sign, which states the title of the work, "Art Official Peace Plan," a pun on the phrase "artificial peace plan."

The meanings conjured-up by *Art Official Peace Plan* can be interpreted on a number of different levels. The slingshot is an ancient weapon which was used by the Biblical hero David to slay the giant Goliath. The obvious irony of associating the shape of this weapon with the emblem of peace is reinforced by the lettering on the strap of each slingshot, which reads, "PEACE." This association is patently humorous, but raises disturbing questions concerning the goal of peace itself. With the slingshots, Wiley questions whether weapons of aggression are a necessary component of peace.

The sign that displays the title in capital letters further enriches the witty irony of Wiley's work. Beyond the clear pun in the title, the slick, commercially-produced appearance of the plaque suggests that it is an "official" sign. It contrasts with the natural, rough-hewn quality of the slingshots and the peace sign, and with the handwritten phrases scrawled on the watercolor above, suggesting that there is a difference between official versions of peace and natural, authentic peace. All of these elements are "signs," or signifiers in a system of specified meanings. Yet, through new associations and combinations, Wiley has opened them up to a multitude of new meanings.

Wiley created this construction during a turbulent year in the history of the United States; one that was marred by the violence of the Kent State and Jackson State protests against the U.S. invasion of Cambodia. Like many artists during the late 1960s and early 1970s, Wiley responded to the disturbing political and social climate by rejecting the hermetic, detached elitism of late modern abstraction, and by producing art loaded with symbolic and metaphorical content. His complex layering of meanings in *Art Official Peace Plan*, at once personal and public, accessible and elusive, produces a work which is rooted in its historical circumstance, yet just as vital and challenging today as it was twenty-five years ago. DM

NOTES

1 Katharine Gregor, "Zen and the Art of William T. Wiley," *ArtNews* 88 (April 1989): 188.

2 Ibid., 189.

PROVENANCE

Allan Frumkin Gallery, New York, 1970; Dr. and Mrs. Irving Forman, 1970–94; Norton Gallery, 1994.

EXHIBITION HISTORY

Allan Frumkin Gallery, New York City, NY, *Summer Group Show*, June–August, 1970.

Allan Frumkin Gallery, New York City, NY, *William T. Wiley*, September 29–October 30, 1970.

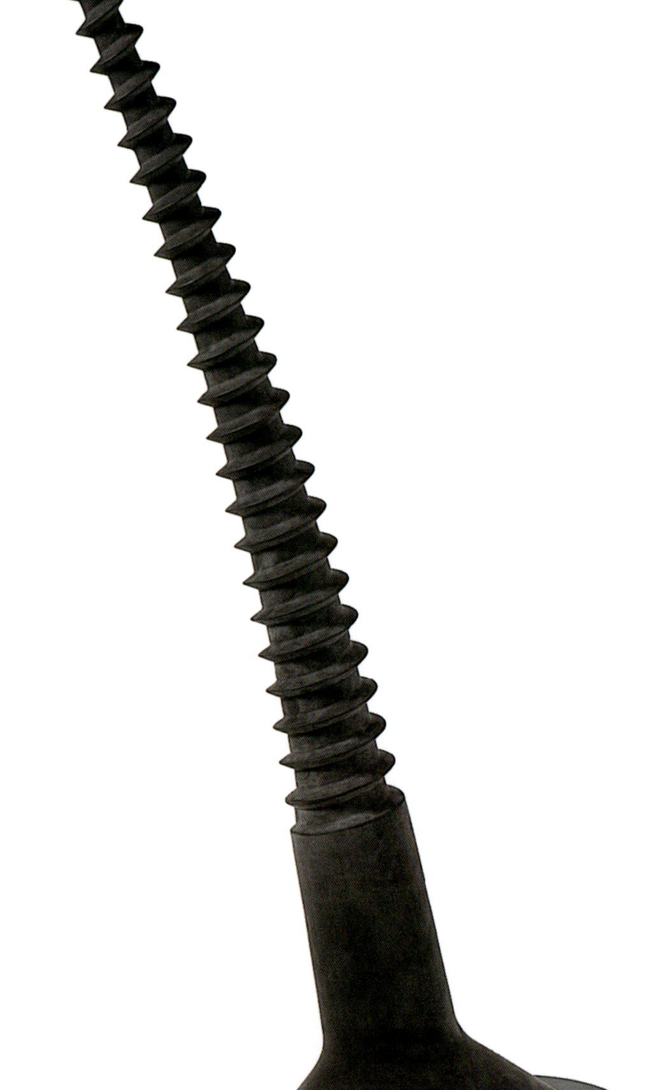

Claes (Thure) Oldenburg

1929–

The outrageous and inventive sculptures of Claes Oldenburg are Pop Art monuments that satirize consumer culture and the synthetic look of modern life. A naturalized American citizen, Claes Oldenburg was born in Stockholm, Sweden. His father was a Swedish diplomat, and the artist's childhood was spent in the cities where his father was assigned: New York, Oslo, and Chicago. The artist attended Yale University from 1946 until 1950, and studied English literature, drama, and art. After graduating from Yale, he returned to Chicago and attended The Art Institute of Chicago from 1952–1954. During this period, he also was an apprentice reporter for the city news bureau and later, in 1955–1956, an illustrator for *Chicago* magazine.

In 1956, Oldenburg moved permanently to New York City. He worked part-time at the Cooper Union Museum and Art School library and spent his first year in the city drawing, making collages, and reading. Following his move to a lower East Side apartment in 1957, he began an association with Red Grooms, Allen Kaprow, and other artists who were creating environments and orchestrating "happenings," the audience-interactive, performance art. Oldenburg exhibited in a group show at Grooms' City Gallery in 1958–1959 and had his first one-man show at the Cooper Union Art School library in 1959. He produced, primarily, drawings of himself and his first wife, Pat, during this period. From his drawings, he constructed collages and objects, among them the "ray gun," a combination object and superhero persona with which he identified. Advertising and other images from the mass media and popular culture intrigued the artist, who had

Soft Screw, 1976
Elastometric urethane on a mahogany base
45 1/2 in.
Gift of Mr. and Mrs. Miles Q. Fiterman

decided that his work would represent his immediate and social environs. His drawings inspired the collages, papier-mâché and found-objects that were incorporated into the installation "The Street," which was exhibited in differing versions at the Judson Gallery and at the Reuben Gallery in 1960.

Oldenburg expanded his sculptural production in 1960, as he explored the possibilities of representing American cultural icons in an innovative, material form. He made reliefs of flags, a motif undoubtedly borrowed from Jasper Johns and Frank Stella, and mixed-media assemblages of the personified and phallic ray gun. In the manner of the Dada and Surrealist artists he admired, Oldenburg discovered an expressive potential in everyday things. In the winter of 1961–1962, he opened "The Store," an installation that consisted of stuffed vinyl and canvas constructions of food and clothes displayed and tagged for sale. The project was a visual commentary on the slick, commercial values of modern society. Oldenburg arranged "The Store" in his own studio, and as a result, he subverted the primacy of the museum and gallery as designated spaces for art viewing. "The Store" generated the idea for another concept, the Ray Gun Theater Plays, in which Claes and Pat Oldenburg, and the artists Lucas Samaras and Gloria Graves, performed loosely scripted dramas of the struggles and passages of working-class life.[1]

An exhibition at the Green Gallery in New York marked the introduction of his large-scale, soft sculptures in 1962. For that exhibition, he enlarged the objects from "The Store," and these huge slices of cake, ice cream cones, and sandwiches became important cornerstones of the Pop Art movement. In subsequent years, he designed other mis-en-scènes, including a motel room and displaced forms, such as car parts, home appliances, and furniture. Oldenburg provocatively brought the ordinary into the fine arts setting. By replacing the conventional qualities of objects with a soft and sensuous malleability, he challenged the viewer's notions about the physical make-up and permanence of worldly things.

In the mid-1960s, Oldenburg developed an interest in permanent, outdoor sculpture, and his designs demonstrated the artist's flair for theatrical presentation. Among his many public commissions is the "Geometric Mouse" sculpture, originally produced for the artist's show at the Museum of Modern Art in 1969, and since then, reproduced for several museums and city plazas.

Soft Screw, 1976
Elastometric urethane on a mahogany base
45 1/2 in.
(no inscription)
Gift of Mr. and Mrs. Miles Q. Fiterman 79.38

The irony, irreverent humor, and innuendo often revealed in Pop Art are embodied in the Norton's *Soft Screw*. It is a cleverly designed work that conveys the characteristics of the screw, down to the energetic and elegant spiral of its threads. Starkly presented as a single image, the object demands aesthetic consideration. Oldenburg's distorted curving of the form, moreover, purposefully contradicts the materiality and utility of the real thing. Tall and kinetically flexible, the simple screw becomes monumental and is invested with a risqué, sexual meaning as well.[2]

The screw form joined the artist's array of

iconic images in 1969. In that year, he participated in the Los Angeles County Museum of Art's Art and Technology program, in which artists took-up brief residencies to produce multi-media and intermedia work. Oldenburg designed a three-part cardboard model of the screw that was constructed at Walt Disney Enterprises. Subsequently, he pursued the concept of a large, kinetic version of the form. Although the expense of building the sculpture prevented it from being realized, the plan for the project illustrates the unboundedness and audacity of Oldenburg's imagination. He envisioned a forty-five-foot-tall work to be sited in a vacant lot next to Gemini G.E.L., a Los Angeles studio with which he was associated. By design, the screw would spiral above and below ground over a 24-hour period, regularly lubricating itself with oil and playing a clocklike role for passing motorists and pedestrians.

The Norton's sculpture is one of 24 commercial editions made by Oldenburg. Discussing the *Soft Screw* design in an exhibition catalogue of 1976, the artist explained that his purpose was to explore the elastic character of its form. The upside-down screw is subject to the whims of gravity and may take three positions: upright, acutely angled, and curved into an arch. Although he has not rejected the anthropomorphic and sexual readings of the sculpture, Oldenburg has maintained that his interest was in its organic character and the transitions between its states of being. He asserted that the screw was "a living thing, one of the many living things of which man is only a category. The screw is as related to a palm or cactus, or any plant, as to a part of the human body or the whole human body."[3] While the related lithographs and drawings of the *Soft Screw* graphically communicate the action of a moving form, the sculpture actually demonstrates it.

Soft Screw generated ideas for a related motif, the "Screw Arch." In 1975–1976, he produced lithographs of screw-shaped bridges spanning a Times Square street in New York. Thereafter, he moved the theme to a Dutch setting, making etchings and models for a two-screw bridge over a Rotterdam waterway. Although this project was never realized, its subject is yet another witty form of the Oldenburg oeuvre. JF

NOTES

[1] Katherine Hoffman, *Explorations: The Visual Arts Since 1945* (New York City, NY: Harper Collins, 1991), 158; Barbara Rose, *American Art Since 1900* (New York City, NY: Holt, Rinehart and Winston, 1975), 189–90; Barbara Rose, *Claes Oldenburg* (New York City, NY: Museum of Modern Art, 1970), 64, 69–70.

[2] Stacia F. Payne, *Contemporary Sculpture from Florida Collections* (Gainesville, FL: University Presses of Florida, 1987), 33.

[3] Gemini G.E.L., *The Soft Screw* (Los Angeles, CA: Gemini G.E.L., 1976), II.

PROVENANCE

Mr. and Mrs. Miles Q. Fiterman, Palm Beach, FL, until 1979; Norton Gallery, 1979.

EXHIBITION HISTORY

Gemini G.E.L., Los Angeles, CA, *The Soft Screw*, February 1976.

University Gallery, College of Fine Arts, University of Florida, Gainesville, FL, *Contemporary Sculpture from Florida Collections*, October 4–November 8, 1987, no. 32.

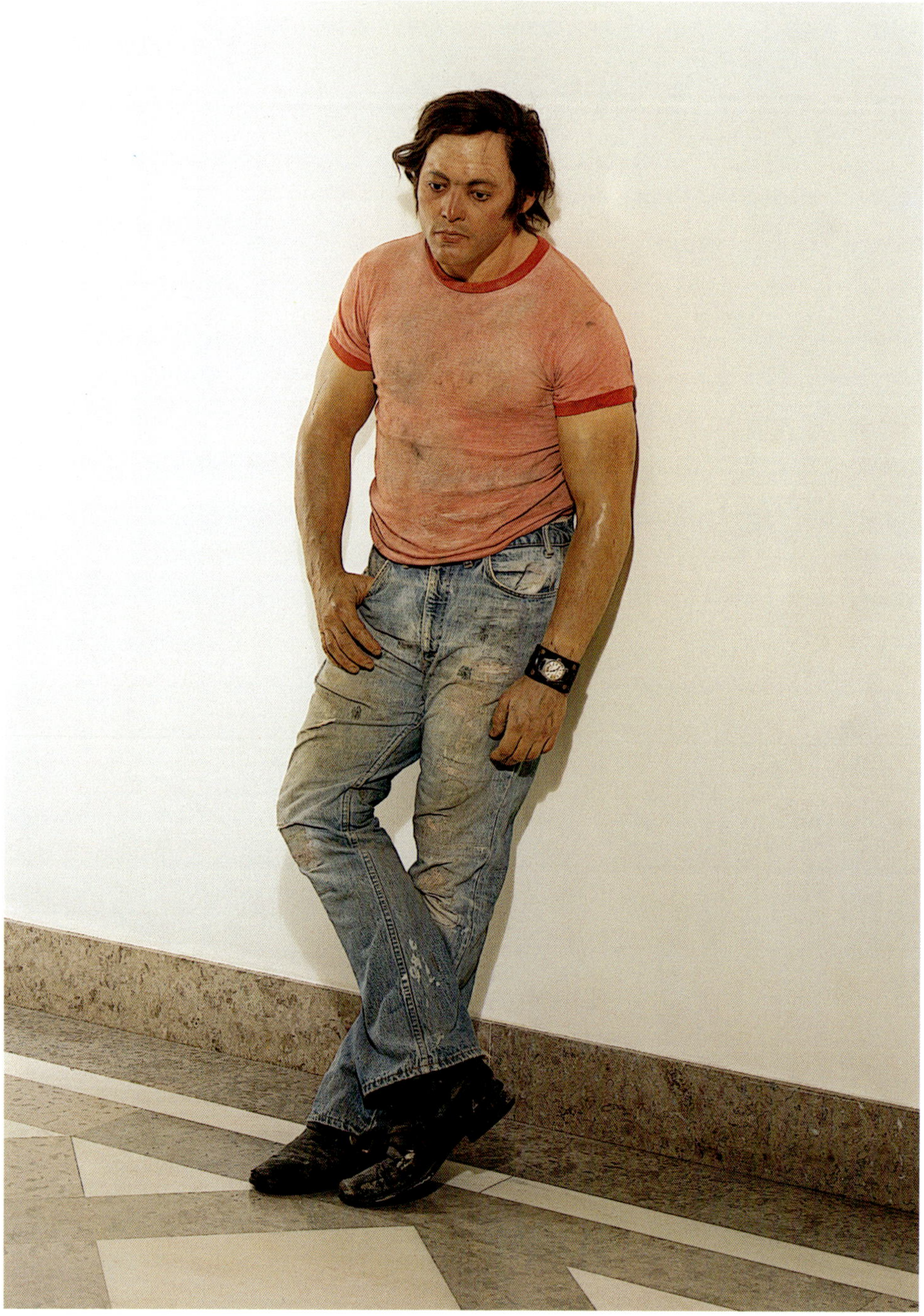

Young Worker, 1976
Polyester resin and fiberglass, polychromed in oil
65 in.
Gift of Joseph Rosenberg

Duane Hanson

1925–

Using familiar, everyday types of people as subjects, Duane Hanson creates an art which is deliberately anti-elitist and accessible to a general audience. The arresting realism of his life-sized figures consistently delights viewers. But the skillful craft and the trompe l'oeil illusionism of Hanson's sculpture are only the means by which the artist communicates the emotional life of ordinary individuals in late twentieth-century America. From his first expressionistic sculptures of the 1960s, to the more subtle, melancholy figures which he creates today, Hanson has reinvigorated the tradition of realism in art.

Born in Alexandria, Minnesota, Hanson grew up in a close-knit Swedish-American family that prided itself on solid, middle-class values. After graduating as an art major from a small college in St. Paul, Minnesota, he entered Cranbrook Academy of Art in Bloomfield, Michigan, where he received a Master of Fine Arts degree in 1951. The artist's attempts to develop an abstract style of art which would be marketable in the United States in the early 1950s met with little success. Hanson explained, "I would try to do abstract work, but I always put a bit of an arm or nose in it. I never could do just nonfigurative work. So it never amounted to much." [1] In 1953, Hanson accepted a teaching position with the United States Army Dependent School system in Germany, where the art world was more receptive to the figurative elements in his work.

Before his return to the United States in 1961, when he accepted a teaching position at Oglethorpe College in Atlanta, Georgia, Hanson met an artist who was using polyester resin and fiberglass to make sculpture. Recognizing this new medium to be easily manipulated and practical, Hanson had some success using it during his tenure at Oglethorpe, but he was still dissatisfied. It was not until 1967, after he had been teaching at Miami-Dade Community College in South Florida for two years, that he discovered his own sculptural mode of expression inspired by the banal vulgarity of Pop Art and the poignant, sculptural environments of George Segal and Edward Kienholz. Over the next few years, Hanson produced several life-sized sculptural groups in polyester resin and fiberglass that focused with graphic realism on the brutality of contemporary existence. The artist had, finally, found a satisfactory way to communicate with a broad audience.

Since the early 1970s, Hanson has turned from the horrific expressionism of his early work, to a more subtle form of satire tinged with sympathy. His recent sculpture is highly illusionistic, focusing on the banality of lower middle-class American life. Typical subjects for his work include working people, housewives, retired citizens, and other common, everyday folk. Because of its deceptive realism, Hanson's work has been associated with the Photorealism of artists such as Richard Estes. But the artist contends, "My art is not about fooling people. It's the human attitudes I'm after—fatigue, a bit of frustration, rejection. To me, there is a kind of beauty in all of this." [2] Hanson's sculptures will be remembered, not only as skillful simulations of physical reality, but also, as highly sensitive records of the emotional reality of contemporary American society.

Young Worker, 1976
Polyester resin and fiberglass, polychromed in oil
65 in.
(no inscription)
Gift of Joseph Rosenberg 81.3

The incredibly lifelike appearance of Hanson's sculptures is largely a result of the painstaking process through which they are cast and then, exactingly, refined and finished down to the smallest detail of a freckle or a single hair. First, the artist conceives of the type of person he wants to portray. Next, he chooses an actual person with the right characteristics to be his model, and after posing and photographing his subject, he applies silicone to make a flexible mold of the model's body, section by section. Polyvinyl acetate is poured into the silicone molds, and the hardened casts of the body parts are reassembled into a figure. After correcting any defects or altering any portions of the figure necessary to produce the envisioned effect, Hanson begins his meticulous work of painting, refining, and finishing the figure. He uses acrylic and oil paints to achieve the proper luminosity in the skin tones and applies individual hairs carefully with a sewing needle. Sometimes, he varnishes fingernails or adds paint to dull the shininess of a watch or other accessory, in order to convey the complete character of the figure which he has conceived.

The man who posed for *Young Worker* was a plastics worker. While the sculpture was being planned, the model had ended a romantic relationship with a woman and had, subsequently, experienced weight loss and a great deal of sadness. In *Young Worker*, Hanson has translated the man's particular sorrow into a universalized image of melancholy, conveyed by the sloping shoulders and weary demeanor of the figure, as well as the slightly wrinkled brow and downturned eyes which seem to stare at nothing.

The body casting with which Hanson begins his sculptures is only an expedient means to an end. Unlike his contemporary John de Andrea, who creates lifelike sculptures of young, beautiful women from body casts, Hanson deliberately chooses common, recognizable types of people as his subjects. If his sculptures seem imbued with pathos, it is because the artist empathizes with them, just as the audience does. Hanson's sculptures are highly evocative because of their startling realism, and because the story of human life, which Hanson writes across their weary physiques and in their melancholy expressions, is as timeless and enduring as the synthetic materials with which his figures are made. DM

NOTES

[1] Martin Bush, *Sculptures by Duane Hanson* (Wichita, KS: Edwin A. Ulrich Museum of Art, Wichita State University, 1985), 27.

[2] Ibid., 95.

PROVENANCE

Joseph Rosenberg, Milwaukee, WI, until 1981; Norton Gallery, 1981.

EXHIBITION HISTORY

Edwin A. Ulrich Museum of Art, Wichita State University, Wichita, KS, *Duane Hanson*, travelling exhibition, November 15, 1976–April 16, 1978, p. 81.

Museum of Fine Arts, Ft. Lauderdale, FL, *Real People: Sculptures by Duane Hanson*, December 14, 1988–January 13, 1989, p. 12.

Florida State University Museum of Fine Arts, Tallahassee, FL, *Duane Hanson: The Politics of Being*, October 1, 1990–June 30, 1991.

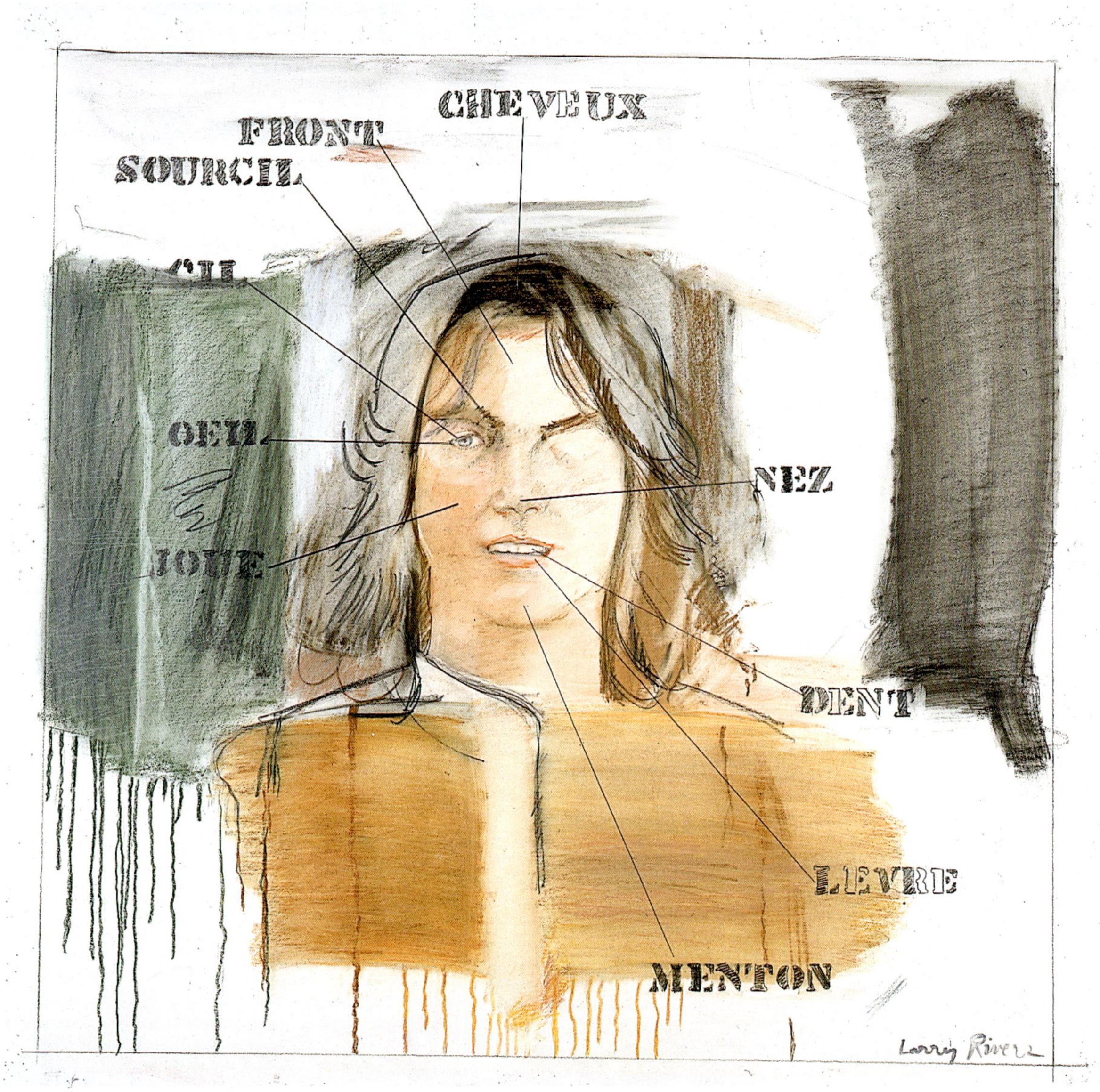

French Vocabulary Lesson, 1978
Colored pencil and charcoal on paper
33 1/8 x 33 1/8 in.
Purchased through the R. H. Norton Fund

Larry Rivers

1923–

Larry Rivers, born Yitzroch Loiza Grossberg in the Bronx, New York, studied at the Juilliard School of Music and began a career as a jazz musician before deciding to become a painter.[1] In 1947, acting on the advice of a friend who witnessed his earliest attempts at abstract representation, he enrolled in Hans Hofmann's progressive art school in New York City. Rivers studied there and at Hofmann's summer school in Provincetown, Massachusetts, through most of 1948, at which point he enrolled for a period in New York University's Art Education Program. At NYU, Rivers studied primarily with the Abstract Expressionist William Baziotes and became acquainted with Willem de Kooning and other prominent New York School artists.

Too young to fully participate in the Abstract Expressionist movement which peaked in the 1940s and early 1950s, Rivers, instead, found his place among a group of younger artists engaged in challenging the hegemony of the older painters. Reactionaries thinking along the same lines as Rivers included Jasper Johns and Robert Rauschenberg, and later, Pop artists, like Roy Lichtenstein, Andy Warhol, and Claes Oldenberg. Abstract Expressionists—inspired by sources as diverse as myths, ancient or "primitive" cultures, and theories of psychology—explored the expression of individual and universal beliefs and emotions in largely nonrepresentational styles. The younger generation, on the other hand, engaged in intellectual projects which, though every bit as earnest, poked fun at the ideas of their elders and irreverently questioned the practice of art-making itself. Rivers contributed to this trend by wittily juxtaposing realism, which was seen as passé, with abstraction, by parodying famous works of art from the past and by creating deliberately humorous works, like his 1960s *Vocabulary Lessons* series.

To the Abstract Expressionists, the naturalistic portrayal of real objects was an enterprise which belonged to an earlier age. They preferred to express weighty concepts through abstract means, especially those which eradicated suggestions of depth and emphasized the flatness of canvas. Though Willem de Kooning, and occasionally others, alluded to general human forms in their compositions, no Abstract Expressionist accorded the figure the primacy that Rivers did. He portrayed the human figure, often in the form of portraiture, while at the same time, ironically retaining Abstract Expressionist traits, such as drips and splatters.

Rivers not only poked fun at Abstract Expressionism, but he viewed society's overly reverent attitude to the art of the past as absurd. He invites his audience to consider this phenomenon by parodying well-known icons from history. Works such as Rivers' two versions of *Washington Crossing the Delaware*, 1953 and 1960, which are based on Emanuel Leutze's 1851 painting of the same name, illustrate this point. Leutze's painting portrays an event in American history in a heroic, grandiose manner, while Rivers' versions parody the concept, as well as Abstract Expressionism, by depicting it in the loose, gestural brushwork associated with the New York School's more cosmic explorations.[2]

The quintessential Rivers surfaces in images such as those from the 1960s *Vocabulary Lessons series*. In 1961, when Rivers studied French at the Alliance Française in Paris, an image in a lesson book caught his eye. It portrayed what he described as a "rather idiotic-looking boy" labeled with French words designating the parts of the body.[3] He appropriated the concept and elevated it, preposterously, in numerous works, to the level of fine art, by painting it in a serious artist's media. The result is non- or anti-art, not unlike Jasper Johns crafting beer cans in bronze in *Painted Bronze (Balantine Ale Cans)*, 1960. Rivers was fascinated with the *Vocabulary Lessons* concept and painted it repeatedly. He eventually created *Vocabulary Lessons* in other languages, including English, Italian, and Polish.

Though misunderstood early in his career—critics failed to see the intellectual content in his approach—today, Larry Rivers is regarded as an important conceptual artist. Like the Dadaist, Marcel Duchamp, earlier in the century, Rivers causes us to re-think the nature and purpose of art and art-making in general, thereby deepening our understanding of one of the most "human" of human activities.

French Vocabulary Lesson, 1978
Colored pencil and charcoal on paper
33 1/8 x 33 1/8 in.
(l.r.: "Larry Rivers")
Purchased through the R. H. Norton Fund 84.1

In 1978, Rivers began work on a group of paintings that he dubbed the "Golden Oldies." Commissioned by the collector and dealer Jeffrey H. Loria, each of the canvases in the series recapitulates an important theme in Rivers' oeuvre. In addition to the *Vocabulary Lessons* paintings, Rivers reworked *Washington Crossing the Delaware*, *The Greatest Homosexual*, *Cedar Bar Menu I*, and others. Having frequently drawn inspiration from the masterpieces of past artists, Rivers, ironically, reached a point where he could parody his own work.[4] But he did not simply re-copy his old paintings, instead, he infused them with new life and additional ironies. Based specifically on a work owned by the Tate Gallery in London, (*Parts of the Face: French Vocabulary Lesson*, 1961), the Norton's *French Vocabulary Lesson* embodies all of Rivers' old cleverness, and more.

Parts of the Face is one of Rivers' earliest *Vocabulary Lesson* pieces. It portrays the head and neck of a young man surrounded by lines leading to the words *joue, oeil, cil, sourcil, front, cheveux, nez, dent, lèvre, and menton* (cheek, eye, eyelash, eyebrow, forehead, hair, nose, tooth, lip, and chin), and it closely resembles the lesson-book image that Rivers described as inspiring the concept. Stylistically, the painting typifies Rivers in the early 1960s, in that it combines the human form portrayed, more or less naturalistically, with elements that poke fun at the painterliness of Abstract Expressionism. Here, consciously applied drips and splatters humorously allude to Jackson Pollock's spontaneous action painting, and several large, nonrepresentational slash marks call to mind the art of Franz Kline. One of the boy's eyes, left unfinished, cleverly alludes to Abstract Expressionism's desire to document the artistic process by intentionally failing to finish the painting.

The "Golden Oldie" version of the Tate Gallery piece, created seventeen years after the first version, utilizes even more innuendoes than the first version, and thus, is more complex. Besides the fact that Rivers parodies his own work in the piece, and in doing so parodies himself parodying other artists, the work further comments on artistic process. At first glance, one assumes that the Norton's piece and the Tate version are identical. Closer examination, however, reveals that the later work is executed in colored pencil, and that the drips, splatters, and brushwork are *drawn on*, rather than real. The irony achieved is similar to the effect created by Roy Lichtenstein who depicted large brush strokes in his famous comic-book-style paintings by using fake Benday dots—the minute dots of color used to create images in commercial imagery. Like Rivers, Lichtenstein meticulously painted the drips onto his canvases to create the effect of spontaneous brushwork.

Larry Rivers oeuvre is rife with parody and witticisms. Though his detractors criticize his irreverence, it is this very quality that makes him valuable. Though brazen at times, his dedication to creating thought-provoking images is sincere. CMC

NOTES

[1] Rivers changed his name around the age of eighteen, when an emcee spontaneously dubbed his jazz group "Larry Rivers and his Mudcats."

[2] See Carol Brightman and Larry Rivers', *Drawings and Digressions by Larry Rivers* (New York City, NY: Clarkson N. Potter, 1979), 58–69, for Rivers' ideas on his two paintings. The second version was intended to replace the first version, which was partially burned in a fire in New York's Museum of Modern Art in 1958, but the piece was bought privately, instead.

[3] Ibid., 139.

[4] Helen A. Harrison, *Larry Rivers* (New York City, NY: Harper and Row, 1984), 100, 103–4.

PROVENANCE

Irving Galleries, 1984; Norton Gallery, 1984.

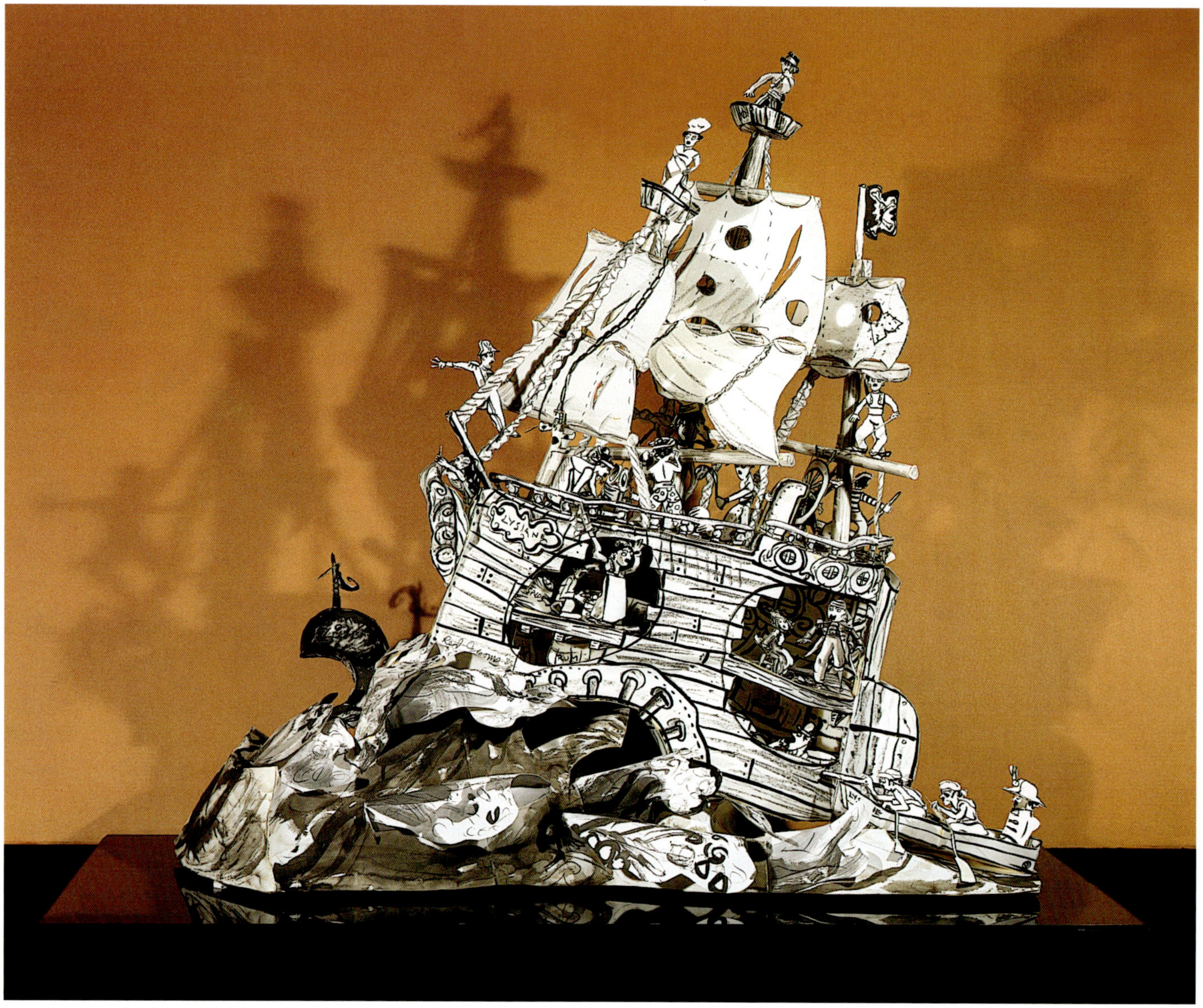

Charlie's Pirate Ship, 1985
Black ink on paper
48 1/4 x 49 1/2 x 22 1/2 in.
Purchased through the R. H. Norton Fund

Red Grooms

CHARLES ROGER (RED) GROOMS, 1937–

Internationally renowned as an artist, set-designer, and moviemaker, Red Grooms has been delighting audiences with whimsical creations of people and places since the early 1960s. Born in Nashville, Tennessee, Grooms made his first colored pencil drawing while in ninth grade, after visiting the Tennessee State Fair. The artist recalled, "There was an energy in places like [the State Fair] which I tried from the beginning to get into my drawings."[1] While still in high school, he learned about European modernism and Abstract Expressionism in New York from the pages of *ArtNews*. By age eighteen, Grooms had decided to become an artist, which made him "a fairly regular kind of oddball" in Nashville during the 1950s.[2]

In 1956, Grooms enrolled as an art student at the New School in New York. He was impressed by "action painters," such as Franz Kline, Philip Guston, and Willem de Kooning, whose work he saw in gallery shows, but the only artist he met outside of the New School faculty was the realist painter Raphael Soyer. The following year, Grooms enrolled in Hans Hofmann's school in Provincetown, Massachusetts, where he was encouraged to explore the expressive possibilities of abstract painting. In Provincetown, Grooms became involved with a group of artists who operated the Sun Gallery, and he collaborated on his first "event," a staged performance with the painter Yvonne Andersen. He also met Allan Kaprow, whose "happenings"—unscripted performances in which people interacted with props and settings—were creating a sensation in the art world.

Returning to New York in 1959, Grooms and some fellow artists opened an alternative exhibition space called the Delancey Street Museum. Grooms spent the next few years exhibiting and staging performances in New York and travelling throughout Europe, Egypt, and Israel. The sculpture, drawings, paintings, etchings, and film which Grooms produced during the early 1960s contained references to personal experiences from his travels.

In 1964, Grooms married the artist Mimi Gross. Over the next decade, he maintained a primary residence in New York, while he and Gross travelled extensively throughout the United States and Europe. Grooms secured funding, in 1975, to begin his most ambitious installation project yet, a collaboration with Gross which they called *Ruckus Manhattan*. The installation featured satirical replicas of familiar Manhattan sights—the Statue of Liberty, Wall Street, the Brooklyn Bridge, and the subway—constructed out of wood, paper, papier-mâché, and a variety of other materials. The objects were painted with bold colors in an exaggerated, cartoon style which led many critics to classify Grooms as a Pop Artist. The artist maintained, however, that his work was too expressive to be associated with the dry, objective style of Pop Art. He explained, "The environment would be lit at night, and people could enjoy it, party around it, just be sociable in its general vicinity. I wanted it to have a nice, romantic atmosphere."[3]

Since the mid-1970s, Grooms has continued to work in a wide variety of media, reworking old memories and developing new themes based on personal experiences. Over the last decade, the artist has continued to travel with his second wife, Lysiane Luong, and has incorporated memories of their travel experiences into his drawings, sculptures, and installations.

Charlie's Pirate Ship, 1985
Black ink on paper
48 1/4 x 49 1/2 x 22 1/2 in.
(bow of ship: "Red Grooms 85")
Purchased through the R. H. Norton Fund 94.10

Like most of Grooms' artwork, *Charlie's Pirate Ship* was inspired by a personal experience. Unlike the majority of the artist's oeuvre, however, the subject matter is not derived from everyday life, but from a dream. One night, Grooms dreamed that he was in a situation similar to that of Charlie Chaplin in his comic film *The Immigrant*. Like Chaplin, Grooms was on a ship sailing the sea, with no crew to perform all of the necessary nautical tasks. The artist had to do everything, and man every station at the same time, to keep the vessel afloat. Greatly amused by this dream, Grooms preserved the memory in his paper pirate ship. He named the ship after his wife, Lysiane, and substituted multiple versions of Chaplin's image for his own. The piece became one of the artist's personal favorites and remained in his possession until acquired by the Norton.

In *Charlie's Pirate Ship*, every character is Charlie Chaplin. Charlie is at the helm and in the galley, way up in the crow's nest, and firing cannons from the gun ports down below. He even appears stepping out of the gaping jaws of a whale that emerges from the surf beneath the starboard side of the ship's bow. The comical quality of *Charlie's Pirate Ship* is enhanced by numerous miniature melodramas being enacted throughout the piece. A cut-away section of the port side of the stern reveals a young maiden tied to a chair, held captive by a menacing, peg-legged Charlie Chaplin pirate. On the deck below, a stow-away Chaplin has popped up among barrels in the cargo hold. In the crow's nest of the foresail, the cook defiantly flings a long string of sausage links at the ungrateful mates below. Pirate Chaplins climb fearlessly through the rigging, securing the masts while the ship rocks in the turbulent sea, and one courageous Chaplin balances precariously on the thin bowsprit which projects from the upper end of the vessel's bow.

Grooms began to make paper sculptures in 1973, when a friend introduced him to the hot-glue gun. Paper is a fitting medium for the pirate ship, which seems as if it sailed right out of a newspaper comics section. The black-and-white drawing of *Charlie's Pirate Ship* recalls the black-and-white, slapstick world of Charlie Chaplin's movies, and its playful, comic-book style suggests childhood fantasies of pirates and buccaneers, Captain Hook and Peter Pan. As in his larger installations, Grooms has drawn on personal experience and popular culture to create a farcical scene that transports the viewer into a romantic world of memories and dreams. DM

NOTES

[1] Red Grooms, unpublished biographical outline (West Palm Beach, FL: Irving Galleries, 1993), 1.

[2] Ibid., 2.

[3] Ibid., 7.

PROVENANCE

Artist, 1985–94; Norton Gallery, 1994.

EXHIBITION HISTORY

Pennsylvania Academy of the Fine Arts, Philadelphia, PA, *Red Grooms, A Retrospective, 1956–1984*, June 21–September 29, 1985.

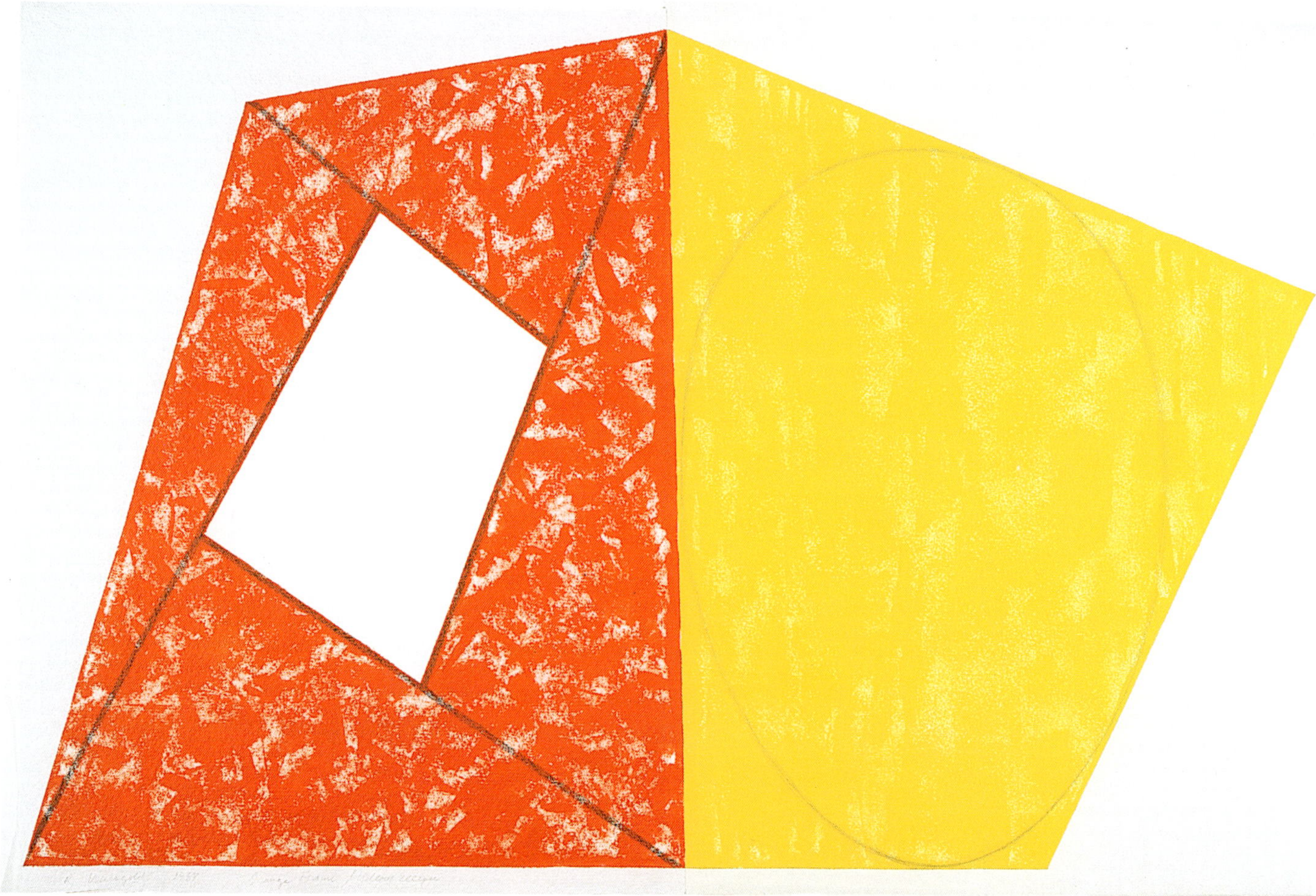

Orange Frame/Yellow Ellipse, 1988
Acrylic, pencil, and oil on two sheets of paper
29 1/2 x 43 1/2 in.
Gift of the Estate of Stephen D. Hassenfeld

Robert Mangold

1937–

Like many artists of his generation, Robert Mangold reacted to the intense romanticism and egotism of Abstract Expressionism by turning to the more rational, objective aesthetic of Minimalism. Yet, within his spare, geometrically inspired, and tightly controlled compositions, Mangold has, increasingly throughout his career, explored the complexities of visual experience with remarkable originality and surprising playfulness.

Growing up in North Tonawanda, New York, Mangold decided to become an illustrator and, in 1956, began studying at the Cleveland Institute of Art. Within two years, he had changed his focus from illustration to fine art, and by the time he graduated in 1959, Mangold was painting in the then dominant Abstract Expressionist style.

In 1960, Mangold began graduate studies at Yale, where he was significantly influenced by Josef Albers' emphasis on formal relationships and color theory. At the same time, he immersed himself in the history of modern art, studying and practicing various styles such as Cubism and Surrealism, from which he gained a thorough understanding of the theoretical and technical developments of twentieth century art. Gradually, Mangold abandoned Abstract Expressionism and began exploring formalist issues in reduced, mathematically inspired compositions which were strongly influenced by Albers' geometric abstractions. Graduating from Yale in 1962 with a Master of Fine Arts degree, Mangold moved to New York City.

Mangold's earliest works as a professional artist reflected many of the ideas behind the Minimalist movement, which had its origins in the 1950s, with the hard-edged imagery of such painters as Ellsworth Kelly. His first solo exhibition, held at the Fischbach Gallery in 1965, for instance, was titled *Walls and Areas*, and featured opaquely painted panels which, in their simplicity, resembled wall sections. Architecturally inspired, they contained none of the content or external references traditionally expected in painting but, in accordance with Minimalist doctrine, insisted instead on the painting as a self-referential object. Mangold's materials and techniques were Minimalist, as well. Rather than painting with traditional brushes on a textured canvas, he sprayed or rolled his paint onto the comparatively smooth and industrial surface of a masonite board. Other works from this period feature single, geometric figures which are pencil drawn on a neutral-color ground and are, thus, similarly uncompromising in their insistence on the 'objectness' of painting and the irrelevance of craftsmanship to art.

In 1969, Mangold received a Guggenheim grant which permitted him to move away from New York City and into the Catskills, where his work developed along increasingly independent lines. He returned to painting with brushes on canvas and began exploring the potential visual effects of color. His paintings of the 1970s and 1980s are, thus, hybrids, employing traditional tools and techniques to explore avant-garde concepts. Often, these works are composed of two or more polygonal canvases which become almost sculptural in their emphasis on form. In recent years, this three-dimensional impulse has been more fully realized in Mangold's colorful, kinetic sculptures.

Yet, what particularly distinguishes Mangold's oeuvre is his sense of playfulness. Mangold is a master at setting-up certain visual expectations in his viewer and, then, confounding those same expectations with a series of surprises. Thus, first impressions of his work are soon amended as subtleties surface, forcing the mental conversion of circles to spirals, figures to ground, or solids to voids. This element of surprise injects even his sparest compositions with a complexity of enduring interest.

Orange Frame/Yellow Ellipse, 1988
Acrylic, pencil, and oil on two sheets of paper
29 1/2 x 43 1/2 in.
(l.l.: "R. Mangold")
Gift of the Estate of Stephen D. Hassenfeld 91.42

Orange Frame/Yellow Ellipse is part of a series in which Mangold pairs two quadrilateral shapes and sets-up a complex dialogue between them. Focusing on his primary concerns of form and color, these paintings are studies in visual contrasts and unexpected juxtapositions.

As with the other works in this series, *Orange Frame/Yellow Ellipse* is an intentionally incongruous composition. The diptych format, enhanced by the quadrilaterals' shared central and bottom edges, raises an expectation of symmetry which is, then, contradicted by multiple contrasts between the two panels.

The painting's most assertive contrast is created with color. The juxtaposition of the bold orange and mustard yellow sets-up a visual competition, and the viewer's eye shifts restlessly from one to the other. Inspired by Henri Matisse's brilliant palette, these colors vibrantly interact and reflect Mangold's absorption of Albers' teaching. Unlike Albers' universally smooth applications of paint, however, Mangold reinforces his color contrast by creating textural surface patterns. With non-Minimalist painterliness, he loosely brushes the orange onto the paper in an erratic, all over pattern reminiscent of Abstract Expressionism. Allowing the white of the paper to gleam through, Mangold adeptly animates the surface of the quadrilateral. Although more thickly applied, the yellow paint, similarly, reveals the hand of the artist through its uneven, and highly visible, vertical brush strokes.

The two panels are further differentiated by their compositions. Sharing two sides, the quadrilaterals are, nevertheless, very different configurations which optically pull in opposite directions. Moreover, their interior compositions are diametrically opposed: a dynamically framed parallelogram within a quadrilateral, versus an oval which is stabilized by its tangential contact with the exterior shape. In his canvas works within this same series, Mangold further stresses these compositional distinctions by making the interior parallelogram on the left an actual hole through the canvas, and by separating the panels in the center, while maintaining the continuous bottom edge.

Typically, Mangold works on an idea for a year or two in a series of related works. In 1977, he began making initial studies on paper, as opposed to masonite, and *Orange Frame/Yellow Ellipse*, thus, represents his early concept of the frame/ellipse series. In subsequent works, Mangold continued to experiment, reversing the ellipse and frame, varying his color combinations, and enlarging the entire composition onto canvas. In all of these works, however, Mangold richly combines tradition and innovation, and reveals his post-Minimalist vision. AMB

PROVENANCE

Artist; Stephen Hassenfeld, New York City, NY; Mrs. Ronald Block, Palm Beach, FL; Norton Gallery, 1991.

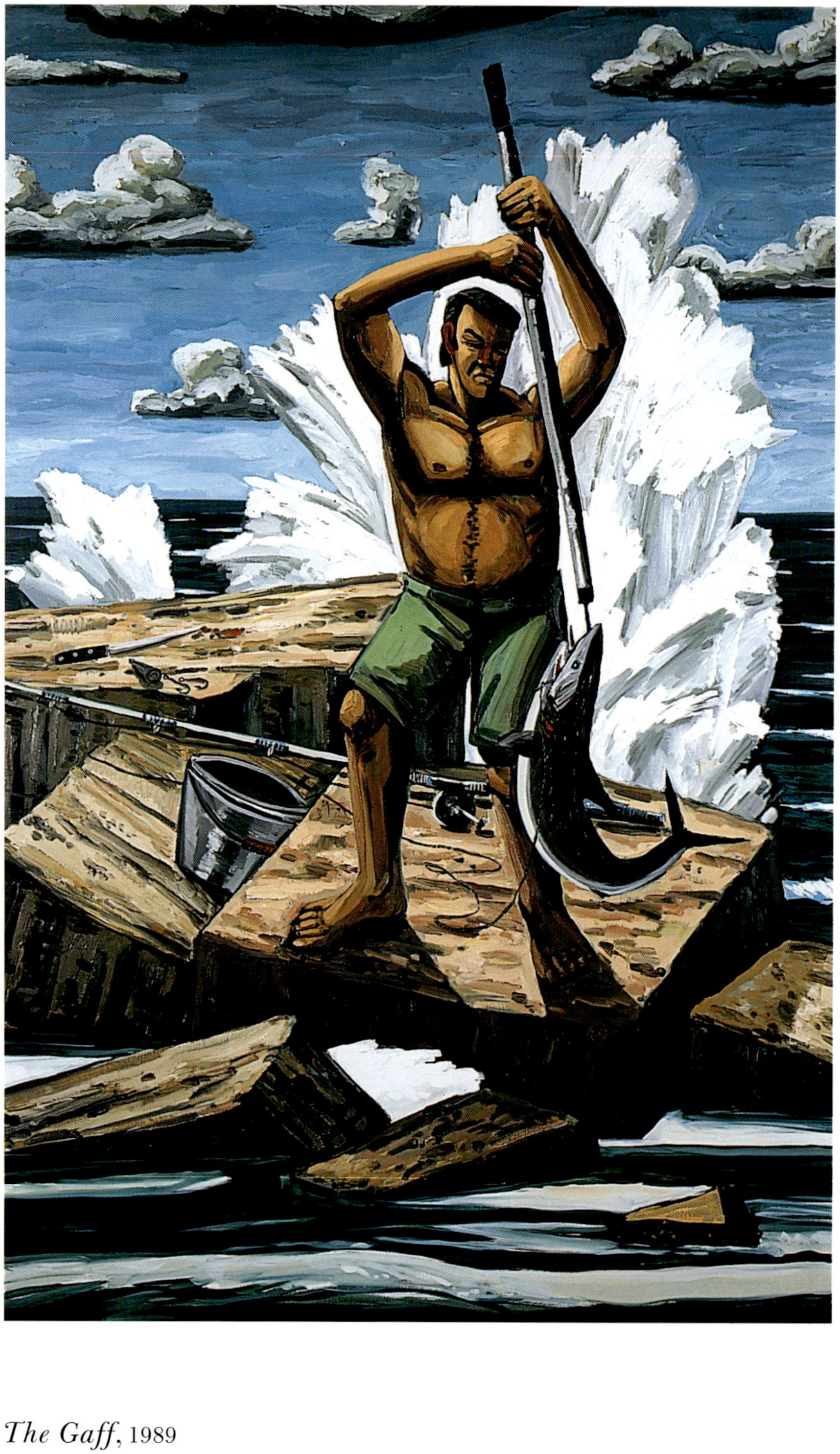

The Gaff, 1989
Oil on canvas
76 x 48 in.
Purchased through the R. H. Norton Fund

David Bates

1952–

David Bates is a Dallas-based painter who gathers the images for his expressionist portraits and landscapes from the rugged environs of rural Arkansas, Florida, and Louisiana. He transforms the outdoor lifestyles common to these locales into high dramas of human interaction with the powerful forces of nature.

An academically trained painter, Bates experimented with several themes and media before arriving at expressionist painting. Born in Garland, Texas, he earned a Bachelor of Fine Arts degree at Southern Methodist University in Dallas in 1975, and in the following year, received a Master of Fine Arts degree from the same institution. Bates then entered the year-long Independent Study Program at the Whitney Museum of American Art. During his New York stay, he practiced contemporary techniques, painting Photorealist portraits of New York indigents and Whitney Museum staff, and creating video and performance art. Still, Bates felt out- of-step with the avant-garde art scene. He was dissatisfied with both his formal approach and his subject matter, and uncertain of his artistic path.

Upon his return to Texas in 1977, Bates settled in Dallas to study art history at his alma mater. He also began to make small, painted carvings based on the people and landscapes he had seen during his hunting and fishing trips in the South. With subject matter drawn from the ordinary happenings in small-town life, these simplified and crudely direct sculptures incorporate the hallmarks of folk art. Bates, in addition, was inspired by the example of Red Grooms, a creator of Pop Art installations. While in New York, Bates had helped Grooms with the construction of *Ruckus Manhattan*, 1975–76 (Marlborough Gallery, New York), and he admired the humor and accessibility of Grooms' art. Starting in the late seventies, Bates carved and created mixed media assemblages. He also translated the everyday subjects of these three-dimensional works into paintings which carried the look of folk art. In this period, his catalogue of painting subjects expanded to include himself, his wife, friends, and family.

The heroic theme of "man in nature" emerged in Bates' painting after the artist visited the western Arkansas area of Grassy Lake in 1981. He was overwhelmed by the unspoiled beauty of this isolated place and its fantastic variety of wildlife and plants. To Bates, the primeval environment of the area explained the impetus of folk art and its independence from the conventional approaches to art. The technical ability and skill of the Grassy Lake hunters and fishermen, especially, impressed him, and the dignity and wisdom that Bates found in them are qualities suggested visually in his paintings.

Since visiting Grassy Lake, Bates has utilized a similarly physical, expressionist approach to interpret other locales, among them, the western coast of Florida. Infrequently, he has produced still lifes and portraits. Although his sitters are posed in studio chairs, they are painted with the same vigorous impasto that is typical of his nature-theme pictures. In these works of the nineties, Bates investigates the emotional impact of color and pattern contrasts and a more linear pictorial structure.

The Gaff, 1989
Oil on canvas
76 x 48 in.
(l.l.: "BATES")
Purchased through the R. H. Norton Fund 92.25

From his contact with the inhabitants of the rural South, David Bates has learned about the rhythms of nature and has come to admire those who move in concert with it. In *The Gaff*, the sportsman's act of fishing is extended into a metaphor of man's relationship with nature. Bates imbues the image of the shark fisherman with a sense of purpose and self-awareness in the world, placing the powerful figure near the canvas center. Posed on the angled surface of the jetty, the sculpted and steady human form matches the magnificence of the breakers. Bates frames the heroic figure with the sea and sky, in such a way as to suggest that the outdoorsman is an inseparable part of the environment in the picture and in the real world he inhabits.

The raw expressionism of Bates' work distinguishes it from ordinary genre scenes. In *The Gaff*, he exaggerates the scale of representative objects to make them larger than life. Everything is big in the world he portrays, from the fisherman and his equipment, to the forces of nature. Furthermore, Bates flattens his forms, organizes them into planes, and selectively eliminates details about them, in order to present the essential. He starkly lights the action, creating value shifts that give volume and texture to forms. The generally dark palette of *The Gaff* is also brightened by the intense, white light emitting from the background spray of water. Together, these simplifying techniques of folk art and the artist's overall reductivist strategy convert the local and particular into a far-reaching, generalized statement.

Bates' paintings are developed conceptions, rather than exact, visual translations of the bayous, coastal towns, and wooded areas he has visited. He customarily observes commercial hunters and fishermen at work and during their leisure time, and sketches their activities in pen and ink. In the studio, he expands his ideas, and these preparatory drawings are enlarged as charcoal-and-sepia washes on canvas. Although Bates makes drawings for exhibition that are not in adjunct relationships with his paintings, a drawing entitled *The Gaff*, 1989 (Charles Cowles Gallery, New York) is likely a preliminary study for the picture of the same name. It presents the same subject as the Norton's painting, but the fisherman and his catch are organized along a central, vertical axis. Parallel strokes of sepia and gray shadow the darkly outlined forms of the Herculean human figure, the struggling fish, and the sea, to indicate the vigorous engagement of these active forces. The Norton's painting is similarly energetic, as a result of Bates' direct painting method and the muscularity of his brushwork. JF

PROVENANCE

John Berggruen Gallery, San Francisco, CA; Norton Gallery, 1992.

EXHIBITION HISTORY

The Art Museum, Florida International University, Miami, FL, *David Bates*, April 30–May 29, 1993, no. 7.

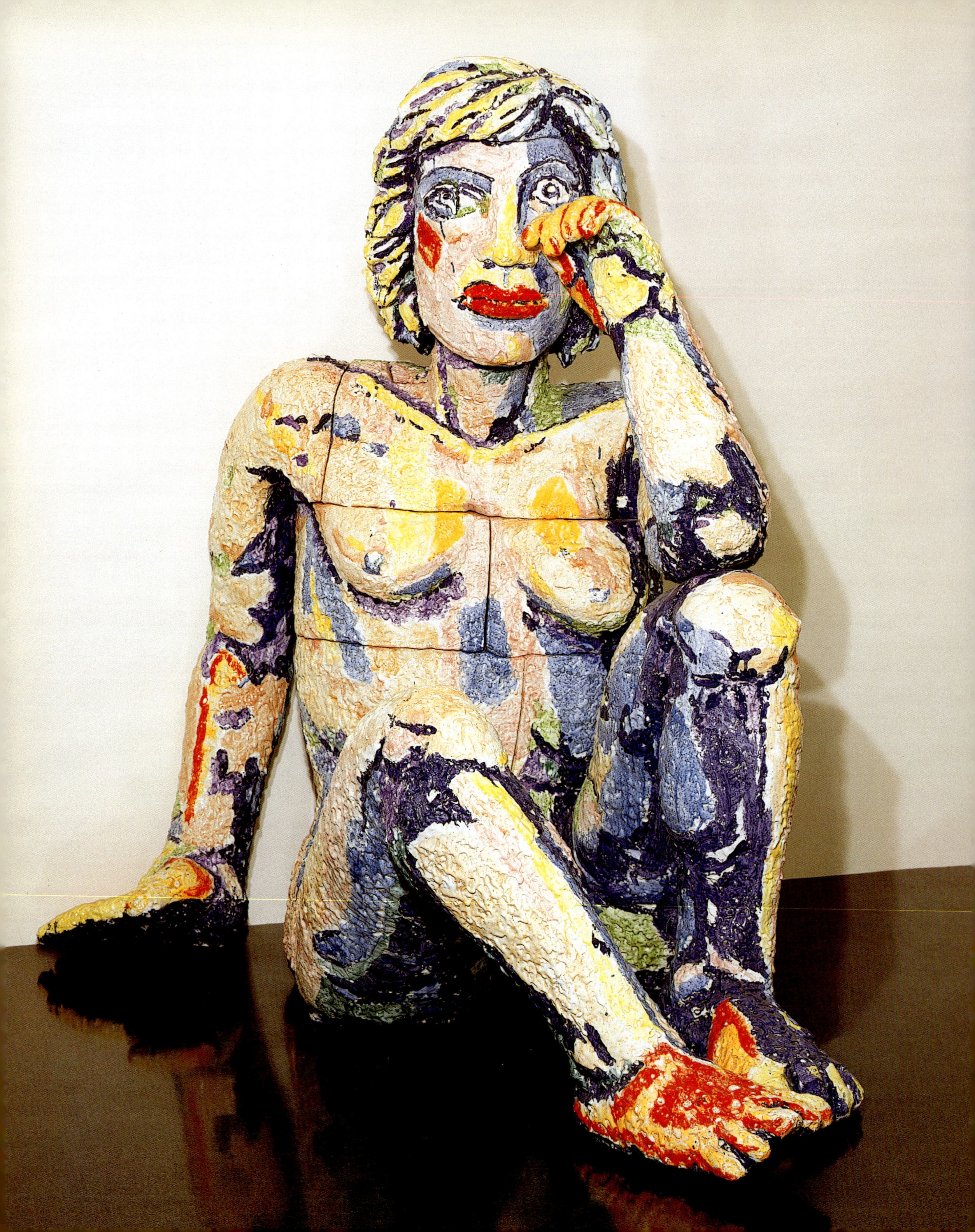

Viola Frey

1933–

Viola Frey has been called a "visual anthropologist of contemporary American culture."[1] The San Francisco Bay area sculptor chooses subject matter from her own experiences, drawing her inspiration from a wide variety of sources ranging from classical antiquity to flea market bric-a-brac. Since the early 1980s, Frey has been producing larger-than-life, ceramic figures which embody a number of paradoxes. The stocky, massive sculptures dominate the three-dimensional space which they inhabit, yet the gestural strokes of brightly-colored glazes which cover their surfaces refer to the flatness of an Abstract Expressionist painting. Frey's figures appear awesome as they tower above the viewer, but the visible seams, where the artist has joined the component sections of each figure, emphasize their fragile nature. A sensitive observer of human nature, Frey endows her figures with humanity, in spite of their powerful monumentality.

Although she is most well known as a sculptor, Frey majored in painting under Richard Diebenkorn at the California College of Arts and Crafts in Oakland, California, from 1953–1956. She switched her emphasis to ceramics when she enrolled at Tulane University in New Orleans in 1957, where she earned a Master of Fine Arts degree. During the winter term at Tulane, she attended a workshop taught by Mark Rothko and was greatly impressed with his manipulation of color. Unlike Rothko, however, Frey eschewed complete abstraction, opting instead to produce work based on the human form. A few years, later she saw an exhibition of figurative paintings by Diebenkorn, and decided to return to

Weeping Woman, 1990–1991
Glazed ceramic
76 x 58 x 80 in.
Purchased through the Rose L. Kraft Fund

the San Francisco Bay area where the figurative tradition in art flourished.

Upon her return to San Francisco in 1960, Frey re-enrolled at the California College of Arts and Crafts to continue her study in ceramics. By 1965, she was teaching there and exhibiting her work in New York and San Francisco Bay area museums. She also began to frequent flea markets, collecting china knickknacks and figurines which she referred to as "cultural artifacts."[2] The flamboyant effect of the colored glazes which cover her figures recalls the flashy quality of these mass-produced items. In 1975, Frey purchased a house in Oakland which finally gave her the room she needed to work on a large scale, and she began to produce male and female figures which became progressively bigger. Although she has continued to paint and to produce smaller-scale ceramics, her emphasis, over the last two decades, has been on the monumental figures.

The gestural quality of the paint and glazes dripped over the surface of Frey's sculptures has been compared to the figurative mode of Abstract Expressionist painting adopted by Diebenkorn and the Bay Area Figurative Painters in the late 1950s and early 1960s. But Frey's art was also influenced by European art, which she saw reproduced in art magazines and catalogues. The artist has explained, "I was aware of [the Bay Area Figurative Painters], of course.... I don't think I felt allied aesthetically to Bay Area figurative art; it's just that its presence was comforting and supportive. Like so many young artists on the West Coast at that time, my strongest single influence came from art publications.... I was strongly attracted to the work of Léger, Giacometti, Dubuffet, Fontana, and others. Books and catalogues were more my mentors than any regional movements."[3] Frey's monumental, archetypal figures derive from a rich body of influences, combined with her personal observations of contemporary culture.

Weeping Woman, 1990–1991
Glazed ceramic
76 x 58 x 80 in.
(no inscription)
Purchased through the Rose L. Kraft Fund 92.2

One of a series of nude female figures which Frey cast in the early 1990s, *Weeping Woman* exemplifies the synthesis of modern popular culture and art historical tradition which characterizes the sculptor's work. The colossal female nude continues a sculptural tradition which reaches back to classical antiquity. The seated position of *Weeping Woman*, leaning back on her right hand, with bent legs partially extended to the front, recalls mythological figures which decorated triangular pediments above the entrances of ancient Greek temples. The massiveness of Frey's sculpture is similar to the cumbersome women in paintings of Picasso's classical period. Unlike the smooth contours of Picasso's women, however, the contours and volumes of *Weeping Woman* are broken by the slashing marks of brilliantly colored paint and glazes which enliven the surface of the figure. Cast in thirty-three separate pieces, the creation of *Weeping Woman* involved an elaborate and painstaking process, during which Frey had to act as sculptor, ceramicist, and painter, all in one.

Frey has been compared to a modern day "cartoonist who thinks big."[4] Like the enlarged, comic-strip characters painted by the Pop artist Roy Lichtenstein during the 1960s, the emphatic, pantomimic gesture of *Weeping Woman* creates a feeling of staged melodrama which minimizes the emotional impact of the image. The effect of caricature is heightened by the magnified eyes of the figure, outlined in dark blue and painted as if wearing azure eye shadow, and her full lips which seem to be painted with brilliant crimson lipstick. The large, fuschia teardrop which falls from her right eye completes the stereotypical representation of sorrow, in her face that is echoed in the hunched position of her body. Using the visual language of the mass media, Frey has created a figure which is instantly recognizable as a representation of sorrow, without overt sentimentality. But, unlike the banal cartoon characters that proliferate in the modern media, *Weeping Woman* conveys a subtle sense of vulnerability. The visible seams between the thirty-three ceramic sections which comprise the work emphasize the fragile nature of this colossal figure. In spite of the sculpture's brassy boldness, the viewer is aware that this monumental clay woman can easily break. In *Weeping Woman*, Frey has preserved the human quality of her tragic-comic figure, and updated the classical tradition of monumental sculpture to include an archetype of modern popular culture. DM

NOTES

[1] Patterson B. Sims, *It's All Part of the Clay: Viola Frey* (Philadelphia, PA: Goldie Paley Gallery, Moore College of Art, 1985), 3.

[2] Charlotte Streiffer Rubenstein, *American Women Sculptors* (Boston, MA: G.K. Hall & Co., 1990), 528.

[3] Viola Frey, interview with Garth Clark, 6 August 1984, in *It's All Part of the Clay: Viola Frey*, 18.

[4] Glenn O'Brien, "Viola Frey," *Artforum* 23 (November 1984); 106.

PROVENANCE

Nancy Hoffman Gallery, New York City, NY, 1991; Norton Gallery, 1992.

EXHIBITION HISTORY

Nancy Hoffman Gallery, New York City, NY, *Viola Frey*, April 27–June 2, 1991.

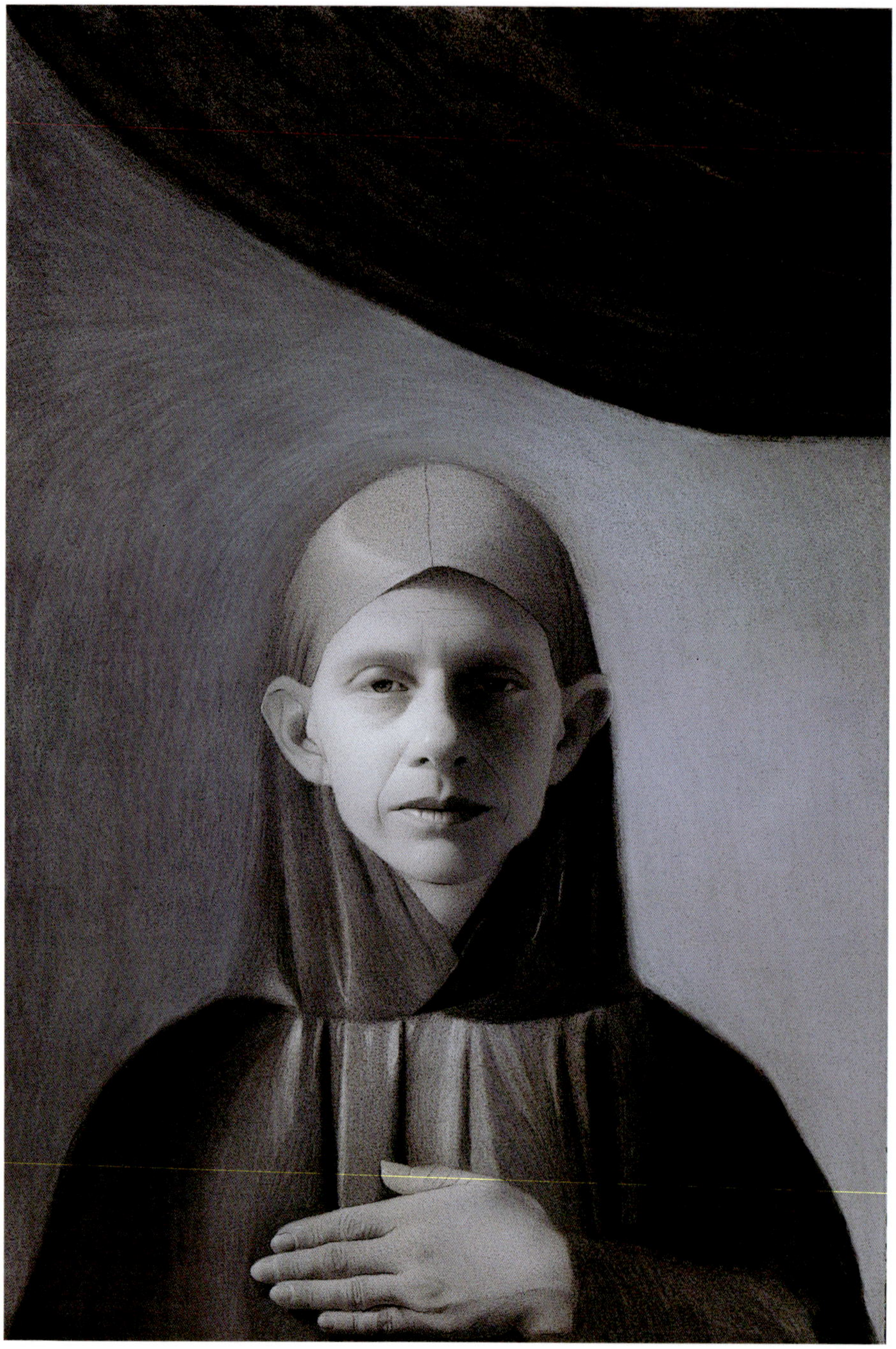

Self-Portrait, 1990
Charcoal and pastel on paper
40 x 26 in.
Purchased through the R. H. Norton Fund

Susan Hauptman

1947–

For Susan Hauptman, who has drawn from a very early age, a broad range of expression is as possible with traditional drawing media as with any other medium. Although she began her graduate training as a painter, she soon turned back to drawing because of its flexibility and its sensuousness. Hauptman was born in Michigan, and after attending a special high school for the arts, she received a Bachelor of Fine Arts degree from the University of Michigan in 1968 and a Master of Fine Arts degree in 1970 from Wayne State University in Detroit. Over the next decade, she taught at the University of Pittsburgh, at St. Lawrence University in Canton, New York, and at Skidmore College in Saratoga Springs, New York.

Hauptman feels that her art began when she first met her husband in 1979.[1] She drew a self-portrait to send to him shortly after their marriage, when he continued to live in California, while she remained in New York. Since then, she has examined her own image in numerous large-scale drawings, sometimes starkly naked, and at other times with curious clothing and props. Because she likes to be alone, she draws for up to twelve hours a day, six days a week, in a solitary working environment conducive to self-examination. Hauptman also produces exquisite, large-scale, still life drawings, often with subtle, personal sexual references.

Hauptman moved to California in 1985, where she was a visiting artist at the University of California, Davis, and later taught at Otis/Parsons Institute in Los Angeles. She has received numerous awards in California, including The Oakland Museum Artist of the Year Award, in 1984, and a Visual Artist Fellowship from the California Arts Council, in 1990. Other awards include two National Endowment for the Arts Fellowships, in 1985 and 1991, that enabled her to live and work in France. The artist currently resides in New York City.

Self-Portrait, 1990
Charcoal and pastel on paper
40 x 26 in.
(no inscription)
Purchased through the R. H. Norton Fund 91.121

Susan Hauptman's meticulously finished *Self-Portrait* is at once a simple expression of self, and a participant in the complex discourse of artistic representation. Although she does not idealize her own image, the exquisitely rendered surface of her drawing is beautiful in its own right. She achieves remarkable precision in her work by carefully reworking her image, often over a period of several months. The artist enjoys unlimited freedom with her drawing media, mixing her charcoal with pencil, pastel, and other materials. The same freedom can be seen in her exaggeration of features, such as hands or ears, which gives her portrait a sense of ambiguity and vulnerability. Opposed to that vulnerability is a self which denies possession by the spectator. Hauptman is not presenting herself to be consumed as an object of pleasure. Rather, through her technical mastery of the medium, she creates her own self on paper.

This *Self-Portrait* relates to Hauptman's experience while vacationing at a remote game preserve in Southern India. She and her husband watched a group of powerful elephants suddenly back away and humble themselves in front of an approaching smaller, horned animal. The enlarged hand, placed across Hauptman's chest in the drawing, refers to those great elephants' lesson of humility. Her visit was during the monsoon season, and the cloak she is wearing, which has been compared to a nun's habit, is actually a plastic rain poncho. Her exaggerated ears protrude because she had to leave them outside of her poncho to hear the animals. The soft, ambiguous, sloping form in the background, and the clear, but unidentified, light which falls on the left side of her face and continues uninterrupted in the right background, are left deliberately ambiguous.

As in many of her self-portraits, Hauptman appears in this drawing as not overly feminine or masculine, but strangely androgynous. This is because Hauptman does not see any clearly defined boundaries in life between men and women.[2] The artist also chooses not to recognize the boundary between drawing and painting in the hierarchy of art forms, which historically has exalted the latter above the former. Although Hauptman does not consider her drawings to be feminist, there is an equalizing process at work in her straightforward presentation of herself to the world. In her own words, she "[does] not take on feminist causes, but art causes."[3]

On a certain level, however, Hauptman's images do enter into the discourse of recent feminist scholarship concerning issues of representation. In the history of Western art, depictions of women have generally emphasized external attributes which make them desirable to the male viewer. John Berger has noted that a woman's "own sense of being in herself is supplanted by a sense of being appreciated as herself by another."[4] The quiet assertiveness of Hauptman's self-representation undermines this tradition. Her gaze is turned back at the viewer, not in militant confrontation, but with a steadfastness that defies possession. With imperfections ruthlessly emphasized through the artist's exaggerations, her self asserts itself as an image which is beautiful on its own terms. For Hauptman, those terms are the formal terms of art: the sinuous line, the carefully modulated play of light and shadow, the exquisitely rendered sheen of reflected light on the slick surface of her plastic poncho. She does not accept the limitations traditionally associated with her gender or chosen medium, placing herself with humility before the world, the dominant gaze being her own. DM

NOTES

[1] Susan Hauptman, telephone interview with author, 15 April 1994.

[2] Ibid.

[3] Ibid.

[4] John Berger, *Ways of Seeing* (London, England: British Broadcasting Corp. and Penguin Books, 1972), 46.

PROVENANCE

Norton Gallery, 1991.

EXHIBITION HISTORY

Norton Gallery and School of Art, West Palm Beach, FL, *Susan Hauptman*, May 2–June 14, 1992.

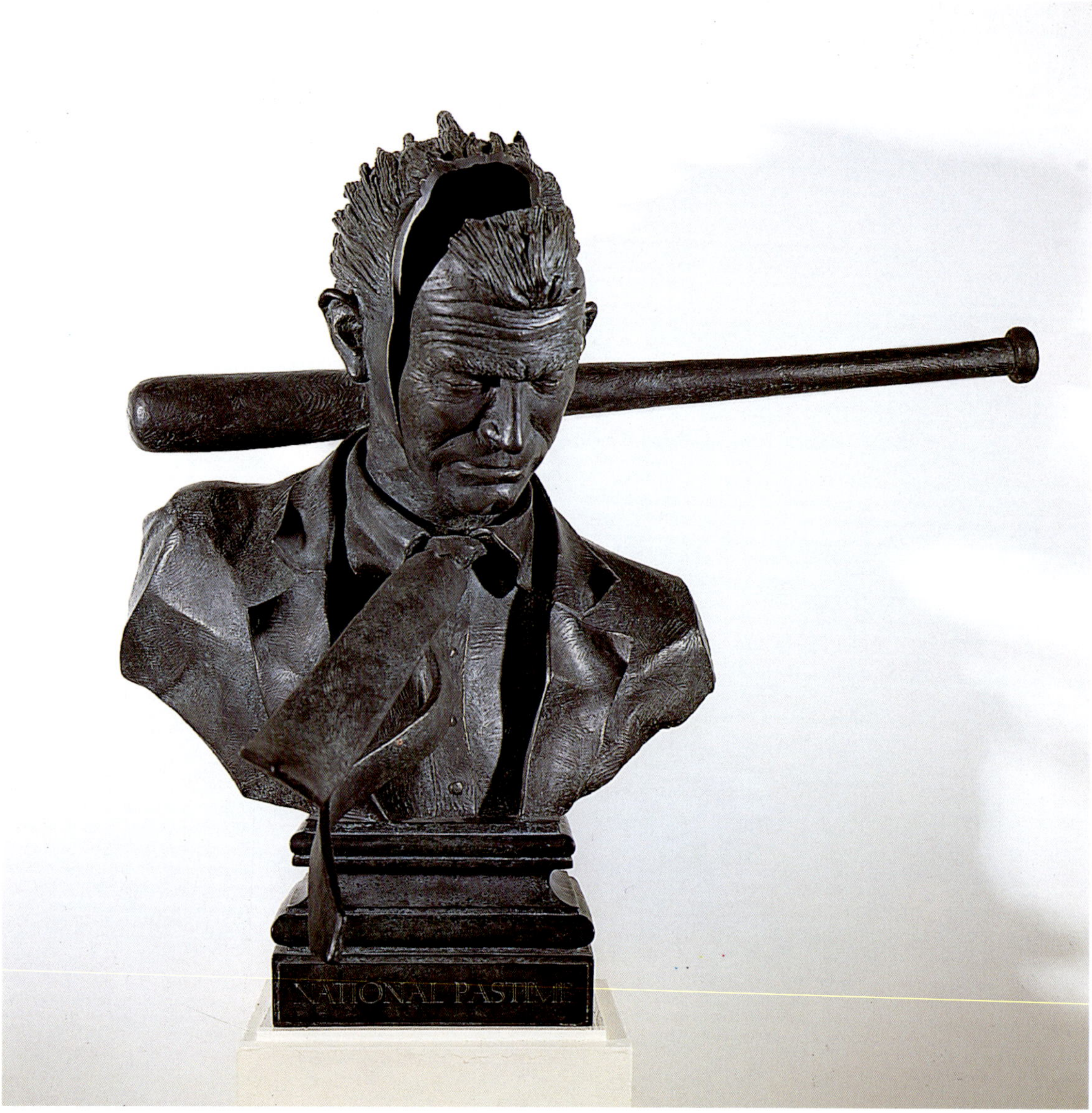

National Pastime I, 1991
Cast bronze, edition 2/3
33 x 23 x 15 in.
Purchased through the R. H. Norton Fund

Terry Allen

1943–

Terry Allen is a musician, songwriter, performance artist, director, installation artist, painter, and sculptor, whose work embodies hilarity and anguish, satire and poignant commentary about the contemporary world. Born in Wichita, Kansas, the artist grew up in Lubbock, Texas. His mother was a ragtime piano player, and his father, Fletcher Mansion "Sled" Allen, was a professional baseball player, turned promoter, who also staged musical evenings in a reconditioned World War II bomber hanger featuring performers, such as T-Bone Walker and Hank Williams.[1] Allen studied at the Chouinard Art Institute in Los Angeles, where he received his Bachelor of Fine Arts in 1966. He returned to teach drawing classes at Chouinard from 1968–1969, and he spent a year as a guest artist at the University of California, Berkeley, in 1971. During the 1970s, Allen was a faculty member in the Art Department of California State University, Fresno. He has exhibited in museums and galleries throughout the world, and he has received numerous awards for his work, including National Endowment for the Arts Fellowships, in 1972 and 1979, a Guggenheim Fellowship, in 1986, and a 1989 National Endowment for the Arts' Adaline Kent Award.

Allen's work mixes his own, personal memories with the collective memories of American society. Much of his creative energy during the 1980s was directed towards his *Youth in Asia* project, a group of mixed-media installations, paintings, drawings, and sculptures which reflected the cultural fragmentation and alienation that resulted from the United States' involvement in the Vietnam War. The irony of the title is typical of Allen's work in all media: the gentle humor of its pun is coupled with serious, far-reaching implications.

In 1991, Allen began to explore the possibilities of using bronze, one of the oldest sculptural mediums, for a commission from Citicorp Plaza in Los Angeles to create a series of busts of *Corporate Heads*. Playfully absurd and humorous at first sight, these busts wittily expose the falsehoods which lie behind the faces of corporate America. The artist has also continued to write and record music, a selection of which appears on David Byrne's album "*UH OH*," and he has worked as writer and set designer for vanguard music-theater performances. Allen currently lives with his wife, performance artist Jo Harvey Allen, in Santa Fe, New Mexico.

National Pastime I, 1991
Cast bronze, edition 2/3
33 x 23 x 15 in.
(on base: "National Pastime I")
Purchased through the R. H. Norton Fund 92.5

National Pastime I continues the series of bronze busts which began with Allen's *Corporate Heads* commission of 1991. Although cast in the tradition of classical Roman portraits, Allen's bust bears little similarity to the commemorative busts of great historical figures which adorn modern banks and government buildings. Typically, Allen's bust does not represent a specific person. Rather, the artist has created a generalized type of individual who is nonetheless an immediately recognizable part of contemporary society. The face is middle-aged, and the figure wears a business suit with a tie—the uniform of corporate America. His tie, flying forward as a symbol of corporate allegiance, can be compared to those featured in New York artist Robert Longo's *Men in the Cities* series of images in the early 1980s. The hair of Allen's figure is blown back from his face, as if by a strong wind, yet it is inconsistent with the direction of the flying tie. The rearward force of the wind is countered by the forward swing of the baseball bat, which cracks the figure from behind, at the base of its head. The paradoxical nature of *National Pastime I* is enhanced by the split in the figure's skull that opens to reveal a hollow cranium.

In characteristic style, Allen has created a jocular image which makes serious commentary on American civilization. The empty shell of the businessman's head suggests a loss of individuality or a lack of intelligence. But, as one critic has noted, Allen's bronze busts "do not merely mock the American corporate male. There is tragedy in the emptiness revealed in these portraits, to which the artist seems sympathetic."[2] The baseball bat and title refer, on one level, to the national popularity of the sport. One is left to wonder, however, if "national pastime" really refers to the playing of baseball, or to the smashing of one's competitors in the brutal games played by corporate America. As the son of a former baseball player and promoter, the artist grew up witnessing the politics which surround America's popular national pastime. In *National Pastime I*, Allen has combined autobiography with the collective experiences of modern American culture. The resulting image is both tragically revealing and comically entertaining. DM

NOTES

[1] Andrea Liss, "Terry Allen," in *Forty Years of California Assemblage* (Los Angeles: University of California, Los Angeles, CA, Wight Art Gallery, 1989), 102.

[2] Saundra Goldman, review, *ArtNews* 91 (May 1992): 136.

PROVENANCE

Moody Gallery, Houston, TX, 1991–1992; Norton Gallery, 1992.

EXHIBITION HISTORY

Moody Gallery, Houston, TX, *Terry Allen*, January 25–February 29, 1992.

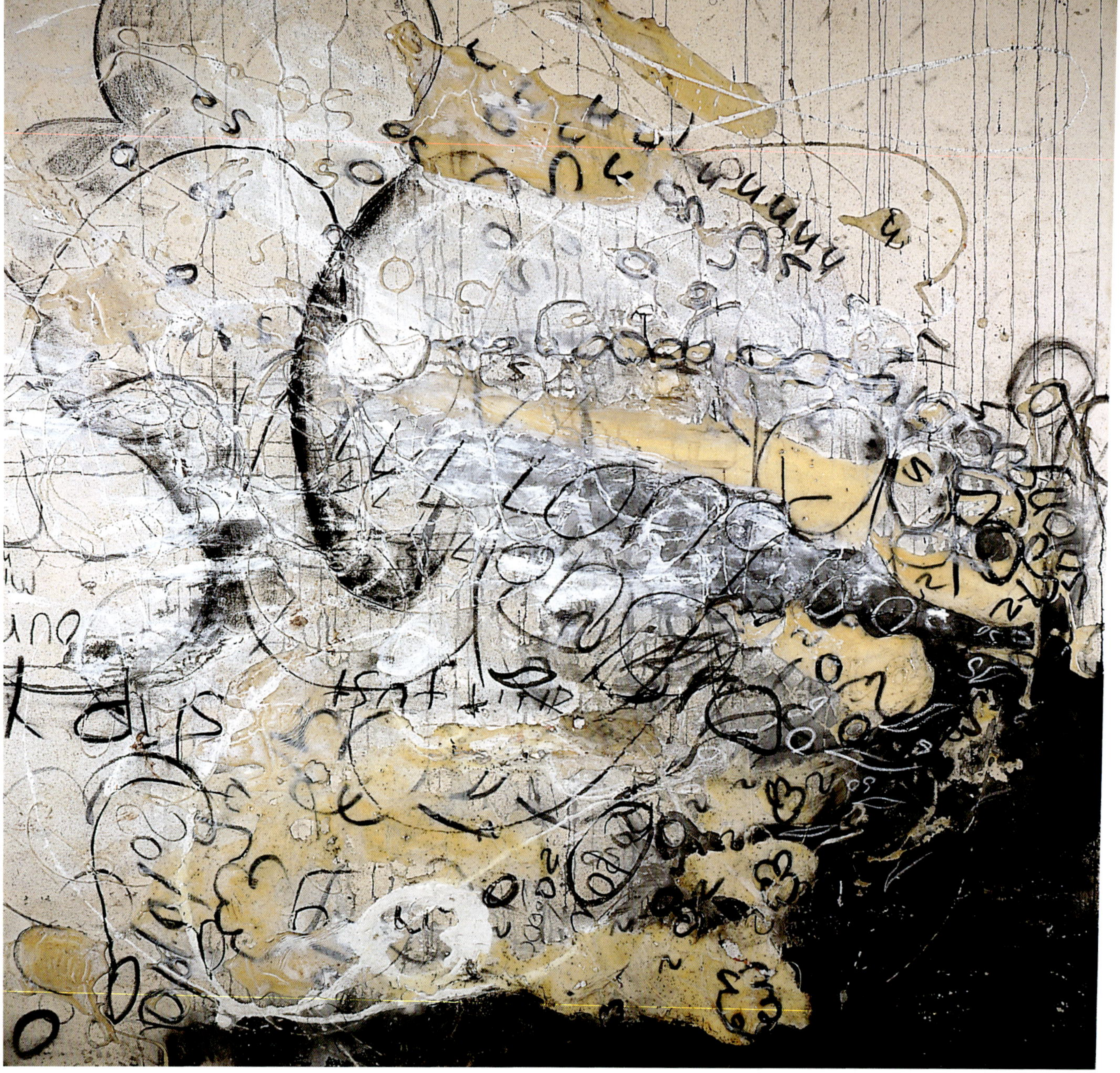

so long, 1992
72 x 72 in.
Acrylic, charcoal, and gesso on canvas
Purchased through the Rose L. Kraft Fund

Suzanne McClelland

1959–

Suzanne McClelland is one of the youngest artists represented in the Norton's collection. She was born in Jacksonville, Florida, and presently lives and works in New York City. McClelland received a Bachelor of Fine Arts degree from the University of Michigan at Ann Arbor in 1981, and a Master of Fine Arts degree from the School of Visual Arts, New York, in 1989. She spent a year abroad, in 1980, at the Universita Italiana per Stranieri, Perugia, Italy.

McClelland is one of a number of contemporary artists to incorporate words into her art, as a means of calling attention to language. Two other artists to do so are Barbara Krueger, who is known primarily for her paintings with texts that comment on gender issues, and Jenny Holzer, whose multi-media works allude to sayings and phrases that, although common, are perfunctory or lacking in meaning. Cy Twombly, however, is McClelland's major influence. Twombly's loosely painted word-paintings, which call to mind graffiti, scribbling, or doodling, most directly inspire McClelland's own scrawling images.

McClelland's use of text in her paintings is unique because she highlights one word, or at most, two related ones, and never entire sentences. She believes that her works make more potent statements this way.[1] Because the words are isolated, they are removed from their broader contexts. Their meaning is thus obscured or left open for the viewer to interpret. Words or phrases are repeated, however, and often fragmented and rearranged, as if spoken in different tones of voice, by different people, or at different times.[2] But, the manner in which paint is applied to the canvas, helps to evoke the effect of varying voices, as well. In McClelland's words, "the 'how' of something and the 'what' of something have to work together, so that how something is conveyed is really how it's painted. If [a word] is written in a heavy-handed, aggressive, assertive way, that gives it its tone, in the same way that if you speak, you can't separate the tone of the spoken word and the content of it."[3]

McClelland's words, which come from conversations she has either participated in or overheard, fall into four or five general categories.[4] The first category consists of words that suggest time—soon, never, till, wait. The second group is made up of words that suggest a person or place other than, or apart from, herself—them, they, there. The third category consists of words that are onomatopoetic or even pre-lingual in character—ow, he-he, ah-ha. (McClelland reports being influenced by her daughter's learning to speak.) A fourth group consists of words that are used as responses or replies—yes, no, maybe, sure. When McClelland employs phrases, they consist of no more than two words, like "My Pleasure" or "While Away."

It is difficult to view McClelland's words, which can be frustratingly vague, without trying to reconstruct the contexts from which they arise. Thus, her greatest contribution may be the fact that she invites us to contemplate the nature of communication. More specifically, McClelland's canvases point to language's power both to provide meaning and to confound it. Though the artist does not see her work as didactic, we, nevertheless, come away richer for having considered it.

so long, 1992
72 x 72 in.
Acrylic, charcoal, and gesso on canvas
(u.c.: signed and dated)
Purchased through the Rose L. Kraft Fund 93.5

McClelland's paintings have an energetic quality similar to those of the 1950s Abstract Expressionists. Like Jackson Pollock's canvases, which are covered with spattered or poured paint, McClelland's works are laced with weblike patterns. McClelland uses a variety of materials to achieve her effect, however, not just paint, as is the case with Pollock. Canvases, such as *so long*, are covered with a mixture of acrylic, charcoal, clay, gesso, and rabbit-skin glue.

The animated quality of McClelland's canvases, coupled with the fragmentation of the word or words that she highlights, force the viewer to examine the entire canvas in order to comprehend what is spelled out. The words that make up the title *so long* become apparent only after close scrutiny. First, one has to differentiate the letters from a tangle of arcs, arabesques, and other abstract lines, and then, one has to rearrange them into an order that makes sense. Most readily apparent in *so long*, are the darker letters. While "LLLLOng," at the center of the piece, is easily read, the upside-down "n n n n," however, and the widely spaced "o"s across the top of the canvas, are not. The letters are repeated in white paint (note the large "o" at the bottom of the canvas) and in clear glue.

"*so long*" is one of few paintings by McClelland to highlight a phrase, rather than a single word. The expression "so long" suggests parting and alludes to time. To utter the phrase "so long," is to imply that a present state is coming to an end, and thus, to suggest the idea of a past. "So long" also alludes to the future, however. Unlike the more permanent "goodbye," the casual "so long" suggests a point at which a reunion will occur. It is this power of suggestion that gives McClelland's canvases the power to intrigue. CMC

NOTES

[1] Jennifer Rubell and Jerry Saltz, *Let It Rain, Suzanne McClelland's Doors of Perception* (Palm Beach, FL: Jason Rubell Gallery, 1992), 52.

[2] Barry Schwabsky, "Suzanne McClelland, Stephanie Theodore Gallery," *Arts Magazine* 66 (December 1991): 63.

[3] Rubell, 52.

[4] Ibid., 12–13.

PROVENANCE

Jason Rubell Gallery, Palm Beach, FL, 1992; Norton Gallery, 1993.

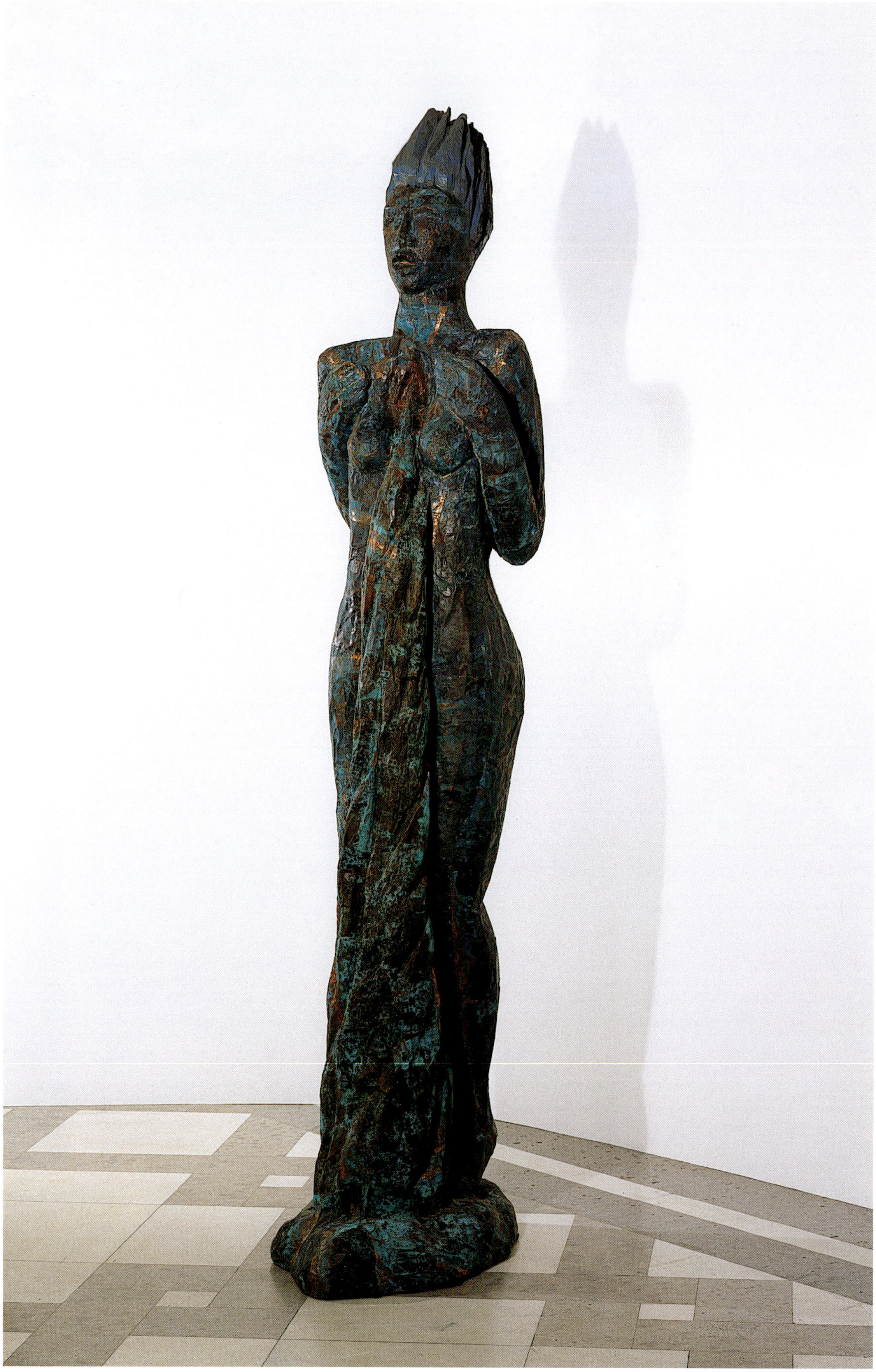

Alison Saar

1956–

Inspired by the folk and ritual art of Africa and the African Diaspora, Alison Saar has created sculpture and installations that incorporate stylistic elements from these varied traditions. The artist, an American of African, Native American, and European descent, determinedly has invested her work with the historical and spiritual legacy of her heritage.

Saar was born in Los Angeles, the daughter of the artists Betye and Richard Saar. As a teenager, she worked for her father, who is also a conservator of African and Asian art. From this experience, Saar acquired a knowledge of ritual objects and artifacts. The ritual arts of the African Diaspora, a central influence in her mother's work, also made an impact upon the young artist. Saar visited Simon Rodia's towers in Watts and Grandma Prisbey's Bottle Village in Simi Valley, and the visionary determination of these artists greatly impressed her. While a student at Scripps College in Claremont, California, she focused her academic research on "outsider" artists who work without the support of artistic institutions and challenge conventional studio methods. She earned a Bachelor of Fine Arts degree in art and art history in 1978 from Scripps, and in 1981, a Master of Fine Arts degree from Otis Art Institute of Los Angeles.

In the manner of the outsider artists she admired, Saar frequently constructed sculpture from salvage. Consistently, she preferred found-objects that cost her nothing and permitted her to economically rework, or even destroy, her creations. The rawness and crudeness of her chosen media is crucial, because Saar believes her materials retain an accumulated, essential energy that

Rio Dulce, 1993
Oxidized copper and enamel on wood
93 x 16 1/2 x 23 in.
Purchased through the R. H. Norton Fund

she must tap, in order to create art with power and presence. Among the first objects she exhibited were books with their covers intact, but their pages removed and replaced with chunks of glass, pottery, metal, and flora. Like the boxes of Joseph Cornell, an influence the artist has acknowledged, her assemblages and three-dimensional figures channel their power through an aggregation of offbeat, disparate elements.[1] Saar's early works, characteristically, were created on a smaller, more intimate scale than her most recent projects. As the art historian Susan Krane has observed, the sculpture in Saar's dramatic installations is visual metaphor that draws upon African, African-American, and Native American cultures and histories.[2]

Saar has steadily gained recognition for her art. She moved to New York in 1983 and was the artist-in-residence at the Studio Museum of Harlem in 1984-1985. In addition, Saar received a National Endowment for the Arts grant in 1988 and a John Simon Guggenheim Foundation fellowship in 1989. Since the 1980s, she has had one-person shows in Los Angeles, New York, and Washington, D.C., and has participated in significant group exhibitions, such as *The Decade Show* of 1990 at the Studio Museum of Harlem and the 1993 Whitney Biennial. The Hirshhorn Museum and Sculpture Garden in Washington, D.C., organized a ten-year retrospective of her work in 1993.

Rio Dulce, 1993
Oxidized copper and enamel on wood
93 x 16 1/2 x 23 in.
(no inscription)
Purchased through the R. H. Norton Fund 93.11

A wealth of cultural allusions saturates *Rio Dulce*, a majestic work that demonstrates the force of Saar's artfully raw style. The sculpture was created for *Fertile Ground*, a 1993 installation of five sculptures engaging the theme of African-American life in the rural South. Specifically, the everyday experiences from the agrarian past are embodied in these monumental figures that celebrate and commemorate southern, black culture.

Rio Dulce engenders numerous interpretative readings to come forth, with no one version crowding out another. Its title, Spanish for "sweet river," evokes the centrality of this natural agent in the history of the African Diaspora and of humankind in general. Sites of ritual celebration and ceremony, rivers are also essential bases in the development and rise of civilizations. The curvaceous female form may refer to Oshùn, the river goddess of the Yorùbá religion observed in Nigeria and transported to the Western hemisphere by African captives in the slavery era.[3] *Rio Dulce*, moreover, may generally represent the nurturing female. The figure symbolically gestures toward its pendulous breasts, and from between them, an abundant stream of milk flows. Yet, with a blank stare and hair (or a headdress) that resembles rivulets, the figure is otherworldly, and appears to possess supernatural powers.

A mysterious rusticity permeates the form and emanative aura of *Rio Dulce*. The quality of the medium and Saar's blunt handling of it, successfully express an essential naturalism. *Rio Dulce* is a towering construction that dwarfs the human viewer and the other figural sculptures of the *Fertile Ground* installation, all of which address the symbolic, natural forces particular to the South, such as the tobacco scourge and the magnolia tree. Each sculpture maintains the unified, singular character of its various media—wood, steel, tin, kaolin, gemstones, cotton bolls—yet together, the five figures appear to constitute a spiritual assembly. At each venue where *Fertile Ground* was exhibited, the installation included strewn red dirt, magnolia leaves, and painted scrims. In this multimedia environment, the sculptures were "actors" in an environment that suggested the primeval, sacred, and venerated. Saar's art, as the art historian Susan Krane has noted, transcends display and approaches "the realm of ritual."[4] JF

NOTES

[1] Judith Wilson, "Down to the Crossroads: The Art of Alison Saar," in *Secrets, Dialogues and Revelations: The Art of Beyte and Alison Saar*, ed. Elizabeth Shepard (Los Angeles, CA: Wight Art Gallery, University of California, 1990), 38.

[2] Susan Krane, *Art at the Edge: Alison Saar (Fertile Ground)* (Atlanta, GA: High Museum of Art, 1993), 6.

[3] Ibid., 10.

[4] Ibid., 6.

PROVENANCE

Norton Gallery, 1993.

EXHIBITION HISTORY

High Museum of Art, Atlanta, GA, *Art at the Edge: Alison Saar (Fertile Ground)*, May 1–July 11, 1993.

Selected Bibliography

Allen, Terry

Johnson, Patricia C. "Artists' explorations offer something to think about." *Houston Chronicle*, 26 January 1992.

Southeastern Center for Contemporary Art. *Youth in Asia: Terry Allen*. Winston-Salem, NC: Southeastern Center for Contemporary Art, 1992.

Wexner Center for the Arts, The Ohio State University. *A Simple Story (Juarez): Terry Allen*. Columbus, OH: Wexner Center for the Arts, 1992.

Avery, Milton

Breeskin, Adelyn. *Milton Avery*. Washington, D.C.: Smithsonian Institution Press, 1969.

Haskell, Barbara. *Milton Avery*. New York City, NY: Whitney Museum of American Art, 1982.

Hobbs, Robert. *Milton Avery*. New York City, NY: Hudson Hills Press, 1990.

Bates, David

Berggruen Gallery. *David Bates: Recent Work*. San Francisco, CA: John Berggruen Gallery, 1992.

Gallati, Barbara Dayer. "Reconciling Places and Process: New Chapters in the Art of David Bates." In *David Bates*. Miami, FL: The Art Museum, Florida International Museum, 1993.

Price, Maria. *David Bates: Forty Paintings*. Fort Worth, TX: Modern Art Museum of Fort Worth, 1988.

Bellows, George Wesley

Doezema, Marianne. *George Bellows and Urban America*. New Haven, CT: Yale University Press, 1992.

Rosen, Steven, et al. *George Wesley Bellows, Paintings, Drawings, and Prints*. Columbus, OH: Columbus Museum of Art, 1979.

Wilmerding, John, et al. *The Paintings of George Bellows*. New York City, NY: Harry N. Abrams, 1992.

Burchfield, Charles Ephraim

Art Museum of the Palm Beaches, Inc. *Catalogue of the Collection: Norton Gallery of Art*. West Palm Beach, FL: Art Museum of the Palm Beaches, Inc., 1979.

Trovato, Joseph S. *Charles Burchfield, Catalogue of Paintings in Public and Private Collections*. Utica, NY: Munson-Williams-Proctor Institute, 1970.

Calder, Alexander

Art Museum of the Palm Beaches, Inc. *Catalogue of the Collection: Norton Gallery of Art*. West Palm Beach, FL: Art Museum of the Palm Beaches, Inc., 1979.

Chapin, James

Art Museum of the Palm Beaches, Inc. *Catalogue of the Collection: Norton Gallery of Art*. West Palm Beach, FL: Art Museum of the Palm Beaches, 1979.

Palm Beach Art Institute, Inc. and the Norton Gallery and School of Art. *Paintings and Sculpture in the Norton Gallery*. West Palm Beach, FL: Palm Beach Art Institute, Inc. and the Norton Gallery and School of Art, 1963.

Palm Beach Art League, Inc. *Norton Collection of Painting and Sculpture*. West Palm Beach, FL: Palm Beach Art League, Inc., 1957.

"Public Favorites (31)," *Time*, September 28, 1953, p. 71–72.

Chase, William Merritt

Pisano, Ronald G. *A Leading Spirit in American Art: William Merritt Chase 1849–1916*. Seattle, WA: University of Washington Press, 1983.

Weinberg, H. Barbara, et al. *American Impressionism and Realism: The Painting of Modern Life, 1885–1915*. New York City, NY: Harry N. Abrams, 1994.

Davidson, Jo

Davidson, Jo. *Between Sittings*. New York City, NY: Dial Press, 1951.

Fort, Elene Susan, and Michael Quick. *American Art: A Catalogue of the Los Angeles County Museum of Art Collection*. Los Angeles, CA: Los Angeles County Museum of Art, 1991.

Jo Davidson Portrait Sculpture. Washington, D.C.: Smithsonian Institution Press, 1978.

Davies, Arthur B.

Czestochowski, Joseph S. *Arthur B. Davies*. Chicago, IL: University of Chicago Press, 1979.

Wright, Brooks. *The Artist and the Unicorn: the Lives of Arthur B. Davies (1862–1928)*. New York City, NY: Historical Society of Rockland County, 1978.

de Creeft, José

Thornton, Gene. "José de Creeft on Art: 'It Doesn't Necessarily Spoil Things If People Enjoy It.'" *ArtNews* 72 (January 1973): 68–70.

Demuth, Charles

Friedman, Martin L. *The Precisionist View in American Art*. Minneapolis, MN: Walker Art Center, 1960.

Gerdts, William H. *Painters of the Humble Truth: Masterpieces of American Still Life 1801–1939*. Columbia, MO: University of Missouri Press, 1981.

Haskell, Barbara. *Charles Demuth*. New York City, NY: Whitney Museum of American Art in association with Harry N. Abrams, 1987.

Murchland, Bernard. "Technology." *Crosstalk: The Cult of Technology* 3 (June–August 1974): n.p.

Norton, Thomas E., ed. *Homage to Charles Demuth: Still-Life Painter of Lancaster*. Ephrata, PA: Science Press, 1978.

Dove, Arthur Garfield

Morgan, Ann Lee. *Arthur Dove: Life and Work, with a Catalogue Raisonné*. London, England: Associated University Presses, 1984.

Palm Beach Art Institute, Inc. and the Norton Gallery and School of Art. *Paintings and Sculpture in the Norton Gallery*. West Palm Beach, FL: Palm Beach Art Institute, Inc. and the Norton Gallery and School of Art, 1963.

Flannagan, John B.

Baro, Gene. Introduction to *John Flannagan: Sculpture and Works on Paper*. Washington, D.C.: International Exhibitions Foundation, 1975–76.

Flannagan, John B. *Letters of John B. Flannagan*. New York City, NY: Curt Valentin, 1942.

Gordon, Jennifer. *John Storrs and John Flannagan: Sculpture and Works on Paper*. Williamstown, MA: Sterling and Francine Clark Art Institute, 1980.

John B. Flannagan: Sculpture/Drawings, 1924–1938. Minneapolis, MN: Minnesota Museum of Art, 1973.

Frey, Viola

Borum, Jennifer. Review. *Artforum* 30 (October 1991): 127.

Grosz, George

Art Museum of the Palm Beaches, Inc. *Catalogue of the Collection: Norton Gallery of Art*. West Palm Beach, FL: Art Museum of the Palm Beaches, Inc., 1979.

Hanson, Duane

Corbino, Marcia. "Duane Hanson's Polymer People." *Sarasota Herald-Tribune* (September 7, 1980): 20–22, 27.

Roberts, Elizabeth Kendrick. "Duane Hanson." *Art Voices/South* 1 (January/February, 1978): 4–5.

Russell, Candice. "Is It Live or is it Hanson?" *Sky* (July 1984): 53–56.

Varnedoe, Kirk. *Duane Hanson*. New York City, NY: Harry N. Abrams, 1985.

Hartley, Marsden

Feininger, Lyonel. *Marsden Hartley*. New York City, NY: The Museum of Modern Art, 1966.

Ferguson, Gerald, ed. *Marsden Hartley and Nova Scotia*. Halifax, Nova Scotia: Mount Saint Vincent University Art Gallery, 1987.

Haskell, Barbara. *Marsden Hartley*. New York City, NY: Whitney Museum of American Art in association with New York University Press, 1980.

Hassam, Childe

Feld, Stuart P. *Childe Hassam 1859–1935*. New York City, NY: Guild Hall Museum, 1981.

Hiesinger, Ulrich W. *Childe Hassam: American Impressionist*. New York City, NY: Prestel, 1994.

Hoopes, Donelson. *Childe Hassam*. New York City, NY: Watson-Guptill, 1979.

Palm Beach Art League, Inc. *Norton Collection of Painting and Sculpture*. West Palm Beach, FL: Palm Beach Art League, Inc., 1957.

Palm Beach Art Institute, Inc. and the Norton Gallery and School of Art. *Paintings and Sculpture in the Norton Gallery*. West Palm Beach, FL: Palm Beach Art Institute, Inc. and the Norton Gallery and School of Art, 1963.

Roque, Oswaldo Rodriguez. "American Impressionist Paintings in the Collection of Dr. and Mrs. John J. McDonough," *Antiques* 128 (November 1985): 1007.

Weinberg, H. Barbara, et al., *American Impressionism and Realism: The Painting of Modern Life, 1885–1915*. New York City, NY: Harry N. Abrams, 1994.

Wheeler, Charles Van Cise. *Sketches*. Privately printed: December 1926.

Hauptman, Susan

Fitzsimmons, Casey. "The One She Loves Best: *In Thine Own Image* at San Jose ICA." *Artweek* 23 (September 5, 1991): 24.

Hays, J. Burstein. "Drawing Broadly Defined." *Artweek* 15 (October 13, 1984): 7–8.

Orr-Cahall, Christina. *Best Pics*. Oakland, CA: The Oakland Museum, 1986.

Sultan, Terrie. *Susan Hauptman: The Obsessive Image*. Washington, D.C: The Corcoran Gallery of Art, 1990.

Henri, Robert

Palm Beach Art Institute, Inc. and the Norton Gallery and School of Art. *Paintings and Sculpture in the Norton Gallery*. West Palm Beach, FL: Palm Beach Art Institute, Inc. and the Norton Gallery and School of Art, 1963.

Palm Beach Art League, Inc. *Norton Collection of Painting*

and Sculpture. West Palm Beach, FL: Palm Beach Art League, Inc., 1957.

Homer, Winslow

Art Museum of the Palm Beaches, Inc. *Catalogue of the Collection: Norton Gallery of Art*. West Palm Beach, FL: Art Museum of the Palm Beaches, Inc., 1979.

Downes, William Howe. *Winslow Homer*. New York City, NY: Burt Franklin Reprints, 1974.

Hendricks, Gordon. *The Life and Work of Winslow Homer*. New York City, NY: Harry N. Abrams, 1979.

Hopper, Edward

Levin, Gail. *Edward Hopper: The Art and the Artist*. New York City, NY: W. W. Norton and Company, 1980.

Inness, George

Art Museum of the Palm Beaches, Inc. *Catalogue of the Collection: Norton Gallery of Art*. West Palm Beach, FL: Art Museum of the Palm Beaches, Inc., 1979.

Cummer Gallery of Art. *George Inness in Florida, 1890–1894, and the South, 1884–1894*. Jacksonville, FL: The Gallery, 1980.

Ireland, LeRoy. *The Works of George Inness, An Illustrated Catalogue Raisonné*. Austin, TX: University of Texas Press, 1965.

Kauffman, Craig

Butterfield, Jan. "Craig Kauffman." *Art in America* 64 (July–August 1976): 81–82.

Clothier, Peter. "Craig Kauffman at Asher/Faure." *Art in America* 74 (February 1986): 139.

Karlstrom, Paul J. "Craig Kauffman." In *Contemporary Artists*, edited by Colin Naylor. Chicago, IL: St. James Press, 1989.

McDonald, Robert. *Craig Kauffman: A Comprehensive Survey, 1957–1980*. Los Angeles, CA: Fellows of Contemporary Art, 1981.

Schipper, Merle. "An Affirmation of Paint." *Artweek* 16 (September 28, 1985): 5.

Schneider, Greg. "Only Skin Deep: Finish Fetish: L.A.'s Cool School at USC Fisher Gallery." *Artweek* 22 (April 4, 1991): 1.

Kuhn, Walt

Adams, Philip Rys. *Walt Kuhn, 1877–1949: A Memorial Exhibition*. Cincinnati, OH: Cincinnati Art Museum, 1960.

—. *Walt Kuhn, Painter: His Life and Work*. Columbus, OH: Ohio State University Press, 1978.

Brown, Milton W. *The Story of the Armory Show*. New York City, NY: Abbeville Press and Joseph H. Hirshhorn Foundation, 1988.

Perlman, Bennard B. "Innocence in Greasepaint." *Art and Antiques* 7 (February 1990).

Riley, Maud. "Cincinnati Re-Enacts Famous Armory Show." *Art Digest* 19 (1 Apr. 1944): 8–9.

Rockefeller, Nelson A. "Back to the Sixty-ninth Regiment Armory." *Art in America* 51 (1963): 59.

"Sale of Quinn Collection Is Completed." *ArtNews* 25 (February 2, 1927): 7.

Tillim, Sidney. "Dissension on the Armory Show." *Arts* 37 (May 1963): 98.

"Whole of John Quinn Collection Announced for Sale Piece Meal." *ArtNews* 24 (January 2, 1926): 1.

Zilczer, Judith. *John Quinn, Patron of the Avant-Garde*. Washington, D.C.: Smithsonian Institution Press, 1978.

Lawrence, Jacob

Nesbett, Peter. *Jacob Lawrence: Thirty Years of Prints (1963–1993), A Catalogue Raisonné*. Seattle, WA: Francine Sedars Gallery and University of Washington Press, 1994.

Turner, Elizabeth Hutten, ed. *Jacob Lawrence: "The Migration" Series*. Washington, D.C.: The Phillips Collection, 1993.

Wheat, Ellen Harkins. *Jacob Lawrence: The Frederick Douglass and Harriet Tubman Series of 1938–40*. Hampton, VA: Hampton University Museum, 1991.

Willis, Garry. "The Real Thing." *The New York Review of Books*, 11 August 1994, p. 6–9.

Lawson, Ernest

Art Museum of the Palm Beaches, Inc. *Catalogue of the Collection: Norton Gallery of Art.* West Palm Beach, FL: Art Museum of the Palm Beaches, Inc., 1979.

Palm Beach Art League, Inc. *Norton Collection of Painting and Sculpture.* West Palm Beach, FL: Palm Beach Art League, Inc., 1957.

Palm Beach Art Institute, Inc. and the Norton Gallery and School of Art. *Paintings and Sculpture in the Norton Gallery.* West Palm Beach, FL: Palm Beach Art Institute, Inc. and the Norton Gallery and School of Art, 1963.

Lever, Hayley

Art Museum of the Palm Beaches, Inc. *Catalogue of the Collection: Norton Gallery of Art.* West Palm Beach, FL: Art Museum of the Palm Beaches, Inc., 1979.

Green, Theodora. "Hayley Lever: An Australian Expatriate Painter." *Art and Australia* 27 (Spring 1989): 103–06.

White, Claire Nicolas. "Hayley Lever." *Arts Magazine* 51 (April 1977): 9.

Louis, Morris

Baker, Elizabeth C. "Morris Louis: Veiled Illusions." *ArtNews* 69 (April 1970): 39–40, 62–64.

Baker, Kenneth. "Reckoning with Notation: The Drawings of Pollock, Newman and Louis." *Artforum* 18 (Summer 1980): 32–36.

Benson, LeGrace G. "The Washington Scene: Some Preliminary Notes on the Evolution of Art in Washington, D.C." *Art International* 13 (1969): 23.

Carmean Jr., E. A. *Morris Louis: Themes and Variations.* Washington, D.C.: National Gallery of Art, 1976.

Fried, Michael. *Morris Louis, 1912-1962.* Boston, MA: Museum of Fine Arts, 1967.

Greenberg, Clement. "Louis and Noland." *Art International* 4 (May 1960): 26–29.

Lipsey, Roger. "Diptych: (1) Veiled Meaning in Morris Louis, (2) Form and Meaning in Criticism Today." *Arts* 57 (November 1982): 142–44.

Murphy, Kay. "A New 'Look' in Palm Beach." *Miami Herald*, 15 August 1964, H1, H7, illus.

Luks, George Benjamin

Milroy, Elizabeth. *Painters of a New Century: The Eight and American Art.* Milwaukee, WI: Milwaukee Art Museum, 1991.

Lundeberg, Helen

La Jolla Museum of Contemporary Art. *Helen Lundeberg: A Retrospective Exhibition.* La Jolla, CA: Museum of Contemporary Art, 1972.

Wechsler, Jeffrey, and Greta Berman. *Realism and Realities.* Camden, NJ: Stedman Art Gallery, Rutgers University, 1981.

MacMonnies, Frederick William

Art Museum of the Palm Beaches, Inc. *Catalogue of the Collection: Norton Gallery of Art.* West Palm Beach, FL: Art Museum of the Palm Beaches, Inc., 1979.

Menconi, Susan E. *Uncommon Spirit, Sculpture in America 1800–1940.* New York City, NY: Hirschl & Adler Galleries, Inc., 1989.

Manigault, Edward Middleton

Columbus Museum of Art. *American Selections from the Columbus Museum of Art.* Columbus, OH: Columbus Museum of Art, 1988.

Manship, Paul

Kittleson, Gloria. *Paul Manship: Changing Taste in America.* Minneapolis, MN: Minnesota Museum of Art, 1985.

Rand, Harry. *Paul Manship.* Washington, D.C.: Smithsonian Institution Press, 1989.

Marin, John

Helm, MacKinley. *John Marin.* New York City, NY: Da Capo Press, 1970.

Reich, Sheldon. *John Marin, Part I: A Stylistic Analysis, and Part II: Catalogue Raisonné.* Tucson, AZ: The University of Arizona Press, 1970.

Mathews, Arthur Frank

Spanierman Gallery, Ira. *American Works on Paper III.* New York City, NY: Spanierman/Drawings, Winter 1989.

Maurer, Alfred Henry

McCausland, Elizabeth. *A. H. Maurer, 1968–1932.* Minneapolis, MN: Walker Art Center, 1949.

Pollock, Peter. *Alfred Maurer and the Fauves, The Lost Years Rediscovered.* New York City, NY: Bernard Danenberg Galleries, 1973.

Taylor, Joshua C., et al. *Alfred H. Maurer 1868–1932.* Washington, D.C.: Smithsonian Institution Press, 1973.

McClelland, Suzanne

Kazanjian, Dodie. "abstract expressions." *Vogue* (June 1992).

Klauss, Kertess. "Three Artists for the '90s." *Elle Decor* (August/September 1992).

Siegel, Jeanne. "Suzanne McClelland." *Tema Celeste* (April/May 1992).

Yau, John. "Suzanne McClelland, Stephanie Theodore Gallery." *Artforum* 30 (February 1992):118–19.

Moran, Thomas

Christie, Manson and Woods, International. *American Paintings, Drawings and Sculpture of the 19th and 20th Centuries.* Auction catalogue, May 23, 1979, no. 52 (as *Florida Landscape*).

Wilkins, Thurman. *Thomas Moran, Artist of the Mountains.* Norman, OK: University of Oklahoma Press, 1966.

Motherwell, Robert

Farber, Manny. "Like a Rock Cast in the Sea." *New Republic* 111 (November 20, 1944).

Harris, Mary Emma. *The Arts at Black Mountain College.* Cambridge, MA: M.I.T. Press, 1987.

Mackie, Alwynne. *Art/Talk: Theory and Practice in Abstract Expressionism.* New York City, NY: Columbia University Press, 1989.

Mattison, Robert Saltonstall. "Robert Motherwell's First Collages: All My Life I Have Been Obsessed by Death." *Studies in Iconography* 12 (1988): 176, fig. 2.

Moholy-Nagy, László. *Vision in Motion.* Chicago, IL: P. Theobald, 1947.

Noland, Kenneth

Moffett, Kenworth. "Noland." *Art International* 17 (Summer 1973): 22–33, 91–93, 100.

Waldman, Diane. *Kenneth Noland.* New York City, NY: Solomon R. Guggenheim Foundation and Harry N. Abrams, 1977.

Wilkin, Karen. *Kenneth Noland.* New York City, NY: Rizzoli, 1990.

O'Keeffe, Georgia

Art Museum of the Palm Beaches, Inc. *Catalogue of the Collection: Norton Gallery of Art.* West Palm Beach, FL: Art Museum of the Palm Beaches, Inc., 1979.

Bry, Doris, and Nicolas Callaway, eds. *Georgia O'Keeffe in the West.* New York City, NY: Alfred A. Knopf, 1989.

Castro, Jan Garden. *The Art & Life of Georgia O'Keeffe.* New York City, NY: Crown Publishers, Inc., 1985.

Duryea, Polly. "Cather and O'Keeffe: Spirits of the Southwest." *Kansas Quarterly*, vol. 19, no. 4 (Fall 1987): 35.

Eldredge, Charles C. *Georgia O'Keeffe.* New York City, NY: Harry N. Abrams, Inc., 1991.

Goddard, Donald, and Robert Rosenblum. *American Painting.* New York City, NY: Hugh Lauter Lavin Associates, Inc., 1990.

Hoffman, Katherine. *An Enduring Spirit, The Art of Georgia O'Keeffe.* Metuchen, NJ: The Scarecrow Press, 1984.

Hough, Katherine Plake, and Michael Zakian. *Transforming the Western Image in 20th-Century American Art.* Palm Springs, CA: Palm Springs Desert Museum, 1992.

Kuh, Katherine. *The Artist's Voice, Talks with Seventeen Artists.* New York City, NY: Harper & Row, 1962.

May, Wilfred. "Art as Investment." *Saturday Review*, December 6, 1958, 19.

Messinger, Lisa Mintz. "Georgia O'Keeffe." *Metropolitan Museum of Art Bulletin* (Fall 1984): 52.

—. *Georgia O'Keeffe*. New York City, NY: Thames and Hudson and the Metropolitan Museum of Art, 1988.

O'Keeffe, Georgia. *Georgia O'Keeffe*. New York City, NY: Viking Press, 1976.

Sweeney, J. Gray. *Masterpieces of Western American Art*. Superstock, NY: M&M Books, 1991.

"The Two Worlds of Georgia O'Keeffe." *Art and Man* 19 (March 1989).

Oldenburg, Claes

Johnson, Ellen H. "Oldenburg's Poetics: Analogues, Metamorphoses and Sources." *Art International* 14 (20 April 1970): 42–45, 51.

Kuspit, Donald. "Material as Sculptural Metaphor." In *Individuals: A Selected History of Contemporary Art, 1945–1986*, edited by Howard Singerman. New York City, NY: Abbeville Press, 1986.

Oldenburg, Claes, and Coosje van Bruggen. *Claes Oldenburg: Large-Scale Projects, 1977–1980*. New York City, NY: Rizzoli, 1980.

Siegel, Jeanne. "How to Keep Sculpture Alive In and Out of a Museum: An Interview with Claes Oldenburg." *Arts Magazine* 44 (September–October 1969): 24–28.

Peterson, Jane

Art Museum of the Palm Beaches, Inc. *Catalogue of the Collection: Norton Gallery of Art*. West Palm Beach, FL: Art Museum of the Palm Beaches, Inc., 1979.

Hirschl and Adler Galleries. *Jane Peterson: A Retrospective Exhibition*. New York City, NY: Hirschl and Adler Galleries, 1970.

Pollock, Jackson

Busignani, Alberto. *Pollock*. New York City, NY: Hamlyn, 1970.

del Guercio, Antonio. "De l'action painting au pop art." *XXe siecle* 40 (June 1973): 148.

Frank, Elizabeth. *Pollock*. New York City, NY: Abbeville Press, 1983.

Hunter, E. R. "An Early Pollock for the Norton Gallery." *Arts Magazine* 46 (November 1971): 56 illus.

Hunter, Sam. *Modern American Painting and Sculpture*. New York City, NY: Dell Publishing Co., 1959.

Landau, Ellen. *Jackson Pollock*. New York City, NY: Harry N. Abrams, 1989.

O'Connor, Francis V., and Eugene Thaw. *Jackson Pollock: Complete Works*. New Haven, CT: Yale University Press, 1978.

Rushing, W. Jackson. "Ritual and Myth: Native American Culture and Abstract Expressionism." In *Concerning the Spiritual in Art*, edited by Maurice Tuchman. Los Angeles, CA: Los Angeles County Museum of Art and Abbeville Press, 1986.

Strauss, Michael. [Review]. *Burlington Magazine* 103 (July 1961): 327.

Prendergast, Maurice

Art Museum of the Palm Beaches, Inc. *Catalogue of the Collection: Norton Gallery of Art*. West Palm Beach, FL: Art Museum of the Palm Beaches, Inc., 1979.

Glavin, Ellen. "Maurice Prendergast: The Development of an American Post-Impressionist." Ph.D. diss., Boston University, 1988.

Goldin, Amy. "How Are the Prendergasts Modern?" *Art in America* 64 (September–October 1976): 60–7.

Green, Eleanor. "Maurice Prendergast, Myth and Reality." *American Art Review* 4 (July 1977): 89–103.

Langdale, Cecily. "The Late Watercolor/Pastels of Maurice Prendergast." *Antiques* 132 (November 1987): 1084–95.

Palm Beach Art Institute, Inc. and the Norton Gallery and School of Art. *Paintings and Sculpture in the Norton Gallery*. West Palm Beach, FL: Palm Beach Art Institute, Inc. and the Norton Gallery and School of Art, 1963.

Palm Beach Art League, Inc. *Norton Collection of Painting and Sculpture*. West Palm Beach, FL: Palm Beach Art League, Inc., 1957.

Rivers, Larry

Hunter, Sam. *Larry Rivers*. New York City, NY: Harry N. Abrams, 1971.

Rivers, Larry. *What Did I Do? The Unauthorized Autobiography*. New York City, NY: Harper Collins, 1992.

Saar, Alison

Hewitt, Mary Jane. "Alison Saar: The Persistence of the Figurative." *International Review of African American Art* 9 (November 1990): 4.

Hugo, Joan. "Sophisticated Ladies." *Artweek* 14 (8 January 1983): 16.

Kuspit, Donald. "Alison Saar." *Artforum* 24 (April 1986): 111–12.

Lippard, Lucy R. *Mixed Blessings: New Art in a Multicultural America*. New York City, NY: Pantheon, 1990.

Van Proyen, Mark. "A Conversation with Betye and Alison Saar." *Artweek* 22 (15 August 1991): 3, 15.

Sheeler, Charles

Adlow, Dorothy. "In the Vanguard of U.S. Art." *Christian Science Monitor*, November 25, 1950, illus.

Art Museum of the Palm Beaches, Inc. *Catalogue of the Collection: Norton Gallery of Art*. West Palm Beach, FL: Art Museum of the Palm Beaches, Inc., 1979.

Friedman, Martin. *Charles Sheeler*. New York City, NY: Watson-Guptill, 1976.

Palm Beach Art Institute, Inc. and the Norton Gallery and School of Art. *Paintings and Sculpture in the Norton Gallery*. West Palm Beach, FL: Palm Beach Art Institute, Inc. and the Norton Gallery and School of Art, 1963.

Shinn, Everett

Art Museum of the Palm Beaches, Inc. *Catalogue of the Collection: Norton Gallery of Art*. West Palm Beach, FL: Art Museum of the Palm Beaches, Inc., 1979.

DeKay, Ormande. "Shinn." *American Heritage* 37 (December 1985): 66–78.

DeShazo, Edith. *Everett Shinn, 1876–1953: A Figure in His Time*. New York City, NY: Crown Publishers, 1974.

Palm Beach Art Institute, Inc. and the Norton Gallery and School of Art. *Paintings and Sculpture in the Norton Gallery*. West Palm Beach, FL: Palm Beach Art Institute, Inc. and the Norton Gallery and School of Art, 1963.

Palm Beach Art League, Inc. *Norton Collection of Painting and Sculpture*. West Palm Beach, FL: Palm Beach Art League, Inc., 1957.

Sloan, John

Art Museum of the Palm Beaches, Inc. *Catalogue of the Collection: Norton Gallery of Art*. West Palm Beach, FL: Art Museum of the Palm Beaches, Inc., 1979.

Baker, John. "Voyeurism in the Art of John Sloan." *Art Quarterly* (Autumn 1978), vol. 1, no. 4: 379–396.

Holcomb III, Grant. *A Catalogue Raisonné of the Paintings of John Sloan, 1900–1913*. Ph.D. diss., University of Delaware, 1972.

Palm Beach Art Institute, Inc. and the Norton Gallery and School of Art. *Paintings and Sculpture in the Norton Gallery*. West Palm Beach, FL: Palm Beach Art Institute, Inc. and the Norton Gallery and School of Art, 1963.

Palm Beach Art League, Inc. *Norton Collection of Painting and Sculpture*. West Palm Beach, FL: Palm Beach Art League, Inc., 1957.

Sloan, John. *Gist of Art*. New York City, NY: American Artists Group, 1939.

Tobey, Mark

Roberts, Collette. *Mark Tobey*. New York City, NY: Grove Press, 1959.

Stanford Art Gallery. *Mark Tobey: Paintings from the Collection of Joyce and Arthur Dahl*. Palo Alto, CA: Stanford Art Gallery, 1967.

Tobey, Mark. *The World of A Market*. Seattle, WA: University of Washington Press, 1984.

Yao, Min-Chih. *The Influence of Chinese and Japanese Calligraphy on Mark Tobey, 1890–1976*. San Francisco, CA: Chinese Materials Center, 1983.

Warhol, Andy

Danto, Arthur C. "Who was Andy Warhol?" *ArtNews* 86 (May 1987): 128–32.

McShine, Kynaston, ed. *Andy Warhol: A Retrospective*. New York City, NY: Museum of Modern Art, 1989.

Swenson, G. R. "What is Pop Art? Answers from Eight Painters." *ArtNews* 62 (November 1963): 26, 60.

Warhol, Andy. *The Philosophy of Andy Warhol: From A to B and Back Again*. New York City, NY: Harcourt Brace Jovanovich, 1975.

Weber, Max

Art Museum of the Palm Beaches, Inc. *Catalogue of the Collection: Norton Gallery of Art*. West Palm Beach, FL: Art Museum of the Palm Beaches, Inc., 1979.

Kootz, Samuel M. *Modern American Painters*. New York City, NY: Brewer and Warren, 1930.

Werner, Alfred. *Max Weber*. New York City, NY: Harry N. Abrams, 1975.

Wiley, William T.

Hudson, Robert, and William T. Wiley. " 'It's Strange to Talk About Art. . .': A Conversation Between Robert Hudson and William T. Wiley." *Artweek* 22 (February 7, 1991): 28.

Perrault, John. "Art Eccentrics." *The Village Voice*, 15 October 1970.

Wellish, Marjorie. "Material Extension in New Sculpture." *Arts Magazine* 45 (June 1971): 26.

Wyeth, Andrew

Andrew Wyeth. Essay by Marina Vaizey. London, England: Royal Academy of Arts, 1980.

Andrew Wyeth: Dry Brush and Pencil Drawings. Greenwich, CT: New York Graphic Society, 1973.

Brandywine River Museum. *An American Vision: Three Generations of Wyeth Art: N. C. Wyeth, Andrew Wyeth, James Wyeth*. Boston, MA: Little Brown, 1987.

Richardson, E. P. "Andrew Wyeth." *Atlantic Monthly* 213 (June 1964): 62–71.

Weber, Bruce. *Master Watercolors and Drawings from the Norton Gallery of Art*. Washington, D.C.: Smithsonian Institution Press, 1988.

Index

Design by Molly Murphy, Red Letter Design Group, West Palm Beach, Florida; Photography by Lucian Capehart, Palm Beach, Florida. This book has been typeset in Monotype Bulmer types. 2,500 copies of this book have been printed by Toppan Printing Co., Japan.